Home Environment and Early Cognitive Development
Longitudinal Research

DEVELOPMENTAL PSYCHOLOGY SERIES

SERIES EDITOR
Harry Beilin

Developmental Psychology Program
City University of New York Graduate School
New York, New York

Published

ALLEN W. GOTTFRIED. (Editor). *Home Environment and Early Cognitive Development: Longitudinal Research*

EUGENE S. GOLLIN. (Editor). *Malformations of Development: Biological and Psychological Sources and Consequences*

DAVID MAGNUSSON AND VERNON L. ALLEN. (Editors). *Human Development: An Interactional Perspective*

DIANE L. BRIDGEMAN. (Editor). *The Nature of Prosocial Development: Interdisciplinary Theories and Strategies*

ROBERT L. LEAHY. (Editor). *The Child's Construction of Social Inequality*

RICHARD LESH and MARSHA LANDAU. (Editors). *Acquisition of Mathematics Concepts and Processes*

MARSHA B. LISS. (Editor). *Social and Cognitive Skills: Sex Roles and Children's Play*

DAVID F. LANCY. *Cross-Cultural Studies in Cognition and Mathematics*

HERBERT P. GINSBURG. (Editor). *The Development of Mathematical Thinking*

MICHAEL POTEGAL. (Editor). *Spatial Abilities: Development and Physiological Foundations*

NANCY EISENBERG. (Editor). *The Development of Prosocial Behavior*

WILLIAM J. FRIEDMAN. (Editor). *The Developmental Psychology of Time*

SIDNEY STRAUSS. (Editor). *U-Shaped Behavioral Growth*

The list of titles in this series continues on the last page of this volume.

Home Environment
and
Early Cognitive Development

Longitudinal Research

EDITED BY

Allen W. Gottfried

Department of Psychology
California State University
Fullerton, California

1984

ACADEMIC PRESS, INC.

(Harcourt Brace Jovanovich, Publishers)

Orlando   San Diego   San Francisco   New York   London
Toronto   Montreal   Sydney   Tokyo   São Paulo

ACADEMIC PRESS, INC.
Orlando, Florida 32887

United Kingdom Edition published by
ACADEMIC PRESS, INC. (LONDON) LTD.
24/28 Oval Road, London NW1 7DX

Library of Congress Cataloging in Publication Data

Main entry under title:

Home environment and early cognitive development.

    (Developmental psychology series)
    Includes bibliographical references and index.
    1. Children--Intelligence levels. 2. Children--
Family relationships. I. Gottfried, Allen W.
II. Series. [DNLM: 1. Child development. 2. Social
environment. 3. Mental processes--In infancy and child-
hood. WS 105.5.D2 H765]
BF432.C48H65 1984   155.4'13   83-13057
ISBN 0-12-293460-1

PRINTED IN THE UNITED STATES OF AMERICA

84 85 86 87   9 8 7 6 5 4 3 2 1

Contents

Contributors

Numbers in parentheses indicate the pages on which the authors' contributions begin.

Kathryn E. Barnard (117), Child Development and Retardation Center, School of Nursing, University of Washington, Seattle, Washington 98195

Leila Beckwith (235), Department of Pediatrics, School of Medicine, University of California, Los Angeles, Los Angeles, California 90024

Helen L. Bee (117), School of Nursing and Department of Psychology, University of Washington, Seattle, Washington 98195

Robert H. Bradley (5), Center for Child Development and Education, University of Arkansas at Little Rock, Little Rock, Arkansas 72204

James N. Breckenridge (151), Center for Study of Psychotherapy and Aging, Palo Alto Veterans Administration Center, Palo Alto, California 94304

Bettye M. Caldwell (5), Center for Child Development and Education, University of Arkansas at Little Rock, Little Rock, Arkansas 72204

Sarale E. Cohen (235), Department of Pediatrics, University of California, Los Angeles, Los Angeles, California 90024

Adele Eskeles Gottfried (57), Department of Educational Psychology, California State University, Northridge, California 91330

Allen W. Gottfried (1, 57, 329), Department of Psychology, California State University, Fullerton, Fullerton, California 92634

Mary A. Hammond (117), Child Development and Retardation Center, School of Nursing, University of Washington, Seattle, Washington, 98195

Dale L. Johnson (151), Department of Psychology, University of Houston, Houston, Texas 77004

Ronald J. McGowan (151), University of New Mexico Medical School, Department of Psychiatry, Programs for Children, Albuquerque, New Mexico 87106

David MacPhee[1] (343), Frank Porter Graham Child Development Center, University of North Carolina, Chapel Hill, North Carolina 27514

Craig T. Ramey (343), Frank Porter Graham Child Development Center, University of North Carolina, Chapel Hill, North Carolina 27514

Linda S. Siegel (197), Department of Psychiatry, McMaster University, Hamilton, Ontario, Canada L8N 325

Theodore D. Wachs (273), Department of Psychological Sciences, Purdue University, West Lafayette, Indiana 47907

Keith Owen Yeates (343), Frank Porter Graham Child Development Center, University of North Carolina, Chapel Hill, North Carolina 27514

[1] Present address: Department of Psychology, University of Denver, Denver, Colorado 80208.

Preface

This book represents the efforts of seven research groups in the United States and Canada investigating the relationship of home environment and early cognitive development. The aim of these investigations has been to determine the specific or process home environmental variables that correlate with and possibly regulate cognitive development during infancy and the preschool years. Thus, the scope of investigation is restricted to the first 5 years, a period that has been given considerable attention in theories of human development.

This book is unique in several ways. First, all of the studies presented are not only longitudinal, but also recent. In fact, several are still underway. Second, some of the researchers have selected similar home and developmental assessments and ages at which to conduct assessments, thus providing a unique opportunity to determine the extent to which findings are generalizable. Third, most of the studies differ widely with respect to the characteristics of the populations investigated. Fourth, the assessments of cognitive development include not only standard psychometric tests of intelligence but also Piagetian-type measures of sensorimotor development, measures of language development, and newly devised measures of recognition memory for infants. Hence, the relationship between home environment and cognitive development can be examined across an array of cognitive abilities. Fifth, the researchers address issues that are traditional as well as those that have been recently defined.

The book contains 10 chapters. The first is a brief introduction to the issues investigated. Each of the following 7 chapters is devoted to a longitudinal investigation. Here, the researchers were given the scholarly freedom of presenting, analyzing, and interpreting their data as they saw best. Because of the complexity of findings in multivariate longitudinal studies, the ninth chapter focuses exclusively on the issue of comparability and generalizability of findings across the longitudinal studies. An integration of the findings at both conceptual and quantitative levels is put forth. The tenth chapter deals with the implications for intervention. It is in this last chapter that the theorizing and empirical findings are turned into applications.

I take this opportunity to thank my colleagues for their eagerness and willingness to contribute their longitudinal findings to this book. The late Leon Yarrow was also to have contributed his knowledge to this book; he has contributed indirectly through his influence on researchers in this area. I am also indebted to the Thrasher Research Fund for its support, which allowed me to pursue my scholarly endeavors in this area. Appreciation is extended to Dr. Chris Cozby, chairperson, Department of Psychology, and Dr. Don Schweitzer, dean, Humanities and Social Sciences at California State University, Fullerton, for awarding me instructionally related research time. This time proved useful in the editing of this book. I am certain the contributors would concur that this book should be dedicated to our species' most valuable resource, our children.

Home Environment and Early Cognitive Development
Longitudinal Research

1

Issues concerning the Relationship between Home Environment and Early Cognitive Development

Allen W. Gottfried

The relationship between home environment and cognitive development has been and continues to be a controversial issue in developmental psychology. It is an issue of both theoretical and practical significance. Theoretically, it is important to ascertain the environmental factors that correlate with cognitive development and the extent to which they account for unique variance in developmental status. This information is necessary for understanding the construct of cognitive development and the degree to which environmental processes regulate it. With respect to the applied significance of this issue, determining the environmental factors that correlate with cognitive development should provide an empirical foundation for the curricula of environmental enrichment and parent education programs aimed at enhancing children's cognitive skills.

The arduous longitudinal investigations presented in this book were not conducted to determine whether there exists a relationship between home environment and cognitive development. It is an empirical fact that environmental variables within the home correlate significantly with cognitive development, and this was demonstrated as early as 1929 by Van Alystne. However, because of advancements in statistical techniques, elaborations in methodological designs, more precise and direct assessments of home environment, and the research questions asked becoming more complex, we are now able to pursue the issue in greater depth.

Although the central issue investigated concerns the proximal home environmental variables that correlate with cognitive development and the magnitudes of these relationships, the researchers of the longitudinal studies presented here have investigated a number of related issues. One of these issues involves the correlations of home environmental variables and cognitive development in different populations. There is no basis to assume that the environmental correlates of cognitive development are the same across populations. In fact, there is evidence indicating differential relationships across populations. Recently, Blau (1981) has shown that the socialization and social structural models that predicted intellectual performance in school children varied for blacks and whites. The researchers in this book examine the relationship between home environment and cognitive development in young children of white, black, and Hispanic families. Furthermore, the home environment–cognitive developmental relations are compared in males and females, first- and later-borns, children differing in perinatal risk and gestational age, and children from different socioeconomic groups and whose parents differ in educational achievement.

By conducting multiple cross-time home and developmental assessments, the investigators are able to address another set of issues:

1. Age trends in magnitudes and patterns of relationships between home environment and cognitive development
2. Stability of home environmental variables across various time intervals during infancy and the preschool years
3. Whether the correlations between early home environment and subsequent cognitive development are due to early home environment per se, or are a function of the stability of home environment during the early years
4. Whether early and later home environments have a cumulative effect in predicting subsequent developmental status
5. The importance of receiving a consistently high quality of home stimulation compared to an inconsistent pattern of stimulation, as they relate to cognitive development
6. Which of the different developmental tests or abilities are the most sensitive to home environmental variables, based on the variety of developmental assessments that have been employed across the time spans investigated.

Another major issue investigated concerns whether there is a direct relationship between home environment and cognitive development or whether the relationship is spuriously due to variables related to both young children's home environment and their cognitive development. Specifically, the authors determine whether there is a significant correlation between home environment and cognitive development when socioeconomic status (SES), and mothers' intelligence and educational achievement are statistically controlled. Similarly the correlations of SES and mothers' intelligence with young children's cognitive development is ascertained when home environmental variables are held constant. These relationships, particularly with that of mothers' intelligence, have recently generated a considerable amount of controversy (see, e.g., Longstreth, Davis, Carter, Flint, Owen, Rickett, & Taylor, 1981; Willerman, 1979).

The predictive value of home environmental variables is an issue of concern to all of the investigators. In addition to determining the bivariate correlations between home environment and subsequent cognitive development, the relative contribution of home environmental variables among a set of preselected predictor variables is examined. In particular, the results of stepwise multiple regression analyses are presented, comparing the relative predictive value of home environmental variables, mothers' intelligence, SES, and developmental tests to young children's subsequent developmental status.

With the relationship of home environment and cognitive development being examined across a wide range of proximal variables, in different populations, at various ages, and on a variety of cognitive abilities, it is important to begin developing a model that would best characterize and explain the network of relationships. Thus, it must be considered whether the most accurate and comprehensive model is one that focuses on specific or on global relationships or one that encompasses both types of relationships or processes. Moreover, whether a home environmental model should be restricted to proximal variables or should include distal variables must be given consideration as well. Certainly, the model would serve as a heuristic for future research investigating functional or causal relationships between home environment and cognitive development and would have implications for intervention programs.

Most of the research presented in this book addresses issues relating home environment to cognitive development. However, several of the researchers are also concerned with the relationships of home environment and demographic factors, social and family configurational variables, and parental characteristics. The quantity and quality of home stimulation is compared in children differing in race, gender, birth order, gestational age, and developmental status (i.e., delayed versus nondelayed). Furthermore, the authors explore the correlations of home stimulation variables and SES, parental education and occupation, mothers' intelligence and attitudes, number of children in the home, crowding, quality of family relationships, and preschool attendance. The results of these analyses should give direction regarding potential mechanisms within the context of the family, which regulate the home stimulation and experiences available to infants and pre-schools.

Finally, an empirical issue that emerges concerns the extent to which there is comparability and generalizability of findings across our current longitudinal studies. This is of utmost importance for developmental psychologists to establish if we are to make rapid progress at both the theoretical and the practical levels (see Bell & Hertz, 1976). This issue is the essence of the integration chapter, Chapter 10.

References

Bell, R. Q., & Hertz, T. W. Toward more comparability and generalizability of developmental research. *Child Development,* 1976, *47,* 6–13.

Blau, Z. S. *Black children/white children: Competence, socialization, and social structure.* New York: Free Press, 1981.

Longstreth, L. E., Davis, B., Carter, L., Flint, D., Owen, J., Rickett, M., & Taylor, E. Separation of home intellectual environment and maternal IQ as determinants of child IQ. *Developmental Psychology,* 1981, *17,* 532–541.

Willerman, L. Effects of families on intellectual development. *American Psychologist,* 1979, *34,* 923–948.

174 Children: A Study of the Relationship between Home Environment and Cognitive Development during the First 5 Years

Robert H. Bradley
Bettye M. Caldwell

During the past quarter century we have been concerned about the environments that children live in, how these environments contribute to optimal development, and how the multiple facets of the environment interact with child characteristics to determine the course of development. We have focused most closely on the home environment and the day care environment, and in the process we have developed a variety of interventions and a variety of measurement procedures to help in understanding the relation between environment and development in young children. The purpose of this chapter is twofold: (1) to describe the development of one of our major environmental assessment procedures and (2) to describe findings from one of our major investigations of the relationship between environment and development.

The Home Observation for Measurement of the Environment (HOME) Inventory

In most of our studies done since 1968 we have used the Home Observation for Measurement of the Environment (HOME Inventory) as a measure of the quality of the environment available to a child in the home. The HOME Inventory is a combination observation–interview technique. It is administered in a child's home at a time when the child is present and awake. The subject for the interview is the child's primary caregiver (usually the mother).

There are currently two versions of the HOME Inventory, one for use with families of infants (birth to age 3 years), and one for use with families of preschoolers (3 to 6 years). The infant version of the HOME was previously referred to as the Inventory of Home Stimulation (STIM), but all references in this book are to the newer name, HOME.

The infant version of the inventory contains 45 items scored in binary ("yes–no") fashion. The 45 items are clustered into six subscales: (1) Emotional and Verbal *Responsivity* of Mother; (2) Avoidance of *Restriction* and Punishment; (3) *Organization* of the Physical and Temporal Environment; (4) Provision of Appropriate *Play Materials*; (5) Maternal *Involvement* with Child; and (6) Opportunities for *Variety* in Daily Stimulation. For ease of discussion, the subscales are often referred to by the shortened name given in italics. It is important to note that we are going to rename the second subscale, "Acceptance of Child"; thereby giving a positive name to all six subscales. However, because most of the existing literature has referred to the second subscale as Avoidance of Restriction and Punishment, that older name is used throughout this book.

Items in the HOME Inventory catalog a variety of interactions, events, and objects from the child's family environment. The items were selected because a review of existing research and theory indicated that such factors were related to children's cognitive, social, and emotional development.

Rationale and Early History of HOME

In the early 1960s, several ideas emerged in the field of child development which gave impetus to the development of the HOME Inventory. First, due to the seminal writings of Bloom (1964) and Hunt (1961), there was greater recognition of the importance of the early environment in children's cognitive development. With that recognition came the observation that more research was needed in order to more accurately map the relationship between environmental factors and aspects of children's development. Second, as scientists began the process of designing studies of environment–development relationships, a consensus developed with respect to the inadequacy of the environmental measures then available. Social class (or socioeconomic status—SES) measures were most frequently used, despite the fact they often provided too crude a picture of the child's actual living conditions—and sometimes even an erroneous picture. They did not provide a precise, sensitive picture of the objects, events, and transactions (processes) of the environment a child was experiencing from moment to moment, day to day, week to week. Moreover, even when an attempt was made to catalog precise transactions, attitudes, and so on, interview or questionnaire techniques were used most often, rather than direct observation of behaviors. The reliability and precision of these techniques were often questionable. Third, as early intervention programs were initiated, there was a growing awareness of the value of having a precise portrait of the child's home environment in planning appropriate interventions. Thus, a valid, yet easy-to-use measure of a child's environment was needed. For these and related reasons, Caldwell and her colleagues at the Syracuse Early Learning Project designed the first version of HOME (the inventory was initially called the Inventory of Home Stimulation, STIM).

Over 200 items were field tested as part of the first version of HOME in Syracuse. Based on the field tests, the inventory was reduced to the 72-item scale described by Caldwell, Heider, and Kaplan (1966). The 72-item version was administered to 113 families, also in Syracuse. A factor analysis and a variety of item analyses were done on the 72 items. It was then reduced to the 45 items in the current scale.

List of HOME Items

(Infant Version)

    I. Emotional and Verbal Responsivity of Mother[1]
1. Mother spontaneously vocalizes to child at least twice during visit (excluding scolding).
2. Mother responds to child's vocalizations with a verbal response.
3. Mother tells child the name of some object during visit or says name of person or object in a "teaching" style.
4. Mother's speech is distinct, clear, and audible.
·5. Mother initiates verbal interchanges with observer—asks questions, makes spontaneous comments.
·6. Mother expresses ideas freely and easily and uses statements of appropriate length for conversation (e.g., gives more than brief answers).
·7. Mother permits child occasionally to engage in "messy" types of play.
8. Mother spontaneously praises child's qualities or behavior twice during visit.
·9. When speaking of or to child, mother's voice conveys positive feeling.
10. Mother caresses or kisses child at least once during visit.
11. Mother shows some positive emotional responses to praise of child offered by visitor.

[1]The term *mother* is used to refer to the primary caregiver, regardless of gender. The term *father* is used to refer to a second caregiver, living in the child's home, generally assumed to be of the opposite gender to the primary caregiver.

II. Avoidance of Restriction and Punishment
12. Mother does not shout at child during visit.
13. Mother does not express overt annoyance with or hostility toward child.
14. Mother neither slaps nor spanks child during visit.
15. Mother reports that no more than one instance of physical punishment occurred during the past week.
16. Mother does not scold or derogate child during visit.
*17. Mother does not interfere with child's actions or restrict child's movements more than three times during visit.
. 18. At least 10 books are present and visible.
19. Family has a pet.
III. Organization of Physical and Temporal Environment
20. When mother is away, care is provided by one of three regular substitutes.
21. Someone takes child into grocery store at least once a week.
22. Child gets out of house at least four times a week.
23. Child is taken regularly to doctor's office or clinic.
24. Child has a special place in which to keep his toys and "treasures."
. 25. Child's play environment appears safe and free of hazards.
IV. Provision of Appropriate Play Materials
. 26. Child has some muscle-activity toys or equipment.
27. Child has push or pull toy.
28. Child has stroller or walker, kiddie car, scooter, or tricycle.
29. Mother provides toys or interesting activities for child during interview.
. 30. Provides learning equipment appropriate to age—cuddly toy or role-playing toys.
31. Provides learning equipment appropriate to age—mobile, table and chairs, high chair, play pen.
. 32. Provides eye–hand coordination toys—items to go in and out of receptacle, fit together toys, beads.
. 33. Provides eye–hand coordination toys that permit combinations—stacking or nesting toys, blocks or building toys.
34. Provides toys for literature or music.
V. Maternal Involvement with Child
35. Mother tends to keep child within visual range and to look at him often.
36. Mother "talks" to child while doing her work.
37. Mother consciously encourages developmental advances.
38. Mother invests "maturing" toys with value via her attention.
39. Mother structures child's play periods.
40. Mother provides toys that challenge child to develop new skills.
VI. Opportunities for Variety in Daily Stimulation
41. Father [1] provides some caretaking every day.
42. Mother reads stories at least three times weekly.
43. Child eats at least one meal per day with mother and father.
44. Family visits or receives visits from relatives.
45. Child has three or more books of his or her own.

In 1970 the Center for Child Development and Education initiated a multidisciplinary, multiphasic study of children's environments and their development. The purpose of this chapter is to describe findings from this investigation known as the Longitudinal Observation and

Intervention Study (LOIS). Some of the data have been previously reported and are only briefly reviewed.

Longitudinal Observation and Intervention Study

The LOIS was designed to explore the very important scientific question of exactly when the decline in rate of development so often observed in children from disadvantaged circumstances begins. A second purpose of the study was to compare the effectiveness of different types of intervention in preventing this decline. LOIS thus represents a continuation of the work begun in Syracuse by Caldwell, Richmond, and their colleagues (Caldwell & Richmond, 1967, 1968; Caldwell, Wright, Honig, & Tannenbaum, 1970) and the work of researchers such as Golden and Birns (1968) and Bayley (1965). Studies of the development of infants from all types of social backgrounds revealed no measurable differences during the first year (Knoblock & Pasamanick, 1960), up to 15 months of age (Bayley, 1965), and at 24 months of age (Golden & Birns, 1968). Yet, comparative studies of children aged 3 years and beyond, from different social class backgrounds, have consistently shown a difference in favor of the more socially and economically privileged children. The studies suggested that the divergence of developmental curves begins somewhere between 24 and 36 months of age. More recently, Wachs, Uzgiris, and Hunt (1971) have documented that such differences occur as early as 7 months of age.

Recruitment of the subjects for this study began in November 1970. Well-baby clinics, birth records from hospitals, and personal contacts in the community all served as sources of subjects, who were drawn from both middle- and lower-SES backgrounds.

Each infant was assigned to one of four groups on the basis of their HOME scores (Caldwell & Bradley, in press). Each group, which consists of 30 to 32 infants, received a different level of educational intervention. For the 2½-year duration of the experiment, there was approximately 30% attrition from the various groups.

Level 1 consisted solely of testing the infant with age-appropriate measures (The Bayley Scales of Infant Development or the Stanford-Binet) at 12, 24, and 36 months of age.

Level 2 consisted of testing the infants every month from 8 through 12 months and then every 3 months from 12 to 36 months. This group was formed as a means of gauging the impact of frequent testing on

the development of children. Because all testing was done in the presence of the mother, the mothers were afforded the opportunity to no-
tice behavior that the examiner considers important. To control for
any modeling or "testing" effects, it was decided to have two groups
that were tested: one infrequently and one frequently.

Level 3 consisted of testing the infant on the same testing schedule
as Level 2. In addition, mother was given some suggestions about ways
to help her baby "learn new things." They were also given a paper bag
full of toys to help teach their babies. The paper bags also contained
some simple suggestions about the interaction between mother and
child during the play sessions which might be most beneficial to the
child. The examiner demonstrated, with the toys contained in the bag,
the kinds of teaching activities likely to be of value to the child. The
toys and the suggested activities are, in effect, transfer items for each
of the items found at a particular age range on the Bayley test. Teaching activities were individualized and were based upon the infant's pattern of strengths and weaknesses as revealed on the Bayley test.

Level 4 infants were tested on the same schedule as in Levels 2 and
3. Unlike Level 3, however, intervention in this group was provided
in the home. Home visitors attempted to establish a relationship with
the mother. In sum, target of the intervention was the parent–child
unit. The home visits occurred biweekly.

Follow-up assessments were done on children from all four levels at
54 months.

Characteristics of the Sample

HOME data were periodically gathered from the 174 families whose
children participated in the study. Characteristics of those families are
presented in Table 1. The psychometric characteristics presented in
this section are based on analyses of HOME data collected on these
Little Rock families.

Descriptive Statistics

HOME Inventory assessments of the 174 Little Rock families of infants and toddlers were used to calculate the mean, standard deviation,
and standard error of measurement for each of the six HOME subscales
and the total HOME score. Results of these calculations can be found
in Table 2. It is notable that the home environment of male and female
children differed very little. In fact, statistically reliable differences be-

TABLE 1

Characteristics of the Little Rock Sample: Family and Child Data

$(N = 174)$

Family data[a]

Educational status: Father = 12.9 Mother = 12.2
(mean number
of years)

Source of income: Welfare = 59 Nonwelfare = 115
Wide range of employment but a high percentage fell into
categories like semiskilled laborers or clerical

Paternal status: Father present = 122 Father absent = 52

Child data[b]

Age status: 4–12 months = 67 13–24 months = 59 25–36 months = 48

Race and gender Black males = 57 Black females = 58
status: White males = 31 White females = 28

Birth order status: First born = 92 Second or third born = 52
Fourth or later born = 30

[a]Complete data were not available on all families. Family data figures are estimates based on the available information.

[b]Complete birth order data were not available on all children. Birth order figures are estimates based on the available information.

tween their home environments were obtained neither with the HOME total score nor any of the subscale scores.

The means and standard deviations for three different age groups (5–8, 10–14, and 23–28 months) are given in Table 2. These results indicated a tendency for the mean scores to increase slightly between 1 and 2 years and to remain fairly stable thereafter. One reason for the increase is that children are usually provided different types of toys as

TABLE 2

Means and Standard Deviations for the Infant HOME Inventory, Comparing Ages of Assessment

| | Time of assessment | | | | | | | | |
| | 6 Months | | 12 Months | | 24 Months | | Total sample | | |
Subscale	Mean	SD	Mean	SD	Mean	SD	Mean	SD	SF_m
Responsivity	7.60	2.40	8.02	2.18	8.57	1.99	8.48	2.09	1.11
Restriction	5.91	1.37	5.29	1.62	5.24	1.64	5.57	1.72	0.98
Organization	4.62	1.14	4.89	1.17	4.93	1.24	4.84	1.13	0.89
Play materials	5.04	2.29	6.36	2.37	6.36	2.03	5.98	2.39	1.14
Involvement	3.01	1.60	3.32	1.59	3.54	1.79	3.45	1.62	0.90
Variety	2.25	1.06	2.97	1.14	3.03	1.52	2.78	1.25	0.94
Total score	28.49	6.59	30.85	7.59	31.69	7.45	31.20	7.31	2.55

they become more mobile and coordinated. Thus, families are more likely to get credit for items such as Item 26 (Child has one or more muscle toys or pieces of equipment) and Item 32 (Provides eye–hand coordination toys) when the child is over 1 year old.

Reliability

The reliability of the HOME Inventory has been examined in a variety of ways. Specifically, the precision of the instrument has been examined in terms of interobserver agreement, internal consistency, and stability. It is important to note that the short-term test–retest reliability procedures were not employed. The reason for this omission is primarily one of practicality. One of the major criteria established for conducting a successful assessment using the HOME is that of "naturalness." It would have been rather difficult for us to have gone into the homes of participants twice in a short interval and not to have seemed pushy or artificial. The nature of the HOME interview process is such that a respondent is quite likely to remember a specific answer given to a question. Thus, the test–retest correlations for the interview—but not the observation—items might have been spuriously inflated.

Interobserver Agreement The traditional interobserver agreement procedures were also not used with regard to scores on the HOME Inventory. In our judgment, such procedures would not have been appropriate because all assessors should be *trained* until they achieve at least a 90% level of agreement with a previously trained HOME administrator. As is mentioned in the section on *Administration*, careful training in the use of the HOME is essential. So, too, is periodic rechecking of all who administer the scale so that the 90% level of agreement is maintained. In our experience, it is generally possible to achieve an acceptable level of agreement if the person being trained accompanies a trained administrator on 10 home visits. In some instances, longer training periods may be required.

Internal Consistency Internal consistency estimates for the HOME were calculated using the Kuder–Richardson Formula 20 (K–R$_{20}$). Estimates were made for the total score and each subscale score. The reliability coefficients are displayed in Table 3. They range from .44 for variety of stimulation to .89 for organization of the environment. The rather low reliability coefficient observed for variety of stimulation resulted partially from the small number of items in the subscale (5). It may have also resulted from the fact that when subscales were

TABLE 3
Internal Consistency (K–R$_{20}$) and Stability Coefficients for the Infant HOME

HOME	K–R$_{20}$	Pearson product–moment coefficients (age in months)			Intraclass coefficients (age in months)		
		6 vs. 12	6 vs. 24	12 vs. 24	6 vs. 12	6 vs. 24	12 vs. 24
Subscale							
Responsivity	.72	.32	.35	.55	.31	.32	.52
Restriction	.67	.29	.32	.30	.23	.25	.30
Organization	.89	.45	.27	.56	.43	.25	.56
Play materials	.77	.40	.48	.70	.30	.35	.69
Involvement	.69	.47	.34	.51	.45	.31	.50
Variety	.44	.62	.64	.77	.57	.58	.76
Total score	.89	.62	.64	.77	.57	.58	.76
N	174	91			91		

composed, not all items included had high factor loadings on the scale (i.e., an inclusion criteria of .30 was used).

Stability HOME data were collected from 91 families in Little Rock, Arkansas when the child was six months, twelve months, and twenty-four months of age. Using these three assessments for each family, it was possible to estimate the stability of the HOME Inventory for families of infants and toddlers. Results for the six subscales and the total scale are located in Table 3. These coefficients indicate a moderate to high degree of stability for all subscales, ranging from $r = .27$ to $r = .77$. The obtained correlations may be somewhat low estimates of the subscales' stability for two reasons. First, none of the subscales contain more than 11 items. Thus a change on only one or two points could significantly affect a family's standing relative to others in the group. Second, the 6-month and 1-year intervals between test sessions represent a considerably longer period of time than is typically used in calculating test–retest reliability coefficients.

Intraclass Correlations Because the mean total score on the HOME increased more than 2 points from the 6- to the 12-month assessment and another point between the 12- and the 24-month assessments, intraclass correlations were also computed as an index of the HOME's stability. These coefficients, found in Table 3, measure the similarity of paired scores in relation to the total variability of all scores (Haggard,

1958). As expected, the intraclass coefficients are slightly lower than the product–moment coefficients. This is because they take account of the fact that retest scores tend to be higher than the original scores whereas product–moment correlations do not. Given that the HOME scores increased during the three test periods, the intraclass coefficients may be considered a more accurate measure of test–retest agreement.

Intercorrelation among Subscales   In Table 4 the intercorrelations among 6-, 12-, and 24-month HOME subscale scores are displayed. The coefficients range from negligible to moderate in size and corroborate the findings of the factor analysis. That is, each subscale contains clusters of items that can be meaningfully interpreted. The subscales cannot, on the other hand, be considered independent home environment factors. In fact, play materials, involvement, and variety appear to share about 20–45% common variance. The primary reason that a moderate level of intercorrelation among subscales was observed is that several of the items loaded significantly on two subscales (e.g., .5 with Subscale A, .3 with Subscale B). The item was then included in the subscale on which it had the higher factor loading.

Despite the significant correlation between some subscales, it is important to look at family performance on each subscale separately. In the profiling of performance on these subscales for individual families, we have observed the same family scoring high on one subscale yet low on another.

Research Note   Children from the LOIS investigation constituted the study samples used in all of the studies reported in this chapter. The specific subsample used in each of the studies reported in the chapter varied by study. The children who attended the Kramer day care center were excluded from all studies except the investigation of early intervention. In most studies the children who were in Level 4 of the LOIS sample were also excluded. The purpose for these exclusions was to eliminate the possible contamination of intervention when examining the relation of home environment and behavioral development.

HOME and Family Demographics

The original intent in designing the Home Inventory was to create a procedure for assessing more specifically the quality of experiences available in a child's home environment than was possible with more

TABLE 4

Intercorrelations among HOME Subscales at 6, 12, and 24 Months

Subscale		Restriction			Organization			Play materials			Involvement			Variety		
		6	12	24	6	12	24	6	12	24	6	12	24	6	12	24
Responsivity	6	.30			.23			.36			.29			.32		
	12		.21			.43			.52			.58			.48	
	24			.32			.30			.51			.64			.36
Restriction	6				.20			.28			.18			.10		
	12					.07			.24			.37			.17	
	24						.23			.43			.40			.24
Organization	6							.40			.23			.16		
	12								.59			.46			.50	
	24									.56			.50			.48
Play materials	6										.62			.21		
	12											.68			.52	
	24												.61			.41
Involvement	6													.30		
	12														.52	
	24															.44

global measures such as SES designations. Despite this clear intention on the part of the instrument developers, some concern has been voiced that most family environment measures may be biased in the sense that they catalog childrearing practices that are more common to particular cultures or classes. Historically speaking, items on family environments instruments have been selected to reflect the quality of support available to a child in the home environment. Some of the items contained in the instruments do involve objects, events, or transactions more often found in affluent than in poor homes. Nonetheless, the extent to which such differences exist is not well established; neither is it clear which differences are associated with ethnic or SES characteristics versus family structure characteristics.

In Table 5 the intercorrelations between the HOME Inventory and six SES variables are given. The SES variables include mother's education, mother's occupation, father's presence, father's education, father's occupation, and a crowding ratio for the home. Data for 6-, 12-, and 24-month HOME were obtained from 91 families and used to examine the relationship between the SES variables and HOME scores for the three testing periods. In general, the correlations remained consistent across the three HOME assessments with only a slight increase at the 24-month assessment.

All of the correlations between HOME subscale scores and SES measures were in the expected direction. However, many of the correlations between mother's occupation and the six home environment factors assessed by HOME were not of sufficient magnitude to be statistically significant. By comparison, mother's education, father's presence, father's education, father's occupation, and crowding in the home all had a significant degree of association with the environment variables. Most notable is the fact that each of the SES variables was related to all six of the home environment variables. Given the rather low intercorrelations among HOME subscales, this finding was surprising but encouraging.

Responsivity of mother toward the child seems significantly related to mother's education, father's education, father's presence, and the amount of crowding in the home. The correlation with crowding was especially high when the child was over a year old.

Avoidance of restriction and punishment appeared most strongly related to father's education and father's occupation. Prior to 1 year, mother's education also seemed to be strongly associated with this subscale. Beyond 1 year, the amount of crowding was significantly related.

Mother's education, father's education, father's presence, father's oc-

TABLE 5

Correlations between HOME Inventory and SES Variables at 6, 12, and 24 Months

Subscale (months)	SES variables					
	Mother education	Mother occupation	Father presence	Father education	Father occupation	Crowding ratio
Responsivity						
6	.22 *	.19	.27 *	.16	.11	.14
12	.30 *	.10	.42 *	.32 *	.36 *	.41 *
24	.25 *	.22 *	.39 *	.30 *	.29 *	.36 *
Restriction						
6	.36 *	.10	.26 *	.35 *	.44 *	.23 *
12	.24 *	.17 *	.04	.39 *	.26 *	.15
24	.29 *	.11	.22 *	.38 *	.37 *	.36 *
Organization						
6	.07	.03	.20	.20	.24 *	.31 *
12	.43 *	.10	.36 *	.36 *	.41 *	.45 *
24	.33 *	.17 *	.30 *	.31 *	.44 *	.23 *
Play materials						
6	.31 *	.20	.19	.39 *	.48 *	.25 *
12	.42 *	.01	.31 *	.48 *	.50 *	.42 *
24	.51 *	.10	.30 *	.50 *	.54 *	.40 *
Involvement						
6	.31 *	.14	.12	.28 *	.34 *	.23 *
12	.29 *	.02	.40 *	.44 *	.39 *	.40 *
24	.35 *	.34 *	.28 *	.52 *	.37 *	.31 *
Variety						
6	.16	.01	.29 *	.11	.14	.24 *
12	.38 *	.01	.38 *	.37 *	.29 *	.25 *
24	.39 *	.10	.31 *	.47 *	.44 *	.21 *
Total scale						
6	.39 *	.20	.34 *	.42 *	.48 *	.34 *
12	.46 *	.08	.44 *	.54 *	.53 *	.48 *
24	.49 *	.24 *	.42 *	.57 *	.56 *	.44 *

* $p > .05$.

cupation, and the amount of crowding were all related to the organization of the environment. In all cases except crowding, moreover, the relationships were stronger when the child was at least a year old.

Mother's education, father's education, and father's occupation had the strongest degree of association with appropriate play materials. Each of these SES characteristics shared between 20 and 30% common variance with this particular home environment variable.

Maternal involvement was significantly related to mother's education, father's presence, father's education, father's occupation, and the crowding ratio. According to our data, father's presence appears to make less difference in the amount of maternal involvement before the child is a year old; similarly, as the child gets older, father's education increases in importance with respect to maternal involvement.

Prior to 1 year of age, only the father's presence was significantly correlated with variety of daily stimulation. Beyond 1 year, mother's education, father's education, and father's occupation were also associated with the opportunity for variety.

In a later study, we studied the relation between HOME and demographic factors in a more detailed way. In addition to the SES factors (education, occupation) and family configuration factors (paternal absence, crowding) used in the first study, the child's gender, race, and birth order were considered. It was anticipated that, except in the case of extreme impoverishment, specific childrearing practices and events are more strongly associated with structural features of the environment such as the degree of crowding than they are with race, SES, or gender differences. This hypothesis was based on the confluence model of family configuration by Zajonc and Markus (1975).

Sample

A total of 79 children and their families from the LOIS sample constituted the sample for the study. Because intactness of the home was confounded with race and SES in our sample, only intact families (mother, father, and one or more children) were included. Description of the sample is provided in Table 6. The Hollingshead Four Factor Index of Social Status (1975) was used to establish social status. The distributions for black and white subsamples within the total sample are highly comparable in all demographic areas except the Crowding Index (number of persons per room in the family living quarters), which remained higher for the black subsample.

TABLE 6
Demographic Characteristics of Sample

		Hollingshead index[a]			Ordinal position			Crowding[b] Index
	N	Lower < 20	L–m 20–39	Middle > 39	1	2–3	> 3	
Total sample	79	6	42	31	36	23	14	.89
Black	42	5	28	9	18	13	11	.98
White	37	1	14	22	18	16	3	.78

[a] Based on the Hollingshead Four-Factor Index of Social Status.
[b] Crowding Index = number of persons per room.

Results

Table 7 displays mean scores on the HOME Inventory at 12 and 24 months by race, gender, and SES. Results generally show that whites have higher scores than blacks, females have higher scores than males, and middle SES have higher scores than lower-middle SES or lower SES. However, the differences appear only to hold for certain small subgroups and only on certain specific subscales. For example, white females score higher than white males, but only in the middle SES. By comparison, it is lower-middle-SES females who score higher than their black male counterparts—and even that only at 2 years. Lower-middle SES black males show no difference from lower-middle SES white males on such HOME subscales as organization of the environment and variety of stimulation, but not on maternal responsivity.

Multivariate analyses of covariance (MANCOVA) were done using a multiple linear regression approach. Predictor variables in each MANCOVA were entered in the following order: degree of crowding, birth order, social status, gender × SES, race × SES, and gender × race. Criterion variables in the analyses were the six HOME subscales. Two separate MANCOVAs were done, one involving 12-month HOME subscale scores and the second involving 24-month HOME subscale scores. Following each MANCOVA, a separate ordered-regression analysis was done for each of the six HOME subscales, using the same predictor variable set used in the MANCOVAs.

Results of the multivariate analyses are shown in Table 8. With respect to 12-month HOME scores, both crowding ($F = 2.93$, $df = 6,61$, $p < .02$) and birth order ($F = 2.46$, $df = 12,120$, $p < .01$) showed significant overall multivariate effects. The ordered regression analyses showed significant prediction for restriction of child, organization of the family, play materials, and maternal involvement. R^2 values ranged from .25 to .43 (see Table 8). As with the total sample, the strongest predictor of HOME scores in the intact family sample was degree of crowding.

Scores for the 24-month HOME were available for 77 of the 79 participants from intact families. Significant overall multivariate effects were noted for birth order ($F = 2.79$, $df = 12,120$, $p < .01$), the race × SES interaction ($F = 1.86$, $df = 12,116$, $p < .05$), and the race × gender interaction ($F = 3.59$, $df = 6,59$, $p < .01$). The race × SES effect appears to have been primarily an artifact of the small number of cases in some cells. However, there is a rather persistent environmental effect favoring black females over black males on the HOME subscales, which account for the gender × race effect. Significant prediction was

TABLE 7

Means on the HOME Inventory for the Intact Family Sample by Gender, Race, and SES

Subscale	Age in months	White male			White female			Black male			Black female		
		MC[a] N = 12	LMC[b] N = 8	LC[c] N = 0	MC N = 10	LMC N = 6	LC N = 1	MC N = 6	LMC N = 14	LC N = 3	MC N = 3	LMC N = 14	LC N = 2
Responsivity	12	8.8	9.1	—	9.3	9.0	10.0	7.0	8.3	10.0	9.3	8.5	6.5
	24	9.8	9.2	—	10.4	8.5	9.0	9.0	8.7	8.0	9.0	8.9	9.0
Restriction	12	4.3	3.4	—	5.5	4.7	7.0	3.8	4.5	4.5	3.0	3.6	6.5
	24	6.2	4.5	—	7.0	5.3	5.0	5.7	5.2	6.0	6.3	4.4	4.5
Organization	12	4.3	4.4	—	4.5	4.5	6.0	4.3	4.2	4.5	3.0	3.4	3.5
	24	5.5	5.3	—	5.9	5.3	6.0	5.8	4.6	4.0	6.0	4.9	3.0
Play materials	12	6.3	5.6	—	7.1	5.7	9.0	5.3	5.2	5.0	4.0	4.1	3.0
	24	8.6	7.5	—	8.8	6.7	7.0	7.3	4.9	6.3	8.7	5.6	4.5
Involvement	12	3.3	2.9	—	4.1	3.2	6.0	2.2	2.7	3.0	2.6	2.7	2.5
	24	5.1	4.3	—	5.5	4.0	6.0	3.7	2.6	2.6	5.3	3.8	1.0
Variety	12	3.2	2.8	—	3.3	2.7	5.0	2.0	2.7	4.0	2.3	2.4	2.5
	24	4.4	3.0	—	3.8	3.3	4.0	3.3	2.5	4.0	4.3	3.1	2.5
Total score	12	30.2	28.2	—	33.8	29.8	43.0	24.6	27.6	31.0	24.2	24.7	24.5
	24	39.6	33.8	—	41.4	33.1	37.0	34.8	28.0	30.9	39.6	30.7	24.5

[a]MC = middle SES: Hollingshead four-factor index > 39.
[b]LMC = lower middle SES: Hollingshead four-factor index 20 = 39.
[c]LC = lower SES: Hollingshead four-factor index < 20.

TABLE 8

Regression of HOME Subscales, Using Degree of Crowding, Birth Order, SES,
Gender, Race, Gender × SES, Race × SES, and Gender × Race
for Intact Families

	Significant predictors	
Subscale	Ordered regression model[a]	Partial correlations[b]
12-Month HOME		
Responsivity n.s.	Crowding	
$R^2 = .25$	Crowding, gender	Crowding, gender
Organization $R^2 = .41$	Crowding, birth order	Crowding, birth order
Play materials $R^2 = .43$	Crowding, SES, race	Crowding
Involvement $R^2 = .35$	Crowding, birth order	Crowding
Variety n.s.	Crowding, race	
24-Month HOME		
Responsivity n.s. n.s.	Crowding, gender × race	Crowding, gender × race
Organization $R^2 = .46$	Crowding, SES, birth order	Birth order
Play materials $R^2 = .52$	Crowding, birth order, SES, race	Birth order, crowding
Involvement $R^2 = .51$	Crowding, birth order, SES, race	Birth order, race
Variety n.s.	Crowding	

[a]Indicates significant contribution to prediction of HOME when used as part of ordered regression model.

[b]Indicates significant correlation with criterion subscale with all other predictor variables partialled out.

observed for three subscales, organization of environment, $(R^2 = .52)$, and maternal involvement $(R^2 = .51)$. Birth order, crowding, and social status showed the highest degree of relationship with these HOME subscales. However, only birth order and crowding consistently showed independent relations with the HOME scales.

Discussion

The results from this study reveal an interesting pattern of relations between the HOME Inventory and a variety of commonly used demographic characteristics: namely, amount of crowding in the home,

birth order, gender, race, SES, and several interactions among the variables. Each of the personal and environmental variables show some
relation to the kinds of objects, events, and transactions cataloged by
the HOME Inventory. However, it appears that none of these variables
by itself accounts for a high degree of variance in HOME scores. More
important is the finding that a great deal of the variance in HOME
scores remains unattributed to any single variable, or even to any combination of these important variables. In only a few instances does any
subscale account for as much as 50% of the variance. Even when error
of measurement is allowed, individual variation in the family environment remains beyond what is attributable to gender, race, SES, birth
order, and the amount of crowding in the home. In many ways these
findings were expected, given previous evidence for within-group differences in childrearing patterns (Baumrind & Black, 1967; Bloom,
1964; Bradley & Caldwell, 1981; Wulbert, Inglis, Kriegsman, & Mills,
1975). The value of these findings would seem to lie in providing a
more complete estimate of the extent to which environmental processes, such as those contained in family environments measures, reflect within-group versus between-group differences.

Among the most salient findings of this study are those pertaining
to racial differences in HOME scores. The first major point to be made
relating to race is that no overall significant multivariate effect was
noted for race. The ordered regression analyses showed a significant
relation between race and HOME subscale scores in the case of availability of play materials and maternal involvement at 2 years. However, the partial sums of squares results showed that little relation
between HOME and race remained once the other factors and their
interactions were statistically controlled. It is perhaps most critical to
note that there were few race effects once the amount of crowding in
the home and a child's birth order were considered. The lower HOME
scores obtained for blacks in other studies (Barkauskas, 1980) may well
reflect the fact that black children often live in more crowded conditions, are most closely spaced, and are more likely to be later born.
Such a finding is consonant with the confluence model proffered by
Zajonc (1976) regarding ethnic, national, and regional differences in
intellectual test scores.

Another interesting finding from the study is the relatively small
number of simple gender differences. No overall multivariate effect for
gender was observed. The only consistent finding pertained to the
higher scores made on the acceptance of child subscale for girls. It was
true for all females when measured at age 1 year, but only for white
females when measured at age 2 years. The sex difference on the re-

striction of child subscale is noteworthy in that the subscale is predictive of mental test scores in girls but not in boys (Bradley & Caldwell, 1980).

As expected, there was a noticeable relationship between SES and types of environmental processes assessed by the HOME Inventory. Walberg and Marjoribanks (1976) suggest that such processes mediate the SES–Achievement relationship. The largest number of significant relations occurred at the 2 year assessment, although a significant multivariate effect was not observed. None of the significant effects survived the partialling of race, gender, crowding and birth order. Thus, the significant relation observed between SES and measures of the family environment observed in other studies (Davé, 1963; Bradley et al., 1977; Walberg & Marjoribanks, 1976) may partially reflect the fact that social status is often confounded with such family configuration variables as paternal absence, spacing of children, and amount of crowding (Zajonc, 1976).

The two family-structure variables examined in the study, crowding and birth order, showed substantial relationships with HOME scores. The amount of crowding showed the strongest, most consistent relation to HOME scores of all variables studied. It was especially strong at the 12-month assessment period. It was related to all six HOME subscales. Most notable is the finding that the amount of crowding remained significantly related to HOME scores even when all other environmental variables were controlled via partial correlation.

The birth order of the child also revealed a substantial relation to the HOME scores with overall multivariate effects observed at 12 months for the intact family subsample and at 24 months for both the total sample and the intact family subsample. Its effects appear to be more restricted than crowding, however. Specifically, birth order appears related to three subscales: organization of the environment, play materials, and maternal involvement. It is important to mention that the effects of birth order appear to hold even after the effects of race, SES, gender, and crowding have been accounted for, a finding that agrees with the confluence model. Given previous findings that play materials, maternal involvement, and organization of the environment are strongly related to child development measures (Elardo, Bradley, & Caldwell, 1975; Wulbert, Inglis, Kriegsman, & Mills, 1975), it may be that it is through such environmental processes that the birth order–achievement relation is mediated. On the other hand, such findings also tend to verify contentions that certain child attributes and behaviors shape parental behavior (Bell, 1968; Lewis & Rosenblum, 1975). Parental behaviors such as having children, but not considering the importance of toys may reflect that parents think children are just something you have—you do not need to be concerned about their development. They themselves are property.

It is interesting to note the types of home environmental processes most strongly associated with family structure and status variables (organization of the environment, play materials, and maternal involvement). These structural variables seem much less highly related to restriction of the child or to the variety of stimulation provided. In general, the findings appear to make some sense. In a family where many people live in limited space, it is likely to be harder for parents to organize the environment and for them to provide constant encouragement for their children's development. The significant relation observed for play materials is less obvious on the surface. It may be that in large families it is generally harder for parents to be mindful of their children's need for developmentally stimulating toys and materials. It may partially reflect that with limited economic resources, it is a problem for parents to provide toys and other materials for all their children. However, because SES never showed a significant partial correlation with provision of appropriate play materials, the economic effect would not seem to be the only one. Finding that organization of the environment, provision of appropriate play materials, and maternal involvement are substantially related to family structure variables is significant in that these three HOME factors have demonstrated a strong relation to children's development (Bradley & Caldwell, 1976; Bradley, Caldwell & Elardo, 1977; Elardo et al., 1975; Wulbert et al., 1975).

The present study begins to delineate what appears to be a complex set of relations between family environment measures and a variety of child development and environmental variables. Only rarely do such measures appear to provide information simply redundant of social class or race—a point cogently made by Bloom (1964). The study did not examine a number of other variables that undoubtedly are related to measures of the family environment, such as maternal IQ.

Correlations with Cognitive Development

The largest number of studies using HOME are those that have investigated the relation of HOME to children's cognitive test performance. Among the earliest was one reported by Elardo, Bradley, and Caldwell (1975). HOME scores obtained when children were 6, 12, and 24 months old were correlated with Bayley Infant Scales scores obtained when the child was 6 and 12 months old and with Stanford–Binet Intelligence Test scores obtained at age 3 years. Results of these analyses can be found in Table 9. A follow-up study by Bradley and Caldwell (1976) included an IQ assessment at 54 months. Seventy-seven children from the LOIS investigation were used in the 1975 study; 49 in the 1976 study.

Age Differences

Six-Month HOME

Table 9 shows the Pearson product–moment and multiple correlation coefficients between HOME scores and Bayley Mental Development Index (MDI) scores at 12 months. The table also shows correlations between 6-month HOME scores and Stanford–Binet scores at 36 and 54 months. An examination of these coefficients indicates that variety in daily stimulation was correlated with the criterion $r = 27$. The multiple correlation between all six scores and the 12-month MDI scores was calculated at $R = .30$.

Correlations between 6-month HOME scores and 36-month Binet scores were generally higher than correlations between 6-month HOME scores and MDI performance at 12 months. This was particularly true of the relationship between 6-month HOME total score and 36-month Binet score ($r = .50$ vs. $r = .16$). It is also interesting to note that appropriate play materials ($r = .41$), maternal involvement ($r = .33$), organization of the environment ($r = .40$), and variety in daily stimulation ($r = .31$) were significantly related to 36-month Binet performance. The multiple correlation between 6-month HOME subscale scores and 36-month Binet IQ was computed at $R = .54$.

Correlations between 6-month HOME scores and 54-month IQ scores were very little different from correlations between 6-month HOME and 36-month IQ. The multiple R was still .50. For only two subscales was there a drop of as much as .10: avoidance of restriction and punishment ($r = .10$), organization of the environment ($r = .31$).

Twelve-Month HOME

Pearson product–moment coefficients and multiple correlation coefficients between 12-month HOME scores and 12-month MDI scores and 36-month and 54-month Binet scores are shown in Table 9. The 12-month MDI scores were most related to appropriate play materials

TABLE 9

Correlations between 6-, 12-, and 24-Month HOME Scores and Cognitive Test Scores Gathered at 1, 3, and 4½ Years

| | Time of HOME assessment | | | | | | | |
| | 6 Months | | | 12 Months | | | 24 Months | |
Subscales	1-Yr. MDI[a]	3-Yr. IQ	4½-Yr. IQ	1-Yr. MDI	3-Yr. IQ	4½-Yr. IQ	3-Yr. IQ	4½-Yr. IQ
Responsivity	.09	.25*	.27	.15	.39*	.34*	.49*	.50*
Restriction	.13	.24*	.10	.01	.24*	.21	.41*	.28*
Organization	.20	.40*	.31*	.20	.39*	.34*	.41*	.33*
Play materials	.05	.41*	.44*	.28*	.56*	.52*	.64*	.56*
Involvement	.08	.33*	.28*	.28*	.47*	.36*	.55*	.55*
Variety	.27*	.31*	.30*	.05	.28*	.32*	.50*	.39*
Total score	.16	.50*	.44*	.30*	.58*	.53*	.71*	.57*
Multiple correlation[b]	.30	.54*	.50*	.40	.59*	.57*	.72*	.63*

[a]MDI—Mental Development Index from Bayley Scales.

[b]This represents the multiple correlation of all six HOME subscales.

* $p < .05$.

($r = .28$) and maternal involvement ($r = .28$). A moderate relationship was also observed for organization of the environment ($r = .20$). A multiple correlation of $R = .40$ was found for six subscales and the 12-month MDI.

Correlations ranging from $r = .24$ to $r = .56$ were observed between 12-month HOME subscale scores and 36-month Binet scores, the highest being for appropriate play materials ($r = .56$) and for maternal involvement ($r = .47$). It was at 12-months that maternal responsivity also showed a strong relationship to mental test performance ($r = .39$). The correlation between 36-month Stanford-Binet scores and total 12-month HOME score was found to be $r = .58$, while the multiple correlation between the six *HOME* subscales and Stanford-Binet scores was $R = .59$.

Correlations between 12-month HOME scores and 54-month Binet IQ scores were quite similar to those between 12-month HOME and 36-month Binet scores. The range was from $r = .21$ to $r = .52$ for the subscales, $r = .53$ for the total score, and a multiple correlation of $R = .57$. The only notable difference in the pattern of correlations for 4½-year IQ scores as compared with 3-year IQ scores was for maternal involvement. For 36 months it was $r = .47$; for 54 months it was $r = .36$.

Twenty-four-Month HOME

In Table 9 the correlations between 24-month HOME scores and 36-month Stanford-Binet scores are listed. Coefficients ranged from $r = .41$ for avoidance of restriction and punishment to $r = .64$ for appropriate play materials. The total HOME score at 24-months and the Binet score at 36 months share about 50% common variance ($r = .72$). The multiple correlation between the six HOME subscales and the 36-month Binet scores was computed at $R = .72$. A multiple R of .77 was computed when using HOME scores at 6, 12, and 24 months, and 36 month Binet scores

All HOME subscale scores at 24 months were significantly correlated with 54-month Binet performance. These coefficients ranged from .28 for avoidance of restriction and punishment to .56 for appropriate play materials and .55 for maternal involvement. The multiple correlation was $R = .63$. In general these coefficients were slightly lower than those between 24-month HOME scores and 3-year IQ.

In Canada, Fowler and Swenson (1975) conducted a 5-year longitudinal study of 23 day care and 23 matched home-reared infants. Correlations between HOME scores and measures of cognitive and social development ranged from moderate to strong (.4 to .8). The coefficients varied as a function of the age at which the child was tested. HOME scores generally showed a stronger relation to verbal than affective or perceptual-motor factors.

Hayes (1977) conducted an investigation of the effects of environmental stimulation on premature infants. Three groups were examined: 17 premature infants who received various forms of visual and tactile stimulation during the weeks immediately after birth, 14 premature infants who received no special enrichment, and 16 full-term infants who received no special enrichment. Performance on the McCarthy Scales of Children's Abilities at age 3 years was used as an index of children's cognitive ability. A higher score on the HOME scale was related to higher developmental scores for all groups.

A more recent study of premature infants from Hamilton, Ontario, Canada by Siegel (1981) revealed a similar portrait. The study involved 148 infants, mostly from lower social-class backgrounds. The infants were administered the Bayley scales at 4, 8, 12, 18, and 24 months; the Uzgiris–Hunt scales at 4, 8, 12, and 18 months; the Reynell Developmental Language Scales at 24 months; and the HOME Inventory at 12 months. The 12-month HOME scores generally showed low to moderate correlations with both Reynell language scores and Bayley scores (.2 to .4), the strongest relation being that for provision of appropriate play materials.

Gender and Race Differences

Research since 1964 has established a strong association between children's mental development and the quality of stimulation available in the home environment during the first 3 years of life (Wachs, 1978). However, a great many questions remain with regard to the relation, including questions about race differences. Many have speculated, with some empirical support, that childrearing practices in black homes differ from those in white homes (Scarr & Weinberg, 1976). In a study of ninth-grade girls, Trotman (1977) found that middle-class black families scored significantly lower on Wolf's (1965) measure of the home environment than did a comparable group of middle-class white families. They employed a home environmental measure consisting of a 63-question interview schedule and an associated set of scales by which a family is rated according to the presence of environmental variables that are related to intellectual development. Still, there are few investigations of young children that have made direct racial comparisons; thus, it is not clear how environment–development relations differ among blacks and whites during infancy.

Similarly, there is some evidence to support sex differences in the relation between home environment and cognitive development (Bayley & Schaefer, 1964; Bradley & Caldwell, 1980; Moore, 1968; Wachs, 1978). For example, Wachs (1978) found a number of sex differences in the correlations between features of the physical environment and IQ at age 2½ years. Again, however, empirical investigations of the differences are limited. Kamin (1978) recently made the point that many of the studies claiming evidence for sex differences do not even statistically show that such differences exist.

It was the purpose of this study to carefully examine both race and sex differences in the pattern of relations among six environmental processes and children's development in the first 3 years of life. In so doing, statistical checks were made of the reliability of the differences.

Sample

A total of 72 children and their families participated in the study (18 white males, 18 black males, 18 white females, 18 black females). Both the black and the white samples were heterogeneous with respect to socioeconomic status (SES). However, the black sample had proportionately more lower SES families and the white sample proportionately more middle SES families. Thus, the sample used accurately reflects the natural confound between race and SES existing in the city. This confound may make comparisons between races somewhat troublesome. However, because both races vary considerably in SES and because it was not mean differences between groups but differences in correlations that were at issue, the confound did not seem likely to pose major problems of interpretation. Previous research (Bradley & Caldwell, 1981) has shown that the home environment scores of children are less strongly related to race, gender, and even SES than they are to family structure variables such as birth order, the amount of crowding, and family intactness. It is important to note, nonetheless, that the inclusion of both racial groups increased the range in SES present in the sample as well as increased the range of scores on the HOME Inventory and Stanford-Binet Intelligence Test mentioned subsequently (see Table 10).

Results

In an effort to unravel race, gender, and age differences in the HOME–IQ relations, two separate strategies were employed. The first strategy

TABLE 10
Characteristics of the Little Rock Sample: Contrast of Whites and Blacks

WHITES

Mean family characteristics
   Two-Factor Index of Social Position: 38.3
   Paternal education: 13.9 years (Educational Scale Score = 5.11)
   Paternal occupation: Wide range including a few in executive or professional posi-
                          tions. Average is about semiprofessional, clerical, or sales. (Oc-
                          cupational Scale Score = 4.61)
   Maternal education: 13.1 years (Educational Scale Score = 4.83)
   Maternal occupation: Mostly housewives. Some teachers, clerical workers, techni-
                          cians, etc. (Occupational Scale Score = 1.36)
Mean child characteristics
   12-Month Bayley MDI: 103.3 SD = 16.6
   36-Month Stanford-Binet Intelligence Test score: 114.3 SD = 14.9

BLACKS

Mean family characteristics
   Two-Factor Index of Social Position: 22.6
   Paternal education: 11.3 years (Educational Scale Score = 3.64)
   Paternal occupation: Wide range but many unemployed or in menial positions. Aver-
                          aged is semiskilled to skilled manual workers. (Occupational
                          Scale Score = 2.33)
   Maternal education: 11.1 years (Educational Scale Score = 3.39)
   Maternal occupation: Mostly housewives. Some in menial or semiskilled positions;
                          a few teachers or clerical workers. (Occupational Scale
                          Score = 1.08)
Mean child characteristics
   12-Month Bayley MDI: 98.7 SD = 24.5
   36-Month Stanford-Binet Intelligence Test Score: 85.3 SD = 17.0

involved collapsing across gender when race differences were examined (e.g., black females [BF] and black males [BM] together were compared to a group composed of white males [WM] and females [WF].)
Similarly, when gender differences were examined, same-gender members of both races were combined for purposes of analyses (BM + WH
vs. BF + WF). The second strategy involved doing comparisons between each of the four gender–race groups used separately. Specifically, when race differences were examined, black males were compared to white males, black females to white females (See Tables 11–
15.) The second strategy was undertaken with great caution given the
small sample size (18) for each group. It was felt that correlation coefficients involving such small samples might well be unreliable.

   When members of both races were combined for purpose of analysis,
no gender differences were observed for 6-month HOME scores. Tests
showed that at 12 months, the correlation between avoidance of re-

TABLE 11

Means and Standard Deviations for the Infant HOME Inventory, Comparing Males and Females, Blacks and Whites

Subscales		Female			Male			Black			White		
		6	12	24	6	12	24	6	12	24	6	12	24
Responsivity	Mean	7.7	7.9	8.7	7.5	8.5	8.7	6.9	7.4	7.8	8.3	9.1	9.5
	SD	2.5	2.4	2.2	2.4	1.8	2.0	2.7	2.1	2.1	1.9	1.6	1.7
Restriction	Mean	5.8	5.8	5.3	5.9	5.4	5.0	5.4	5.4	4.6	6.3	5.7	5.8
	SD	1.9	1.7	1.9	1.0	1.2	1.6	1.3	1.1	1.6	1.5	1.8	1.6
Organization	Mean	4.7	4.8	5.9	4.6	4.9	4.9	4.3	4.3	4.6	5.0	5.4	5.4
	SD	1.1	1.2	1.1	1.3	1.2	1.2	1.3	1.2	1.2	1.0	0.9	0.9
Play materials	Mean	5.5	6.5	6.6	5.6	6.7	6.8	4.5	5.2	5.4	6.6	8.0	8.0
	SD	2.6	2.5	2.1	2.2	2.2	2.0	2.2	2.3	1.7	2.0	1.3	1.5
Involvement	Mean	3.4	3.5	3.8	3.2	3.5	3.8	2.8	2.7	2.8	3.8	4.3	4.8
	SD	1.6	1.7	1.8	1.9	1.6	1.7	1.4	1.3	1.5	1.9	1.6	1.4
Variety	Mean	2.5	3.0	3.1	2.3	3.1	3.1	2.1	2.3	2.5	2.7	3.8	3.7
	SD	1.0	1.3	1.3	1.2	1.4	1.4	1.1	1.2	1.3	1.1	1.1	1.2
Total score	Mean	29.8	31.5	32.7	29.0	31.9	32.2	25.9	27.2	27.8	32.9	36.3	37.1
	SD	7.5	8.6	8.0	6.9	6.8	8.5	6.2	6.1	5.9	6.3	6.3	6.3

TABLE 12

Partial Correlations between 6-Month and 12-Month HOME Scores and 3-Year IQ,
Comparing Males and Females[a]

Subscales	6-Month HOME and IQ controlling for 12-month HOME				12-Month HOME and IQ controlling for 6-month HOME			
	Male		Female		Male		Female	
Responsivity	.19	(.37*)	−.01	(.27)	.25	(.39*)	.49**	(.54**)
Restriction	.23	(.26)	.04	(.27)	.09	(.16)	.42**	(.48**)
Organization	.34*	(.50**)	.14	(.40*)	.25	(.46**)	.42**	(.54**)
Play materials	.46**	(.62**)	.21	(.49**)	.64**	(.74**)	.53**	(.65**)
Involvement	.01	(.35*)	.12	(.47**)	.45**	(.55**)	.49**	(.64**)
Variety	.37*	(.41*)	.21	(.30)	.14	(.23)	.37*	(.43**)
Total score	.34*	(.63**)	.05	(.55**)	.31*	(.62**)	.51**	(.70**)

[a] Simple correlations are displayed in parentheses.
*p < .05.
**p < .01.

striction, organization of the environment, and variety of stimulation all showed statistically higher correlations for females. With regard to gender, some interesting differences were noted in shifts of correlations across time. For example, correlations between total HOME score and IQ showed no change from 6 to 24 months for males. By contrast, for females the total HOME score at 6 months was correlated $r = .55$

TABLE 13

Partial Correlations between 12- and 24-Month HOME Scores and 3-Year IQ,
Comparing Males and Females[a]

Subscales	12-Month HOME and IQ controlling for 24-month HOME				24-Month HOME and IQ controlling for 12-month HOME			
	Male		Female		Male		Female	
Responsivity	.17	(.39*)	.30*	(.54**)	.45**	(.55**)	.35*	(.56**)
Restriction	.07	(.16)	.26	(.48**)	.27*	(.30)	.45**	(.58**)
Organization	.36**	(.46**)	.25	(.54**)	.17	(.34*)	.37*	(.59**)
Play materials	.38**	(.74**)	.26	(.65**)	.32*	(.72**)	.53**	(.74**)
Involvement	.29*	(.55**)	.34*	(.64**)	.45**	(.62**)	.49**	(.70**)
Variety	−.12	(.23)	.27	(.43**)	.45**	(.49**)	.60**	(.66**)
Total score	.17	(.62**)	−.06	(.70**)	.43**	(.70**)	.65**	(.84**)

[a] Simple correlations are displayed in parentheses.
*p < .05.
**p < .01.

TABLE 14

Partial Correlations between 6- and 12-Month HOME Scores and 3-Year IQ, Comparing Blacks and Whites[a]

Subscales	6-Month HOME and IQ controlling for 12-month HOME				12-Month HOME and IQ controlling for 6-month HOME			
	Black		White		Black		White	
Responsivity	−.01	(.04)	.26	(.39*)	.15	(.16)	.06	(.31)
Restriction	−.18	(.05)	−.01	(.18)	.28*	(.23)	.45**	(.47**)
Organization	.48**	(.52**)	.01	(.14)	.00	(.23)	.20	(.24)
Play materials	.19	(.28)	.30*	(.46**)	.41**	(.45**)	.29*	(.45**)
Involvement	−.07	(.09)	.25	(.46**)	.27	(.27)	.27	(.47**)
Variety	.14	(.08)	.47**	(.48**)	−.28*	(.26)	.10	(.12)
Total score	.09	(.25)	.39**	(.58**)	.21	(.31)	.13	(.48**)

[a] Simple correlations are displayed in parentheses.
*p < .05.
**p < .01.

with IQ, whereas at 24 months it was $r = .84$. The z test was significant using the formula presented by Peters and VanVoorhis (1940).

The number of racial differences in the relation between HOME scores and 3-year IQ was substantial. For four of the six HOME subscales measured at 6 months, whites had statistically stronger correlations with IQ than blacks. One interesting exception was organi-

TABLE 15

Partial Correlations between 12- and 24-Month HOME Scores and 3-Year IQ, Comparing Blacks and Whites[a]

Subscales	12-Month HOME and IQ controlling for 24-month HOME				24-Month HOME and IQ controlling for 12-month HOME			
	Black		White		Black		White	
Responsivity	−.05	(.16)	.15	(.31)	.42**	(.44**)	.28*	(.38*)
Restriction	.20	(.23)	.29*	(.47**)	.15	(.19)	.22	(.44**)
Organization	.15	(.23)	.05	(.24)	.16	(.23)	.34*	(.41*)
Play materials	.23	(.45**)	.20	(.45**)	.34*	(.51**)	.25	(.47**)
Involvement	.14	(.27)	.30*	(.47**)	.30*	(.38*)	.34*	(.49**)
Variety	−.38**	(.26)	−.12	(.12)	.49**	(.41*)	.37*	(.37*)
Total score	−.13	(.31)	.09	(.48**)	.54**	(.59**)	.36*	(.57**)

[a] Simple correlations are displayed in parentheses.
*p < .05.
**p < .01.

zation of the environment where blacks showed the stronger relation-ship. At the 12-month HOME assessment the differences were not quite so pronounced. Only avoidance of restriction and maternal in-volvement showed stronger relationships for whites. Total HOME scores at 12 months correlated .31 with 3-year IQ for blacks, .48 for whites. Even less race difference was noted in correlations between 24-month HOME and 3-year IQ. Avoidance of restriction and organization of the environment showed stronger relations for whites; but correla-tions between the total HOME score and IQ were almost identical (.59 vs. .57).

Correlations between HOME and IQ for each of the four gender–race groups separately are displayed in Tables 16 and 17. These results, while quite tenuous due to restricted sample size, nonetheless, are of-fered as useful in understanding the analyses on combined groups. Be-cause of the small sample (18) in each group, no attempt was made to determine the reliability of observed differences. Statements about the differences are offered tentatively.

The most notable finding from these analyses is the unusual pattern of HOME–IQ correlations among black males. It is only at 24 months

TABLE 16

Partial Correlations between 6- and 12-Month HOME Scores and 3-Year IQ, Comparing WM, WF, BM, and BF[a]

	6-Month HOME and IQ controlling for 12-month HOME				12-Month HOME and IQ controlling for 6-month HOME			
Subscales	White male	White female	Black male	Black female	White male	White female	Black male	Black female
Responsivity	.18	.34	.09	−.22	.15	−.01	.07	.40
	(.34)	(.45)	(12)	(−.10)	(.33)	(.32)	(.11)	(.35)
Restriction	.25	−.18	−.02	−.25	.41	.48	−.05	.52
	(.39)	(.02)	(−.02)	(.02)	(.49)	(.45)	(−.06)	(.47)
Organization	−.12	.27	.66	.20	.37	−.12	−.32	.40
	(.03)	(.28)	(.61)	(.33)	(.36)	(.15)	(.07)	(.47)
Play materials	.53	.06	.28	.17	.32	.38	.54	.32
	(.59)	(.34)	(.39)	(.26)	(.44)	(.49)	(.59)	(.37)
Involvement	.17	.38	−.06	−.06	.41	.05	.14	.49
	(.40)	(.53)	(.05)	(.10)	(.53)	(.40)	(.14)	(.49)
Variety	.55	.40	.05	.02	.13	.09	−.50	.07
	(.55)	(.41)	(.01)	(.05)	(.14)	(.13)	(−.50)	(.08)
Total score	.41	.37	.29	−.27	.30	.03	−.03	.59
	(.61)	(.55)	(.33)	(.14)	(.56)	(.43)	(.18)	(.55)

[a] Coefficients in parentheses represent the simple correlation between HOME and IQ Coefficients > .40 are significant for simple correlations, > .41 for partial correlations.

TABLE 17

Partial Correlations between 12- and 24-Month HOME Scores and 3-Year IQ, Comparing WM, WF, BM, and BF[a]

| Subscales | 12-Month HOME and IQ controlling for 24-month HOME | | | | 24-Month HOME and IQ controlling for 12-month HOME | | | |
	White male	White female	Black male	Black female	White male	White female	Black male	Black female
Responsivity	.24	.12	.00	.13	.06	.45	.41	.29
	(.33)	(.32)	(.11)	(.35)	(.24)	(.53)	(.42)	(.43)
Restriction	.32	.29	−.05	.39	.28	.15	.13	.17
	(.49)	(.45)	(−.06)	(.47)	(.47)	(.39)	(.14)	(.33)
Organization	.27	−.21	.04	.28	.15	.53	.08	.24
	(.36)	(.15)	(.07)	(.47)	(.29)	(.52)	(.10)	(.45)
Play materials	.33	.03	.28	.23	.17	.41	.27	.35
	(.44)	(.49)	(.59)	(.47)	(.35)	(.61)	(.59)	(.45)
Involvement	.46	.06	−.08	.43	.37	.39	.33	.44
	(.53)	(.44)	(.14)	(.49)	(.46)	(.53)	(.35)	(.51)
Variety	−.05	−.16	−.63	.09	.21	.57	.48	.69
	(.14)	(.13)	(−.50)	(.08)	(.24)	(.56)	(.22)	(.69)
Total score	.39	−.33	−.25	.10	.20	.63	.51	.63
	(.56)	(.43)	(.18)	(.55)	(.47)	(.67)	(.49)	(.76)

[a]Coefficients in parentheses represent the simple correlation between HOME and IQ.
Coefficients > .40 are significant for simple correlations, > .41 for partial correlations.

that they begin to resemble findings from the other three groups. Several of the findings observed on the combined groups seem primarily attributable to differences in the black male sample. For example, the gender differences observed on the restriction of child subscale appear almost wholly due to black males; similarly, the gender difference on variety of stimulation at 12 months. The race difference on organization of the environment at 6 months, maternal involvement at 12 months, and organization of the environment at 24 months seemed also to come from differences in the black male group. An extremely unusual correlation for black males was also noted on the 12-month variety of stimulation scale.

A number of apparent within-race gender differences and within-gender race differences are displayed in Tables 16 and 17—albeit statistical checks for reliability were not performed. Among the more interesting age trends are the following: (1) a slight decrease for white males in HOME–IQ correlations as the time of HOME assessment approached the 3-year IQ assessment; (2) a substantial increase in HOME–IQ correlations for black females as the time of HOME assessment approached the 3-year IQ assessment; (3) a variable but increasing trend for both black males and white females. A second noticeable trend was that when black and white males were combined for analyses, the resulting correlation was often higher for the combined group than for either group separately. The same pattern emerged for females. These findings probably resulted from the fact that the range of scores on all variables increased when racial groups were combined.

Correlations with Language Performance

Closely related to studies of HOME and intelligence are studies of HOME and language development. Several investigators have examined this relationship. Our own study included 74 children and their families (48 black, 26 white). The sample was of heterogeneous SES, but a disproportionate number of children were from lower and lower middle SES families. For purposes of this investigation (Elardo, Bradley & Caldwell, 1977) HOME scores taken at 6 and 24 months were correlated with 37-month performance on the Illinois Test of Psycholinguistic Abilities (ITPA).

The Pearson Product–Moment and Multiple correlation coefficients for 6-month HOME scores and 37-month ITPA scores are displayed in Table 18. An examination of these coefficients reveals a substantial relationship between the two sets of variables. Variety in daily stimulation and appropriate play materials appear particularly salient for the early growth of language. The subscales maternal involvement and responsivity of mother also showed a strong relationship to several aspects of language, although their correlation with ITPA total score was not as significant. The types of stimulation assessed by HOME demonstrated a reasonably strong association with Auditory Reception, Auditory Association, Visual Association, Verbal Expression, and Grammatical Closure. The multiple correlation coefficients indicate that HOME subscale scores share between 18% and 21% common variance with these five psycholinguistic abilities. The multiple correlation for HOME subscales and the ITPA total scores was $R = .41$.

The Pearson product–moment and multiple correlation coefficients for 24-month HOME scores and 37-month ITPA scores are also displayed in Table 18. As expected, 24-month HOME scores show an even stronger association with 37-month ITPA scores than do 6-month HOME scores. In fact, all six HOME subscales and each of the ITPA subtests was significant. Responsivity of mother, appropriate play materials, maternal involvement, and variety in daily stimulation re-

TABLE 18
Intercorrelations among 6-Month and 24-Month HOME Scores and 37-Month ITPA Scores for the Total Sample[a]

ITPA scales	Age in months	HOME subscales						Total score	Multiple R[b]
		Responsivity	Restriction	Organization	Toys	Involvement	Variety		
Auditory reception	6	.34**	.19	.32**	.37**	.32**	.28*	.46**	.47**
	24	.42**	.27*	.38**	.62**	.53**	.44**	.60**	.65**
Visual reception	6	.29**	.14	.17	.27*	.21	.27*	.35**	.37
	24	.36**	.28*	.25*	.45**	.39**	.31**	.47**	.48**
Visual memory	6	.13	.04	.20	.10	.14	.11	.17	.25
	24	.17	.09	.09	.12	.04	.18	.14	.24
Auditory association	6	.30**	.20	.29**	.37**	.28*	.25*	.43**	.43*
	24	.46**	.34**	.39**	.62**	.54**	.46**	.64**	.66**
Auditory memory	6	-.05	.02	.13	.09	.03	-.09	.04	.21
	24	.28*	.05	-.01	.14	.14	.28*	.21	.37
Visual association	6	.26*	.05	.24*	.37**	.31**	.35**	.41**	.46**
	24	.40**	.24**	.40**	.52**	.49**	.42**	.55**	.58**
Visual closure	6	.14	.09	.14	.12	.04	.01	.15	.19
	24	.36**	.17	.10	.27*	.29**	.27*	.34**	.39
Verbal expression	6	.21	.18	.31**	.37**	.16	.22	.37**	.43*
	24	.41**	.24*	.25*	.41**	.39**	.45**	.48**	.53*
Grammatical closure	6	.33**	.27*	.17	.29**	.25*	.41**	.41**	.44*
	24	.42**	.45**	.35**	.57**	.51**	.62**	.62**	.63**
Manual expression	6	.22	-.11	.14	.21	.16	.22	.22	.37
	24	.47**	.20	.22	.36**	.37**	.47*	.47**	.55**
Total ITPA score	6	.28*	.13	.27*	.33**	.25*	.39**	.39**	.41*
	24	.52**	.30**	.32**	.55**	.51**	.61**	.61**	.65**

[a] $N = 74$.
[b] This represents the multiple correlation of all six HOME subscales and ITPA scores.
* $p < .05$.
** $p < .01$.

vealed the highest degree of relation to language growth. Variety in daily stimulation had the highest overall correlation to total language development ($r = .62$), whereas appropriate play materials showed highest relations with Auditory Reception, Auditory Association, Visual Association, and Grammatical Closure (coefficients ranged from .52 to .62).

Tables 19 and 20 display correlations between HOME and ITPA scores for males and females, respectively. As expected, 24-month HOME scores are more strongly associated with 37-month ITPA scores than are 6-month scores. For males, maternal responsivity and play materials revealed the highest degree of relation to language capacity. Four aspects of language (auditory reception, auditory association, visual association, grammatical closure) produced the highest correlations with environmental quality. For females, all six HOME subscales were significantly correlated with language performance; the strongest relations observed were those for subscales play materials, involvement, and variety. Additionally, a greater number of significant correlations among HOME scores and psycholinguistic abilities appeared for females than for males.

In Tables 21 and 22 the correlations between HOME and ITPA scores are displayed for blacks and whites, respectively. Substantial correlations between 24-month HOME scores and 37-month ITPA scores were observed for both races. It is only in the white sample, however, that significant correlations were obtained for 6-month HOME scores. Among blacks, responsivity, play materials, and variety appeared most strongly related to language competence; while among whites, involvement and variety appeared most strongly related. Among whites, environmental quality, as measured by the HOME Inventory, was significantly related to 9 of the 10 psycholinguistics abilities tested, this figure being 5 out of 10 for blacks. The multiple correlation coefficient between the six HOME subscales at 24 months and the ITPA total score was somewhat higher for whites ($R = .74$) than for blacks ($R = .57$).

Stability of the Home Environment and Early Cognitive Development

Beyond interest in the general strength of the relation between home environment and cognitive development, there have been a number of postulations with regard to the mechanisms whereby the environment

TABLE 19

Intercorrelations among 6-Month and 24-Month HOME Scores and 37-Month ITPA Scores for Males[a]

ITPA scales	Age in months	HOME subscales						Total score	Multiple R[b]
		Responsivity	Restriction	Organization	Toys	Involvement	Variety		
Auditory reception	6	.38*	.25	.41**	.37*	.27	.42**	-.51**	.61*
	24	.45**	.04	.32*	.58**	.48**	.38*	.55**	.63**
Visual reception	6	.24	.19	.14	.17	-.01	.36*	.26	.48
	24	.31	.11	.14	.36*	.25	.23	.35*	.40
Visual memory	6	-.09	-.25	.27	.00	.11	.17	.03	.43
	24	.00	.02	.05	-.07	-.16	.06	-.03	.28
Auditory association	6	.39*	.22	.34*	.35*	.19	.37*	.46**	.56*
	24	.52**	.17	.29	.60**	.46**	.45**	.59**	.66**
Auditory memory	6	.00	.08	.25	.08	-.13	-.07	.05	.35
	24	.38*	.18	-.10	.14	.03	.13	.20	.49
Visual association	6	.38*	.15	.21	.39*	.25	.41**	.46**	.55
	24	.49**	.07	.31	.50**	.43**	.39*	.52**	.59*
Visual closure	6	.07	.11	.17	.23	.03	.14	.19	.30
	24	.47**	.26	.01	.24	.30	.14	.36*	.50
Verbal expression	6	.27	.11	.34*	.46**	.02	.15	.37*	.58*
	24	.51**	.09	.13	.30	.25	.26	.38*	.54
Grammatical closure	6	.30	.19	.08	.12	.00	.39*	.25	.53
	24	.44**	.28	.20	.49**	.41**	.31	.51**	.54
Manual expression	6	.18	-.23	.18	.15	.03	.21	.14	.48
	24	.40**	-.15	.22	.39*	.33*	.33*	.43**	.45
Total ITPA score	6	.31	.13	.32*	.33*	.11	.35*	.39*	.52
	24	.57**	.19	.23	.50**	.41**	.36*	.55**	.62**

[a] N = 38.
[b] This represents the multiple correlation of all six HOME subscales and ITPA scores.
* p < .05.
** p < .01.

TABLE 20

Intercorrelations among 6-Month and 24-Month HOME Scores and 37-Month ITPA Scores for Females[a]

ITPA scales	Age in months	HOME subscales						Total score	Multiple R[b]
		Responsivity	Restriction	Organization	Toys	Involvement	Variety		
Auditory reception	6	.32	.15	.20	.38*	.36*	.15	.41**	.41
	24	.38*	.43**	.45**	.65**	.57**	.50**	.65**	.70**
Visual reception	6	.34*	.11	.19	.39*	.46**	.15	.43**	.48
	24	.41**	.43**	.39*	.55**	.55**	.39*	.60**	.60*
Visual memory	6	.28	.22	.08	.18	.16	.05	.26	.31
	24	.30	.13	.08	.27	.18	.09	.25	.36
Auditory association	6	.22	.18	.23	.38*	.39*	.10	.39*	.42
	24	.40*	.50**	.52**	.65**	.61**	.48**	.69**	.69**
Auditory memory	6	-.10	-.03	-.02	.10	.19	-.10	.01	.31
	24	.18	-.05	.07	.13	.22	.42*	.20	.50
Visual association	6	.17	-.01	.24	.36*	.37*	.31	.36*	.47
	24	.31	.35*	.49**	.52**	.52**	.45**	.57**	.60*
Visual closure	6	.18	.07	.06	.01	.04	-.12	.10	.28
	24	.25	.10	.15	.27	.26	.38*	.31	.44
Verbal expression	6	.16	.24	.24	.27	.32	.32	.37*	.50
	24	.29	.37*	.38*	.52**	.52**	.65**	.58**	.69**
Grammatical closure	6	.35*	.32	.22	.43**	.45**	.22	.51**	.52
	24	.39*	.56**	.49**	.64**	.58**	.50**	.69**	.70**
Manual expression	6	.24	-.03	.05	.26	.31	.11	.28	.40
	24	.54**	.24	.19	.30	.40*	.60**	.50**	.74**
Total ITPA score	6	.26	.12	.18	.33*	.38*	.17	.38*	.40
	24	.46**	.38*	.42**	.59**	.59**	.59**	.66**	.71**

[a] N = 36.

[b] This represents the multiple correlation of all six HOME subscales and ITPA scores.

*p < .05.

**p < .01.

TABLE 21

Intercorrelations among 6-Month and 24-Month HOME Scores and 37-Month ITPA Scores for Blacks[a]

ITPA scales	Age in months	HOME subscales						Total score	Multiple R[b]
		Responsivity	Restriction	Organization	Toys	Involvement	Variety		
Auditory reception	6	.14	.08	.23	.14	.21	.09	.22	.30
	24	.34*	.10	.17	.48**	.41**	.37**	.47**	.55**
Visual reception	6	.11	.03	.02	.07	.07	.23	.13	.24
	24	.21	.16	.05	.31*	.15	.22	.28	.39
Visual memory	6	.10	−.07	.22	.08	−.01	.28	.13	.42
	24	.09	−.04	−.01	−.00	−.07	.02	.00	.20
Auditory association	6	.07	.11	.19	.13	−.12	.10	.17	.23
	24	.35*	.25	.23	.55**	.40**	.43**	.54**	.61**
Auditory memory	6	−.25	.01	.18	.01	−.04	−.16	−.09	.37
	24	.26	−.02	−.07	.13	.02	.24	.15	.41
Visual association	6	.20	.02	.07	.21	.13	.23	.23	.33
	24	.24	.14	.29*	.40**	.35*	.29*	.41**	.44
Visual closure	6	.03	.06	.13	.09	.06	−.04	.08	.15
	24	.34*	−.00	−.07	.14	.13	.23	.21	.41
Verbal expression	6	.01	.14	.18	.25	−.04	−.05	.13	.36
	24	.28	.06	−.02	.19	.18	.31*	.25	.39
Grammatical closure	6	.12	.13	−.04	−.02	.06	.25	.11	.31
	24	.31*	.24	.12	.40**	.26	.31*	.41**	.48
Manual expression	6	.07	−.27	.08	.02	.04	.15	.02	.37
	24	.40**	.13	.10	.28	.23	.40**	.38**	.51*
Total ITPA score	6	.06	.02	.18	.13	.09	.14	.14	.22
	24	.44**	.14	.10	.41**	.30*	.40**	.45**	.57**

[a]N = 48.
[b]This represents the multiple correlation of all six HOME subscales and ITPA scores.
*p < .05.
**p < .01.

41

TABLE 22
Intercorrelations among 6-Month and 24-Month HOME Scores and 37-Month ITPA Scores for Whites[a]

ITPA scales	Age in months	HOME subscales						Total score	Multiple R[b]
		Responsivity	Restriction	Organization	Toys	Involvement	Variety		
Auditory reception	6	.54**	−.03	−.03	.44*	.24	.37	.49**	.64
	24	.28	.06	.38	.63**	.50**	.41	.50*	.73*
Visual reception	6	.54**	.09	.18	.43*	.22	.18	.49**	.57
	24	.48**	.22	.46*	.50**	.67**	.29	.59**	.69
Visual memory	6	.05	.02	−.19	−.10	.22	−.38	−.04	.54
	24	.11	.08	−.03	−.06	−.03	.01	−.03	.25
Auditory association	6	.46*	.00	.05	.44*	.25	.26	.45*	.52
	24	.51**	.15	.33	.61**	.56**	.41	.58**	.73*
Auditory memory	6	.57**	.12	.14	.41	.23	.14	.49**	.58
	24	.53**	.42*	.43*	.56**	.61**	.48**	.68**	.70*
Visual association	6	.18	−.30	.06	.36	.30	.40	.33	.55
	24	.48**	−.01	.32	.47*	.48**	.48**	.50**	.69*
Visual closure	6	.26	−.02	−.15	−.01	−.13	−.06	.03	.44
	24	.27	.33	.25	.37	.44*	.21	.42*	.48
Verbal expression	6	.36	−.08	.18	.32	.17	.46*	.50	.55
	24	.43*	.15	.35	.39	.43*	.52**	.51**	.58
Grammatical closure	6	.52*	.18	−.02	.41	.22	.18	.48*	.54
	24	.39	.57**	.40	.65**	.67**	.42	.69**	.77**
Manual expression	6	.51**	.07	.07	.55**	.28	.35	.55**	.62
	24	.59**	.21	.47*	.53**	.60**	.53**	.66**	.70*
Total ITPA score	6	.48**	−.05	.03	.39	.23	.27	.44*	.54
	24	.55**	.22	.42*	.62**	.65**	.46*	.66**	.74*

[a] N = 26.
[b] This represents the multiple correlation of all six HOME subscales and ITPA scores.
* p < .05.
** p < .01.

exerts an influence on development. However, data pertinent to this relationship are meager. It is unclear whether the correlation between early environment and later IQ results primarily from the salience of early experience or because the quality of children's environments remains generally stable. There is theory to support each position (Bloom, 1964; White, Watts, & Associates, 1973); but no specific empirical investigations. Thus, we attempted to examine the issue using partial correlations.

Sample

The same 72 children and their families who participated in the study of gender and race differences in the relation between HOME and IQ were included in this study. The participants were part of the larger Longitudinal Observation and Intervention Study (LOIS) (Caldwell, Elardo, & Elardo, 1972). From the larger study, subjects were selected from which there was a full complement of data. Both the black and the white samples were heterogeneous with respect to SES. However, the black sample included proportionately more lower and the white sample proportionately more middle SES families.

Instruments

As described previously, each of the 72 participating families was administered the HOME Inventory when the child was 6 months, 12 months, and 24 months old. The Stanford-Binet Intelligence Test was given to each child at age 3 years.

Results

To examine the question of whether correlations between early HOME scores and later IQ represent the unique contribution of the early environment, or whether they result from the fact that early environment tends to be highly correlated with later environment, a series of partial correlations were performed. Specifically, 6-month HOME scores were correlated with 3-year IQ, controlling for 12-month HOME scores. Then 12-month HOME scores were correlated with 3-year IQ, controlling for 6-month HOME scores. A similar set of partial correlations was done examining 12-month versus 24-month HOME scores. Separate analyses were done for males and females and for blacks and whites. Results of these analyses on combined race and sex groups can be found in Tables 12–15.

For females, no significant residual correlations between 6-month HOME scores and IQ were observed with 12-month HOME scores partialled out. By contrast, a significant partial correlation between 12-month HOME scores and IQ was observed when 24-month HOME was controlled. All 24-month HOME subscales revealed significant partial correlations with IQ when 12-month HOME scores were controlled.

For males, three of the six HOME subscales (organization of the environment, provision of appropriate play materials, and maternal involvement) measured at 6 months showed significant partials with IQ when 12-month HOME scores were controlled. Almost the same picture emerged when partial correlations between 12-month HOME scores and IQ were calculated, regardless of whether 6-month or 24-month HOME scores were partialled out of the relationship.

For blacks, a rather inconsistent pattern of partial correlations was obtained. At 6 months, only organization of the environment showed a significant partial correlation with 12-month HOME controlled. By comparison, correlations between three 12-month HOME subscale scores and IQ were noted with 6-month HOME scores partialled out (restriction of child, provision of appropriate play materials, and a variety of daily stimulation). Among the partial correlations between 12-month HOME subscales and IQ with 24-month HOME subscale scores controlled, only one subscale reached significance, variety of stimulation, and that was negative ($r = .38$). By contrast, four of the six subscales at 24 months showed significant partial correlation—the total HOME score having a very strong partial correlation ($r = .54$).

For whites, the pattern of partial correlations is a bit more consistent. With 12-month HOME scores partialled out, the correlation between two subscales at 6 months and later IQ was significant (provision of appropriate play materials, variety of stimulation). A very strong partial correlation was observed between 12-month scores on restriction of child and IQ with 6-month score controlled ($r = .47$). A significant partial was also obtained for provision of appropriate play materials. Twelve-month HOME scores from two subscales (restriction of child and maternal involvement) showed significant partial correlations with 24-month scores controlled. All partials except two (restriction of child and provision of appropriate play materials) were significant when 24-month HOME scores were correlated with 3-year IQ. Perhaps the most interesting finding was that 6-month total HOME score and 24-month total HOME score both had significant partials with IQ when 12-month HOME scores was controlled; but the reverse was not true.

In an effort to more fully explain the results of the partial correlation analyses on combined groups, two additional types of statistical analyses were done. First, as with simple correlation analyses described earlier, partial correlations were performed separately on each of the four race–gender subgroups (WM, WF, BM, BF). Results of these analyses are contained in Tables 16 and 17. Second, autocorrelations between HOME subscale scores at 6, 12, and 24 months were calculated to determine the stability of each subscale.

An examination of the partial correlations for the four separate groups showed the following. Except for two subscales (restriction of child, and play materials), the significant partials for females between 12-month HOME scores and IQ controlling for 6-month HOME scores were primarily attributable to black females. As a matter of fact, the nonsignificant trends for white females on the remaining four subscales tended to show a greater residual correlation for 6-month than for 12-month HOME. Looking at the residuals for 24-month HOME scores, it appears that black and white females show nearly identical patterns. However, there is much greater difference between the 12-month and 24-month residuals for whites (see Table 15). For example, among white females the 12-month partials for organization of environment, variety of stimulation, and total score were $-.21$, $-.16$, and $-.33$, respectively. The corresponding partials at 24 months were .53, .57, and .63. As with the simple correlations, the partial correlations on combined groups were frequently higher—albeit not statistically.

In the case of males, one of the four significant partials for 6-month HOME was almost solely attributable to white males (see Table 12), one to black males. Significant 12-month partials for maternal involvement and total score appear mostly due to white males. Moreover, in one instance where white males had a significant partial (restriction of child), the combining of male subgroups reduced the correlation. The significant 24-month partial for maternal responsivity seems primarily due to black males, whereas the significant partial for restriction of child seems primarily due to white males. Unlike the situation that obtained with females, the magnitude of correlations for the combined male group rarely exceeded the magnitude in at least one of the subgroups.

The partial correlation results for the four race–gender subgroups (see Tables 16 and 17) show that the significant 6-month partial for whites in play materials is most closely associated with white males. Similarly, the significant 12-month partials for maternal involvement in the case of white males was reduced to nonsignificance when both gender subgroups were combined. Among the most interesting results in the white subsample was the substantial difference in partials for the total HOME score, especially the 12-month partials, where 24-month HOME was controlled (.39 and −.33 for males and females respectively). Among the five significant 24-month partials recorded for whites, four were principally due to white females.

In the black subgroup, the significant 6-month partial for organization of the environment reflects black males performance. Among the significant 12-month partials, the one for restriction of child reflects black females, the one for variety of stimulation reflects black males.

In an effort to more fully dilineate the relative importance of consistency across time in the home environment versus the unique salience of the early period, the autocorrelations for each HOME subscale were examined. The stability of these six factors varied considerably across the four subgroups (BM, WM, BF, WF). For black males, there was little evidence for consistency for the HOME scores across the three time-points studied. Most coefficients were in the .2–.4 range. For black females there was little consistency from 6 to 12 months, slightly more from 12 to 24 months. The correlation between 12-month and 24-month total scores was .66. For white males, there was modest consistency across the three periods (a number of coefficients in the .3–.6 range). The greatest consistency observed was for white females. The correlation betweem 6- and 12-month total scores was .76; between 12- and 24-month scores was .87.

Discussion

The major question addressed in this study was whether experiences in the early environment were especially significant for later development or whether the observed correlations between early environment and later intelligence primarily reflected the correlation between early environment and later environment. Evidence in favor of the second position would essentially indicate that the early environment per se is not so critical for development; rather the environment tends to be consistent and it is a type of cumulating relationship between environmental experiences and intellectual capability that develops. Results from this study provide some support for each position, albeit more support for the second. In general there were few significant partial correlations between 6-month HOME scores and 3-year IQ with 12-month HOME scores controlled. None were noted for females, three for males. Two were noted for whites and only one for blacks. More significant partial correlations were observed between 12-month HOME scores and IQ with 6-month HOME scores controlled, especially for females, where all six HOME subscales showed significant partials. Relatively few significant partials were observed between 12-month HOME subscales and IQ with 24-month HOME scores controlled (two for females, three for males, two for whites, one for blacks). By contrast, when 24-month HOME scores were correlated with 3-year IQ, partialling out the effect of 12-month HOME scores, over 80% of the partial correlations were significant. For three of the four race–sex subgroups (WF, BF, BM), the 24-month partials were the highest of the three time-periods examined.

HOME–IQ Correlation: Direct or Indirect Relationship

In addition to our attempts at trying to clarify the salience of the early environment versus the cumulating and continuous effect of the environment, it has been our interest to delineate the mechanisms through which the environment influences development. Wachs *et al.* (1971) suggested that environmental stimulation promotes or retards certain processes or functions that are crucial for later development. Central to their model is the idea that "abilities develop sequentially and those coming later build, through maturation and experience, upon those appearing earlier" (p. 305). Yarrow, Rubenstein, Pederson, and Jankowski (1973) argued that certain classes of cognitive variables such as attention, foresight, and goal orientation may be the essential mediators through which the environment impacts development. Their investigation of the relation between early social- and inanimate-environmental events and these cognitive variables, among 6-month old infants, reveals a moderate degree of association. However, they did not determine whether or not it was through these early cognitive variables that the early environment was related to later intelligence test scores. Thus, we attempted to determine whether the early cognitive variables mediate the association we previously observed between early HOME scores and later IQ scores.

Ninety-three of the children (31 white, 62 black) who are a part of our longitudinal study were used in this study. HOME scores were available on participants at 6 and 12 months. Bayley scores were also available. Three differentiated clusters of items from the Bayley were identified as measuring cognitive functions by Yarrow *et al.* (1973): goal-directedness, social responsiveness, and language use. Children's performance on these three groups of items were examined to determine the extent to which they mediated the HOME–IQ relationship.

Results from the study revealed that the three behavioral clusters derived from the Bayley Scales when assessed at 6 months do not appear to mediate the relation between home environment and IQ. The path coefficients between HOME scores and IQ indicate that most of the correlation could be considered a "direct effect." When 12-month Bayley scores were examined to determine the extent to which they might mediate the relation between HOME and IQ, a somewhat different picture emerged. First, all three Bayley behavior clusters showed significant correlation with IQ. Second, the path coefficients between HOME scores and IQ indicated a measurable "indirect" effect for both goal-directedness and language competence. For five of the six HOME subscales, an indirect effect greater than .05 was observed (Kerlinger & Pedhazur, 1973).

In sum, it appears that the relation between early environmental experiences and later is mediated to a limited degree through several diverse capabilities manifested during infancy. Of course, it is important to remember that path models do not allow for strict causal interpretations. In particular, from the present study it is not possible to rule out a mutually facilitative effect between HOME scores and Bayley scores because the alternative models using HOME scores as mediating variables were not investigated. In addition, the generally low stability or early developmental measures make it difficult to draw strong conclusions from the results.

HOME, SES, Family Structure, and Cognitive Abilities

The final way we have attempted to delineate the relation between early home environment and cognitive development is by considering the environmental processes measured by HOME in the context of several SES and family structure variables. Further, it seemed useful to consider the relationship in terms of the fact that both mental test performance and the quality of the environment may change across time and the probability that human cognitive functioning is more amenable to environmental influence at different time points during infancy.

There is some evidence that cognitive measures taken after infancy are more strongly related to environment than measures taken during

TABLE 23

Correlations between Home Environment, 12-Month Cognitive Process Scores, and 3-Year IQ Scores

Environment variables	Social responsiveness		Bayley clusters						IQ	
			Goal directedness		Language					
	6 Month[a]	12 Month[b]	6 Month	12 Month	6 Month	12 Month			6 Month	12 Month
Responsivity	.00	–.12	.23*	–.07	–.03	.00			.07	.28*
Restriction	.23*	.24*	.02	.22*	.06	.33**			.38**	.34**
Organization	.23*	.23*	.13	.32**	.08	.37**			.56**	.58**
Toys	.17	.08	.20	.24*	.08	.26*			.55**	.60**
Involvement	.12	.14	.10	.18	.05	.19			.42**	.55**
Variety	.07	.08	.14	.11	–.03	.18			.29*	.35**
3-Year IQ	.28	.33	.33	.38	.42	.46			—	—

[a] Home assessed when child was 6 months old.
[b] Home assessed when child was 12 months old.
* $p < .05$.
** $p < .01$.

infancy (Elardo, Bradley, & Caldwell, 1975). According to McCall
(1981), development during the earliest months of life may be less amenable to environmental influence than thereafter. There has been some
evidence, however, that certain specific environmental processes may
be significantly related to early measures of competence (Wachs, 1976;
Wachs et al., 1971; Yarrow et al., 1973). Furthermore, there is some
evidence that competence assessed early in life may be related to later
measures of environmental quality. That is, more competent children
may elicit more involvement from parents and encourage them to provide more resources for learning (Bell, 1974; Bradley, Caldwell &
Elardo, 1977). Conversely, less competent children may discourage parental attention and involvement.

The study involved an examination of both mental test performance
and environmental transactions and objects present across the first 3
years of life. Measures of children's development change across time.
Measures of the environment include family status (education and occupation), family structure (degree of crowding), and environmental
process variables. A canonical analysis similar to that used by Walberg
and Marjoribanks (1973) to investigate home environment and differential mental abilities was employed in the study.

A total of 94 children and their families participated in the study (53
males, 41 females). Thirty-eight were white, 56 black. Fathers were
absent in 30 families. All participating children were given the Bayley
Scales of Infant Development at 6 months, 12 months, and 24 months
and the Stanford-Binet Intelligence Test at age 3 years. Families were
administered the HOME Inventory at 12 and 24 months.

Results

Canonical correlations were computed between environmental and
developmental variable sets. The environmental set included maternal
education, occupation of head of household, paternal presence, amount
of crowding, 6 HOME subscales measured at 12 months, and 6 HOME
subscales measured at 24 months. The developmental variable set included Bayley MDI at 6, 12, and 24 months, Bayley Psychomotor Development Index (PDI) at 6 and 12 months, and IQ at age 3 years.

The analysis revealed that only the first canonical variate was significant (.77). As canonical loadings in Table 24 reveal, 3-year IQ was
by far the most strongly loaded on the variate (.88), with MDI at 6
months much less highly loaded (.30). Among the status and structure
variables, amount of crowding was most highly loaded on the canon-

TABLE 24
Canonical Loadings of Environmental
and Developmental Measures

Environmental data set	
SES factors	
Mother's education	− .04
Father presence	− .17
Occupation of head of household	− .15
Amount of crowding	− .22
HOME Inventory—12 months	
Responsivity	.00
Restriction	− .09
Organization	− .12
Play materials	.45
Involvement	.04
Variety	− .20
HOME Inventory—24 months	
Responsivity	.29
Restriction	.09
Organization	− .18
Play materials	.18
Involvement	.13
Variety	.38
Developmental data set	
Bayley MDI—6 months	.30
Bayley PDI—6 months	− .13
Bayley MDI—12 months	.07
Bayley PDI—12 months	.11
Bayley MDI—24 months	− .16
Stanford-Binet IQ—36 months	.88

ical variate (− .22), whereas 12-month play materials, 24-month maternal responsivity, and 24-month variety of stimulation scores were loaded (.45, .29, .38 respectively).

Discussion

The canonical analysis revealed only a single statistically significant canonical variate, one dominated in the developmental sphere by IQ measured at age 3 years. None of the status or structure variables had substantial loadings; the highest was amount of crowding (− .22). Higher loadings were noted for environmental process variables as measured by the HOME Inventory. Play materials had the highest loading on the first canonical variate (.45). Maternal responsivity assessed at 24 months had a .29 loading and variety of stimulation had

a .38 loading. The results seem to suggest that intelligence at age 3 years is most strongly associated with a rich, manipulable object environment beginning in the first year of life. As the child increases in cognitive competence and encounters a larger social and physical world, a responsive and varied environment becomes more highly associated with intelligence test performance.

While the canonical analysis was not intended as a direct test of McCall's (1981) "scoop" model of cognitive development, the results generally seem to fit. Early measures of cognitive development were not as highly loaded on the first canonical variate as was 3-year IQ. (The 2-year Bayley assessment proved problematical in this sample). Furthermore, a somewhat broader array of environmental events in the second year of life appeared related to cognitive performance than was true in the first year. Play materials showed a high degree of stability between the 1-year and the 2-year assessments (.74). Additional follow-ups on a larger sample would be helpful in determining the extent of fit with the scoop model.

Summary

In general, the series of investigations using the HOME Inventory based on the sample obtained in Little Rock may be summarized as follows.

1. The Home Inventory, based on observation and interview with the infant's primary caregiver in the home, provides a reliable, easy-to-use assessment of the quality of the cognitive, social, and emotional environment available to the infant in the home.

2. There is little evidence that the home environments of males and females differ in terms of the mean level of stimulation available during infancy.

3. There appears to be a moderate level of stability in the quality of stimulation available in the home environments of most children throughout infancy.

4. In terms of mean performance, there appear to be differences in HOME scores as a function of race, SES, and family configuration. However, there is evidence that many of the differences reflect the natural confound that exists between many of these demographic variables (i.e., black children tend to live more often in large families where there is little money and only one poorly educated parent who has limited social and economic support). When each of these demographic

factors was examined controlling for all others, the degree of crowding and birth order appeared to account for the greatest variance in HOME scores, with SES, race, and gender contributing less. Over half the variance in HOME remained unaccounted for even when all the factors were added together.

5. There is a substantial relation between the HOME and measures of cognitive development throughout the preschool period. Correlations with Bayley scores in the first year of life tend to be slight. However, correlations with IQ scores at 3 years and 4 ½ years are moderate to strong (.4 to .7). Correlations between HOME and intelligence test scores tend to increase, the closer the timing of the environmental and developmental measures. Correlations between 24-month HOME scores and later IQ were stronger than those between 12-month HOME and later IQ.

6. There is some evidence for race and gender differences in the pattern of our correlations between HOME and later intelligence test scores. Correlations tended to be a little stronger for whites than for blacks and a little stronger for males than for females. However, the differences were more pronounced for correlations between 6-month HOME scores and later IQ than for 24-month HOME and later IQ. Furthermore, the race and gender differences tended to be restricted more to certain subscales rather than to the total HOME score. Correlations between HOME and IQ tended to be more independent of social status for blacks than whites.

7. Correlations between HOME and language performances were similar to those between HOME and IQ.

8. There is evidence that the correlation between early environment and later IQ may reflect the fact that the quality of the home environment tends to remain stable across time and the fact that the later home environment is highly correlated with IQ. On the other hand, there is some (albeit lesser) evidence that certain early home factors may have a more lasting impact, independent of the intervening environment.

9. There is only a limited amount of evidence that the correlation between early HOME scores and later IQ is mediated through some early cognitive motivational variables such as the infant's goal-directedness.

10. In terms of the relationship between HOME and intelligence test performance, there is evidence for some consistency in the relation across time, populations, and aspect of the environment studied. However, there is also some evidence for specificity of effect on each of these dimensions.

References

Barkauskas, V. *Effects of public health nursing interventions with primiparous mothers and their infants.* Unpublished doctoral dissertation, University of Illinois, 1980.

Baumrind, D., & Black, A. Socialization practices associated with dimensions of competence in preschool boys and girls. *Child Development,* 1967, *38,* 291–327.

Bayley, N. Comparisons of mental and motor test scores for ages 1–15 months by sex, birth order, race, geographic location, and education of parents. *Child Development,* 1965, *36,* 379–412.

Bayley, N., & Schaefer, E. Correlations of maternal and child behaviors with the development of mental abilities: Data from the Berkeley Growth Study. *Monographs of the Society for Research in Child Development,* 1964, *29* (Whole No. 6).

Bell, R. A reinterpretation of the direction of effects in studies of socialization. *Psychological Review,* 1968, *75,* 81–95.

Bell, R. Contributions of human infants to caregiving and social interaction. In M. Lewis & L. Rosenblum (Eds), *The effect of the infant on its caregiver.* New York: Wiley, 1974.

Bloom, B. *Stability and change in human characteristics.* New York: Wiley, 1964.

Bradley, R., & Caldwell, B. Early home environment and changes in mental test performance from 6 to 36 months. *Developmental Psychology,* 1976, *12,* 93–97.

Bradley, R., & Caldwell, B. Home environment, cognitive competence and IQ among males and females. *Child Development,* 1980, *51,* 1140–1148.

Bradley, R., & Caldwell, B. The HOME Inventory: A validation of the preschool scale for black children. *Child Development,* 1981, *52,* 708–710.

Bradley, R., Caldwell, B., & Elardo, R. Home environment, social status, and mental test performance. *Journal of Educational Psychology,* 1977, *69,* 697–701.

Bradley, R., Caldwell, B., & Elardo, R. Home environment and cognitive development in the first two years: a cross-lagged panel analysis. *Developmental Psychology,* 1979, *15,* 246–250.

Caldwell, B., & Bradley, R. *Home Observation for measurement of the environment.* New York: Dorsey, in press.

Caldwell, B., Elardo, R., & Elardo, P. *The longitudinal observation and intervention study.* Paper presented at the Southeastern Conference on Human Development, Williamsburg, VA, 1972.

Caldwell, B., Heider, J., & Kaplan, B. The inventory of home stimulation. Paper presented at the annual meeting of the American Psychological Association. Washington, DC, 1966.

Caldwell, B., Wright, C., Honig, A., & Tannenbaum, J. Patterns of information processing used by and with young children in a nursery school setting. *Child Development,* 1970, *41,* 1045–1065.

Caldwell, B., & Richmond, J. Social class level and the stimulation potential of the home. *The Exceptional Infant,* 1, 1967, 453–466.

Caldwell, B., & Richmond, J. The children's center in Syracuse, New York. In L. Dittman (Ed.) *Early child care: The new perspectives.* New York: Atherton, 1968.

Dave, R. *The identification and measurement of environmental process variables that are related to educational achievement.* Unpublished doctoral dissertation, University of Chicago, 1963.

Elardo, R., Bradley, R., & Caldwell, B. The relation of infant's home environments to mental test performance from six to thirty-six months: A longitudinal analysis. *Child Development,* 1975, *46,* 71–76.

Elardo, R., Bradley, R., & Caldwell, B. A longitudinal study of the relation of infants' home environments to language development at age three. *Child Development*, 1977, *48*, 595–603.

Fowler, W., & Swenson, A. *The influence of early stimulation on language development.* Ontario Institute for Studies in Education, Department of Applied Psychology, Toronto, 1975.

Golden, M., & Birns, B. Social class and cognitive development in infancy. *Merrill-Palmer Quarterly*, 1968, *14*, 139.

Haggard, E. *Intra-class correlation and the analysis of variance.* New York: Dryden, 1958.

Hayes, J. *Premature infant development: An investigation of the relationship of neonatal stimulation, birth condition and home environment to development at age three years.* Unpublished doctoral dissertation, Purdue University, 1977.

Hollingshead, A. The Four-Factor Index of Social Status. Unpublished manuscript. 1975.

Hunt, J. *Intelligence and experience.* New York: Ronald, 1961.

Kamin, L. Sex differences in susceptibility of IQ to environmental influence. *Child Development*, 1978, *49*, 517–518.

Kerlinger, F., & Pedhazur, E. *Multiple Regression in Behavioral Research.* New York: Holt, Rinehart, Winston, 1973.

Knobloch, H., & Pasamanick, B. Environmental factors affecting human development before and after birth. *Pediatrics*, 1960, *26*, 210–218.

Lewis, M., & Rosenblum, L. Friendship and peer relations. *The origins of behavior* (Vol. 4), New York: Wiley, 1975.

McCall, R. Nature–nurture and the two realms of development: A proposed integration with respect to mental development. *Child Development*, 1981, *52*, 1–12.

Moore, T. Language and intelligence: A longitudinal study of the first eight years (Part 2): Environmental correlates of mental growth. *Human Development*, 1968, *11*, 1–24.

Peters, C., & VanVoorhis, W. *Statistical procedures and the mathematical bases.* New York: McGraw-Hill, 1940.

Scarr, S., & Weinberg, R. IQ. test performance of black children adopted by white families. *American Psychologist*, 1976, *31*, 726–739.

Siegel, L. Infant tests as predictors of cognitive and language development at two years. *Child Development* 1981, *52*, 545–557.

Trotman, F. Race, IQ and the middle class. *Journal of Educational Psychology*, 1977, *69*, 266–273.

Wachs, T. Utilization of a Piagetian approach in the investigation of early experience effects: A research strategy and some illustrative data. *Merrill-Palmer Quarterly*, 1976, *22*, 11–29.

Wachs, T. The relationship of infants' physical environment to their Binet performance at 2½ years. *International Journal of Behavioral Development*, 1978, *1*, 51–65.

Wachs, T. Uzgiris, I., & Hunt, J. Cognitive development in infants from different age levels and different environmental backgrounds: An explanatory investigation. *Merrill-Palmer Quarterly*, 1971, *17*, 283–317.

Walberg, H., & Marjoribanks, K. Differential mental abilities and home environment: A canonical analysis. *Developmental Psychology*, 1973, *3*, 363–368.

Walberg, H., & Marjoribanks, K. Family environment and cognitive development: Twelve analytic models. *Review of Educational Research*, 1976, *45*, 517–552.

White, B., Watts, J. and Associates. *Experience and environment.* New Jersey: Prentice-Hall, 1973.

Wolf, R. The measurement of environments. In Anastasi (Ed.), *Testing problems in per-spective.* Princeton, NJ: Educational Testing Service, 1965.

Wulbert, M., Inglis, S., Kriegsman, E., & Mills, B. Language delay and associated mother–child interactions. *Development Psychology,* 1975, *11,* 61–70.

Yarrow, L., Rubenstein, J., Pederson, F., & Jankowski, F. Dimensions of early stimula-tion and their differential effects on infant development. *Merrill-Palmer Quarterly,* 1973, *19,* 205–218.

Zajonc, R. Family configuration and intelligence. *Science,* 1976, *197,* 227–236.

Zajonc, R., & Markus, G. Birth order and intellectual development. *Psychological Bul-letin,* 1975, *82,* 74–88.

3

Home Environment
and Cognitive Development in Young Children
of Middle-Socioeconomic-Status Families[*]

Allen W. Gottfried
Adele Eskeles Gottfried

Introduction

The relationship between children's home environment and their cognitive development is a significant issue which has produced a substantial body of literature. This literature has demonstrated that measures of children's home environments are correlated with their intellectual status at a variety of ages (Elardo & Bradley, 1981; Wachs, 1978; Walberg & Marjoribanks, 1976). However, regardless of this general finding, and despite the increasing sophistication by which this issue is studied, there are numerous areas that remain to be resolved. Moreover, it is becoming necessary to refine our understanding of the relationships between environmental factors and cognitive development within designated populations (Wachs & Gruen, 1982; Walberg & Marjoribanks, 1976). The present chapter focuses on the relationship between home environment and cognitive development in a middle-SES sample of children studied longitudinally from infancy through the preschool years.

Socioeconomic status (SES) has been widely used as a measure of home environment, and found to be positively related to intellectual development (see Golden & Birns, 1976). Measures of SES have typically included parental occupation and education, and family income. However, significant limitations have emerged with regard to the use of SES as a measure of environment. First and foremost, SES, a distal variable, provides an index of a family's relative standing with regard

[*]This research was supported by a grant from the Thrasher Research Fund.

57

to these demographic factors, but it provides no direct evidence about proximal experiences that impinge on or interact with the child to influence cognitive development (Bloom, 1964; Deutsch, 1973; Wolf, 1966; Yarrow, Rubenstein, & Pedersen, 1975). Further, SES and proximal environmental variables have been found to contribute separately to ability scores. For example, Whiteman, Brown, and Deutsch (1967) employed a Deprivation Index consisting of proximal home environmental factors such as engaging in dinner conversation and exposure to cultural activities, and found that this index and SES each contributed independently to depressed IQ scores of inner-city elementary school children. Marjoribanks (1972) found that proximal home environmental measures, such as achievement oriented and intellectual activities, correlated with cognitive ability scores of 11-year-old boys at a higher level than did SES.\Proximal home environment has also been shown to add to the prediction of intelligence beyond SES in preschool and school-aged children (Bradley, Caldwell, & Elardo, 1977; Jordan, 1978; Marjoribanks, 1972; Moore, 1968). Hence, to determine the role of experience on cognitive development it is necessary to include measures of the proximal home environment as well as SES.

The emphasis on studying proximal home environmental variables in relation to children's cognitive development is not new. As far back as 1929, Van Alstyne conducted pioneering research on the relationship of the home environment to the intelligence of 3-year-olds. In Van Alstyne's (1929) research, the home environment was assessed through maternal interview, and this interview encompassed specific social and physical aspects that are comparable to the contents of contemporary home environment measures (e.g., Caldwell & Bradley, 1979; Wachs, 1976a). Skodak (1939) also measured the proximal home environments of foster children through ratings based on an interview with the foster mother. Both Skodak and Van Alstyne found that home environment was positively correlated with children's IQ. What is new in contemporary research is the development of inventories for measuring the home environment that have known psychometric properties and that use observational as well as interview formats (Caldwell & Bradley, 1979; Wachs, 1976a). Use of inventories permits generalization and comparability across studies. Time sampling observations of home environments have also been used (Beckwith, Cohen, Kopp, Parmelee, & Marcy, 1976; Clarke-Stewart, 1973; Yarrow *et al.*, 1975).

A second limitation regarding use of SES as an environmental measure concerns the variability of individuals within SES categories. Deutsch (1973) has cogently argued that because SES is a conglomerate of variables, and not a unitary dimension, individuals within an SES group are likely to exhibit considerable heterogeneity on variables related to their children's development. Others have pointed out that there is heterogeneity of home environments within a given SES (Bradley & Tedesco, 1982; Wachs & Gruen, 1982) and that more knowledge about home environment within SES groups is needed (Bradley & Tedesco, 1982; Ramey, Farran, & Campbell, 1979). In this research, we examined the relationship between home environment and cognitive development of young children within a specific SES group that has been largely overlooked in the recent literature on home environment. This research deals with a middle-SES sample.

The importance of studying middle-SES samples include the following reasons.

1. It has been assumed that the middle-SES home environment is facilitative of intellectual development, and that the stimulation provided in middle-SES homes is at a maximum (see Metzl, 1980). However, even within the middle-SES there is considerable variability in children's intellectual development. The extent to which differences in intellectual development within a middle-SES population are accounted for by their home environment has not been extensively investigated. Further, Metzl (1980) found that teaching middle-SES parents to stimulate their infants' language significantly increased both the developmental scores of the infants at 6 months, as well as the level of their home environment as measured by the HOME scale. Therefore, it is apparent that middle-SES parents are not in actuality providing maximal environmental experiences for their young children. Determining the home environmental factors that relate to cognitive development in middle-SES children is of value for enhancing our knowledge about the role of home environment in this extensive portion of the population.

2. Because middle-SES individuals comprise a large segment of the United States population as a whole, it is of importance to obtain data that may be generalized to individuals within this group. Recent longitudinal studies on the relationship between home environment and cognitive development in young children have not focused on middle-SES families, but rather have concentrated on lower-SES samples (Johnson & Breckenridge, 1981), samples inclusive of variation across social classes (Bradley & Caldwell, 1980; Wachs, 1976b; Wachs, Uzgiris, & Hunt, 1971; Yarrow et al., 1975), and at-risk populations (Beckwith et al., 1976; Siegel, 1981). One cannot assume that the relationship between home environment and cognitive development obtained in one population necessarily generalizes to another. Generalizing across pop-

ulations is not a logical but an empirical step. Therefore, if statements are to be made about the relationship of home environment to cognitive development in middle-SES children, research must address this relationship within middle-SES families. This study provides such data.

The major issues that are addressed in this research include the following:

1. What aspects of home environment are correlated with children's cognitive development from infancy through early childhood?
   a. The home environment is differentiated into social and physical components (Caldwell & Bradley, 1979; Parke, 1978; Wachs & Gruen, 1982; Yarrow et al., 1975). While these components may not be totally independent of each other, there may be differential relationships between the social and physical aspects of home environment and children's cognitive development. In this research, we examined the patterns and magnitudes of relationships of both the social and physical aspects of home environment with children's cognitive development.
   b. Are there age trends in the relationships between home environment and cognitive development? We addressed this issue by examining the patterns and magnitudes of relationships across the various ages.
   c. The impact of home environment may differ depending on what particular developmental ability is measured (Yarrow et al., 1975). We examined the relationship of home environment to a variety of measures of development, including both general psychometric and Piagetian sensorimotor scales, a recently devised measure of recognition memory for infants, language development, and the various scales of the McCarthy Test of Children's Abilities.
2. Are the correlations between home environment and cognitive development significant when SES, maternal intelligence, and nursery school attendance are controlled? The importance of this issue is to determine whether home environment contributes significantly to children's cognitive development with these latter three variables held constant.
   a. Regarding SES, determining which of the proximal home environmental variables contribute to cognitive development beyond SES in a middle-SES population enhances our understanding of the impact of home environmental processes.

b. Regarding maternal intelligence, it has been contended that parental intelligence contributes substantially to the correlation between home environment and children's cognitive development (Scarr & Weinberg, 1978; Willerman, 1979). Willerman (1979) has argued that parental intelligence should be included in studies of the relationship between home environment and children's intellectual development to account for genetic variance. While we find this latter point debatable because environment may play a role in parental as well as child intelligence, we agree that a measure of parental intelligence should be included in studies of the relationship of home environment to children's cognitive development to determine the extent to which a child's home environment is mediated through parental intelligence, and the extent to which the home environment contributes to children's cognitive development beyond the variance contributed by parental intelligence.

c. Analyses were also conducted to determine whether SES and maternal intelligence related to cognitive development controlling for home environment.

d. Attendance of children in preschool may also have an impact on the relationship between home environment and cognitive development as Van Alstyne (1929) and Wellman (1940) have suggested. The role of the home environment may change in relation to experiences encountered in nursery school. Therefore, in the present research, attendance of children in nursery school was partialed out of the relationship between home environment and cognitive development.

3. The relative contributions of home stimulation, SES, and mothers' intelligence as predictors of children's cognitive development were examined. It was our purpose to determine which of these predictors was most potent and pervasive.

4. Both earlier and later home environmental assessments have been found to positively correlate with children's subsequent intellectual performance (Bradley & Caldwell, 1980). Significant developmental issues concerning this finding are whether:

a. Earlier and later home environments independently relate to children's subsequent intelligence

b. Early environment relates to subsequent intelligence because of the cross-time consistency in home environment (see, e.g., Bradley & Caldwell, 1980; Kagan, 1979), and

c. Earlier and later home environments are additive in their relationship to subsequent intelligence. In the present study, we have examined these issues.

5. The relationships of mothers' intelligence, family demographic factors, and family social climate with home stimulation variables were examined. The importance of examining these relationships is to elucidate the context and network of relationships of home stimulation.

Method

Subjects

In September 1979, a longitudinal investigation of early development was launched. One hundred and thirty 12-month-old infants were selected from birth notifications of hospitals surrounding California State University, Fullerton. Families were invited by mail and telephone, just prior to the infants' 1-year birthday, to participate in the study. The only criteria used in the selection process were that infants were free of neurological and visual abnormalities. Infants were recruited at 12-months of age because certain measures of cognitive development used in this study (e.g., tactual–visual recognition memory) can be reliably assessed at this age. A total of 130 infants were chosen for the practical reason that this was the maximum number of infants and families that could fit into the study-design time sequence. It is noteworthy that an additional cohort of 40–50 infants selected from the same populations were also longitudinally studied for the purpose of staff training, pilot testing procedures, and establishing initial interobserver reliabilities. However, no data collected on these latter subjects were included in the statistical analyses.

Of the 130 infants recruited at 12-months, 52% were males, 48% were females, 90% were white, and 10% were from other racial or ethnic groups. Fifty-five percent of the infants were firstborns, 32%, 10%, 3%, and 2% were second-, third-, fourth-, and fifth-borns, respectively. Ninety percent of the firstborns had no other siblings. At birth, all of the infants were fullterm and of normal weight ($M = 3591$g, $SD = 894$). On the average, parents were in their late twenties when the infants were born. The sample represented a wide range of middle-SES families as measured by the Hollingshead Four Factor Index of Social Status (Hollingshead, 1975), the Revised Duncan Socioeconomic Index (Stevens & Featherman, 1981), and the Siegel Prestige Scores (Hauser

& Featherman, 1977). The occupational status of 94% of the families ranged from business people and professionals to skilled workers. The remaining 6% were semiskilled. Paternal employment exceeded 96% throughout the course of the study. When the infants entered the study, 36% of the mothers were gainfully employed and by age 3-years, 52% were employed. All families were English speaking. The average years of education of the mothers and fathers were 14.3 ($SD = 2.0$) and 15.2 ($SD = 2.5$), respectively, indicating that most families were composed of parents whose educational achievement ranged from high school to college graduates. Most of the families remained intact with the number married varying between 92% and 94% in the course of investigation. During the study period, 80% of the families lived in the same residence. The number of children attending nursery school increased during the preschool years, with 50% enrolled in nursery school by age 3 years. The demographic characteristics of the sample at the onset of the study are presented in Table 1.

TABLE 1
Demographic Characteristics of Sample

Variable	Mean (SD) or frequency[a]	
Gender		
Males	68	
Females	62	
Race		
White	117	
Chicano	7	
Oriental	1	
East Indian	1	
Hawaiian	1	
Iranian (Arabic)	1	
Interracial	2	
Birth order		
First	71	
Second	40	
Third	13	
Fourth	4	
Fifth	2	
SES		
Hollingshead Four Factor Index of Social Status	45.6	(11.7)
Revised Duncan Socioeconomic Index	46.5	(20.5)
Siegel Prestige Scores	47.9	(14.2)
Parents' age		
Mothers	28.6	(4.2)
Fathers	31.5	(5.1)

(continued)

TABLE 1 (*Continued*)

Mothers' education	
Below high school	3
High school—no college	39
Some college	49
College graduate—no post graduate	23
Post graduate	16
Fathers' education	
Below high school	3
High school—no college	28
Some college	39
College graduate—no post graduate	32
Post graduate	28
Mothers' employment status	
Fulltime	26
Part-time	21
Unemployed	83
Fathers' employment status[b]	
Fulltime	124
Part-time	1
Unemployed	0
Marital status	
Married	121
Unmarried	9

[a] Means are presented for SES and Parents' age; all other values are frequencies.

[b] Five unmarried mothers did not have exact knowledge of fathers' employment status.

Procedure

Commencing at age 12 months the children were tested in the laboratory every 6 months until they reached 42 months of age. Thus, there were a total of six developmental assessments conducted in the laboratory. Subject attrition was minimal throughout the study with 99% (128), 95% (123), 94% (122), 92% (119), and 91% (118) of the children returning at 18, 24, 30, 36, and 42 months, respectively. The small number of families that did not continue was primarily the result of relocating out of state. At each laboratory assessment, which almost always involved a single 1½-hour session, a battery of tests was administered to the child and data were also collected from the mother. Because the focus of this investigation was on individual differences, all tests were administered to all of the children in exactly the same sequence. The amount of missing data was minimal because every attempt was made to completely test all children. This meant accommodating to children's as well as parents' schedules and on occasion scheduling a second session when children were not cooperative on the first.

At an average of 15 months (SD = 1.0 month) and 2 years later at an average age of 39 months (SD = 1.0 month), the homes of the children were visited and directly assessed. Of the 130 children originally in the sample, 99% (129) and 89% (116) had their homes visited at the preceding two ages, respectively. Of the 119 children returning for the 36 month laboratory assessment, 97% had their homes visited at 39 months. Each home assessment was conducted typically in 1 hour with a rule that no assessment be completed in less than 45 minutes. Furthermore, the home assessments were conducted when children were awake.

Measures

Over the course of this longitudinal investigation, numerous tasks were administered. However, only the major measures bearing on the issues at hand are presented here.

Home and Family Environment

The HOME (Home Observation for Measurement of the Environment) developed by Caldwell and Bradley (1979) was designed to measure the social and emotional aspects of home environment by means of direct observation and interview with the mother. The HOME served as the major measure of home environment in this study because: (1) there is an emerging body of literature using this scale, (2) there are several other investigators employing this scale in longitudinal studies, thus, allowing for comparability and generalizability to be determined, and (3) there is an infant and preschool version of this scale. The former version of this scale was administered when the infants were 15 months. This version contains 45 items divided into six subscales and has a total score based on all items. The six subscales are I. Emotional and Verbal Responsivity of Mother, II. Avoidance of Restriction and Punishment, III. Organization of the Physical and Temporal Environment, IV. Provision of Appropriate Play Materials, V. Maternal Involvement with the Child, and VI. Opportunities for Variety in Daily Stimulation. At the 39-month home visit, the preschool version was administered. This version contains 55 items forming eight subscales and a total score. The eight subscales are I. Stimulation Through Toys, Games, and Reading Materials; II. Language Stimulation; III. Physical Environment: Safe, Clean, and Conducive to Development; IV. Pride, Affection, and Warmth; V. Stimulation of Academic Behavior; VI. Modeling and Encouragement of Social Maturity; VII. Variety of Stimulation; and VIII. Physical Punishment. The HOME has been found to be a reliable and valid measure of home stimulation during the early years (Caldwell & Bradley, 1979; Elardo & Bradley, 1981).

During the 1-hour home visit at 15 months of age the physical sections of the Purdue Home Stimulation Inventory (PHSI) (Wachs, 1976a) were administered concurrently with the HOME. The PHSI contains 30 items measuring specific physical aspects of infant home environment and is also based on direct observation and interview.[1] Because of Wachs' focus on environmental specificity in human development (Wachs & Gruen, 1982), he has not derived subscores or a total score for this inventory. The rationale for using both the HOME and the PSHI is that the former was designed to measure socioemotional aspects whereas the latter was constructed to focus on physical characteristics of the environment, thereby providing a more thorough assessment of the home experiences and stimulation available to infants.

An aspect of home environment given little attention in the recent literature on the relationship of home environment to cognitive development in young children is the quality of social relationships among family members. We deemed this to be important because it is reasonable to assume that the social climate of the household would relate to the quality and quantity of home stimulation received by the children and possibly to their cognitive development. For example, households typified by a high degree of family accord may attend more to stimulating and fostering intellectual skills of children compared to families characterized as discordant. In this research, we examined family climate variables in relation to home stimulation and children's cognitive development. At the 36-month laboratory assessment, the mothers filled out the Family Environment Scale (FES) (Moos & Moos, 1981). This scale evaluates the social climate of the family along 10 dimensions: cohesion, expressiveness, conflict, independence, achieve-

[1]Twenty-seven of 30 PHSI items were used. Items measuring change in home environment over time and the state of the infant were not included.

ment orientation, intellectual-cultural orientation, active-recreational orientation, moral-religious emphasis, organization, and control.
The scale is a reliable and valid measure of the quality of social relationships within families and a sensitive indicator of psychological
maladjustment in the family (Holahan & Moos, 1981; Moos & Moos,
1981).

Because variety of stimulation proved to be an important environmental factor during infancy at the 15-month assessment, it was
reasoned that this dimension should be expanded upon at the 39-month
assessment. Therefore, at the 39-month visit, mothers filled out a Variety of Experience Checklist (VEC) (developed by the authors). Mothers checked off the type of experiences their children had in the past
year on three categories. The three categories were: Travel—Type of
Vehicle (car, plane, boat, train, bus, other), Entertainment (TV, movie
theater, circus, aquarium or marineland, museum, amusement park,
zoo or wild animal park, live theater or show, library, special lessons,
other), and Travel—Visit (large city, mountains, desert, forest, beach
or seashore, an island, a different state in the United States, other). The
score on this checklist was the total number of different experiences
the child had received.

Cognitive Development

The infants were tested on the Mental Scale of the Bayley Scales of
Infant Development (Bayley, 1969) at 12, 18, and 24 months. The Bayley was selected because it (1) is the most extensively standardized
infant scale, (2) readily serves as a marker variable or empirical anchor
for the study population (Bell & Hertz, 1976), and (3) has been widely
used, thus, permitting a comparison with other longitudinal studies of
early development. The Mental Development Index (MDI) was used
in all analyses.

At 12 and 18 months, object permanence was assessed (Corman &
Escalona, 1969). The Object Permanence Scale was chosen because it
has been theoretically considered the most important sensorimotor ac-
complishment (Piaget, 1954), and relative to other Piagetian sensorimotor scales, it correlates more highly with subsequent intellectual
performance (Wachs, 1975). The scale yields a single score indicating
the highest level passed in the object permanence progression.

A series of visual recognition memory of objects tasks (visual to visual and tactile to visual) using the paired-comparison technique was
administered at 12, 24, 30, and 36 months (Gottfried, Rose, & Bridger,

1977).[2] Infants' preferences for novel over familiar stimuli, beyond chance expectation, has been used as the index of recognition memory. Measures of recognition memory represent a recent advancement in the assessment of infant cognition, are becoming more widely investigated, and have been found to be sensitive to environmental and risk factors (Rose, Gottfried, & Bridger, 1978; Sigman, 1976; Yarrow et al., 1975). A composite score based on the novelty percentages across the series was derived and used in the analyses.[3]

The McCarthy Scales of Children's Abilities (McCarthy, 1972) were administered at 30, 36, and 42 months. These scales were developed specifically to test children between 2.5 and 8.5 years. The McCarthy was chosen because (1) it allows for analyses to be conducted on separate abilities, and (2) recent evidence is favoring the use of the McCarthy Scales over other intelligence tests during the preschool and early school-age years (Kaufman & Kaufman, 1977). The test comprises 18 subtests, which form six indexes: verbal, performance, quantitative, memory, motor, and a general cognitive index based on the first three indexes.

At the completion of the 39-month home assessment, the Test of Early Language Development (TELD) (Hresko, Reid, & Hammill, 1981) was administered to the children in a quiet location in their homes. This test was given in the home for both practical reasons in the study design and because it was recommended in the test manual that optimal performance for young children is obtained in their regular environment. Hence, testing the children at home was feasible and suitable for assessing their language development. This recently published test was designed to identify children with possible language deficits between the ages of 3 and 7 years. Two of the three dimensions from the Bloom and Lahey (1978) model provided the basis of this test. These two dimensions are form (syntax, morphology, and phonology) and content (encode and decode meaning). The TELD also assesses the expressive and receptive modes of communication. The test is based on a standardization sample of approximately 1200 subjects from several states, has high internal consistency coefficients (.88 to .91) and moderate to high test–retest reliability (.57 to .87). The test permits the computation of several normative scores; however, for the present

[2]Recognition memory tasks were also administered at 18 mo; however, these tasks involved parametric manipulations.

[3]A composite score was used in order to enhance the reliability of these measures. Analyses were conducted directly on the novelty percentages as well as the arcsin transformations of these percentages. The results did not differ.

analyses the total number of items passed on the scale sequence was used.

Mothers' Intelligence

At the 36-month laboratory assessment, the mothers' intellectual performance was tested. It was not feasible to give an entire general intelligence test, therefore, the Vocabularly and Block Design subtests of the Wechsler Adult Intelligence Scale-Revised (WAIS-R) (Wechsler, 1981) were administered. The Vocabulary and Block Design subtests have the highest internal consistency and stability coefficients and smallest standard errors of measurement among the verbal and performance subtests, respectively. Furthermore, among the verbal subtests, Vocabularly correlates the highest with the verbal IQ score (.85) and the highest with the full scale IQ score (.82) compared to the entire set of subtests in the scale. Among the performance subtests, Block Design correlates the highest with the performance IQ score (.74). These two subtests were administered to 115 mothers and their scaled scores used in the analyses.

Social History

At each laboratory assessment, a standard interview was conducted with the mothers. The information collected included such factors as marital status, maternal and paternal education and occupation, changes in family structure (e.g., births); methods of child's caretaking (e.g., whether in nursery school), and whether child has any illnesses, accidents, and/or hospitalizations. This information provided a continuous update of the children's family and health status. From these data, the social status of the families was derived. The Hollingshead Four Factor Index of Social Status based on occupation, education, marital status, and gender (only the former three factors actually enter into the computation) served as the major index of social status in this study because it (1) is the only extant measure suitable for estimating SES of unmarried individuals and heads of households of both genders as well as for families, and (2) correlates more highly with young children's developmental status compared to other contemporary measures of SES (Gottfried, 1983).

Reliabilities

Interobserver reliabilities were conducted on the cognitive tests and home environment inventories at every assessment period. The use of the pilot longitudinal sample helped to establish a high degree of interobserver agreement just prior to each phase of assessment. Furthermore, ongoing interobserver reliabilities were conducted on the actual study sample. For the cognitive tests, reliabilities were conducted on a random sampling of subjects (except for the visual recognition memory tests in which reliabilities were conducted on every subject). In the study sample, all reliabilities in the cognitive tests exceeded .92 with an average of .96 across all tests at all periods. Reliabilities for the study sample were systematically conducted every week during the home assessments phase. Interobserver agreement on the HOME and PHSI across both ages ranged from 91 to 100% on all protocols with an average of 97%.[4]

Results

Environmental Measures: Means, Standard Deviations, and Percentages

The means and standard deviations, or percentages, for the 15- and 39-month HOME (and VEC), PHSI, and FES are presented in Tables 2, 3, and 4, respectively. The first stage in the analyses was to determine whether there were any significant mean differences between the genders and between first- and later-borns on the environmental variables. Multivariate analyses of variance (MANOVAs) with the factors of Gender × Birth Order (2 × 2) were conducted on (1) the 15-month HOME scales, (2) the 39-month HOME scales, (3) the PHSI items with interval scores, and (4) the scales of the FES. These analyses revealed no significant multivariate effects for gender or for the interactions between gender and birth order. Hence, boys and girls did not differ with regard to their mean environment scores.

There were significant multivariate effects for birth order on the HOME at 15-months, $(\lambda = .85)$, $F(7, 119) = 3.06$, $p < .01$, the HOME at 39-months $(\lambda = .78)$, $F(9,104) = 3.17$, $p < .001$, the PHSI $(\lambda = .39)$, $F(13,112) = 13.70$, $p < .001$, and the FES $(\lambda = .62)$, $F(10,105) = 6.43$, $p < .001$. Univariate analyses of variance (ANOVAs) were then conducted on the scales of the HOME, the FES, and on the items of the PHSI, to determine which specific variables were significantly differ-

---

[4]The recommendation by Zimmerman (1981) that the Kappa be used to analyze the interobserver reliability on HOME was found to be not suitable because of the lack of variability that resulted between the concordant cells.

TABLE 2
Means and Standard Deviations on HOME scales and VEC[a]

HOME subscale	Total sample		Firstborn	Later-born	F
15-Month (N = 129)					
Responsivity	8.7	(1.5)			
Restriction and punishment	6.4	(1.1)			
Organization	5.2	(0.9)	5.4	5.0	5.92*
Play materials	8.6	(0.7)			
Maternal involvement	4.0	(1.2)			
Variety of stimulation	3.4	(1.1)	3.7	3.1	8.14***
Total score	36.4	(3.7)			
39-Month (N = 116)					
Toys, games, and materials	8.8	(1.8)			
Language stimulation	5.6	(1.2)	6.0	5.2	12.99***
Physical environment	6.6	(0.7)			
Pride, affection, and warmth	4.8	(1.6)			
Stimulation of academic behavior	3.4	(1.4)	3.7	3.0	9.89***
Modeling of social maturity	3.4	(1.4)			
Variety of stimulation	6.7	(1.4)	7.0	6.3	5.24*
Physical punishment	3.4	(0.8)			
Total score	42.8	(5.9)	43.9	41.4	4.82*
VEC (N = 116)	12.7	(3.8)			

[a] Standard deviations in parentheses; df = 1,125 for 15-month HOME and 1,112 for the 39-month HOME.
 *$p \leq .05$.
 **$p \leq .01$.
 ***$p \leq .005$.

ent for the birth orders. The means and significant univariate F values for these variables are presented in Tables 2 through 4.

For the PHSI items based on categorical data, chi square (χ^2) analyses (correcting for continuity) were conducted to determine whether gender or birth order were significantly associated with responses on the item. There were no significant gender differences; however, birth order differences emerged (see Table 3). For the VEC, an ANOVA was conducted and results revealed neither significant main effects nor a signficant interaction for gender and birth order.

The differences for the birth orders generally revealed higher quantity and quality of stimulation for firstborns. On the HOME, firstborns had a more organized environment, received a greater variety of stimulation at both 15- and 39-months, had more stimulation of their language and academic behavior, and had a higher total score at 39-months. On the PHSI items, homes of firstborns had a greater room:person ra-

TABLE 3
Means and Standard Deviations or Percentages on PHSI[a]

Item	Total sample		Firstborn	Later-born	F or χ^{2} [b]
Ratio of rooms:people	2.7	(0.8)	3.0	2.4	19.91***
Number of categories in which child received training	4.6	(0.5)	4.7	4.4	12.76***
Time per day reading to child (minutes)	12.6	(23.3)	18.3	5.7	9.85***
Number of children's books	17.7	(21.4)	11.9	24.6	12.45***
Number of audio-visual response toys	9.8	(5.0)	8.7	11.0	7.26**
Number of siblings in home	0.73	(0.9)	.2	1.4	122.69***
Number of people in home during interview	2.1	(1.2)	1.8	2.6	16.83***
Times per month child taken out of neighborhood	32.3	(17.8)			
Times per week child visits neighbors	1.5	(0.7)			
Number of adults in home	2.1	(0.4)			
Number of caretaking adults	1.8	(0.4)			
Number of strangers in home during interview	0.2	(0.5)			
Toys exclusively child's					
Yes	70.6		97.1	39.0	
No	29.4		2.9	61.0	52.11***
Activity in home					
Slow	59.2		78.6	37.3	
Active	38.5		21.4	59.3	
Constant rush half-time	0.8		0.0	1.7	
Constant rush most-time	0.8		0.0	1.7	23.37***
Child has place to escape from noise and people					
Yes	93.0		98.6	88.1	
No	6.2		1.4	11.9	5.80*
Child has regular nap time					
Yes	81.4				
No	18.6				
Child has regular supper time					
Yes	94.6				
No	5.4				
Access to newspapers, magazines, and adult books					
Yes	77.5				
No	22.2				

TABLE 3 (*Continued*)

Item	Total sample	Firstborn	Later-born	F or χ^{2b}
Adequate supply of and access to manipulable items				
Yes	70.5			
No	29.5			
Rating of maternal speech				
Average	98.4			
Constant	1.6			
Mobile over crib				
Yes	38.8			
No	61.2			
Decorations in child's room				
Yes	83.7			
No	16.3			
Toys kept in one place				
Yes	88.4			
No	11.6			
Home restricts child's view to interior				
Yes	8.5			
No	91.5			
Stimulus sources on during interview				
None	58.1			
TV	20.2			
Radio	19.4			
Phonograph	1.6			
Any combination	.8			
Rating of sound level				
Only human voices	55.1			
Noise level low to moderate	46.2			
Noise level high half-time	.8			
Noise level high most-time	1.6			
Child's floor freedom restricted				
Yes	2.3			
No	97.7			

[a] N = 129; standard deviation in parentheses; df for ANOVAs = 1,124.

[b] χ^2 values are presented for toys exclusively child's, activity in home, and child having a place to escape from noise and people; all others are F values.

* $p \leq .05$.

** $p \leq .01$.

*** $p \leq .005$.

TABLE 4
Means and Standard Deviations on FES[a]

Subscale	Total sample		Firstborn	Later-born	F
Cohesion	8.1	(1.4)	8.3	7.8	3.75*
Expressiveness	6.8	(1.5)	7.1	6.5	5.40*
Conflict	2.6	(1.8)	2.0	3.4	22.98***
Independence	6.4	(1.5)	6.6	6.1	4.19*
Achievement orientation	5.1	(1.9)			
Intellectual–cultural orientation	6.2	(1.9)			
Active–recreation orientation	5.9	(2.0)			
Moral–religious emphasis	6.1	(2.1)	5.6	6.6	6.16**
Organization	6.3	(2.0)			
Control	4.9	(2.0)	4.0	6.0	34.61***

[a]N = 118; Standard deviation in parentheses; df = 1,114.
  *$p \le .05$.
 **$p \le .01$.
***$p \le .001$.

tio, had less activity (i.e., not as rushed), and were more likely to have a place where the child could escape from noise. Firstborns had fewer books and audio-visual response toys than laterborns but were read to more, had toys that were exclusively theirs, and received training in a greater number of areas (e.g., dressing, self- feeding). Firstborns had fewer siblings and there were fewer people in the home of firstborns during the interview, but these differences appeared to be due to first-borns being mostly only-borns at age 15-months. Being only-borns may also account for firstborns having toys that are exclusively theirs. On the FES, the family climate of firstborns was characterized as more cohesive, expressive, and having a greater emphasis on independence of family members. Furthermore, firstborns' families had less conflict, less moral–religious emphasis, and less control by means of rules or authoritarian techniques.

Standardized Developmental Scales: Means and Standard Deviations

Gender × Birth Order ANOVAs were conducted on the standardized developmental scales (i.e., Bayley and McCarthy).[5] Results revealed significant main effects for gender at 12 months, $F(1,126) = 10.37$, p

[5]MANOVAs were not conducted because of an undue loss of cases for analysis resulting from the use of listwise deletion of missing data in the computer program. ANOVAs gave a more accurate picture because of the inclusion of actual sample sizes at each age.

< .01, and 42 months $F(1,111) = 4.05$, $p < .05$. Girls' scores were significantly higher than boys' at each of these ages. Significant birth order differences were obtained at the consecutive ages of 24-months, $F(1,117) = 6.82$, $p = .01$; 30 months, $F(1,100) = 3.80$, $p = .05$; and 36 months, $F(1,108) = 8.10$, $p < .01$. Firstborns had higher scores at these three ages. There were no significant interactions between gender and birth order. Means and standard deviations for these cognitive scales are displayed in Table 5.

Relationships between Home Environment and Cognitive Development

Bivariate correlations were conducted between the home environment and cognitive measures. We first examined whether there were significant differences between the genders and between the birth orders in the correlations of these variables. There were no significant differences between the correlational matrices of boys and girls, and of first- and later-borns. Heretofore, all data presented are collapsed across gender and birth order. Correlations between the environmental and visual recognition memory measures at 30 and 36-months are not included in the tables because all were nonsignificant.

Correlations with the HOME Scales

Positive, significant correlations emerged between the HOME scales and the cognitive measures across all of the ages. The correlations be-

TABLE 5
Means and Standard Deviations on Standardized Developmental Scales[a]

Scale		Total sample	Firstborns	Later-borns	Males	Females
Bayley 12-month	M	113.3 (10.3)	114.5	111.8	110.8 *	116.2
	N	130	71	59	68	62
Bayley 18-month	M	113.4 (16.6)	115.3	111.2	112.0	115.2
	N	128	70	58	68	60
Bayley 24-month	M	115.0 (20.3)	119.1 *	109.9	112.0	117.8
	N	121	65	56	65	56
McCarthy 30-month	M	112.2 (13.9)	114.3 *	109.4	110.6	114.1
	N	104	59	45	55	49
McCarthy 36-month	M	108.3 (13.0)	111.4 *	104.5	107.3	109.5
	N	112	62	50	60	52
McCarthy 42-month	M	112.4 (10.7)	113.9	110.6	110.7 *	114.6
	N	115	64	51	63	52

[a] Standard deviations in parentheses.
* Significant group differences.

tween the HOME scales and the cognitive measures are presented in
Tables 6 and 7 for the 15- and 39-month HOME, respectively. The significant correlations were low to moderate, with magnitudes ranging
from .15 to .50.

On the 15-month HOME, the variety of stimulation subscale bore
the most consistent relationship with cognitive development. At each
age this subscale correlated with at least one measure of cognitive development, with the correlations tending to increase in magnitude with
advancement in age. Other scales showing significant correlations with
cognitive development over time were the total score, maternal involvement, and responsivity of mother. Play materials was significantly correlated with cognitive development only at one age.
Avoidance of restriction and punishment and organization of environment subscales showed no significant correlations at any age.

The 15-month variety of stimulation subscale was significantly correlated with recognition memory at 12 and 24 months; Bayley at 18
and 24 months; all of the McCarthy mental indexes at 30, 36, and 42
months (except with perceptual-performance at 30 months); the motor
index at 42 months, and the TELD. The 15-month total HOME score
was significantly correlated with recognition memory at 12 and 24
months; with the Bayley at 18 and 24 months; with all of the Mc-
Carthy mental indexes at 36 and 42 months; and with the TELD. The
maternal involvement subscale was significantly correlated with recognition memory at 12 and 24 months; with all of the McCarthy mental indexes at 36 months; and with the verbal, general cognitive, and
memory indexes at 42 months. Responsivity of mother significantly
correlated with recognition memory at 12 and 24 months object permanence at 18 months; with the McCarthy verbal, general cognitive,
and memory indexes at 36; and with the memory index at 42 months.
The play materials subscale showed only a single significant correlation with recognition memory at 12 months.

Examination of the developmental trends showed that recognition
memory at 12 and 24 months correlated with more of the 15-month
HOME scales than did any other infant measure. Further, recognition
memory was the only 12-month infant measure to show a relationship
with the 15-month HOME. The Bayley was correlated with the HOME
at 18 and 24 months whereas object permanence showed only a single
significant correlation at 18 months. There were a considerable number of correlations between the HOME and the McCarthy scales, with
the 36- and 42-month McCarthy showing a greater number of significant correlations than the 30-month McCarthy. The correlations with
the highest magnitudes, between the 15-month HOME scales and the
cognitive measures, emerged with the 36- and 42-month McCarthy. Of

TABLE 6
Correlations between 15-Month HOME and Cognitive Development[a]

HOME	12-Month B	12-Month OP	12-Month RM	18-Month B	18-Month OP	18-Month M	18-Month MT	24-Month B	24-Month V	24-Month RM	30-Month PP	30-Month Q	30-Month GC	30-Month M	30-Month MT
Subscales															
1. Responsivity	-.04	-.01	.17*	.06	.15*	.16*	.04	.09	.11	.15*	.05	.06	.07	.07	.09
2. Restriction and punishment	-.06	-.07	.04	.09	.04	-.03	.11	.08	.06	-.02	.06	-.10	.01	-.01	-.03
3. Organization	-.07	.12	.03	.02	-.04	.05	-.09	.00	.10	.00	-.13	-.07	-.01	-.06	.03
4. Play materials	-.13	-.04	.19**	.05	-.01	-.10	-.08	.02	-.09	.10	-.05	-.07	-.09	-.01	.03
5. Involvement	-.05	.06	.18*	.03	.01	.21*	.07	.10	.06	.18*	.03	.02	.08	.07	-.08
6. Variety	.12	.07	.19**	.24***	-.01	.22**	.11	.31***	.22**	.19**	.14	.27***	.28***	.25***	-.01
Total	-.07	.03	.25***	.15*	.07	.20*	.07	.20*	.14	.18*	.06	.06	.13	.11	-.01
Multiple R (subscales)	.15	.14	.30*** (4,1,6,5)	.30*** (6,5,4)	.15			.38*** (6,3,5,2)		.24* (5,6)			.34*** (6,4,5,1,2)		

HOME	36-Month V	36-Month PP	36-Month Q	36-Month GC	36-Month M	36-Month MT	42-Month V	42-Month Q	42-Month PP	42-Month GC	39-Month TELD
Subscales											
1. Responsivity	.20*	.11	.15	.18*	.21*	-.01	.07	.07	.11	.11	.13
2. Restriction and punishment	.09	.09	.15	.11	.06	-.06	.05	.15	.12	.11	.11
3. Organization	.05	.01	.03	.03	.06	-.02	.06	-.10	-.07	.01	-.02
4. Play materials	-.07	.02	-.03	-.05	-.08	-.07	-.09	-.11	.03	-.04	-.08
5. Involvement	.33***	.18*	.25***	.31***	.18*	.14	.06	.13	.03	.16*	.14
6. Variety	.34***	.35***	.20*	.36***	.39***	.25***	.22**	.22**	.32***	.40***	.25***
Total	.33***	.25***	.25***	.33***	.29***	.20*	.14	.16*	.18*	.26***	.20*
Multiple R (subscales)				.44*** (6,5,4,-2,1,3)						.42*** (6,4,5,2,3)	.31* (6,4,5,2)

[a] B = Bayley, OP = object permanence, RM = recognition memory, V = McCarthy verbal index, PP = perceptual-performance, Q = quantitative, GC = general cognitive, M = memory, MT = motor; $N = 103$–129.

* $p \le .05$.
** $p \le .01$.
*** $p \le .005$.

TABLE 7
Correlations between 39-Month HOME, VEC, and Cognitive Development[a]

Ages 12–30 Months

Scales	12-Month B	12-Month OP	12-Month RM	18-Month B	18-Month OP	24-Month B	24-Month RM	30-Month V	30-Month PP	30-Month M	30-Month Q	30-Month GC	30-Month MT
HOME													
1. Toys, games	.07	.12	.02	.24***	.09	.38***	.13	.26***	.28***	.23**	.16	.29***	.11
2. Language	.02	-.02	.17*	.07	-.05	.17*	.02	.21*	.22**	.21*	.09	.21*	-.04
3. Physical environment	.13	.11	.09	.06	.02	.07	.01	.04	.00	.11	.17*	.07	.19*
4. Pride, affection and warmth	.08	.15*	.12	.12	.06	.22**	.08	.22**	.14	.24**	.11	.21*	-.13
5. Academic behavior	.30***	.17*	.17*	.27***	.13	.37***	.11	.23**	.30***	.21*	.27***	.29***	.00
6. Social maturity	.00	.08	.10	.17*	.12	.19*	.04	.23**	.22**	.23**	.18*	.23**	.10
7. Variety	.13	.23***	-.06	.23**	.04	.28**	.09	.39***	.21*	.27**	.24**	.34***	.12
8. Punishment	-.11	-.10	.08	-.11	-.05	.00	.16*	.12	.14	.19*	.05	.15	.12
Total	.14	.17*	.11	.24***	.09	.42***	.13	.40***	.36***	.38***	.29***	.42***	.08
Multiple R	.39*	.32*	.17			.46***						.44***	
(subscales)	(5,8,3,6,7,1,24)	(7,2,5,4,3)		(5,7,8,2,6,4,1)		(5,1,7,2,4,3,6,8)						(7,5,8,1,4,6,3)	
VEC	.18*	.05	-.01	.24***	.11	.15*	.12	.15	.13	.15	.22**	.23**	-.07

Ages 36–42 Months and 39-Month TELD

Scales	36-Month V	36-Month PP	36-Month M	36-Month Q	36-Month GC	36-Month MT	42-Month V	42-Month PP	42-Month M	42-Month Q	42-Month GC	42-Month MT	39-Month TELD
HOME													
1. Toys, games	.36***	.27***	.20*	.25***	.35***	.11	.35***	.30***	.30***	.27***	.37***	.24***	.29***
2. Language	.29***	.15	.24***	.12	.25***	.10	.27***	.18*	.21*	.16*	.25***	.08	.18*
3. Physical environment	.22**	.06	.23**	.33***	.21*	.10	.20*	.09	.32***	.18*	.18*	.10	.17*
4. Pride, affection and warmth	.35***	.21*	.26***	.27***	.33***	.13	.29***	.27***	.25***	.36***	.34***	.21*	.31***
5. Academic behavior	.37***	.30***	.33***	.28***	.39***	.15	.38***	.29***	.36***	.31***	.39***	.13	.28***
6. Social maturity	.25***	.19*	.23**	.23**	.27***	.08	.24**	.13	.19*	.18*	.23**	.04	.12
7. Variety	.32***	.16*	.17*	.09	.27***	.02	.41***	.21*	.36***	.26***	.39***	.20*	.17*
8. Punishment	.02	-.05	.00	.05	.01	.01	.08	-.02	.05	.00	.04	-.07	.02
Total	.48***	.29***	.35***	.36***	.46***	.13	.50***	.33***	.45***	.41***	.50***	.21*	.35***
Multiple R					.49***						.54***		.39*
(subscales)					(5,4,1,6,3,7,2,8)						(7,5,4,1,3,2,6,8)		
VEC	.21*	.12	.00	-.02	.16*	.05	.20*	.03	.14	.15	.16*	.06	.19*

[a] N = 98–118.
* $p \leq .05$.
** $p \leq .01$.
*** $p \leq .001$.

the McCarthy scales, the verbal, general cognitive, and memory indexes generally had the correlations of the highest magnitudes. The McCarthy motor index showed only a single significant correlation.

To determine which of the 15-month HOME subscales contributed most to the prediction of the cognitive measures, and the magnitudes of multiple correlations between the HOME subscales and the cognitive measures, stepwise multiple regressions and multiple correlations were conducted. The six HOME subscales were the predictors, that is, independent variables, and the cognitive measures were the dependent variables. A separate multiple regression and correlation analysis was conducted for each of cognitive measures (for the 30-, 36-, and 42-month assessments, only the McCarthy general cognitive index was included in these analyses). All of the resulting multiple correlations appear in Table 6 for the 15-month HOME. Significant multiple correlations were obtained for recognition memory at 12 and 24; for the Bayley at 18 and 24; for the McCarthy general cognitive indexes at 30, 36, and 42 months; and for the TELD. The 15-month HOME subscales that contributed to the significant multiple correlations of the cognitive measures differed only slightly across the ages and are indicated in their descending order of contribution, within parentheses, beneath their respective multiple correlation in Table 6. The variety of stimulation subscale contributed most variance to the prediction of all cognitive measures except the 12- and 24-month recognition memory, and thus proved to be the most important and consistent predictor. The magnitudes of the significant multiple correlations were higher than those of any of the respective bivariate correlations. The strongest multiple correlations occurred at 36 and 42 months.

The 39-month HOME scales revealed a greater number of significant correlations with the cognitive measures across the ages that are generally of higher magnitudes than those obtained for the 15-month HOME. The stimulation of academic behavior subscale of the 39-month HOME proved to be the most consistent in its correlation with cognitive development. This subscale correlated with all of the cognitive measures at every age, except for object permanence at 18 and recognition memory at 24 months. Two other 39-month HOME scales, variety of stimulation and the HOME total score, also correlated with cognitive development at every age, with a highly similar pattern to stimulation of academic behavior, albeit with slightly fewer significant correlations than the last-mentioned scale. Variety of stimulation and the total score were significantly correlated with object permanence at 12; with the Bayley at 18 and 24; with virtually all of the McCarthy mental indexes at 30, 36, and 42; with the motor index at 42 months; and with the TELD. The variety of stimulation subscales on the 15- and 39-month HOME consistently correlated with cognitive development across all ages.

Four additional subscales showed a consistent pattern of correlations with the cognitive measures. These are the subscales measuring toys, games, and reading materials; language stimulation; pride, affection, and warmth; and modeling of social maturity. The toys, games, and reading materials subscale was significantly correlated with the Bayley at 18 and 24; with all of the McCarthy mental indexes at 30, 36, and 42 (except the quantitative index at 30); with the motor index at 42 months; and with the TELD. Language stimulation was significantly correlated with recognition memory at 12; with the Bayley at 24; with all of the 30, 36, and 42 McCarthy mental indexes (except quantitative at 30 and 36; and perceptual performance at 36 months); and with the TELD. Pride, affection, and warmth was significantly correlated with object permanence at 12; with the Bayley at 24; with all of the McCarthy mental indexes (except quantitative and perceptual-performance at 30); with the motor index at 42 months; and with the TELD. Modeling of social maturity was significantly correlated with the Bayley at 18 and 24, and with all of the McCarthy cognitive indexes (except perceptual-performance at 42 months). These last four 39-month HOME subscales correlated with fewer infant measures relative to the stimulation of academic behavior and 39-month variety of stimulation subscales.

The physical environment subscale showed fewer significant correlations than those previously discussed. Physical environment was uncorrelated with all of the infant measures from 12 to 24 months. It was significantly correlated with the McCarthy quantitative indexes at 30, 36, and 42; with the verbal, general cognitive, and memory indexes at 36 and 42; with the motor index at 30 months; and with the TELD. The physical punishment subscale was uncorrelated with almost all of the cognitive measures. It was significantly correlated only with recognition memory at 24 and the McCarthy memory index at 30 months.

The developmental trends indicated that the patterns of correlations between the 39-month HOME scales and the McCarthy cognitive indexes were consistent from 30 months on. Moreover, there was an increase in the number of significant correlations from 30 to 42 months, with the highest correlations generally appearing on the McCarthy verbal and general cognitive indexes at 36 and 42 months. The highest correlation was obtained between the 39-month HOME Total score and the 42-month McCarthy verbal and general cognitive indexes (.50). The McCarthy motor index showed relatively few correlations with the 39-month HOME scales. As in the case with the 15-month HOME, the 39-month HOME was correlated with the cognitive abilities on the McCarthy scales as well as with those measured in infancy, albeit more strongly with the former. Of the infant measures, the Bayley showed the highest proportion of significant correlations.

Stepwise multiple regression and correlation analyses were conducted with the eight subscales of the 39-month HOME serving as the predictors, and the cognitive measures as the dependent variables. A separate multiple regression and multiple correlation was conducted for each of the cognitive measures (for the 30-, 36-, and 42-month assessments, only the McCarthy general cognitive index was included in these analyses). The multiple correlations appear in Table 7. Significant multiple correlations were obtained for the Bayley at 12, 18, and 24; object permanence at 12; the McCarthy general cognitive index at 30, 36, and 42 months; and the TELD. The 39-month HOME subscales that contributed to the significant multiple correlations, are indicated in their descending order of contribution within parentheses beneath their respective multiple correlation in Table 7. Stimulation of academic behavior contributed the most variance to the significant multiple correlations of all three Bayley scores and the 36-month McCarthy general cognitive index. The 39-month variety of stimulation subscale contributed the most variance to the multiple correlation of the 12-month object permanence, and the 30- and 42-month McCarthy general cognitive index. Pride, affection, and warmth emerged as the most important predictor of the TELD. These analyses indicate that of the 39-month HOME subscales, stimulation of academic behavior and variety of stimulation were the most important predictors of children's cognitive development. The magnitudes of the significant multiple correlations were higher than any of the respective bivariate correlations. The strongest multiple correlation was obtained for the 42-month McCarthy general cognitive index. The significant multiple correlations between the 39-month HOME and the cognitive measures were higher than those obtained with the 15-month HOME.

Correlations with the Variety of Experience Checklist

The VEC showed low, positive, and significant correlations with the measures of cognitive development. The VEC was significantly correlated with the Bayley at 12, 18, and 24; with the McCarthy general cognitive index at 30, 36, and 42; with the verbal index at 36 and 42; with the quantitative index at 30 months and with the TELD. This checklist, which deals exclusively with the variety of experiences outside the home, related to cognitive development from infancy through 42 months. These findings correspond with those obtained for the 15-

and 39-month variety of stimulation subscale of the HOME, which measures such experiences primarily within the home environment.

Correlations with the Purdue Home Stimulation Inventory

Because of the numerous correlations resulting from 27 PHSI items and 28 cognitive measures, and the need to find reliable interpretation of the data, we selected those items for presentation in the table with an element of consistency. Items not presented are those which (1) were uncorrelated with the cognitive measures (i.e., number of care-taking adults, number of strangers in home during interview, place to escape from noise and people, mobile over crib, toys kept in one place), (2) showed only one significant correlation (i.e., number of adults in home, number of audio-visual response toys, rating of maternal speech, and regular supper time), or (3) resulted in correlations that fluctuated in direction with no discernible trend (i.e., number of people in home during interview, toys exclusively child's, activity in home, regular nap time, decorations in child's room). Thus, 13 of the 27 PHSI items are presented in Table 8.

As previously noted, Wachs did not develop a summary score for the PHSI because of his emphasis on specificity (see Wachs and Gruen, 1982). However, we deemed it important to develop a total score in order to enter it into multiple regression analyses. It was not feasible to enter the extensive number of PHSI items into such analyses; therefore, a PHSI total score or aggregate of the overall physical environment was obtained by summing individual items.[6] Correlations with the PHSI total score are also presented in Table 8.

The PHSI items in Table 8 display both patterns of positive and negative significant correlations. The magnitudes of the positive correlations were of low to low moderate levels with the range from .15 to .45. Negative correlations were low with the range from −.15 to −.33. The items showing significant positive correlations are presented first. Both of the items involving the number of times the child was taken out of the home, either out of the neighborhood or to visit neighbors, correlated with cognitive development. The former correlated with recognition memory at 24, with all of the McCarthy mental indexes at 30, and with the quantitative and general cognitive indexes at 42 months. The latter item correlated with recognition memory at 12; with the Bayley at 18; and with the McCarthy verbal index at 36

---

[6]Items were reversed where appropriate so that a high Purdue Total score represents a more favorable physical environment.

Correlates between PHSI and Cognitive Development[a]

Items	12-Month			18-Month					24-Month		30-Month					
	B	OP	RM	GC	B	M	OP	MT	B	RM	V	PP	Q	GC	M	MT
Taken out of neighborhood	.08	-.03	.11	.13	.08	.05	.06	.04	.03	.19*	.26***	.16*	.17*	.25**	.21*	.12
Visits neighbors	.12	.14	.18*	.09	.19*	.06	-.10	.07	.03	-.05	.00	-.05	.03	-.03	-.03	-.09
Categories of training	.15*	-.03	.03	.21*	.24***	.15	-.04	.13	.22**	.21**	.23**	.09	.20*	.22**	.10	-.03
Time per day reading	.10	.12	.13	.26***	.30***	.19*	.07	.13	.25***	.03	.18*	.00	.13	.15	.13	-.05
Manipulable items	-.03	.03	-.10	.08	.03	.07	.17*	-.11	.13	.10	.16*	.17*	-.04	.13	.02	.12
Ratio of rooms:people	.09	.07	.09	.41***	.30***	.32***	.06	.10	.42***	.02	.32***	.23***	.26***	.33***	.28***	-.07
Floor freedom	.03	.05	.04	.13	-.10	.07	-.09	.09	.06	-.03	.12	.15	.12	.16*	.19*	.07
Number of siblings	-.05	-.07	.11	-.29***	-.19*	-.21*	.04	.00	-.19*	-.01	-.23*	-.08	-.20*	-.21*	-.20*	.04
Restricted view	-.30***	-.14	-.02	.14	-.08	.12	.03	-.28***	-.15*	-.17*	-.16*	-.11	-.14	-.17*	-.18*	.05
Noise sources	-.07	-.11	.03	-.01	-.08	.05	-.16*	.00	-.03	.05	-.11	-.05	-.06	-.10	-.14	-.11
Noise level	-.13	-.11	-.08	-.11	-.16*	-.14	-.10	.01	.06	.12	-.11	-.12	-.10	-.12	-.12	-.02
Children's books	-.07	-.16*	-.08	.02	.00	-.19*	.04	.11	.01	.00	-.18*	-.05	-.20*	-.17*	-.19*	.15
Access to newspapers, magazines, books	-.09	.00	.09	-.02	.02	.01	.08	-.00	.06	.01	.05	.12	-.17*	-.01	-.08	-.02
PHSI total	.05	.04	.11	.23**	.25***	.05	.09	.19*	.18*	.11	.13	.05	.04	.11	.07	-.08

Items	36-Month						42-Month						39-Month
	V	PP	Q	GC	M	MT	V	PP	Q	GC	M	MT	TELD
Taken out of neighborhood	.14	.11	.00	.13	.05	.04	.12	.10	.20*	.19*	.09	.13	.06
Visits neighbors	.17*	.03	-.02	.09	.06	.07	.03	.12	.04	.03	.09	.11	.06
Categories of training	.22***	.12	.16*	.21*	.15	.13	.28***	.09	.23**	.23**	.12	.03	.27***
Time per day reading	.25***	.18*	.26***	.26***	.19*	.13	.27***	.03	.26***	.21**	.24***	-.03	.21**
Manipulable items	.07	.02	.09	.08	.07	-.11	.20*	-.04	.10	.15	.08	.08	.11
Ratio of rooms:people	.43***	.28***	.28***	.41***	.32***	.10	.45***	.07	.26***	.35***	.35***	.22**	.22**
Floor freedom	.08	.09	.19*	.13	.07	.09	.05	.18*	.13	.12	.06	.14	.11
Number of siblings	-.33***	-.19*	-.15	-.29***	-.21*	.00	-.30***	-.02	-.07	-.19*	-.29***	.11	-.24*
Restricted view	-.11	-.20*	.03	.14	.12	-.28***	-.05	-.18*	.13	-.15	-.02	.11	-.10
Noise sources	.00	.01	-.04	-.01	.05	.00	-.12	-.02	-.03	-.07	-.07	.08	-.16*
Noise level	-.08	-.09	-.13	-.11	-.14	.01	-.19*	-.13	-.07	-.17*	-.08	-.09	-.20*
Children's books	-.08	.18*	.04	.02	-.19*	.11	-.03	.08	-.01	.02	-.11	-.14	-.03
Access to newspapers, magazines, books	-.01	-.03	.01	-.02	.01	-.00	.00	-.01	.06	.00	.00	.02	-.02
PHSI total	.18*	.28*	.19*	.23**	.05	.19*	.22**	.13	.24***	.24***	.14	.09	.15

[a] N = 100–129.
* p ≤ .05.
** p ≤ .01.
*** p ≤ .005.

months. The number of categories in which the child received training showed a systematic as well as specific pattern across the ages. It correlated with the Bayley at 12, 18, and 24; with recognition memory at 24; with the McCarthy verbal, quantitative, and general cognitive indexes at 30, 36, and 42 months and with the TELD. Beginning at 18 months, amount of time per day reading to child correlated with a measure of cognitive development at every age. It correlated with the Bayley at 18 and 24; the McCarthy verbal index at 30, 36, and 42; perceptual-performance at 36-mo; the quantitative, general cognitive and memory indexes at 36 and 42 months; and the TELD. Having an adequate supply and access to manipulable items in the home correlated with object permanence at 18; the McCarthy verbal index at 30, and 42; and the perceptual-performance and memory indexes at 30 and 42 months, respectively. The item measuring rooms:people ratio showed the most pervasive and highest correlations with cognitive development. It correlated with the Bayley at 18 and 24; all of the McCarthy indexes at 30, 36, and 42 (except perceptual-performance at 42 months); and the TELD. The amount of floor freedom the child was permitted correlated with the McCarthy general cognitive and memory indexes at 30; quantitative at 36; and perceptual-performance at 42 months. The PHSI total score also revealed significant positive correlations with the Bayley at 18 and 24; McCarthy verbal, quantitative, and general cognitive indexes at 36 and 42; and perceptual-performance and motor at 36 months.

The items showing significant negative correlations are now presented. The number of siblings in the home correlated with the Bayley at 18 and 24; the McCarthy verbal, general cognitive, and memory indexes at 30, 36, and 42; quantitative at 30; perceptual-performance at 36 months; the TELD. The child's view being restricted to the interior correlated with the Bayley at 12 and 24; recognition memory at 24; the McCarthy verbal, general cognitive, and memory indexes at 30; perceptual-performance at 36 and 42; and motor index at 36 months. Both items assessing noise in the home (i.e., number of noise sources and rating of noise level) correlated with cognitive development. The former correlated with object permanence at 18 months and with the TELD, and the latter item correlated with object permanence at 12; the Bayley at 18; the McCarthy verbal and general cognitive indexes at 42 months; and also with the TELD. The items involving the number of children's books and the access to newspapers, magazines, and adult books correlated with the cognitive measures. The former correlated with the McCarthy verbal, quantitative, general cognitive, and memory indexes at 30, and memory index at 36 months (a positive correlation emerged with the perceptual-performance index at 36 months). The latter item correlated with object permanence at 12 and the McCarthy quantitative index at 30 months.

The PHSI items correlated most with the Bayley during infancy (i.e., up to 24 months) and with the McCarthy verbal index between 30 and 42 months. There were virtually no significant correlations between the PHSI items and motor development as measured by the McCarthy (only one significant negative correlation with restrictions of view to interior). The correlations between the PHSI and the cognitive measures tended not to increase or decrease with increasing age, and there was no change in proportion of significant correlations between infancy and the preschool years.

Correlations with the Family Environment Scale

The correlations between the FES and cognitive measures are displayed in Table 9. Only the cohesion, expressiveness, and intellectual–cultural scales showed a pattern of significant correlations with the cognitive measures. These correlations were all positive and of low magnitude ranging from .16 to .36. There was a greater proportion of significant correlations during the preschool period compared to infancy, but no substantial increase in the magnitude of the correlations going from infancy to the preschool period, despite the fact that the FES was administered at the 36 month assessment. All significant correlations were with the sensorimotor and McCarthy scales. Cohesion of the family correlated with object permanence at 12; the Bayley at 24; all of the McCarthy mental indexes at 30, 36, and 42 (except quantitative index at 30); and the motor index at 36 months. Family expressiveness correlated with object permanence at 12; the McCarthy memory index at 30; the verbal index at 36; the quantitative index at 30, 36, and 42; and the perceptual-performance and general cognitive indexes at 36 and 42 months. The intellectual–cultural atmosphere of the family correlated with object permanence at 12, as did the other two scales, the Bayley at 18 and 24 months, and all of the McCarthy indexes at 30, 36, and 42 months (except memory index at 42). The other seven FES scales showed at best a few significant correlations with the direction of the correlations inconsistent in several of the scales.

Correlations with Mothers' Intelligence and Family Demographic Variables

The correlations between mothers' intelligence, family demographic variables, and the children's cognitive development are presented in Table 10. The variables included are mothers' verbal and perceptual

TABLE 9
Correlations between FES and Cognitive Development[a]

Scale	12-Month			18-Month				24-Month		30-Month					
	B	OP	RM	B	OP	M	MT	B	RM	V	PP	Q	GC	M	MT
Cohesion	.10	.17*	.09	.14	-.07	.20*	.20*	.24***	.12	.31***	.24**	.15	.31***	.32***	.14
Expressiveness	.09	.17*	.10	.11	.01	.14	.12	.13	.03	.05	.14	.25**	.14	.16*	-.08
Conflict	.02	.03	-.04	-.01	.07	-.11	-.09	-.13	.12	-.17*	.09	.12	-.10	-.07	.07
Independence	.04	-.03	.00	-.06	.02	.07	.20*	.05	.09	.12	.10	.13	.14	.06	-.12
Achievement	-.02	-.17*	.09	-.02	.12	.05	.25***	.04	.04	-.08	.12	-.03	-.02	-.07	.07
Intellectual–cultural	.13	.20*	-.03	.17*	.01	.18*	.26***	.28***	.10	.27***	.25***	.19*	.30***	.27***	.21*
Active–recreational	.10	.10	.17*	-.06	-.09	-.11	.04	-.01	.04	-.02	.06	-.12	.00	.00	-.10
Moral–religious	.13	.13	.00	.12	.08	-.05	.05	-.01	-.01	-.11	-.03	-.12	-.10	-.08	.04
Organization	.03	.05	.04	.10	.09	.07	.24**	.08	.02	.09	.13	.04	.09	.05	.13
Control	-.08	-.04	-.03	-.01	-.01	-.08	.03	-.19*	-.04	.00	.05	-.02	.02	.00	.15

Scale	36-Month							42-Month						39-Month
	V	PP	Q	GC	M	OP	MT	V	PP	Q	GC	M	MT	TELD
Cohesion	.33***	.28***	.29***	.36***	.20*	-.07	.20*	.27***	.18*	.17*	.28***	.20*	.13	.14
Expressiveness	.24**	.22**	.20*	.27***	.14	.01	.12	.13	.19*	.16*	.21*	.14	.11	.03
Conflict	-.14	-.15	-.14	-.17*	-.11	.07	-.09	-.09	.08	.05	-.02	-.07	.17*	-.07
Independence	.10	.26***	-.03	.12	.07	.02	.20*	.07	.07	.13	.07	-.02	.07	.09
Achievement	-.03	.05	.01	-.01	.05	.12	.25***	-.03	.06	-.05	.00	.03	.13	.09
Intellectual–cultural	.25***	.31***	.22**	.29***	.18*	.01	.26***	.20*	.30***	.28***	.28***	.10	.26***	.15
Active–recreational	-.06	.01	-.16*	.07	-.11	-.09	.04	-.01	.00	-.05	-.02	-.01	.11	-.09
Moral–religious	-.10	-.07	.03	-.08	-.05	.08	.05	-.14	.01	-.08	-.10	-.07	.04	-.17*
Organization	.07	.11	.14	.10	.07	.09	.24**	.02	.03	-.03	.01	.05	.04	.00
Control	-.17*	-.10	-.04	-.14	-.08	-.01	.03	-.08	-.07	-.11	-.13	-.05	.03	-.03

[a] N = 100–118.
* $p \leq .05$.
** $p \leq .01$.
*** $p \leq .005$.

86

TABLE 10
Correlations between Mothers' Intelligence, Family Demographic Variables, and Cognitive Development[a]

Variable	12-Month			18-Month				24-Month		30-Month					
	B	OP	RM	B	OP	M	MT	B	RM	V	PP	Q	GC	M	MT
Mothers' verbal intelligence	−.01	−.02	.05	.03	.09	.24***	.12	.18*	.13	.18*	.19*	.10	.21*	.13	−.01
Mothers' perceptual intelligence	−.03	.00	.29***	−.05	.09	.02	−.15	.03	−.08	−.13	−.14	−.16	−.18*	−.13	−.08
SES	.09	.01	−.07	.29***	.17*	.33***	.21*	.41***	.18*	.33***	.32***	.20*	.34***	.28***	.08
Mothers' education	.10	.02	.10	.29***	.13*	.30***	.18*	.40***	.12	.26***	.29***	.24**	.30***	.21*	−.04
Fathers' education	.04	.08	.03	.22**	.18*	.38***	.13	.34***	.15*	.32***	.20*	.17*	.28***	.26***	.05
Nursery school	.10	.03	.23**	.15*	−.05	.11	.13	.08	.14	.00	−.08	.08	.04	.07	−.13
Children in the home	−.05	.06	−.14	−.16*	.00	−.16*	.00	−.08	.02	−.21*	−.06	−.17*	−.19*	−.19*	.00

Variable	36-Month			42-Month						39-Month
	V	PP	Q	V	PP	Q	GC	M	MT	TELD
Mothers' verbal intelligence	.26***	.33***	.17*	.23**	.09	.21**	.24**	.21**	.01	.16*
Mothers' perceptual intelligence	−.04	.09	−.01	−.05	.04	−.01	−.02	−.10	−.09	−.08
SES	.38***	.36***	.30***	.37***	.28***	.35***	.39***	.21**	.22**	.30***
Mothers' education	.43***	.37***	.25***	.38***	.20*	.38***	.37***	.25***	.08	.26***
Fathers' education	.44***	.27***	.27***	.36***	.23**	.34***	.38***	.28***	.17*	.32***
Nursery school	.17*	.19*	.15	.10	.05	−.01	.06	.12	−.01	.04
Children in the home	−.26**	−.12	−.12	−.21*	.07	−.09	−.10	−.22**	.17**	−.22**

[a] N = 95–130.
* p ≤ .05.
** p ≤ .01.
*** p ≤ .005.

intelligence, family SES, parental education, attendance in nursery school, and the number of children in the home. As previously noted, the verbal and perceptual intelligence of the mothers were assessed at 36 months with the WAIS-R vocabulary and block design subtests. SES was measured with Hollingshead's four factor index, based on data collected at the 12-month assessment. The mothers' and fathers' educational attainment at the time of the 12-month assessment are included because in many cases the educational level of the mother (and in some instances the father) was not calculated into the SES of the family. Although education is a factor in the Hollingshead, it only enters if one is gainfully employed. Nursery school attendance and number of children in the home were based on figures up to and including 36 months of age.

These variables revealed patterns of significant correlations with the cognitive measures. These significant correlations tended to emerge at 18, increase in magnitude at 24 or 30 months on the psychometric tests, and maintained a similar magnitude thereafter. The positive correlations were of low to low-moderate magnitude ranging from .15 to .44, and the negative correlations were of low magnitude ranging from −.16 to −.26.

Mothers' perceptual intelligence bore no relationship with the cognitive measures whereas their verbal intelligence did show a pattern of significant positive correlations beginning at 24 months. Mothers' verbal intelligence correlated with the Bayley at 24; the McCarthy verbal and general cognitive indexes at 30, 36, and 42; the perceptual-performance index at 30 and 36; the quantitative index at 36 and 42; the memory index at 36 months, and the TELD. SES showed a consistent positive relationship with all cognitive measures from 18 to 42 and with the McCarthy motor index at 36 and 42 months. Correlations with mothers' and fathers' education were highly similiar to each other in pattern and magnitude. Both correlated positively with the Bayley at 18 and 24 months, all of the McCarthy mental indexes, and the TELD. Mothers' education also correlated with the McCarthy motor index at 36, and fathers' correlated with object permanence at 18, recognition memory at 24, and the motor index at 42 months. Attendance in nursery school correlated positively with recognition memory at 12; the Bayley at 18; and the McCarthy verbal, perceptual-performance and the general cognitive indexes at 36 months. The number of children in the home at 36 months, like the PHSI number of siblings item, correlated negatively with cognitive development (except for a single positive correlation with the McCarthy motor index at 42 months). Number of children correlated with the Bayley at 18; the McCarthy verbal and memory indexes at 30, 36, and 42; the general cognitive index at 30 and 36; the quantitative index at 30 months; and the TELD.

There were few significant correlations at 12 months, and those emerging during later infancy were mostly with the Bayley, followed by recognition memory. Of the McCarthy cognitive measures, there were slightly more significant correlations with the verbal and general cognitive indexes. As with the HOME, PHSI, and FES, there were few significant correlations with motor development.

Relationship between Home Environment and Cognitive Development, Controlling for SES, Mothers' Intelligence, and Nursery School Attendance

To determine whether the correlations between the home-environmental variables and measures of cognitive development continued to be significant when the effects of SES, mothers' intelligence (verbal), and nursery school attendance were controlled, first-order partial correlation analyses were conducted holding the latter three variables constant. With SES held constant, the percentages of correlations that remained significant for the 15-month HOME scales, 39-month HOME scales, PHSI (those items and the total in Table 8), VEC, and FES (Cohesion, Expressiveness, and Intellectual–Cultural) were 64, 66, 81, 40, and 66, respectively. With mothers' intelligence held constant, the percentages of correlations that remained significant for the 15-month HOME, 39-month HOME, PHSI, VEC, and FES were 75, 96, 98, 50, and 89, respectively. With nursery school attendance held constant, the percentages of correlations that remained significant for the 15-month HOME, 39-month HOME, PHSI, VEC, and FES were 75, 99, 98, 70, and 98, respectively. The magnitudes of the significant partial correlations were highly similar to those of their respective Pearson correlations. Partial correlatons that were nonsignificant involved Pearsons of the weakest magnitudes. These nonsignificant partials showed no trends with regard to age or developmental measure.

Controlling for mothers' intelligence and nursery school attendance produced the largest percentage of significant partial correlations. Moreover, the partial correlations of the 39-month HOME, PHSI, and FES showed a negligible percentage of nonsignificance when mothers' intelligence and nursery school attendance were held constant. Thus, the relationship between home environment and cognitive development was virtually unchanged when mothers' intelligence and nursery school attendance were controlled. When controlling for SES, the majority of partial correlations were significant (except for the VEC), though the percentages of significant partials were somewhat lower than those obtained when controlling for mothers' intelligence and nursery school attendance. Across all three control variables, the 39-month HOME, PHSI, and FES showed the greatest number of significant partials compared to the 15-month HOME and VEC.

Overall, there continued to be a preponderance of significant correlations between the home environmental variables and measures of cognitive development when SES, mothers' intelligence, and nursery school attendance were controlled. Thus, the relationship between home environment and cognitive development continued to be significant independent of the variance attributable to SES, mothers' intelligence, and nursery school attendance.

Home Environment and Cognitive Development: Multiple Regression Analyses

Stepwise multiple regression analyses were conducted to determine the relative contributions of home stimulation, SES, and mothers' intelligence as predictors of children's cognitive development. All of the infant cognitive measures, the general cognitive index of the 30-, 36-, and 42-month McCarthy, and the TELD were the dependent variables in separate multiple regression analyses. The predictor variables were the subscales of the 15-month or 39-month HOME, the PHSI total score, SES, and mother's intelligence (verbal). The results of these analyses appear in Table 11. For each cognitive measure, the significant predictors are presented in their descending order of contribution as well as the significant multiple correlations and R^2 based on the significant predictors.

Analyses with the 15-month HOME revealed a consistent pattern. The variety of stimulation subscale of the HOME and SES were the only significant predictors of the 18- and 24-month Bayley, the 30-, 36-, and 42-month McCarthy general cognitive index, and the TELD. Variety of Stimulation was the primary predictor of the 18- and 24-month Bayley, and the 42-month McCarthy general cognitive index, whereas SES was the primary predictor of the 30- and 36-month McCarthy and the TELD. The play materials and maternal involvement subscales of the HOME were the only significant predictors of 12- and 24-month recognition memory, respectively.

Analyses with the 39-month HOME revealed that the significant predictors of the cognitive measures consisted predominantly of a small set of HOME subscales and SES. The two most consistent predictors were the stimulation of academic behavior subscale and SES. Stimulation of academic behavior was the primary predictor (and at 12 months the only predictor) of the 12-, 18-, and 24-month Bayley; the secondary predictor of the 30-, 36-, and 42-month McCarthy general cognitive index; and the tertiary predictor of the TELD. SES was the primary predictor of 24-month recognition memory, and the 30- and 36-month McCarthy general cognitive index; the secondary predictor of the 24-month Bayley and the TELD; and the tertiary predictor of the 18-month Bayley and the 42-month McCarthy general cognitive index. The variety of stimulation subscale was the primary predictor of the 42-month McCarthy general cognitive index and the only predictor of 12-month object permanence. The pride, affection, and warmth subscale was the primary predictor of the TELD, and was the tertiary predictor of the 36-month McCarthy general cognitive index. The PHSI total score was the secondary predictor of the 18-month Bayley.

Mothers' intelligence, as well as the 15- and 39-month HOME subscales not included in Table 11, failed to be significant predictors of the cognitive measures in these analyses. In all but one instance, the PHSI total score did not significantly predict the cognitive measures. Cognitive measures that were not significantly predicted when the 15-month HOME subscales were entered into the multiple regressions were the 12-month Bayley and the 12- and 18-month object permanence. When the 39-month HOME subscales were entered, the cognitive measures that were not significantly predicted were 12-month recognition memory and 18-month object permanence.

The findings showed that home stimulation variables predicted children's cognitive development more strongly than SES throughout infancy, whereas SES emerged as the strongest predictor of some of the cognitive measures beginning at 24 months. In general, these multiple regressions with the 15- and 39-month HOME subscales revealed that home environment and SES independently and significantly predicted young children's cognitive development. Of the home stimulation variables, the 15-month variety of stimulation subscale and the 39-month stimulation of academic behavior subscale were the most pervasive and potent.

Examination of the multiple correlations revealed a trend for the magnitudes to increase with age for the psychometric tests (i.e., Bayley and McCarthy general cognitive index). The weakest multiple correlations appeared for the 12-month cognitive measures, whereas the strongest appeared for the 24-month Bayley, and the 36- and 42-month McCarthy general cognitive index. Comparing the multiple correlations obtained in these analyses with those appearing in Tables 6 and 7 (in which the multiple correlations are based only on the 15- or 39-month HOME subscales, respectively) revealed that they were of similar magnitudes.

To further address the controversial issue regarding whether the correlation between home environment and children's intelligence is ac-

TABLE 11
Stepwise Multiple Regressions for Cognitive Measures as Predicted by the HOME, PHSI, SES, and Mothers' Intelligence

Cognitive measures	Regressions with the 15-month HOME			Regressions with the 39-month HOME		
	Significant predictors	R	R^2	Significant predictors	R	R^2
12-Month Bayley	NS[a]			Stimulation of academic behavior	.31***	.09
Object permanence	NS			Variety of stimulation	.20*	.04
Recognition memory	Play materials*	.21*	.04	NS		
18-Month Bayley	Variety of stimulation*			Stimulation of academic behavior**		
	SES*	.34***	.12	PHSI total*		
				SES*	.41***	.17
Object permanence	NS			NS		
24-Month Bayley	Variety of stimulation***			Stimulation of academic behavior***		
	SES***	.45***	.20	SES***	.48***	.23

92

Recognition memory	Maternal involvement*	.21*		SES*	.21*	.04
30-Month McCarthy general cognitive index	SES** Variety of stimulation*	.40***	.16	SES*** Stimulation of academic behavior*	.41***	.17
36-Month McCarthy general cognitive index	SES*** Variety of stimulation**	.46***	.21	SES*** Stimulation of academic behavior*** Pride, affection, and warmth*	.53***	.28
42-Month McCarthy general cognitive index	Variety of stimulation*** SES***	.48***	.23	Variety of stimulation*** Stimulation of academic behavior*** SES**	.53***	.28
39-Month TELD	SES* Variety of stimulation*	.34***	.12	Pride, affection, and warmth* SES* Stimulation of academic behavior*	.41***	.17

[a]NS = not significant.
* $p \leq .05$.
** $p \leq .01$.
*** $p \leq .005$.

counted for by their relationship with mothers' intelligence, we conducted hierarchical multiple regression analyses to determine the separate contributions of home environment and mothers' intelligence as predictors of children's 42-month McCarthy general cognitive index scores. The 42-month McCarthy general cognitive index was the dependent variable with mothers' intelligence (verbal) and the 39-month HOME total score the predictors. Two hierarchical regression analyses were performed to examine this issue in two different ways. In the first regression analysis, mothers' intelligence was entered first and the HOME score second, to determine whether the latter variable significantly and independently predicted children's intelligence beyond mothers' intelligence. In the second regression analysis, the HOME score was entered first and mothers' intelligence second, to determine whether the latter variable significantly and independently predicted children's intelligence beyond home environment.

In the first regression analysis mothers' intelligence significantly predicted children's McCarthy scores when it entered the regression analysis on the first step, $F(1,107) = 6.64, p < .01$. When the HOME score was entered on the second step, mothers' intelligence was no longer a significant predictor, $F(1,107) = 1.19, p > .05$, whereas the HOME score did significantly predict the McCarthy, $F(1,107) = 25.76$, $p < .001$. The R^2 of the 42-month McCarthy with mothers' intelligence was .05 $(R = .24, p < .01)$, and when home environment was added, the R^2 was .24 $(R = .49, p < .001)$.

In the second regression analysis the HOME score was entered first and it significantly predicted children's McCarthy scores, $F(1,107) = 32.68, p < .001$. Mothers' intelligence entered on the second step and was not a significant predictor, $F(1,107) = 1.19, p > .05$, whereas home environment continued to be significant, $F(1,107) = 25.76, p < .001$. The R^2 between the HOME and McCarthy was .23 $(R = .48, p < .001)$ and when mothers' intelligence was added the R^2 was .24 $(R = .49, p .001)$.

In both of the hierarchical regression analyses, the interaction between mothers' intelligence and home environment was entered as a third predictor. This interaction was a multiplicative function consisting of mothers' intelligence by home environment. In both analyses, the interactions were nonsignificant. These analyses revealed that when both mothers' intelligence and the HOME total score were included in hierarchical multiple regression analyses, mothers' intelligence was not a significant predictor regardless of its order of entry. Holding mothers' intelligence constant, home environment significantly and independently predicted children's McCarthy scores. However, holding home environment constant, mothers' intelligence was not a significant predictor of children's McCarthy performance. There-fore, the relationship between home environment and children's cog-nitive development was not accounted for by mothers' intelligence. These results complement those of the stepwise regressions in that the findings were consistent regardless of whether the predictors were en-tered hierarchically based on a theoretical rationale guiding their order of entry, or whether the predictors entered the regression due to sta-tistical criteria as in stepwise regression. These findings were also con-sistent with the preceding partial correlations.

Relationships between Early versus Later Home Environment and Cognitive Development

It was found in our data that the infant (15-month) and preschool (39-month) home assessments correlated significantly and positively with the last intellectual assessment (42-month). To address the develop-mental issues regarding these relationships, hierarchical multiple regression analyses were conducted. The 42-month McCarthy general cognitive index was the dependent variable and the 15- and 39-month HOME total scores were the predictors. These latter two variables served as the early and later environmental predictors because the HOME was the only environmental inventory repeated across time, and the total score provided a composite of the environment at each point in time. It should be noted that the correlation between the 15- and 39-month HOME total scores was .58, $p < .001$, indicating a mod-erate degree of consistency in home environment across this time in-terval.

Two hierarchical regression analyses were performed. In the first analysis, the 15-month HOME score was entered first, and the 39-month HOME score second, to determine whether later environment predicts children's intelligence beyond the contribution of early en-vironment. In the second analysis, these variables were entered in the reverse sequence to determine whether early environment predicts children's intelligence beyond the contribution of later environment. Furthermore, by conducting these analyses we were able to determine whether early environment relates to later intelligence due to cross-time consistency in home environment, and whether early and later environment were additive in their relationship to subsequent in-telligence.

In the first regression analysis, the 15-month HOME score signifi-cantly predicted children's McCarthy scores when it entered the regression analysis on the first step, $F(1,110) = 7.59$, $p < .01$. When the 39-month HOME score was entered on the second step, the 15-month HOME score was no longer a significant predictor, $F(1,110) = .88$, $p > .05$, whereas the 39-month HOME score significantly predicted the McCarthy, $F(1,110) = 27.62$, $p < .001$. The R^2 for the McCarthy and the 15-month HOME was .06 ($R = .25$, $p < .01$), and when the 39-month HOME was added the R^2 was .25 ($R = .50$, $p < .001$).

In the second regression analysis, the 39-month HOME score entered first and significantly predicted children's McCarthy scores, $F = 37.27$, $p < .001$. The 15-month HOME score was entered on the second step, and was not a significant predictor, $F = .88$, $p > .05$, whereas the 39-month HOME remained significant $F(1,110) = 27.62$, $p < .001$. The R^2 for the McCarthy and the 39-month HOME was .25 ($R = .50$, $p < .001$), and when the 15-month HOME was added there was virtually no increment in the R^2 (and R). The multiplicative interaction between the 15- and 39-month HOME scores was included as the third predictor in each regression analysis, and was nonsignificant in each case.

These results showed that the later home environment score was a significant and independent predictor of children's subsequent intelligence beyond the contribution of early home environment. Early home environment did not significantly predict children's subsequent intelligence when later home environment was controlled, indicating that the correlation between early home environment and subsequent intellectual status may be accounted for by the cross-time consistency in home environment. Early and later home environment were not additive in predicting intelligence in preschoolers.

Relationships between Family Characteristics and Home Stimulation

To gain knowledge about family characteristics that may play a role in the provision of home stimulation to young children, we examined the correlations between these variables. Mothers' intelligence, family demographic variables, and the quality of social relationships as measured by the FES were correlated with the HOME scales, VEC, and PHSI.

Correlations between mothers' intelligence, family demographic variables and the home stimulation inventories are presented in Tables 12 and 13. The matrix with the HOME scales and VEC showed a substantial number of significant correlations. These correlations were of

TABLE 12

Correlations between Mothers' Intelligence, Family Demographic Variables and Home (and VEC)[a]

HOME or VEC	Mothers' intelligence		SES	Mothers' education	Fathers' education	Nursery school	Children in home
15-Month HOME							
Responsivity	.17*	(.08)	.20*	.27***	.23***	.20*	−.09
Restriction and punishment	.27***	(.13)	.20*	.18*	.21**	.07	−.02
Organization	−.03	(.07)	−.07	.07	.09	.15	−.29***
Play materials	.03	(.18*)	.03	.04	.08	.17*	−.17*
Involvement	.36***	(.09)	.26***	.33***	.25***	.35***	−.21*
Variety	.23**	(.20*)	.25***	.28***	.28***	.21*	−.19*
Total	.35***	(.22**)	.28***	.39***	.36***	.34***	−.27***
39-Month HOME							
Toys, games	.32***	(.17*)	.49***	.47***	.41***	.22**	−.13
Language	.27***	(.19*)	.24***	.36***	.29***	.19*	−.34***
Physical environment	.08	(.06)	.09	.14	.02	.19*	−.25***
Pride, affection and warmth	.17*	(.00)	.26***	.27***	.30***	.19*	−.11
Academic behavior	.01	(.00)	.21*	.24***	.18*	.10	−.26***
Social maturity	.27***	(.21*)	.29***	.25***	.36***	.20*	−.19*
Variety	.19*	(.04)	.38***	.45***	.45***	.06	−.12
Punishment	.03	(−.09)	.01	.10	.12	−.09	−.02
Total	.32***	(.14)	.46***	.53***	.48***	.23**	−.30***
VEC	.32***	(.04)	.31***	.46***	.26***	.25***	−.19*

[a] Mothers' perceptual intelligence in parentheses; $N = 115–129$.

* $p \leq .05$.
** $p \leq .01$.
*** $p \leq .005$.

TABLE 13

Correlations between Mothers' Intelligence, Family Demographic Variables and PHSI[a]

Items	Mothers' intelligence		SES	Mothers' education	Fathers' education	Nursery school	Children in home
Taken out of neighborhood	-.07	(-.13)	-.07	.04	.04	-.06	.06
Visits neighbors	-.11	(-.05)	.00	.15*	.02	.09	-.10
Categories of training	.08	(.00)	.21**	.24***	.11	.09	-.17*
Time per day reading	.02	(.05)	.17*	.18*	.22**	.11	-.19*
Manipulable items	.22**	(.04)	.05	.00	.01	.06	.07
Ratio of rooms:people	.39***	(.08)	.44***	.49***	.45***	.25***	-.39***
Floor freedom	-.01	(-.06)	-.10	-.07	-.10	.07	.06
Number of siblings	-.18*	(-.17*)	-.04	-.29***	-.17*	-.36***	.85***
Restricted view	-.01	(.08)	-.11	-.13	-.18*	.01	.00
Noise sources	-.04	(.07)	-.01	-.11	.03	-.18*	.23**
Noise level	-.05	(-.02)	-.07	-.20**	-.09	-.15*	.37***
Children's books	.17*	(.11)	.15*	.24***	.12	.01	.19*
Access to newspapers magazines, books	.28***	(.07)	.21*	.08	.14	.03	.19*
PHSI total	.10	(.02)	.19*	.28***	.24***	.08	.00

[a] $N = 115–129$.
* $p \leq .05$.
** $p \leq .01$.
*** $p \leq .005$.

low to moderate magnitudes with the positive and negative correlations ranging from .15 to .53 and −.15 to −.34, respectively. Mothers' intelligence (verbal), SES, and parents' education showed a highly similar and pervasive pattern of positive correlations with the home stimulation inventories. Families with mothers of relatively higher intelligence, of higher SES, and with parents of higher educational achievement tended to score higher on the following scales: responsivity of mother; avoidance of restriction and punishment; maternal involvement; variety of stimulation at 15 and 39 months; toys, games, and materials; language stimulation; pride, affection, and warmth; modeling of social maturity; the total HOME scores at 15 and 39 months; and the VEC. Although mothers' intelligence did not relate to stimulation of academic behavior, SES and parents' education did relate to this subscale. Mothers' verbal, in contrast to perceptual, intelligence showed a greater number of correlations with the home stimulation variables. Attendance in nursery school was positively related to responsivity of mother; play materials; maternal involvement; variety of stimulation at 15 months; toys, games, and materials; language stimulation; physical environment; pride, affection, and warmth; modeling of social maturity; the total HOME scores at 15 and 39 months; and the VEC, indicating that parents who provided more home stimulation to their children were more likely to send them to nursery school. The number of children in the home correlated negatively with organization of the environment, play materials, maternal involvement, variety of stimulation at 15 months, language stimulation, physical environment, stimulation of academic behavior, modeling of social maturity, HOME total scores at 15 and 39 months, and the VEC.

These family characteristics also correlated significantly with the quantity and quality of stimulation assessed on the PHSI. Again, the significant correlations were of low to moderate magnitudes (with the exception of the correlation between siblings at 15 and children in the home at 39 months) with the positive and negative correlations ranging from .15 to .49 and −.15 to −.39, respectively. Mothers' intelligence (verbal) correlated positively with access to manipulable items; rooms:people ratio; number of children's books; and access to newspapers, magazines, and adult books; and negatively with number of siblings. Mothers' perceptual intelligence correlated significantly only with number of siblings. Family SES correlated positively with categories of child training; time per day reading; rooms:people ratio; children's books; access to newspapers, magazines, and adult books; and the PHSI total score. Both mothers' and fathers' education correlated positively with time per day reading, rooms:people ratio, PHSI total score, and negatively with number of siblings. Mothers' education also correlated positively with visits to neighbors, categories of child training, and children's books, and negatively with rating of noise level. Fathers' education also correlated negatively with restricted view to interior of the home. Nursery school attendance correlated positively with rooms:people ratio and negatively with number of siblings, and noise sources and level. The number of children in the home correlated positively with noise sources and level, children's books, and access to newspapers, magazines, and adult books, and correlated negatively with categories of child training, time per day reading, and rooms:people ratio. The high correlation between number of siblings and children in the home indicates that there was consistency between 15 and 36 months in the number of children in the home.

The correlations between the FES and home stimulation inventories are presented in Tables 14 and 15. A considerable number of significant correlations resulted between the FES and HOME scales and VEC. These correlations were of low magnitude with the positive and negative correlations ranging from .15 to .38 and −.15 to −.33, respectively. Although the cohesion, expressiveness, and intellectual–cultural scales were the only ones related to children's cognitive development, most of the FES scales showed a pattern of significant correlations with the HOME scales and VEC. However, the largest number of significant correlations were found with these three FES scales. Moreover, these last scales showed a highly similar pattern of positive correlations. All three correlated with maternal involvement, variety of stimulation at 15 and 39 months; games, toys, and reading materials; stimulation of academic behavior; the 15- and 39-month HOME total scores, and the VEC. The cohesion and intellectual–cultural scales both correlated with responsivity of mother; avoidance of restriction and punishment; language stimulation; and pride, affection, and warmth. The cohesion, expressiveness, and intellectual–cultural scales also correlated with organization of environment, modeling of social maturity, and physical punishment, respectively. The independence and active–recreational scales resulted in positive correlations as well. Independence correlated with toys, games, and materials; stimulation of academic behavior; and the VEC. Active–recreational correlated with maternal involvement; variety of stimulation at both 15 and 39 months; the 15-month HOME total score; toys, games, and materials; and the VEC. A highly similar pattern of negative correlations resulted with the conflict and control scales. Both correlated with variety of stimulation at 15 and 39 months; toys, games, and materials; language stimulation; stimulation of academic behavior; and the 15- and 39-

TABLE 14

Correlations between FES and HOME (and VEC)[a]

HOME or VEC	Coh	E	Cf	I	Ach	I-C	A-R	M-R	O	Ct1
15-Month HOME										
Responsivity	.20*	.06	-.07	.08	.07	.22**	.11	-.08	.11	-.01
Restriction and punishment	.20*	.04	-.07	.12	-.15	.18*	.07	-.12	.06	-.02
Organization	.15*	.02	-.11	.08	-.13	.12	.07	-.09	-.03	-.16*
Play material	.01	.07	-.10	-.04	.01	.03	.12	-.07	-.20*	-.08
Involvement	.29***	.21**	-.24***	.08	.06	.28***	.16*	-.02	.04	-.12
Variety	.33***	.25***	-.26***	.03	.09	.28***	.27***	.00	.10	-.20*
Total	.38***	.20*	-.22**	.13	-.09	.36***	.23**	-.11	.07	-.17*
39-Month HOME										
Toys, games	.34***	.15*	-.16*	.19*	-.03	.33***	.20*	.01	.14	-.18*
Language	.21**	.11	-.33***	.07	-.07	.18*	.10	-.21**	.06	-.17*
Physical environment	.03	.03	-.07	-.03	.04	.09	-.05	.00	.24***	-.06
Pride, affection and warmth	.16*	.12	-.11	.07	-.06	.29***	.05	-.10	-.03	-.07
Academic behavior	.25***	.21**	-.20*	.18*	.07	.18*	.10	.03	.07	-.17*
Social maturity	.13	.19*	-.06	-.09	-.12	.14	.05	-.07	.04	-.13
Variety	.33***	.24***	-.16*	.03	-.14	.33***	.29***	-.03	.04	-.22**
Punishment	.03	-.02	-.05	-.06	-.07	.17*	-.04	-.17*	.00	.00
Total	.35***	.24***	-.25***	.11	-.09	.38***	.14	-.10	.11	-.23**
VEC	.26***	.25***	-.09	.20*	-.08	.35***	.34***	-.05	.17*	-.09

[a] Coh = cohesion, E = expressiveness, Cf = conflict, I = independence, Ach = achievement, I-C = intellectual-cultural, A-R = active-recreational, M-R = moral-religious, O = organization, Ct1 = Control; N = 117.

* p ≤ .05.
** p ≤ .01.
*** p ≤ .005.

TABLE 15

Correlations between FES and PHSI[a]

Items	Coh	E	Cf	I	Ach	I-C	A-R	M-R	O	Ctl
Taken out of neighborhood	.14	.07	.03	-.14	.01	.05	.26***	-.16*	-.01	-.01
Visits neighbors	.04	.14	.08	-.07	.00	.01	.19*	.16*	.18*	.12
Categories of training	.19*	.02	-.21**	.33***	.00	.16*	.09	.11	.16*	-.14
Time per day reading	.25***	.16*	-.21**	.11	-.07	.16*	.22**	.20*	.05	-.17*
Manipulable items	.04	.06	.06	-.05	.06	.04	.10	.05	.12	.18*
Ratio of rooms:people	.26***	.24***	-.19*	.16	-.02	.19*	.17*	-.10	.08	-.26***
Floor freedom	.21*	.13	-.07	.00	.10	.13	.10	-.05	.05	-.04
Number of siblings	-.21**	-.25***	.35***	-.25***	.08	-.08	-.01	.28***	.06	.49***
Restricted view	.01	-.07	-.11	-.04	.00	.07	.09	.04	.04	.07
Noise sources	.01	-.05	.13	.00	-.04	-.15*	-.07	.05	.08	.13
Noise level	-.05	-.02	.19*	-.20*	-.07	-.03	-.10	.06	-.02	.30***
Children's books	.10	.13	-.06	-.07	-.11	.13	.12	.11	.09	.13
Access to newspapers, magazines, books	-.02	-.11	.05	.00	-.03	.13	.17*	.17*	-.01	.12
PHSI total	.27***	.19*	-.14	-.02	-.08	.21**	.33***	.12	.09	-.03

[a] Coh = cohesion, E = expressiveness, Cf = conflict, I = independence, Ach = achievement, I-C = intellectual-cultural, A-R = active-recreational, M-R = moral-religious, O = organization, Ctl = control; $N = 117$.

* $p \leq .05$.

** $p \leq .01$.

*** $p \leq .005$.

month HOME total scores. Conflict and control also correlated with maternal involvement and organization of environment, respectively. The FES organization scale correlated positively with physical environment and the VEC, and negatively with play materials. The moral–religious scale correlated negatively only with the language stimulation and physical punishment subscales. Achievement showed no significant correlations with any of the scales.

A number of significant correlations of low to moderate magnitude resulted between the FES and PHSI. The significant positive and negative correlations ranged from .16 to .49 and −.15 to −.26, respectively. The pattern of relationships among the FES scales with the PHSI was similar to those found with the HOME and the VEC. The cohesion, expressiveness, and intellectual–cultural scales correlated positively with time per day reading, rooms:people ratio, and PHSI total score. The cohesion and intellectual–cultural scales correlated positively with categories of child training, and cohesion and expressiveness correlated negatively with number of siblings. The cohesion and intellectual–cultural scales also correlated positively with floor freedom and negatively with noise sources, respectively. Active–recreational correlated positively with being taken out of the neighborhood and to visit neighbors; time per day reading; rooms:people ratio; access to newspapers, magazines, and adult books; and the PHSI total score. Independence correlated positively with categories of child training, and negatively with number of siblings and noise level. Organization correlated positively with visits neighbors and categories of child training. The moral–religious scale correlated negatively with taken out of the neighborhood and positively with visits neighbors, time per day reading, number of siblings, and access to newspapers, magazines, and adult books. Conflict and control correlated positively with number of siblings and noise level, and negatively with time per day reading and rooms:people ratio. Conflict also correlated negatively with categories of child training, and control also correlated positively with access to manipulable items. All correlations with the achievement scale were nonsignificant.

Discussion

This longitudinal study reveals that within a middle-SES sample there are aspects of the social and physical home environment that relate to young children's cognitive development. The findings showed that several of these home environmental variables were related to cognitive development from infancy through the preschool years. The relations between home environment and cognitive development were characterized by positive and negative directions.

The home stimulation variables that were positively related to cognitive development may be conceptualized into the following categories: variety of experiences, stimulation of educational abilities, enhancement of skills, maternal involvement, provision for exploration, and physical home setting. The variety of experience category includes the variety of stimulation subscales on the 15- and 39-month HOME, the VEC items that measured the diversity of experiences outside of the child's home, and PHSI items involving visitation to neighbors, and being taken out of the neighborhood. Stimulation of educational abilities encompasses the stimulation of academic behavior subscale, time per day reading to the child, and the subscale measuring stimulation through toys, games, and reading materials (which involves educational types of toys and games). Enhancement of skills includes the number of categories of child training (i.e., social, self-help, language, and motor skills), the modeling and encouragement of social maturity, and language stimulation subscales. The last subscale, may also come under the rubric of stimulation of educational abilities. The maternal involvement category incorporates the emotional and verbal responsivity of the mother; maternal involvement; and pride, affection, and warmth subscales. The provision for exploration category consists of floor freedom, and access to manipulable items. Another variable falling under the exploration category, albeit having a negative relationship is the child's view being restricted to the interior of the home. The physical home setting category includes the room: people ratio, and the physical environment being clean, safe, and conducive to development.

Positive relationships were also found between cognitive development and family climate as assessed by the cohesion, expressiveness, and intellectual–cultural scales of the FES. The cohesion scale measures commitment, help, and support among family members; expressiveness measures encouragement of family members to act openly and express their feelings; intellectual–cultural orientation measures family interest in political, social, intellectual, and cultural activities.

Patterns of variables that were negatively related to children's cognitive development predominantly involved aspects of the physical environment. Distractability appears to be an element of several of these variables. These include the number of noise sources and rating of noise level during the interview; number of children's books; and access to newspapers, magazines, and adult books. The negative relationships with the last two variables are surprising in view of the fact that toys, games, and reading materials correlated positively with cognitive development. While the nature of this discrepancy is not readily apparent, it may be speculated that sheer number and accessibility of books and reading materials without reference to type or use of these materials indicates distraction and clutter in the home environment. The toys, games, and materials subscale primarily assesses the type and use of these materials. Restriction of child's view to the interior of the home (i.e., inaccessible view through windows) negatively correlated with cognitive development, and as noted, involves restriction of visual exploration. The number of siblings in the home also correlated negatively with cognitive development and involves diminution of home stimulation across a wide range of variables (this is discussed here subsequently).

Several variables showed few or no relationships with cognitive development. These may be categorized as infant toys and decorations, organization of environment, discipline, and people and activity in the home. The category, infant toys and decorations, includes play materials, number of audio-visual toys, mobile over crib at 15 months, and decorations in the child's room. Organization of the environment encompasses the temporal and physical organization subscales, items assessing regular naptime and suppertime, toys in one place in the home, toys belonging exclusively to the child, a place for the child to escape from noise and people, and the organization scale on the FES. Discipline incorporates the avoidance of restriction and punishment and physical punishment subscales, and the control scale on the FES. People and activity in the home consists of number of adults in the home, number of caretaking adults, number of people and strangers in the home during interview, and activity of the home during interview. In addition to items and scales falling within these categories, rate of maternal speech and the other FES scales (conflict, independence, achievement, active–recreational, and moral–religious) did not relate to cognitive development.

The variables having the most pervasive relationships with cognitive development (i.e., correlating with cognitive development at every age) included the 15- and 39-month variety of stimulation subscales, the 39-month stimulation of academic behavior subscale and HOME total score, the number of categories of child training, and the VEC. Where the highest correlations were obtained, they appeared on the variety of stimulation and stimulation of academic behavior subscales, 39-month HOME total score, and the rooms:people ratio item. The highest amount of variance accounted for by the bivariate correlations was 25%. Slightly more variance in cognitive development was accounted for by the multiple correlations with the HOME subscales, with the maximum amount of variance being 29%. Moreover, the HOME subscales that contributed the most variance to the multiple correlations were 15- and 39-month variety of stimulation and 39-month stimulation of academic behavior. Therefore, in a middle-SES sample of children, variety of stimulation and stimulation of academic behavior emerge as the most pervasive and relatively most potent home stimulation variables related to early cognitive development.

With regard to age trends in the correlations between home environment and cognitive development, the significant bivariate and multiple correlations for both the 15- and 39-month HOME scales tended to be higher at the 36- and 42-month McCarthy assessments. This finding of higher correlations at later ages is consistent with those of Bradley and Caldwell (1976) and Elardo et al. (1975). Across all ages, the 39-month HOME, compared to the 15-month HOME assessment, showed a greater number of significant correlations that were generally of higher magnitudes with cognitive development. The finding that the 39-month HOME postdicted cognitive development during infancy suggests that (1) infants differing in cognitive development elicit correspondingly different levels of home stimulation in the preschool years, and (2) the quality and quantity of stimulation assessed on the preschool version of the HOME may actually exist in the home environments of middle-SES infants. It may be possible to assess these preschool home dimensions during infancy in middle-SES homes. Although both the 15- and 39-month HOME assessments correlated with subsequent cognitive development, the hierarchical multiple regression analyses showed that the early HOME correlated with subsequent cognitive development because of the cross-time consistency in home environment. There was no independent or unique contribution of early home environment to preschool cognitive development. These results corroborate the findings of Bradley and Caldwell (1980, 1981), and are consistent with the view that early environment does not play a unique or critical role in later development (Clarke & Clarke, 1976). On the PHSI, there were no age changes in the magnitude or number of significant correlations. On the FES, there were also no changes in the magnitude of the correlations; however, there was a greater proportion of significant correlations during the preschool years.

There are several trends pertaining to the relationships of the cognitive measures with the home environmental variables. During infancy, there was a higher proportion of significant correlations for recognition memory and the Bayley compared to object permanence. Among these infant measures the highest correlations were found with the Bayley. Recognition memory showed no significant correlations beyond 24 months. Although recognition memory as indexed by novelty preferences may be sensitive to home environment during infancy, this measure may assess a cognitive skill that is too rudimentary to be sensitive to environmental differences in the preschool years. During the preschool years, the McCarthy verbal and general cognitive indexes showed the greatest number and strongest correlations with home environment. In view of the fact that the 36- and 42-month McCarthy generally showed stronger correlations than infant measures, it appears that verbal and symbolic abilities are most sensitive to variation in home environment, a finding that corresponds with those of Marjoribanks (1972). Motor development showed few relationships with home environment.

Distal variables (i.e., mothers' verbal intelligence and the demographic factors) related to the children's cognitive development with correlations of comparable magnitude to those of the proximal (home stimulation) variables. However, the distal variables tended to relate to cognitive development beginning at age 18 months, whereas the proximal variables related as early as age 12 months. The finding that proximal variables correlated significantly with cognitive development earlier than has been typically found for distal variables is in accord with other studies (Elardo et al., 1975; Wachs, 1979; Wachs et al., 1971). Distal variables begin to correlate significantly with cognitive development typically around 2 years of age (see Golden & Birns, 1976; Gottfried, 1983; Wilson, 1978).

When SES was controlled in the partial correlation analyses, home environment continued to be significantly related to cognitive development in the large majority of cases, indicating that home environment contributes to cognitive development independently of this demographic factor. Only for the VEC did controlling for SES substantially reduce the number of correlations to nonsignificance revealing that for variety of experiences outside of the home, SES does play an important role.

The multiple regression analyses revealed that both home environment and SES were significant predictors of cognitive development from 18 months on, indicating that both proximal and distal environmental variables independently contribute to variance in cognitive development. These results are in agreement with those of Jordon (1980), Marjoribanks (1972), and Whiteman et al. (1967) who also found independent contributions for proximal home environment and status variables to cognitive development. For most of the assessments during infancy, home environment proved to be a stronger predictor than SES. During the preschool years, SES was more often a stronger predictor than home environment. This latter finding is not entirely in agreement with the view that proximal home environment variables are more strongly related to children's cognitive development than SES as espoused by Bradley *et al.* (1977) and Walberg and Marjoribanks (1976) and in disagreement with the position of Wachs and Gruen (1982) that only proximal environmental variables are relevant to differences in development. We advocate the inclusion of both proximal environmental and SES variables as part of a comprehensive model of the relationship of environment to cognitive development because each contributes uniquely and additively to the prediction of children's cognitive development. Perhaps SES itself allows for children's experiences to be expanded beyond those present in the home environment, such as variety of experience outside of the home, or, there may be additional home proximal variables for which SES is a marker, which are not measured by the current inventories.

The present study reveals that within the middle-SES, there is variability in home environment. Further, middle-SES families are not providing maximal stimulation. Both the significance and magnitudes of correlations found between home environment and cognitive development, and the presence of negative correlations, support these two conclusions. The negative correlations also indicate that there are conditions within middle-SES homes that may impede cognitive development. Our findings support views of heterogeneity of environment within SES (Bradley & Tedesco, 1982; Wachs & Gruen, 1982), and also complement the conclusions of Metzl (1980) regarding home stimulation provided by middle-SES parents.

A controversial issue that we addressed concerned whether the correlation between home environment and cognitive development is accounted for by their relationships with mothers' intelligence. The results of partial correlations controlling for mothers' verbal intelligence, stepwise and hierarchical regression analyses all supported the conclusions that (1) home environment is significantly and independently related to children's cognitive development controlling for mothers' intelligence, and (2) mothers' intelligence does not significantly predict children's cognitive development whereas home environment is a significant predictor, when both are included in regression analyses. These results show that despite the significant bivariate correlations among mothers' intelligence, children's cognitive development, and home environment, the relative contribution of mothers' intelligence when compared to home environment, is insignificant in predicting children's cognitive development. We conclude that the relationship between home environment and children's cognitive development is not spuriously due to their relationship with mothers' intelligence. These findings are in contrast to those of Campbell (1979) and Longstreth, Davis, Carter, Flint, Owen, Rickert, and Taylor (1981). These two studies put forth data that the relationship between home environment and cognitive development is due to their correlation with mothers' intelligence. In each of these studies, the sampling procedures employed were highly questionable. In the former study, the relatively small sample was constructed of a lower SES intervention group (Abecerdarian study) and a middle-SES group from the general population. In the latter study an admittedly haphazard procedure generated the sample including the use of personal acquaintances or mutual contacts who served as referrals. The extent to which these unusual sampling procedures biased the results is unknown. However, these samples should not be taken as representative of any population, and more importantly, the validity of the findings of Campbell (1979) and Longstreth et al. (1981) is questionable.

Examining the relationships of mothers' intelligence, family demographic factors, and family social climate as related to home stimulation variables is important for construct validation of home stimulation inventories, but more important for (1) gaining a comprehensive and deeper understanding of the relationships between home environment and early cognitive development, and (2) developing theories and causal explanations of home environment and young children's cognitive development. Based on our data, we emphasize the need to take into account the intellectual, social, and physical ecology of the family (also see Belsky, 1981; Bradley & Caldwell, 1978; Bronfenbrenner, 1979).

Mothers' intelligence and family demographic factors related not only to children's cognitive development, but also pervasively to the provision of their social and physical home stimulation. Mothers of higher intelligence (i.e., verbal intelligence), education, and SES provided a social and physical environment that was generally more enriched and conducive to enhancing children's cognitive development (also see Clarke-Stewart, 1973). Additionally, it is interesting to note that studies have shown that mothers with higher educational achievement have been found to have more knowledge about the environmental factors that influence children's development (Clarke-Stewart, 1973; Stevens, 1982) and are more accurate in assessing their children's developmental skills (Gottfried, Guerin, Spencer, & Meyer, in press). Thus, mothers of higher intelligence, education, and SES may be intentionally instituting a child development and academically oriented curriculum in the home for their young children. The predominance of stimulation of academic behavior subscale as a predictor of the infants' and preschoolers' cognitive development supports this position. It appears that these mothers are more aware of what is necessary for intellectual development and school success and are acting on their knowledge to provide the experiences and the setting that facilitate such achievements.

Where nursery school attendance correlated significantly with cognitive development, these relationships were positive in all instances. Controlling for nursery school attendance did not substantially reduce the number of significant correlations between home environmental variables and cognitive development. In most cases, it had a negligible effect on the correlations, indicating that the relationship between home environment and cognitive development is independent or not influenced by nursery school attendance. However, what is interesting is the finding that mothers who provided more home stimulation, particularly social stimulation were more likely to send their children to nursery school. Thus, those mothers who provide more stimulation may appreciate the value of schooling earlier, and choose to expand their children's experiences beyond that of the home.

Number of children in the home correlated negatively with cognitive development as early as age 12 months and with all but one age. Furthermore, a greater number of children was associated with a less favorable social and physical home environment. These results coincide with those comparing first- and later-borns. It it likely that as the number of children in the home increases, the opportunity to interact with, and be stimulated by the mother diminishes. For example, later-borns had more books but were read to less. It may be speculated that this less advantaged environment of later-borns may be a factor accounting for their significantly lowered cognitive scores compared to firstborns.

Although only the cohesion, expressiveness, and intellectual–cultural scales of the FES correlated with cognitive development, virtually all of the FES scales correlated with the social and physical home stimulation variables. A major role or influence of the social climate of the family may reside in its indirect rather than its direct relationship with cognitive development. The quality of social relationships in the home may influence the level and quality of home stimulation provided for the child, which in turn may account for individual differences in children's developmental status.

Moos and Moos (1981) have conceptualized the ten scales into three dimensions: relationship (cohesion, expressiveness, and conflict), personal growth (independence, achievement, intellectual–cultural, active–recreational, and moral–religious), and system maintenance (organization and control). Our data show that more favorable stimulating environments for children are associated with families in which (1) relationships are characterized by more cohesion, and expressiveness, and less conflict; (2) personal growth is stressed predominantly by greater independence, intellectual–cultural, and active–recreational orientations, and (3) system maintenance is conducted by more organization in planning and structuring activities and less control by rigid rules and authoritarian techniques.

In summary, our findings show that social and physical home environment variables are uniquely related to cognitive development in young children of middle-SES families. These variables which displayed positive and negative relations were independent of SES, mothers' intelligence, and nursery school attendance. The most pervasive and potent social environmental variables were variety of stimulation and stimulation of academic behavior, and among the physical variables, rooms:people ratio was the strongest. Age trends showed that the highest correlations between environment and cognitive development tended to be found during the preschool years. The correlation between early home environment and subsequent cognitive development was due to the cross-time consistency of early and later home environment. During infancy, home stimulation correlated most with recognition memory and the Bayley and during the preschool years with the verbal and general cognitive indexes of the McCarthy. Mothers' intelligence and family demographic factors such as SES and parental education related to cognitive development as well as home stimulation variables. SES proved to be independently related to cognitive development; however, mothers' intelligence was not related to cognitive development independently of home stimulation. Variables measuring family social climate, which included cohesion, expressiveness, and intellectual–cultural orientation, were related to cognitive development and virtually all social climate variables were related to home stimulation variables. It was suggested that mothers of higher intellect, education, and SES knowledgeably provide more stimulating home environments to facilitate their children's cognitive development.

Acknowledgment

Deepest appreciation is extended to Connie Meyer, Diana Guerin, Steve Renfeldt, Debbie Schmierer, Joan Spencer, and Chava Pollack for their dedicated and conscientious work. The parents and young children in this study deserve special thanks for their effort and continuous participation.

References

Bayley, N. *Bayley Scales of Infant Development.* New York: Psychological Corporation, 1969.

Beckwith, L., Cohen, S., Kopp, C., Parmelee, A., & Marcy, T. G. Caregiver–infant interaction and early cognitive development in preterm infants. *Child Development,* 1976, *47,* 579–587.

Bell, R. Q., Hertz, T. W. Toward more comparability and generalizability of developmental research. *Child Development,* 1976, *47,* 6–13.

Belsky, J. Early human experiences: A family perspective. *Developmental Psychology.* 1981, *17,* 3–23.

Bloom, B. *Stability and change in human characteristics.* New York: Wiley, 1964.

Bloom, L., & Lahey, M. *Language development and language disorders.* New York: Wiley, 1978.

Bradley, R. H., & Caldwell, B. M. The relation of infants' home environments to mental test performance at fifty-four months: A follow- up study. *Child Development,* 1976, *47,* 1172–1174.

Bradley, R. H., & Caldwell, B. M. Screening the environment. *American Journal of Orthopsychiatry,* 1978, *48,* 114–130.

Bradley, R. H., & Caldwell, B. M. The relation of home environment, cognitive competence, and IQ among males and females. *Child Development,* 1980, *51,* 1140–1148.

Bradley, R. H., & Caldwell, B. M. *Home environment and cognitive development in the first three years: Race and sex differences.* Paper presented at the Biennial Meeting of the Society for Research in Child Development, Boston, March, 1981.

Bradley, R. H., Caldwell, B. M., & Elardo, R. Home environment, social status, and mental test performance. *Journal of Educational Psychology,* 1977, *69,* 647–701.

Bradley, R. H., & Tedesco, L. A. Environmental correlates of mental retardation. In J. Lachenmeyer & M. Gibbs (Eds.), *The psychology of the abnormal child.* New York: Gardner, 1982.

Bronfenbrenner, U. *The ecology of human development.* Cambridge, MA: Harvard University Press, 1979.

Caldwell, B. M., & Bradley, R. H. *Home Observation of measurement of the environment.* Little Rock: University of Arkansas, 1979.

Campbell, F. *How may we best predict the child's IQ?* Paper presented at the Biennial Meeting of the Society for Research in Child Development, San Francisco, March, 1979.

Clark, A. M., & Clarke, A. D. B. Overview and implications. In A. M. Clarke & A. D. B. Clarke (Eds.), *Early experience: Myth and evidence.* New York: Free Press, 1976.

Clarke-Stewart, K. A. Interactions between mothers and their young children: Characteristics and consequences. *Monographs of the Society for Research in Child Development,* 1973, *38,* (6-7, Serial No. 153).

Corman, H. H., & Escalona, S. K. Stages of sensorimotor development: A replication study. *Merrill-Palmer Quarterly*, 1969, *15*, 351–361.

Deutsch, C. Social class and child development. In B. Caldwell & H. Ricciuti (Eds.), *Review of child development research* (Vol. 3). Chicago: University of Chicago press, 1973.

Elardo, R., & Bradley, R. H. The HOME Observation for Measurement of the Environment (HOME) Scale: A review of research. *Developmental Review*, 1981, *1*, 113–145.

Golden, M., & Birns, B. Social class and infant intelligence. In M. Lewis (Ed.), *Origins of intelligence*. New York: Plenum, 1976.

Gottfried, A. W. *Measures of socioeconomic measures in child development research: Data and recommendations.* Presented at the Biennial Convention of the Society for Research in Child Development, Detroit, April 1983.

Gottfried, A. W., Guerin, D., Spencer, J. E., & Meyer, C. Validity of Minnesota Child Development Inventory in screening young children's developmental status. *Journal of Pediatric Psychology*, in press.

Gottfried, A. W., Rose, S. A., & Bridger, W. H. Cross-modal transfer in human infants. *Child Development*, 1977, *48*, 118–123.

Hauser, R. M., & Featherman, D. L. *The process of stratification: Trends and analyses.* New York: Academic Press, 1977.

Holahan, C. J., & Moos, R. H. Social support and psychological distress. *Journal of Abnormal Psychology*, 1981, *90*, 365–370.

Hollingshead, A. B. *Four Factor Index of Social Status*, Unpublished manuscript, Yale University (available from Department of Sociology), 1975.

Hresko, W. P., Reid, D. K., & Hammill, D. D. *The test of early language development.* Austin, TX: Pro-ed, 1981.

Johnson, D. L., & Breckenridge, J. N. *The impact of a parent education program on the home environment and cognitive development of Mexican-American children.* Paper presented at the Biennial Meeting of the Society for Research in Child Development, Boston, March, 1981.

Jordan, T. E. *Development in the Preschool Years.* New York: Academic Press, 1980.

Jordan, T. E. Influences on vocabulary attainment: A five-year prospective study. *Child Development*, 1978, *49*, 1096–1106.

Kagan, J. Family experience and the child's development. *American Psychologist*, 1979, *34*, 886–891.

Kaufman, A. S., & Kaufman, N. L. *Clinical evaluation of young children with the McCarthy scales.* New York: Grune & Stratton, 1977.

Longstreth, L. E., Davis, B., Carter, L., Flint, D., Owen, J., Rickert, M., & Taylor, E. Separation of home intellectual environment and maternal IQ as determinants of child IQ. *Developmental Psychology*, 1981, *17*, 532–541.

Marjoribanks, K. Environment, social class, and mental abilities. *Journal of Educational Psychology*, 1972, *43*, 103–109.

McCarthy, D. *McCarthy Scales of Children's Abilities.* New York: Psychological Corporation, 1972.

Metzl, M. N. Teaching parents a strategy for enhancing infant development. *Child Development*, 1980, *51*, 583–586.

Moore, T. Language and intelligence: A longitudinal study of the first eight years. *Human Development*, 1968, *11*, 1–24.

Moos, R. H., & Moos, B. S. *Family Environmental Scale manual.* Palo Alto, CA: Consulting Psychologists Press, 1981.

Parke, R. D. Children's home environments: Social and cognitive effects. In I. Altman & J. F. Wohlwill (Eds.), Children and the environment. New York: Plenum, 1978.

Piaget, J. *The construction of reality in the child.* New York: Basic Books, 1954.

Ramey, R., Farran, D., & Campbell, F. Predicting IQ from mother–infant interaction. *Child Development,* 1979, *50,* 804–814.

Rose, S. A., Gottfried, A. W., & Bridger, W. H. Cross-modal transfer in infants: Relationship to prematurity and socioeconomic background. *Developmental Psychology,* 1978, *14,* 643–652.

Scarr, S., & Weinberg, R. A. The influence of "family background" on intellectual attainment. *American Sociological Review,* 1978, *43,* 674–692.

Siegel, L. S. Infant tests as predictors of cognitive and language development at two years. *Child Development,* 1981, *52,* 545–557.

Sigman, M. Early development of preterm and full-term infants: Exploratory behavior in eight-month-olds. *Child Development,* 1976, *47,* 606–612.

Skodak, M. Children in foster homes: A study of mental development. Iowa: University of Iowa City, 1939.

Stevens, J. H., Jr. *Child development knowledge and parenting skills.* Paper presented at the Annual Meeting of the American Educational Research Association, New York, March 1982.

Stevens, G., & Featherman, D. L. A revised socioeconomic index of occupational status. *Social Science Research,* 1981, *10,* 364–395.

Van Alstyne, D. *The environment of three-year-old children: Factors related to intelligence and vocabulary tests.* New York: Columbia University, Bureau of Publications, 1929.

Wachs, T. D. Relation of infants' performance on Piaget scales between twelve and twenty-four months and their Stanford-Binet performance at thirty-one months. *Child Development,* 1975, *46,* 929–935.

Wachs, T. D. *Purdue Home Stimulation Inventories* (Sections I, II, and III). Unpublished manual, Purdue University, 1976.(a)

Wachs, T. D. Utilization of a Piagetian approach in the investigation of early experience effects: A research strategy and some illustrative data. *Merrill-Palmer Quarterly,* 1976, *22,* 11–30.(b)

Wachs, T. D. The relationship of infants' physical environment to their Binet performance at 2½ years. *International Journal of Behavioral Development,* 1978, *1,* 51–65.

Wachs, T. D. Proximal experience and early cognitive–intellectual development: The physical environment. *Merrill-Palmer Quarterly,* 1979, *25,* 3–41.

Wachs, T. D., & Gruen, G. E. Early experience and human development. New York: Plenum, 1982.

Wachs, T. D., Uzgiris, I., & Hunt, J. McV. Cognitive development in infants of different age levels and from different environmental backgrounds. *Merrill-Palmer Quarterly,* 1971, *17,* 283–317.

Walberg, H. J., & Marjoribanks, K. Family environment and cognitive development: Twelve analytic models. *Review of Educational Research,* 1976, *46,* 527–551.

Wechsler, D. *Wechsler Adult Intelligence Scale-Revised.* New York: Psychological Corporation, 1981.

Wellman, B. L. The meaning of environment. In G. M. Whipple (Ed.), *The thirty-ninth yearbook of the National Society for the study of education.* In *Intelligence: Its nature and nurture* (Part 1). Bloomington, IL: Public School Publishing, 1940.

Whiteman, M., Brown, B. R., & Deutsch, M. Some effects of social class and race on children's language and intellectual abilities. In M. Deutsch (Ed.), *The disadvantaged child.* New York: Basic Books, 1967.

Willerman, L. Effects of families on intellectual development. *American Psychologist,* 1979, *34,* 923–928.

Wilson, R. S. Synchronies in mental development: An epigenetic perspective. *Science,* 1978, *202,* 939–948.

Wolf, R. The measurement of environments. In A. Anastasi (Ed.), *Testing problems in perspective. Twenty-fifth anniversary volume of topical readings from the invitational conference on testing problems.* Washington, DC: American Council on Education, 1966.

Yarrow, L. J., Rubenstein, J., & Pedersen, F. *Infant and environment.* New York: Wiley, 1975.

Zimmerman, M. The Home Observation for Measurement of the Environment: A rejoinder to Elardo and Bradley's comment. *Developmental Review,* 1981, *1,* 322–329.

4

Home Environment and Cognitive Development in a Healthy, Low-Risk Sample: The Seattle Study*

Kathryn E. Barnard
Helen L. Bee
Mary A. Hammond

Introduction

In the late 1960s and early 1970s there was widespread interest among developmental psychologists in the relationship between early environmental quality and later cognitive outcomes for children. The stage was set a decade earlier when Hunt (1961) argued forcefully that a child's early environment had a potent influence on measured intelligence and cognitive development. But what specific features of the environment mattered? Early results from several major longitudinal studies (Smith, Flick, Ferriss, & Sellman, 1972; Werner, Bierman, & French, 1971) indicated that assessments of infant perinatal status were poor predictors of long-term outcomes for the child. Broad indicators of socioeconomic status (SES), such as the mother's education or the family SES, appeared to be much better predictors. But most of us assumed that maternal education or SES was simply a marker variable for differences in actual rearing environments, and that the actual quality of the encounters between parent and child and the stimulation provided to or available to the child, were causally related to the child's later cognitive performance. Many of us took this chain of reasoning one step further and concluded that if we could adequately assess the

*This research was supported by the Division of Nursing, Health Resources Administration, Public Health Service, Department of Health & Human Services, Contract #NO1-NU-14174 and Grants #NU-00559 and NU-00816.

crucial qualities of the early environment, we could devise screening methods that would permit identification of families that were at high risk for later poor cognitive performance by the child (see Bradley & Caldwell, 1978; Ramey, MacPhee, & Yeates, 1982). If we could identify such families early, before a child's poor cognitive performance actually emerged, genuine primary prevention might be possible through special interventions.

Out of such interests and assumptions emerged the set of independently conceived, but remarkably parallel, short-term longitudinal studies represented in this volume. The data we report are part of just such a longitudinal study in which a group of mothers and infants has been followed from birth through age 4 years. (We are presently collecting data at age 7½, but cannot report on these findings at this stage.)

Our own goals, broadly stated, were three: (1) to identify early precursors of later success or problems for children and families, both so that we could trace the links more systematically and so that we might develop screening strategies; (2) more narrowly, to amplify our knowledge about environmental precursors, particularly aspects of the parent–infant interactional system; and (3) to develop or identify methods for measuring those precursors that could be used by health professionals who regularly come into contact with families, such as public health nurses, pediatricians, day care workers, and the like.

The present chapter focuses primarily on the second of these goals, and on only one of several methods of assessing parent–infant interaction and environmental quality included in our study, namely the HOME Inventory. Results from two other methods of assessing parent–infant interaction—an observation of feeding, and an observation of teaching interactions—are described elsewhere (Bee, Barnard, Eyres, Gray, Hammond, Spietz, Snyder, & Clark, 1982), as are results of assessments of perinatal status and of parent perceptions of the child. In this report we are thus describing only a subset of the findings of a much larger study.

Because the several longitudinal projects described in this volume share many design features and measurement strategies, interpretation of the collective body of data requires that each of us makes clear the ways in which our sample and procedure differs from those in other studies. In our case, the most important difference is the sample we studied. Our subjects are overwhelmingly healthy working- and middle-SES mothers and their healthy, normally developing children. At 48 months of age, only a few of the children showed any significant problems. For example, only 10 out of 163 subjects for whom we have Stanford-Binet IQ scores at 48 months have scores below 90; 60 children scored at 120 or above. The group is predominantly Caucasian, with intact families. This is clearly a mainstream, low-risk sample, similar to the general population sample described by Ramey, Farran and Campbell (1979).

We selected this low-risk sample for two reasons. First and foremost, they were accessible to us (pragmatism rides again!). We were able to establish a good working relationship with a large, well-established Health Maintenance Organization (HMO) in Seattle whose clients included families of employees of many of the major companies and educational institutions in the region. The participants in this HMO tend to remain as clients over long periods of time, which meant that attrition might be less of a problem than is often the case in longitudinal studies. The obstetricians and pediatricians in this group practice were also willing to have study-personnel contact mothers during regular clinic visits, and encouraged mothers to find out about the study, which increased the likelihood that we could locate a large and willing sample within the intake period we had available. We were aware from the beginning that a sample drawn from such a source would not be typical of those studied by others. But this sample *is* typical of the working population of this region of the country.

Our second reason for choosing a healthy, stable sample was that we wanted to discover whether strong environment–outcome relationships could in fact be found within a relatively low-risk group. What are the characteristics of otherwise stable and intact families that might be related to good or poor cognitive performance by the child? For both of these reasons—one pragmatic and one empirical–theoretical—we chose to study a normal rather than an atypical or high-risk group.

Within this healthy, normal population, however, we intentionally sampled from as wide a range of maternal education as was possible among the clients. The median educational level of mothers at the HMO is 12 years (completion of high school); our goal was to achieve a sample in which half the mothers had high school or less, and half had more than high school education. In this way we could ensure as much variability as possible on a dimension that others had found to be an important predictor of child outcome (see Broman, Nichols, & Kennedy, 1975). Such a sample would also permit us to look at predictor–outcome relations separately within high- and low-education groups. This broad distribution on maternal education makes our sample quite distinct from others described in this volume. Our low-education mothers (high school or less) are roughly comparable in education (although not in racial composition) to the samples described by Bradley and Caldwell and by Ramey; the high-education mothers are more similar to samples studied by Siegel (1981), whereas Wachs's sample (1979) cuts across the educational spectrum. Where necessary, we report relations between early home environment and cognitive outcomes separately for the two education groups, so that comparability of findings (or lack of it) may be seen more clearly.

Another way in which the present study differs from others in this group of parallel studies is in the number of contacts and observations we have for each family. We observed–interviewed–tested families at birth, and at 1, 4, 8, 12, 24, 36, and 48 months, with the infant version of the HOME inventory completed at 4, 8, 12, and 24 months.

The size of our sample, the repeated measurements, and the broad distribution on maternal education also allows us to examine two other issues of considerable current theoretical and practical importance. The first of these concerns what Wachs (1981) has called *age specificity*. There appears to be an emerging consensus that the impact of the early environment is far more specific than the early theories had led us to believe. For example, Ramey and Haskins (1981) have speculated that "there are key intellectual deficits that occur in intellectually nonsupportive environments at times of rapid transitions in developmental processes" (p. 15). Hunt (1981) agrees that growth-fostering experience is specific to particular points in the developmental progression, although not necessarily at points of rapid transition: "For any experience to have maximal effect, however, it is essential that it match the existing achievements of the infant and utilize them in the new coordinations in the epigenetic sequence" (p. 23). Whether one defines the crucial environment–child linkages in terms of periods of rapid development, or in terms of the specific match between the child's developmental level and the properties of the environment, it is clear that we must begin to explore longitudinal data for age specificities in environmental effect.

A variant of this issue concerns the relative importance of early versus later environmental enrichment. Kagan (1979) has argued that correlations are found between early environmental features and later cognitive performance not because the early stimulation is causally significant, but because parents tend to be consistent over time in the way they treat the child and in the richness or barrenness of the environment they provide. Middle-SES parents clearly create a different environment than do working-SES parents (see Bee, Van Egeren, Streissguth, Nyman, & Leckie, 1969), and the children of middle-SES parents typically do better in school and score higher on standarized IQ or achievement tests. This may indicate causal connections between the environment provided and the outcome for the child, but it need not indicate that it was *early* stimulation that was critical. Obviously this point has both theoretical and practical implications. Is development so highly "canalized" during the first 12–18 months, as McCall has suggested (1981, p. 732), that specific environmental features matter little? Or are there aspects of the environment during those early months that are vital for optimal development? The point is obviously critical for the design of intervention programs, as well as for theoreticians. In one of the few analyses directly addressing this question, Bradley & Caldwell (1980) examined the relations between an early HOME score (6 months) and later IQ with a later HOME score (12 months) partialed out. Except in the case of the toys and materials subscale for boys, no significant residual correlation remained between 6-months HOME and IQ under these conditions, suggesting that it was not the 6-month stimulation per se that was critical. Our data permit us a second look at this set of relations.

A second vital theoretical issue is whether the relations between environment and child outcome are causal at all, whatever the age of the child. A number of researchers who have taken a strong genetic view of IQ, most notably Longstreth (1978; Longstreth, Davis, Carter, Flint, Owen, Rickert, & Taylor, 1981) have argued that the observed environment–outcome relationships are largely genetic variance in disguise. Bright parents provide more enriched environments, but they also pass on genetic material to their children. In most studies, heredity and environment are thus entirely confounded in a measure of environmental quality. Longstreth has reported that in a sample of 12-year-old children, a correlation between a measure of environmental quality (Wolf's Home Environment Interview) and the child's IQ was attenuated to the point of nonsignificance when maternal IQ was partialed out. Longstreth reports that Campbell (1979) found a similar loss of significance when maternal IQ was partialed out of a correlation between Caldwell and Bradley's HOME Inventory and IQ in a younger, higher-risk sample than Longstreth studied. These findings obviously raise serious questions about assumptions of causal links between early environmental quality and the child's cognitive skills. It is incumbent on those of us who have similar data to examine the relations more fully.

Method

Subjects

The sample for the longitudinal study consisted of 193 primiparous mothers and their infants, all of whom were clients of a major HMO in Seattle, Washington at the beginning of the study. All infants were born during 1973 and 1974. Maternal education was used as a blocking variable during subject selection in order to achieve a sample that included approximately half mothers who had a high school education or less, and half with more than high school. The final sample of 193 actually included 84 mothers with low education and 109 mothers with higher education. The presence or absence of perinatal risk factors was also used as a blocking variable in the hopes of securing a sample that would vary as widely as possible on perinatal status. The final sample included 80 completely healthy mother–infant pairs: the mother had had no complications of pregnancy or delivery, and the infant had shown no postnatal complications. The remaining 113 mother-infant pairs had shown *at least one* complication out of a list of 36 possible complications either during pregnancy, delivery, or in the postnatal period. The most common maternal risk-factors were age under 18 or over 30 years ($N = 32$), weight gain under 10 or over 40 pounds ($N = 20$), and previous history of stillbirth or neonatal death ($N = 14$). The most common infant risk-factors were fetal heart tones below 120 or above 160 beats per minute ($N = 46$), meconium staining ($N = 24$), and Apgar of 6 (out of 10) or below at 1 or at 5 minutes after birth ($N = 23$). The number of such complications in the 113 mother–infant pairs with at least one complication ranged from 1 to 6, with a mean of 2.0.

Despite the use of perinatal complications as a subject selection-factor, this sample is basically healthy. The list of complications we used was very wide-ranging, and included many items indicative of only marginal risk. Thus the "some risk" subgroup should more appropriately be called "minimal perinatal risk." Because subsequent comparisons of outcomes for the zero risk and the minimal risk groups showed essentially no differences, and because inspection of correlational patterns also suggested few differences between risk groups, we have combined the two-risk groups in all analyses reported here.

Subject Recruitment

Initial contact with potential subjects normally occurred in the hospital at the time of the mother's 8-month prenatal visit. Mothers were told about the study by the clinic staff, and those who were interested talked at greater length with study personnel who were present during the clinic hours. Mothers who expressed a willingness to participate, and who fit the study criteria, completed the antenatal questionnaires at that time. At the time of delivery, if the mother and infant continued to meet the criteria, and if there had not been more than three deliveries that day, the mother and infant remained part of the study sample. (For logistical reasons we were unable to handle more than three new subjects per day). A few of the subjects (39 mothers) expressed some interest initially, but did not want to commit themselves to participation until they knew the outcome of the pregnancy. These mothers were contacted again at the time of delivery.

Sample Retention

We went to considerable pains to remain in contact with subjects over the ensuing years. This was aided by the fact that the sample is primarily made up of stable families, and that those who have remained in the Northwest area have tended to maintain contact with the HMO. At 36 and 48 months, we made a special effort to relocate families who had moved from the area, and to arrange for testing of those children by psychometrists in their new locale. Approximately 5% of the cases at these ages were tested in this fashion. Table 1 gives the retention figures for the full sample of 193, and for the original high- and low-education subsamples. It is evident that we were more successful in retaining contact with the high-education families, but retention levels were quite high in both groups.

Sample Analyzed in the Present Report

As anyone knows who has done longitudinal research, retention of a subject at a particular data collection point need not imply that com-

TABLE 1
Sample Retention during each Year of the Study

Time since delivery	Number remaining in each group					
	High education		Low education		Total sample	
Original sample	109	(100%)	84	(100%)	193	(100%)
1 Year	105	(96%)	72	(86%)	177	(92%)
2 Years	97	(89%)	64	(76%)	161	(83%)
3 Years	95	(87%)	72	(86%)	167[a]	(86%)
4 Years	100	(92%)	69	(82%)	169[a]	(87%)

[a] At 3 and 4 years of age, additional efforts were made to test children who were no longer living in the Seattle area; thus the sample size increased somewhat at these time points.

plete data are available for that subject. If we were to use the most stringent requirements and include in the analyses only those subjects for whom we had complete data at all points, the sample would be 125—far smaller than the numbers shown in Table 1. For this report we have chosen a looser requirement. We have included in the analyses all subjects for whom we had at least one cognitive test score for the infant and at least one HOME score at 4, 8, 12, or 24 months. One hundred and seventy-nine subjects meet this criterion, and all descriptive information about the sample is based on this subset of 179. Individual analyses, of course, are frequently based on smaller samples than this. Table 2 sets out the basic demographic characteristics of the sample of 179, and of the high- and low-education subgroups. The data in the table underline the point we have already made: this is fundamentally a working-SES and middle-SES sample of mothers with their healthy infants. The group is primarily Caucasian, and the vast majority were married at the time of intake into the study. The fact that these are all primiparous mothers is another important feature of this sample—one that distinguishes this group from those studied by others.

A word is in order about the Hollingshead Four-Factor Index of Social

TABLE 2

Demographic Characteristics of Total Sample, and High- and Low-Education Subsamples

	Total sample N = 179		High education N = 105 subsample		Low education N = 74 subsample	
Demographic characteristic	Mean or %	SD	Mean or %	SD	Mean or %	SD
Mother's years of schooling	14.1	2.5	15.9	1.8	11.7	0.8
Mother's age at delivery	25.2	4.1	27.0	3.0	22.6	4.1
Hollingshead four-factor index	45.3	12.6	51.5	10.1	35.9	9.7
Gestational age of infants at birth, in weeks	39.2	1.3	39.3	1.2	39.0	1.5
Race of mother[a]						
% White	87.4%		92.2%		80.8%	
% Black	8.0%		2.9%		15.1%	
% Other	4.6%		4.9%		4.1%	
Mother's marital status:[a]						
% Married at delivery	90.5%		97.1%		81.1%	
Child's gender: % boys	48.6%		50.5%		45.9%	
Premature (<37 weeks gestational age)	5.0%		3.8%		6.8%	

[a] Significant difference between high- and low-education subsamples (χ^2, $p < .05$).

Status (Hollingshead, 1975) reported in Table 2. All information about the mother's and father's occupation and education was collected from the mother in questionnaire form. We asked about the father's occupation at the 12-month contact, and in some detail about the mother's occupation at the 48-month contact. Father's and mother's education were reported at the antenatal or the hospital contact. Because we did not set out to obtain the level of detail on occupation required for the Hollingshead Four-Factor Index, the quality of information on which the classification is based is not always remarkably high. In 3% of the cases, in which the mother's report of her own or her partner's occupation was ambiguous, we listed all the occupational categories that *could* apply and then chose the median value. This may result in a somewhat lower estimate of SES than actually obtains for our sample; in any case it clearly introduces some error variance into individual scores. For purposes of this volume, however, the Hollingshead scores given in Table 2 are probably sufficiently reliable to permit general comparison of the sample in this study with the samples studied by others.

Procedure

Cognitive development in the infants was assessed at 12 and 24 months with the Bayley Scales of Infant Development (BSID) (Bayley, 1969), and at 48 months with the Stanford-Binet (Terman & Merrill, 1973). The quality of the home environment was assessed with the HOME inventory (Caldwell & Bradley, 1978) at 4, 8, 12, and 24 months. This inventory consists of 45 binary items describing 6 dimensions of the home environment. It yields six separate subscores: Emotional and Verbal Responsivity of the Parent, Avoidance of Restriction and Punishment, Organization of the Physical and Temporal Environment, Provision of Appropriate Play Materials, Maternal Involvement with the Child, and Opportunities for Variety in Daily Stimulation. A total score is simply the sum of the subscale scores.

At 4, 8, and 12 months, this inventory was completed in the customary manner. A home visitor went to the family home, interviewed the mother, observed the mother interacting with her child, and noted specific features of the home environment. At 24 months, no home visit was included in our regular data collection procedure, but we nonetheless wanted to obtain some estimate of the quality of the home environment. We therefore adapted the HOME to a questionnaire–observation format that could be used during a clinic visit. Items normally obtained by interviewing the mother were revised into multiple choice and open-ended questions, which the mother responded to as part of a questionnaire (Items 7, 15, 18, 19, 20–24, 26–28, 30–34, and 36–45). Observation items were completed by an interviewer who had seen the mother and child interact during the clinic visit. Two items that could not be adapted to either system (Item 25, relating to the safety of the child's play environment, and Item 29, relating to the provision of toys by the mother during the interview) were omitted, and scores on the two subscales on which these items appear were prorated using the formula:

$$\text{Subject's modified subscale score} \times \frac{\text{Number of items in original subscale}}{\text{Number of items in modified version of subscale}}$$

to make the scores comparable to those collected in the normal home-visit manner. Note that most of the items in Subscales 1 and 2 (emotional and verbal responsivity, and avoidance of restriction and punishment) were primarily based on observation of the mother and child, whereas information for Subscales 3, 4, 5, and 6 was primarily provided through questionnaire. As it happened, arrangements to have the interviewers fill out the observation items during the clinic visits were not completed until several dozen subjects had already been tested, so the N for analyses involving the 24-month HOME scores is consistently lower than for other analyses to be reported.

Obviously this modification of the HOME represents a major change. Because we have never used both systems with the same sample at the same time, we have no direct comparative data. However, the predictive validity of the total score from the questionnaire form of the instrument appears to be as good as what others have reported for the home-visit version at the same ages. Nonetheless, this difference in method should be kept in mind whenever we examine results from the 24-month assessment or compare results from this age with results from other studies.

Reliability of the HOME Inventory

We have examined the reliability of this instrument in four ways. The information most commonly provided is interobserver agreement. Three home-visitors participated in data collection, and all possible pairs of these three made joint home-visits in a subsample of families. A total of 42 dual observations were made at 4 months, of 22 at 8 months, and of 22 at 12 months. Percent agreement of individual items in the several subscales and in the total score are given in Table 3. Interobserver agreement ranged from 86% to 97%.

These agreement figures are high, but as Mitchell (1979) pointed out, interobserver agreement percentages can be misleading because they carry no information about individual differences among subjects. An interobserver reliability coefficient, on the other hand, partitions the variance of a set of scores into a true score (individual differences) and an error component (differences among observers as well as other random error). To examine interobserver reliability, a two-factor (subjects by observers) analysis of variance (ANOVA) design was used. The obtained Mean Squares were then used to compute the interobserver reliability coefficients presented in Table 3. An example of the difference between agreement and reliability can be seen clearly in the organization of the environment subscale at 8 months. Here the percent of agreement between observers is relatively high (92%) while the low reliability-coefficient (.34) reflects the low variability among subjects relative to the variability among observers; even though percent agreement is high, the organization of the environment score at 8 months does not differentiate among the children in this sample. In general, the interobserver reliability coefficients range from moderate to high.

Still a third method of looking at reliability is developmental generalizability (explored in an earlier paper based on these data by Mitchell & Gray, 1981). Cronbach, Gleser, Nanda, & Rajartnam's (1972) theory of generalizability can be used to look at the stability of scores over time. An ANOVA design is used with multiple scores for each subject. From the obtained Mean Squares, variance components are computed which represent the independent contributions of each factor. In this instance, four HOME-scores (4, 8, 12, and 24 months) were entered into a one-factor repeated-measures ANOVA, and the Mean Squares were used to calculate generalizability coefficients, which we have shown in Table 3, along with the other estimates of reliability. To the extent that the HOME is intended to tap ongoing qualities of the environment, we would expect the developmental generalizability score to be quite high. To the extent that individual items, or subscale scores, would normally change with the child's development, we would expect somewhat lower generalizability. The results suggest that both forces are at work. The generalizability of the total score is remarkably high, whereas the coefficients for the individual subscales are more moderate. That is, individual families tend to be quite stable in their total scores over the 20-month period in question (4–24 months), but the specific things they are doing, or not doing, to achieve those scores change. Some of that change may represent unreliability in the instru-

TABLE 3
Comparison of Four Methods of Estimating Instrument Reliability for the HOME Inventory

HOME subscale	Percent agreement between observers (HOME age in months)			Interobserver reliability coefficients (HOME age in months)			Developmental generalizability	Internal consistency (alpha) (HOME age in months)			
	4	8	12	4	8	12		4	8	12	24
1. Emotional and verbal responsivity	95	93	92	.83	.81	.67	.63	.68	.68	.65	.57
2. Avoidance of restriction and punishment	95	91	93	.67	.48	.91	.66	.38	.52	.64	.63
3. Organization of the environment	94	92	92	.80	.34	.60	.44	.27	.27	.39	.12
4. Play materials	94	97	92	.80	.88	.38	.44	.59	.62	.74	.72
5. Maternal involvement	96	86	91	.91	.46	.73	.42	.66	.58	.64	.12
6. Variety in daily stimulation	96	97	96	.90	.95	.93	.65	.00	.32	.37	.19
Total score	97	96	95	.93	.81	.76	.79	.77	.81	.86	.69

ment itself. But some of that change undoubtedly represents response to changing needs or demands by the child. For example, a parent who achieved a high score on the avoidance of restriction and punishment scale at 4 months, when the baby was not yet mobile and required little restriction, may have a lower score when the child was 24 months old and asserting more independence. But this change might be compensated by a higher score on the play materials subscale.

A final dimension of instrument reliability is internal consistency, which we computed for the HOME using Cronbach's *alpha* (corrected for number of items in each scale). These figures are also presented in Table 3, calculated separately for each subscale at each age at which HOME assessments were made. Note that the internal consistency of the total score is high at every age, but that individual subscales are considerably less consistent at some or all time points. In particular, Subscales 3 and 6 have low internal consistency at most ages. Note also that *alphas* are lower for the 24-month score obtained from questionnaire–observation, than for the traditional interview–observation method at earlier ages.

It is instructive to compare these several reliability estimates with those reported by Caldwell (1978) for the original study samples used in the development of the HOME Inventory. For a sample of 174 children ranging in age from 6 to 36 months, from a racially mixed, primarily working-SES population, Caldwell reports internal consistencies (Kuder–Richardson split-half correlations) ranging from .44 for Subscale 6 to .89 for Subscale 3. The median value was approximately .70. In contrast, Cronbach's *alphas* in the present sample are generally much lower.

Caldwell also reports intraclass coefficients for a sample of 91 subjects observed at 6, 12, and 24 months. Such coefficients are statistical cousins to the developmental generalizability-coefficients reported here; the generalizability coefficient describes common variance over more than two age-points simultaneously, whereas the intraclass coefficient covers only two age-points. In this instance, evidence for consistency over time is slightly stronger for the present sample than in Caldwell's original analyses. The intraclass coefficients in Caldwell's longitudinal sample ranged from .23 to .76, with a median value of approximately .40. As is clear from Table 3, the developmental generalizability coefficients in the present data range from .42 to .66. In particular, the generalizability for Subscales 1 (emotional and verbal responsivity) and 2 (avoidance of restriction and punishment) are considerably higher in our sample than in Caldwell's.

The most likely explanation of these discrepancies lies in differences in the heterogeneity of the samples studied. The internal consistency data reported by Caldwell are based on a sample that not only varies more in maternal education and race than does our sample; it also includes children of widely varying ages. Because HOME Inventory scores increase consistently with age, the use of an age-varying sample automatically increases the variance of each subscale. Because estimates of internal consistency are sensitive to the variance of the scores, it is not surprising that our estimates of internal consistency are lower than those obtained by Caldwell. In general, we report the best internal consistency for those subscales with the largest number of items (Subscales 1, 2, 4, and the total score). As will become clear in the results section, these are also the subscales that are most strongly predictive of intellectual outcomes in our sample.

In sum, in the present study the total HOME score appears to be reliable in several senses: observers can agree on what they see; items are internally consistent; and scores are stable over time. Subscale scores in our homogeneous sample are generally less reliable, or less consistent, in all of these ways. However, reliability and consistency are generally adequate for those subscales with a larger number of individual items. We conclude that some caution is in order in using individual subscale scores for analysis (or for interpretation of individual family patterns) particularly in relatively homogeneous samples such as ours. The total HOME score, however, appears to be very robust, even within a generally well-educated, middle-SES sample.

Results

Means and standard deviations for HOME subscores and total scores at each age are given in Table 4. Note that the standard deviations for Subscales 3, 4, 5, and 6, at 24 months, are considerably lower than at earlier ages, presumably due to the questionnaire form of the HOME used at that age. Subscales 1 and 2, at 24 months, based primarily on observation, show more typical variance.

Table 4 also provides a comparison of the scores for the high- and low-education subgroups. It is evident that in 20 of the 24 subscale comparisons, and in all the total score comparisons, the high-education mothers have achieved a significantly higher score than the low-education mothers. This is least true for 24 months, where again we find that the subscales with scores based most heavily on maternal self-report show the smallest education differences.

Significant gender differences in HOME subscale or total scores were found in only one out of 28 comparisons: mothers of girls had significantly higher scores on avoidance of restriction and punishment at 24 months than did mothers of boys (for girls, $M = 6.2$, $SD = 1.4$; for boys, $M = 5.6$, $SD = 1.9$, t diff = 2.09, $p < .05$).

TABLE 4

Means, Standard Deviations, and Education Differences for HOME Inventory at Four Ages

HOME subscale	Total sample		High education		Low education		t Education difference
	Mean	SD	Mean	SD	Mean	SD	
4-Month scores (N's = 178, 105, and 73)[a]							
Emotional and verbal responsivity	9.2	1.9	9.6	1.7	8.6	1.9	3.57***
Avoid restriction and punishment	6.7	1.1	7.0	0.9	6.3	1.4	3.31***[b]
Organization of the environment	4.8	1.1	4.9	1.0	4.5	1.1	2.60**
Play materials	4.8	1.7	5.3	1.6	4.2	1.5	4.42***
Maternal involvement	4.7	1.5	5.0	1.3	4.4	1.6	2.38*
Opportunities for variety	2.5	0.9	2.5	0.9	2.4	1.0	.59
Total score	32.7	5.1	34.3	3.8	30.4	5.7	4.88***[b]
8-Month scores (N's = 162, 100, and 62)							
Emotional and verbal responsivity	9.4	1.8	10.0	1.2	8.4	2.6	5.49***[b]
Avoid restriction and punishment	5.8	1.4	6.1	1.2	5.2	1.5	4.07***
Organization of the environment	4.9	1.0	5.1	0.9	4.5	1.2	3.04**[b]
Play materials	6.8	1.6	7.3	1.5	6.2	1.7	4.20***
Maternal involvement	4.8	1.3	5.2	1.0	4.1	1.5	5.05***[b]
Opportunities for variety	2.8	1.2	3.1	1.1	2.4	1.2	3.62***
Total score	34.4	5.4	36.7	3.7	30.7	5.6	7.38***[b]
12-Month scores (N's = 169, 103, and 66)							
Emotional and verbal responsivity	9.7	1.6	10.2	1.1	9.0	1.9	4.75***[b]
Avoid restriction and punishment	5.4	1.7	5.8	1.4	4.8	2.0	3.51***[b]
Organization of the environment	4.8	1.0	5.0	0.9	4.5	1.1	3.69***
Play materials	7.9	1.5	8.4	0.9	7.2	1.9	4.90***[b]
Maternal involvement	5.0	1.3	5.3	1.0	4.5	1.4	4.33***[b]
Opportunities for variety	3.4	1.2	3.7	1.2	3.0	1.2	3.73***
Total score	36.3	5.6	38.4	3.6	33.0	6.5	6.32***[b]

(continued)

TABLE 4 (Continued)

HOME subscale	Total sample		High education		Low education		t Education difference
	Mean	SD	Mean	SD	Mean	SD	
24-Month scores (N's = 144–155; 86–96; 54–72)[c]							
Emotional and verbal responsivity	9.9	1.4	10.4	0.9	9.3	1.7	4.37***[b]
Avoid restriction and punishment	6.0	1.7	6.4	1.4	5.2	1.8	4.19***[b]
Organization of the environment	4.4	0.7	4.4	0.7	4.4	0.7	0.01
Play materials	7.6	0.9	7.8	0.6	7.4	1.3	1.94
Maternal involvement	5.7	0.5	5.8	0.5	5.6	0.5	2.08*
Opportunities for variety	4.3	0.8	4.3	0.8	4.4	0.9	0.63
Total score	37.9	3.5	39.1	2.6	36.1	4.1	4.71***[b]

[a] N's are given for the total group, high-education, and low-education samples, respectively.

[b] Variances also differ between high- and low-education group. t for the mean difference is based on separate variances.

[c] N's vary from one subscale to the next because observation items were not completed for all subjects.

* $p < .05$.
** $p < .01$.
*** $p < .001$.

Equivalent comparisons for the three cognitive development scores are given in Table 5. Two aspects of these findings in Table 5 are worth emphasis. First, the high level of performance in both high- and low-education subgroups underlines once again the healthy, well-developing character of the sample we are studying. Second, the fact that education differences in performance on intelligence tests do not emerge until 24 months of age is consistent with findings from a number of other studies (see Bayley, 1965; Farran & Ramey, 1980; Golden, Birns, Bridger, & Moss, 1971). Given the results in Table 5, and the findings from earlier studies (reviewed by McCall, 1979), it should not be surprising that we found only modest correlations between the 12-month MDI score and the 24-month MDI ($r = .29$, $p < .001$), and between the 12-month MDI and the 48-month Stanford-Binet IQ ($r = .21$, $p < .01$). In contrast, the 24-month MDI and Stanford-Binet IQ scores were more strongly related ($r = .53$, $p < .001$). Thus in this sample, as in many other longitudinal samples, 12-month Bayley MDI scores are not particularly good predictors of the child's performance on standarized tests of cognitive development at later ages. By 24 months,

TABLE 5
Means, Standard Deviations, and Education Differences
for Three Measures of Cognitive Development

Measure	Total sample			High education			Low education			t difference in education
	Mean	SD	N	Mean	SD	N	Mean	SD	N	
12-Month Bayley Mental Development Index (MDI)	117.1	10.7	172	117.7	9.0	103	116.2	12.9	69	.81[a]
24-Month Bayley Mental Development Index (MDI)	116.8	18.2	159	121.1	16.3	96	110.3	19.1	63	3.78*
48-Month Stanford-Binet IQ	114.2	16.9	161	118.3	16.6	99	107.6	15.1	62	4.12*

[a] Variances differ significantly between high- and low-education groups.
* p < .001.

however, we not only see consistent SES or parent education-differences in the MDI scores of toddlers, but also find that the MDI at this age is a reasonably good predictor of later IQ.

To complete the basic descriptive picture, Table 6 shows the correlations between the two major demographic measures we have used—maternal education and family SES—and the child's cognitive development scores and the HOME Inventory total scores. Except for the MDI at 12 months, we see that both education and SES are moderately related to cognitive development and HOME scores at every age tested.

TABLE 6
Correlations between Demographic Measures, Total HOME Scores,
and Intelligence Test Performance of the Child

Variable	Demographic measure	
	Maternal education	Family SES[a]
12-Month MDI	.07	.06
24-Month MDI	.24*	.32*
48-Month Stanford-Binet IQ	.38*	.45*
4-Month total HOME score	.42*	.37*
8-Month total HOME score	.50*	.46*
12-Month total HOME score	.45*	.41*
24-Month total HOME score	.44*	.42*

[a] Based on Hollingshead Four-Factor Index of Social Status.
* p < .001.

Basic Predictive Relationships

The correlations between HOME scores and the three cognitive development scores for the sample as a whole are given in Table 7. The findings show no predictive relationship between the HOME at 4 and 8 months and the 12-month MDI, although the concurrent relationship between the 12- month HOME and 12-month MDI is significant. Predictions of the 24-month MDI and 48-month IQ, however, are stronger and more consistent. Of the six subscales, Subscales 3 and 6, (organization of the environment and variety in daily stimulation) are the poorest predictors of 48-month IQ, whereas Subscales 1, 2, 4, and 5 all show consistently significant relationships to both 24- and 48-month cognitive development.

These findings confirm the basic results reported by others (see Bradley & Caldwell, 1976; Ramey et al., 1979), and tell us little that is new. What is important at this stage is to go beyond these basic numbers to look at possible education-level differences, gender differences, and the contribution of education or social class to the observed correlations. In these more detailed analyses we concentrate our attention on the 24-month MDI and the 48-month IQ scores. There seems little point in pursuing more complex analyses of the extremely weak relationship between HOME scores and the 12-month MDI.

Education Level and Sex Differences in Predictive Relationships

Tables 8 and 9 give the correlations between HOME Inventory scores and outcome measures separately for the two education-groups, and for boys and girls. After a while, examining tables of correlations like these begins to feel a bit like reading tea leaves; one must be cautious about seeing things that are not really there. On the other hand, one does not want to let the mind-boggling number of correlations lead one to miss some pattern that does really exist. In the present case, the most important point to be made is that the patterns are highly similar in all four subgroups. At the same time there are some suggestions of differences that are worth exploring.

Looking first at Table 8, the first impression is that the magnitude of the correlations is somewhat higher within the low education group, particularly for Subscales 3 and 6. In fact, of the 48 pairs of correlations between HOME subscales and the two outcomes, the larger correlation of the pair is in the low-education group in 32 cases ($p < .05$). However,

TABLE 7

Correlations between HOME Scores at Ages 4, 8, 12, 24 Months, and 12-Month and 24-Month Bayley MDI Scores, and 48-Month Stanford-Binet IQ

HOME subscales	Correlations with 12-month (HOME age in months)				Correlations with 24-month MDI (HOME age in months)				Correlations with 48-month MDI Stanford-Binet IQ (HOME age in months)			
	4	8	12	24	4	8	12	24	4	8	12	24
Responsivity of mother	.07	.00	.10	.08	.20**	.25***	.29***	.23**	.20**	.28***	.27***	.42***
Restriction and punishment	.12	-.15*	.19**	.17*	.19***	.10	.20**	.51***	.27***	.28***	.29***	.56***
Organization of environment	-.07	.02	.09	.02	.23**	.24**	.37***	.12	.15*	.16*	.18*	.05
Play materials	.04	.13	.27***	.22**	.21**	.29***	.36***	.31***	.22**	.38***	.32***	.21**
Maternal involvement	-.05	.04	.18*	.07	.26***	.36***	.39***	.24**	.20**	.25***	.35***	.37***
Variety of stimulation	.06	.13	.20**	.14	.15*	.22**	.27***	.26***	.10	.21**	.18*	.20**
Total score	.05	.04	.26***	.19*	.34***	.38***	.45***	.53***	.34***	.42***	.44***	.60***
N	168	158	165	142	156	148	155	139	157	148	153	133

* $p < .05$.
** $p < .01$.
*** $p < .001$.

TABLE 8

Correlations between HOME Scores at 4, 8, 12, and 24 Months, and 24-Month MDI and 48-Month IQ for High- and Low-education Mothers

| HOME subscales | High-education mothers (more than high school education) | | | | | | | | Low-education mothers (high school or less) | | | | | | | |
| | 24-Month MDI (HOME age in months) | | | | 48-Month IQ (HOME age in months) | | | | 24-Month MDI (HOME age in months) | | | | 48-Month IQ (HOME age in months) | | | |
	4	8	12	24	4	8	12	24	4	8	12	24	4	8	12	24
Responsivity of mother	.12	.10	.15	.19*	.12	.07	.17	.29**	.16	.21	.30*	.11	.17	.31*	.26*	.49***
Restriction and punishment	.14	.10	.25**	.49***	.10	.20	.32***	.60***	.14	−.08	.04	.43***	.36**	.22	.13	.39**
Organization of environment	.14	.28**	.31***	.08	.02	.13	.01	−.04	.25*	.09	.34**	.17	.24*	.05	.35**	.33*
Play materials	.12	.20*	.15	.23*	.09	.34***	.16	.32***	.18	.28*	.40***	.31*	.27*	.30*	.37***	.07
Maternal involvement	.19	.19*	.28**	.24*	.12	.19*	.29**	.17	.25*	.41***	.40***	.17	.24*	.14	.30*	.33*
Variety of stimulation	.17	.14	.15	.14	.13	.07	−.01a	.12	.09	.19	.32**	.39**	.04	.29*	.41***a	.39**
Total HOME score	.28**	.29***	.39**	.49***	.20*	.32***	.31***	.55***	.27*	.31**	.41***	.47***	.36**	.38**	.46***	.61***
N	96	92	95	85	99	94	98	85	60	56	60	54	58	54	55	48

a Significant difference between the correlations for high and low education.
* p < .05.
** p < .01.
*** p < .001.

136

TABLE 9

Correlations between HOME Scores at Four Ages and 24-Month MDI and 48-Month Stanford-Binet IQ for Boys and Girls Separately

HOME subscales	Boys								Girls							
	24-Month MDI (HOME age in months)				48-Month Stanford-Binet IQ (HOME age in months)				24-Month MDI (HOME age in months)				48-Month Stanford-Binet IQ (HOME age in months)			
	4	8	12	24	4	8	12	24	4	8	12	24	4	8	12	24
Responsivity of mother	.19	.20	.31**	.21	.13	.15	.21*	.37**	.23*	.30**	.29**	.26*	.28**	.39***	.35***	.51***
Restriction and punishment	.21*	.15	.20*	.60***	.19*	.23*	.23*	.60***	.19*	.07	.20*	.42***	.33***	.33**	.35***	.48***
Organization of environment	.27*	.31**	.44***	.18	.09	.19	.30**	.16	.22*	.21*	.32**	.07	.24*	.15	.11	.01
Play materials	.29**	.46***	.53***a	.46***a	.15	.47***	.39***	.37***a	.17	.19*	.20*a	.12a	.32**	.34***	.24*	.03a
Maternal involvement	.31**	.34**	.48***	.25*	.13	.06a	.29**	.30**	.22*	.38***	.28**	.23*	.28**	.40***a	.40***	.22*
Variety in stimulation	.01	.24*	.29**	.26*	.03	.22*	.30**	.29*	.29**	.22*	.28**	.26**	.18*	.22*	.09	.10
Total score	.38***	.45***	.52***	.59***	.23*	.37***	.46***	.65***	.33***	.35***	.38***	.47***	.46***	.50***	.42***	.55***
N	72	68	71	62	75	70	73	60	84	80	84	77	82	78	80	73

a Significant difference between the correlations for boys and for girls, p < .05.

* p < .05.
** p < .01.
*** p < .001.

in only 3 pairs is the difference in magnitude of the two correlations significant, and in 1 of those 3 cases the larger correlation is in the high-education group. The most parsimonious description of the findings in Table 8 is that the patterns of predictions are basically the same in the two education-groups, and that any differences in magnitude is due to the somewhat larger variance in HOME scores within the low-education sample.

Table 9 presents a similar picture of basic similarity of predictive relationships for boys and girls. There is no apparent trend for either gender to show stronger correlations over time or over outcomes, and only 4 of the 56 pairs of correlations are significantly different from one another. However, 3 of those 4 pairs occur in Subscale 4, (play materials) and in all 3 cases the correlation for boys significantly exceeds the correlation for girls. In other analyses, we have found the same pattern of higher correlation among boys for this subscale in predictions of language outcomes as well, which increases our confidence that this is not a chance phenomenon. (Bee, Mitchell, Barnard, Eyres, & Hammond, 1982). Thus, against the backdrop of similar correlation patterns for boys and girls is at least a suggestion of some gender-specificity in the importance of toys and materials. Note that this occurs despite the fact that there are no gender differences in the actual scores on the toys and materials subscale at any age. In this one area at least, the possibility is raised that boys and girls are receiving similar treatment, but responding differently to it.

Comparison of Early versus Late Influences of the Home Environment

Analysis of the relative contribution of early versus late stimulation could be accomplished through the use of partial correlations, as Bradley and Caldwell (1980) have done. But because we have four measures of the HOME, instead of two, a partial correlation strategy becomes cumbersome. A logical extension of this method is to use hierarchical multiple regressions. For each subscale, and for the total score, we have computed two hierarchical regressions predicting 48-month IQ: (1) a *forward* regression, in which the 4-month HOME score was entered first, followed by the 8-month, the 12-month, and the 24-month scores, and (2) a *reverse* regression, in which the 24-month score was entered first, followed by the 12-month, the 8-month, and the 4-month scores. Thus, in the reverse regression, when we look at the contributions of the HOME scores at 4 months, we are asking whether the 4-month score is significantly related to IQ when all the later HOME variance has been removed. If this step is not significant, it suggests that there is no unique variance associated with 4-month scores and thus that the uncorrected correlation between 4-month HOME and outcome is due primarily to the consistency of the environment over time.

Table 10 shows the results of these two sets of regressions in summary form. For simplicity, we have shown the p value for the F to enter each step, and the beta weight for that step in the full regression equation (when all four steps have been entered either in forward or reverse sequence). The multiple R is also given.

By combining the information from the forward and reverse analyses, we can gain some hints of age specificities of several types. At least three patterns are possible. First, we might find an *early age-specific effect*. This would be indicated by a subscale that showed significant early steps but *not* significant late steps in the forward analysis, and significant residual effects for the early points in the reverse analysis. That is, a subscale for which early data points contribute significant *unique* variance whereas later observations do not. Subscale 4 is a case in point. Significant relationships exist for the 4- and 8-month steps, but not for the 12- and 24-month steps in the forward analyses, whereas in the reverse analyses the 12- and 8-month steps are significant. This suggests that the 8-month period may be especially important for the facets of the environment measured by this subscale: 8 months is the only age at which uniquely predictive variance is found in both forward and reverse analyses. This same pattern occurs when these analyses are done separately for boys and girls, except that for boys the 24-month score also appears to contribute unique variance.

Two other subscales also show patterns that suggest the possibility of early age-specific effects. Both 8- and 12-month scores on the maternal involvement subscale (Subscale 5) contribute unique variance in both forward and reverse analyses, whereas the 8-month score on opportunities for variety shows a significant contribution.

A second possible pattern would be a *late age-specific effect*, illustrated by the results for Subscale 2, avoidance of restriction and punishment. This score shows no significant relationship to 4-year IQ until 12 months in the forward analysis, and only at 24 months in the reverse analysis, suggesting that it is the 24-month restrictiveness that is most critical.

A *cumulative effect* is a third logical pattern. A cumulative effect might be demonstrated in the hierarchical regressions if each step in both forward and reverse analyses was significant. If this occurred, it

TABLE 10

Comparison of Temporally Forward and Reverse Hierarchical Regressions Predicting 48-Month IQ from HOME Inventory Scores at Four Ages for Full Sample $(N = 126)$

| | Forward sequence | | | | | | | | |
| | Step 1 4-month HOME | | Step 2 8-month HOME | | Step 3 12-month HOME | | Step 4 24-month HOME | | |
HOME subscales	p	beta	p	beta	p	beta	p	beta	Multiple R
1. Emotional and verbal responsivity	.001	(.14)[b]	.052	(.01)	.01	(.14)	<.001	(.34)	.47
2. Avoid restriction and punishment	n.s.	(.03)	n.s.	(−.04)	.005	(.08)	<.001	(.56)	.57
3. Organization of the environment	n.s.	(.03)	n.s.	(.14)	n.s.	(.10)	n.s.	(.04)	.21
4. Play materials	.01	(.11)	<.001	(.31)	n.s.	(.13)	n.s.	(.13)	.45
5. Maternal involvement	.02	(.12)	.001	(.17)	<.001	(.32)	n.s.	(.06)	.47
6. Opportunities for variety	n.s.	(.05)	.04	(.21)	n.s.	(.05)	n.s.	(.15)	.26
Total score	<.001	(.04)	<.001	(.11)	<.005	(.06)	<.001	(.50)	.62

[a] Scores given are the p values for the F to enter the HOME score at that step in the hierarchical regression.
[b] beta weight for that step when all four steps have been entered.

would indicate that at each age a particular subscale was tapping some unique variance that was independently related to later IQ. No subscale matches this pattern, although the emotional and verbal responsivity subscale shows significant Fs at each step in the forward analysis, as does the total score. The absence of significant Fs at each step in the reverse analysis in both instances, however, need not indicate that there is no cumulative effect; it merely tells us that the later measurements have captured the significant variance that was also tapped at earlier points. For both the total score, and the emotional and verbal responsivity subscale, then, the issue remains open. The pattern shown in Table 10 could point to a late age-specific effect for both scores or to a cumulative effect.

One other finding to note in Table 10: In the reverse analysis, no subscale adds significantly at 4 months. This suggests that the aspects of the home environment tapped by this instrument, while measurable and modestly predictive of later IQ when measured as early as 4 months, are probably not causally significant at that age. If we are cor-

TABLE 10 (*Continued*)

Reverse sequence								
Step 1 24-month HOME		Step 2 12-month HOME		Step 3 8-month HOME		Step 4 4-month HOME		
p	beta	*p*	beta	*p*	beta	*p*	beta	Multiple *R*
<.001[a]	(.34)[b]	.03	(.14)	n.s.	(.01)	n.s.	(.14)	.47
<.001	(.56)	n.s.	(.08)	n.s.	(−.04)	n.s.(−.03)		.57
n.s.	(.04)	n.s.	(.10)	n.s.	(.14)	n.s.	(.03)	.21
n.s.	(.13)	.002	(.13)	<.001	(.31)	n.s.	(.11)	.45
.01	(.06)	<.001	(.32)	.03	(.17)	.ns.	(.12)	.47
n.s.	(.15)	n.s.	(−.05)	.04	(.21)	n.s.	(.05)	.26
<.001	(.50)	n.s.	(.06)	n.s.	(.11)	n.s.	(.04)	.62

rect in this conclusion, then the primary purpose in using the HOME in the first 6 months of life would be as a predictor of the child's *future* environment.

Causal Relationships or Genetic Variance?

Lacking a measure of parental IQ, we cannot precisely match the procedure used by Longstreth *et al.* (1981). The closest we can come is to use maternal education and family SES as estimates of parental IQ—a procedure quite commonly used in adoption and twin studies when measures of parental intelligence are not available. Because education and IQ are not perfectly correlated, this is clearly not an ideal procedure. But removing the variance associated with education or SES from the relationship between the HOME scores and later IQ is still informative. The relevant partial correlations are shown in Tables 11 and 12 for 24-month MDI and 48-month IQ, respectively.

TABLE 11
Correlations between HOME Scores and 24-Month MDI with Maternal Education and SES Partialed Out

Home subscale	4-Month HOME (N = 152)			8-Month HOME (N = 144)			12-Month HOME (N = 151)			24-Month HOME (N = 136)		
	A^a	B^b	C^c	A	B	C	A	B	C	A	B	C
1. Emotional and verbal responsivity	.20**	.15*	.09	.25***	.18*	.17*	.29***	.24**	.16*	.23**	.15*	.13
2. Avoid restriction and punishment	.19**	.17*	.05	.10	.02	−.03	.20**	.13	.07	.51***	.45***	.41***
3. Organization of environment	.23**	.19**	.14*	.24**	.19*	.20**	.37***	.34***	.32***	.12	.13	.13
4. Play materials	.21**	.15*	.09	.29***	.24**	.20**	.36***	.31***	.27***	.31***	.27***	.24***
5. Maternal involvement	.26**	.29**	.18*	.36**	.31***	.29***	.39***	.34***	.30***	.24**	.19*	.20**
6. Opportunities for variety	.15*	.13*	.12	.22**	.18*	.17*	.27***	.23**	.20**	.26***	.25***	.24**
Total score	.34***	.27***	.20**	.38***	.31***	.29***	.45***	.40***	.35***	.53***	.47***	.44***

[a] Uncorrected correlation.
[b] Partial correlation with mother's education controlled.
[c] Partial correlation with Hollingshead Four-Factor Index of Social Status controlled.

* $p < .05$.
** $p < .01$.
*** $p < .001$.

142

TABLE 12
Correlations between HOME Scores and 48-Month IQ with Maternal Education and SES Partialed Out

HOME subscale	4-Month HOME (N = 157)			8-Month HOME (N = 148)			12-Month HOME (N = 153)			24-Month HOME (N = 133)		
	A[a]	B[b]	C[c]	A	B	C	A	B	C	A	B	C
1. Emotional and verbal responsivity	.20*	.12	.12	.28***	.16*	.17*	.27***	.19*	.17*	.42***	.34***	.34***
2. Avoid restriction and punishment	.27***	.22**	.13	.27***	.17*	.09	.29***	.21**	.19*	.56***	.48***	.45***
3. Organization of the environment	.15*	.07	.01	.16*	.08	.09	.18*	.15*	.12	.05	.08	.09
4. Play materials	.22**	.12	.09	.38***	.30***	.27***	.32***	.25***	.21**	.21**	.17*	.16*
5. Maternal involvement	.20**	.11	.13	.25**	.14*	.12	.35***	.28***	.26***	.27***	.20*	.20*
6. Opportunities for variety	.10	.08	.07	.21**	.15*	.13	.18*	.13	.09	.20**	.20*	.18*
Total score	.34***	.22**	.17*	.42***	.30***	.27***	.44***	.35***	.31***	.60***	.53***	.51***

[a] Uncorrected correlation.
[b] Partial correlation with mother's education controlled.
[c] Partial correlation with Hollingshead Four-Factor Index of Social Status controlled.

* $p < .05$.
** $p < .01$.
*** $p < .001$.

143

The findings show that there is some attenuation of the correlations in every instance but that in the substantial majority of cases the attenuated correlation remains statistically significant. A significant correlation remained 46 out of 52 times (88%) when maternal education was partialed out, and 36 times out of 52 times (65%) when SES was partialed out. Further, in every instance the correlation between the total HOME score and either outcome remained significant when the corrections were made. Inspection of the tables also shows that the degree of attenuation is similar across correlations. Thus, whether the partialing reduced a correlation to nonsignificance was primarily a function of the size of the original r and not due to the specific aspect of the home environment assessed. In sum, while a portion of the variance in child IQ may be attributable to parental education or SES (and thus possibly to heritable factors), a significant amount of variance is also independently predicted by a measure of environmental quality. The fact that significant correlations between HOME and IQ can also be found within subgroups that are relatively homogeneous in SES (as we have already reported) is further support for this same conclusion.

Discussion

The findings in this study replicate those in several parallel longitudinal studies in showing moderate to strong correlations between a measure of the quality of the home environment (the HOME) during the first 2 years of life and the child's performance on IQ tests at later ages. Caldwell's HOME Inventory appears to be an excellent instrument for measuring those aspects of the early environment that are related to later cognitive performance; at this stage the HOME appears to be the best single such instrument available. It is, of course, tempting to take the large leap from this basic finding to causal statements about crucial aspects of the environment, or to methods for screening families for "environmental risk." But some caution is in order before we take that leap. Important questions have been raised about the appropriate interpretation of findings such as those we have given here. How strong is the case for causal links between environment and IQ generally? Equally interesting to us, can we make a case for age specificities in the environment–outcome relationships? If both of those cases can be made persuasively, then there are clear implications for screening and for intervention.

We have attempted to address both of these questions with the data available from our longitudinal project, and while we think that our analyses show that some early environmental events or qualities are significant, and that the relationship cannot be entirely explained by SES variance, we recognize that there is still work to be done on both questions.

The genetic argument, as we indicated earlier, is basically that bright parents create "better" environments. Longstreth *et al.* (1981) and Campbell (1979) both found that environment–IQ corrrelations vanished when parental IQ was partialed out. The Longstreth study seems questionable to us on several grounds, the most compelling of which is that the basic correlation between their measure of the home environment (Wolf's Home Environment Interview) and the child's IQ was only .28 for the Raven Progressive Matrices, and .25 for the PPVT. This environment–IQ correlation is markedly lower than those reported here, and much lower than the correlation reported by Wolf (1966) in his early work with the interview ($r = .69$ in Wolf's study). With a sample size of 80 in the Longstreth study, it would not take a very large attentuation of a .25 correlation to reduce it to insignificance. It is not clear from the information given why the environment–IQ correlation is so unusually low in this sample, but it seems unwarranted to base a sweeping rejection of causal explanations of environment–IQ relationships on such a sample.

The same cannot be said, however, for the North Carolina study (Campbell, 1979). As described by Longstreth *et al.* (1981), Campbell found sizable correlations between early HOME Inventory scores and 48-month Stanford-Binet IQ ($r = .59$ for a 6-month HOME, and .69 for an 18-month HOME), both of which were eliminated when maternal IQ was partialed out. However, in this same study (Ramey & Haskins, 1981) maternal IQ was not significantly related to child IQ in a subgroup of children who had been in a special enriched day-care program since early infancy. That is, when the environment was markedly altered, the mother's IQ failed to predict the child's IQ.

Because we have no independent measure of the mother's IQ, the results from the present study cannot be compared directly to Longstreth's or Campbell's. However to the extent that SES or maternal education are highly correlated with maternal or paternal IQ, our analyses have shown that significant residual correlations remain when SES or education are removed. Whether those residuals would be further attenuated if we removed maternal IQ we cannot say.

The early versus late environmental influence is perhaps easier to answer with our findings. If we can assume for the moment that we are, in fact, dealing with causal relationships, then it looks very much as if those aspects of the environment assessed at 4 months by the HOME are not causally related to later IQ. For such very early measurements, Kagan's argument seems to have some validity. But Bradley and Caldwell's analysis (1980) suggests that beginning at 6 months, the availability of suitable toys and materials becomes significant. Our data indicate that this relationship is still stronger by 8 months. Maternal involvement and variety of stimulation appear to be important at 8–12 months, whereas the level of restriction and punishment appears to be particularly relevant at 24 months. Our reply to Kagan, then, is not that *all* aspects of the environment are important in the first year or 2 of life, but that *specific aspects* of the environment appear to be important at particular points in the child's development, which is consistent with the positions taken by both Hunt (1981) and Wachs (1981).

Obviously the particular age-specificities that have emerged from our data must remain as hypotheses until they are confirmed by others with similar analyses on parallel data, and with other measures of the environment. It is important to bear in mind as well that the HOME measure we used at 24 months is the questionnaire–observation form, and not the interview–observation form, which also limits what we are able to say about 24-month specificities. Nonetheless, the possible existence of any age specificities at all is intriguing, and worth further exploration. Should the pattern of results we have reported prove replicable, it would have obvious implications for intervention. For example, if appropriate toys and materials do in fact become particularly critical in the middle of the child's first years, then intervention programs aimed at that age level should focus on this facet of the mother's knowledge, and of the child's environment. Emphasis on disciplinary techniques, on appropriate and inappropriate restrictiveness or punitiveness, could be delayed until the child's second year. Such age specificities illustrate the increasingly obvious conclusion that relationships between environmental properties and intellectual development are far more complex than most of us had originally hypothesized. Further understanding of the complexities will require more detailed analyses of the role of external stimuli in the achievement of particular cognitive skills at particular points in development. What is occurring cognitively at 6–12 months, for example, that would make the availability of varied toys and materials especially critical? And what is happening at 24 months that would make restriction particularly detrimental? Intervention studies based on such analyses will then be required to check for causal links. If we are to achieve a more subtle understanding of environment–outcome relationships, we must move beyond the basic work reported in this volume.

In sum, our findings suggest the following conclusions:

1. The HOME Inventory, measured at 4, 8, 12, and 24 months of age, is moderately to strongly correlated with later measures of IQ. This finding strengthens the conclusions drawn from other studies, on less advantaged populations, that aspects of the home environment have a significant impact on the child's development of cognitive skills.

2. As a general rule, however, the later the assessment of the environment takes place (at least within the first 2 years), the stronger the predictive correlation with IQ becomes. This may mean that early environment is not causally significant in shaping cognitive development, or it may merely indicate that those critical elements of the early environment continue to be important and are more fully assessed at later ages.

3. Preliminary analyses of age specificities of impact of facets of the early environment suggest that we need to go beyond discussions of the general effect of the child's home environment, and look at the timing of specific types of experiences. In particular, evidence from our analyses suggests that the availability of stimulating toys and materials may be especially critical (causally significant) during the second 6 months of life.

4. These patterns are found for both sexes and for both well-educated and less well-educated families. Furthermore, the relationships continue to be statistically significant is most instances when education or SES are partialed out. Thus, the relationship between the HOME Inventory and later IQ cannot be laid entirely at the door of genetic variance.

References

Bayley, N. Comparisons of mental and motor test scores for ages 1–15 months by sex, birth order, race, geographical location, and education of parents. *Child Development,* 1965, 36, 379–411.

Bayley, N. *Bayley Scales of Infant Development: Birth to two years.* New York: Psychological Corporation, 1969.

Bee, H. L., Barnard, K., Eyres, S. J., Gray, C. A., Hammond, M. A., Spietz, A. L., Snyder, C., & Clark, B. Prediction of IQ and language skill from perinatal status, child performance, family characteristics, and mother–infant interaction. *Child Development,* 1982, 53, 1134–1156.

Bee, H. L., Mitchell, S. K., Barnard, K. E., Eyres, S. J., & Hammond, M. A. Predicting intellectual outcomes: Sex differences in response to early environmental stimulation. *Sex Roles*, in press.

Bee, H. L., Van Egeren, L. F., Streissguth, A. P., Nyman, B. A., & Leckie, M. A. Social class differences in maternal teaching strategies and speech patterns. *Developmental Psychology*, 1969, *1*, 726–734.

Bradley, R. H., & Caldwell, B. M. The relation of infants' home environment to mental test performance at fifty-four months: A follow-up study. *Child Development*, 1976, *47*, 1172–1174.

Bradley, R. H., & Caldwell, B. M. Screening the environment. *American Journal of Orthopsychiatry*, 1978, *48*, 114–129.

Bradley, R. H., & Caldwell, B. M. The relation of home environment, cognitive competence, and IQ among males and females. *Child Development*, 1980, *51*, 1140–1148.

Broman, S. H., Nichols, P. L., & Kennedy, W. A. *Preschool IQ: Prenatal and early developmental correlates*. Hillsdale, NJ: Erlbaum, 1975.

Caldwell, B. M., & Bradley, R. H. *Manual for the Home Observation for Measurement of the Environment*. Little Rock, AR: University of Arkansas, 1978.

Cronbach, L. J., Gleser, G. C., Nanda, H., & Rajaratnam, N. *The dependability of behavioral measurements: Theory of generalizability for scores and profiles*. New York: Wiley, 1972.

Farran, D., & Ramey, T. Social class differences in dyadic involvement during infancy. *Child Development*, 1980, *51*, 254–257.

Golden, M., Birns, B., Bridger, W., & Moss, A. Social class differentiation in cognitive development among black preschool children. *Child Development*, 1971, *52*, 37–46.

Hollingshead, A. B. *Four-Factor Index of Social Status*. Unpublished manuscript, 1975. (Available from P. O. Box 1965, Yale Station, New Haven, CN 06520).

Hunt, J. McV. *Intelligence and experience*. New York: Ronald Press, 1961.

Hunt, J. McV. Comments on "The modification of intelligence through early experience" by Amey and Haskins. *Intelligence*, 1981, *5*, 21–27.

Kagan, J. Family experience and the child's development. *American Psychologist*, 1979, *34*, 886–891.

Longstreth, L. E. A comment on "Race, IQ, and the middle class" by Trotman: Rampant false conclusions. *Journal of Educational Psychology*, 1978, *70*, 469–472.

Longstreth, L. E., Davis, B., Carter, L., Flint, D., Owen, J., Rickert, M., & Taylor, E. Separation of home intellectual environment and maternal IQ as determinants of child IQ. *Developmental Psychology*, 1981, *17*, 532–541.

McCall, R. B. The development of intellectual functioning in infancy and the prediction of later IQ. In J. D. Osofsky (Ed.), *Handbook of infant development*. New York: Wiley, 1979.

McCall, R. B. Nature–nurture and the two realms of development: A proposed integration with respect to mental development. *Child Development*, 1981, *52*, 1–12.

Mitchell, S. K. The interobserver agreement, reliability, and generalizability of data collected in observational studies. *Psychological Bulletin*, 1979, *86*, 376–390.

Mitchell, S. K., & Gray, C. A. Developmental generalizability of the HOME Inventory. *Educational and Psychological Measurement*, 1981, *41*, 1001–1010.

Ramey, C. T., Farran, D. C., & Campbell, F. A. Predicting IQ from mother–infant interactions. *Child Development*, 1979, *50*, 804–814.

Ramey, C. T., & Haskins, R. The modification of intelligence through early experience. *Intelligence*, 1981, *5*, 5–19.

Ramey, C. T., MacPhee, D., & Yeates, K. O. Preventing developmental retardation: A general systems model. In L. Bond & J. Joffe (Eds.), *Facilitating infant and early childhood development.* Hanover, NH: University of New England, Press 1982.

Siegel, L. S. Infant tests as predictors of cognitive and language development at two years. *Child Development,* 1981, *52,* 545–557.

Smith, A. C., Flick, G. L., Ferriss, G. S., & Sellman, A. H. Prediction of developmental outcome at seven years from prenatal, perinatal, and postnatal events. *Child Development,* 1972, *43,* 495–507.

Terman, L. M., & Merrill, M. A. *Stanford-Binet Intelligence Scale—Manual for the third revision form L–M.* Boston: Houghton Mifflin, 1973.

Wachs, T. D. Proximal experience and early cognitive–intellectual development: The physical environment. *Merrill-Palmer Quarterly,* 1979, *25,* 3–41.

Wachs, T. D. *Models of early environmental action: Implications for research and intervention.* Paper presented at the Biennial Meetings of the Society for Research in Child Development, Boston, 1981.

Werner, E. E., Bierman, J. M., & French, F. E. *The children of Kauai.* Honolulu: University of Hawaii Press, 1971.

Wolf, R. The measurement of environment. In A. Anastasia (Ed.), *Testing problems in perspective.* Washington, DC: American Council of Education, 1966.

5

Home Environment and Early Cognitive Development in Mexican-American Children

Dale L. Johnson
James N. Breckenridge
Ronald J. McGowan

Introduction

Considerable evidence has accumulated for the usefulness of the HOME measure in research and applied settings involving young children (Caldwell & Bradley, 1979); a usefulness documented in other chapters in this volume. There are, however, a number of unclear issues involving the measure, some of which we intend to explore in this paper. HOME was used to evaluate the effectiveness of the Houston Parent–Child Development Center (PCDC), a 2-year program of parent–child education directed at optimizing the competence of the child. Families begin the program when the child is 1 year old and complete it when the child is 3 years old. With goals similar to those of Head Start, it was designed for very low-income families. Families entered the project in annual groups called "cohorts." A pilot cohort began in 1970 and the first cohort to be reported here began in 1971. In evaluating the program, HOME was used along with a large number of other measures. As data from the various cohorts accumulated, fairly large sample sizes became available.

First on our list of concerns about HOME is that virtually all work with the measure reported in the literature is with Anglo or black families. Our research is with another United States ethnic group, Mexican-Americans. HOME results for this group may differ from those of other ethnic and SES groups in a number of ways unspecified as yet.

While the literature on Mexican-American parent–child and home–child relationships has grown rapidly in the past two decades it is still comparatively sparse and much of it concerns school-age children. We have found no studies of home environmental or parental effects on infants or very young children for this ethnic group. Nevertheless, a number of relevant issues have been examined by other investigators and their results will be reviewed briefly here.

The question of whether Mexican-American students differ from those of other ethnic groups in educational aspirations was studied by Anderson and Johnson (1971). Both personal and parental expectations were reported by the secondary-school students who participated in the study. Mexican-American students had a greater desire to achieve high grades than Anglos and they reported as much parental pressure to succeed as Anglo students.

Results of studies using measures of the home environment to predict school achievement are rather mixed. Henderson and Merritt (1968) predicted "school potential" as measured by the Goodenough–Harris Drawing Test and Van Alstyne Picture Vocabulary Test for Mexican-American first graders using a multidimensional measure of the home environment. They found that means for high-potential children were higher than those for low-potential children in all of the home environment process measures. Variables yielding significant differences included "periodicals in the home," "engage in weekend travel" and "engage in active diversions." Other significant discriminators were "number of children in family," "father's occupational level," and "mother's educational level."

Henderson (1972) followed 35 of the 80 subjects in the preceding study and found that reading achievement in the third grade was significantly predicted by first-grade home-environmental process variables. The best predictors were Achievement Press (.61), Total (.55), and Activeness of Family (.54). Saldate (1972) found no relationship between a measure of home environmental stimulation and school achievement. High and low achievers had been matched for level of intelligence and apparently the home environment measure added nothing to the prediction. Seguesta (1976) used Wolf's home environment scale to predict the reading achievement of Mexican-American fifth-graders. She found a significant relationship for boys, but not for girls.

Gill and Spilka (1962) compared mothers' child-rearing attitudes of achieving and nonachieving Mexican-American secondary students. They found significant sex differences on the Maternal Dominance scale: High-achieving girls and low-achieving boys had more dominant mothers. There were no significant differences on the Possessive and the Ignoring scales.

Child-rearing beliefs of Anglo, black, and Mexican-American mothers of second-grade children were compared by Strom, Griswold, and Slaughter (1981). They found significant differences between Anglos and blacks, but Mexican-Americans gave responses that placed them between the other two groups on all measures used. Their results are in sharp contrast to those of Durrett, O'Bryant, and Pennebaker (1975), who compared the child-rearing attitudes of Anglo, black, and Mexican-American parents of 5-year-olds. After controlling for level of educational attainment, they found significant differences on five of six categories: Mexican-American parents were less authoritarian (demanding less respect from child), less achievement-oriented (fathers only), and had less concern for individual responsibility. They were also more protective, placed more emphasis on controlling emotions, and were more consistent in their methods of reward and punishment.

There have been several reports using mother–child interaction techniques with Mexican-American subjects. Kagan and Ender (1975) found that Mexican-American mothers more often than Anglo mothers used noncontingent reinforcement of child behavior in a level-of-aspiration game. Steward and Steward (1973) found Mexican-American mothers differed from Anglo and Chinese-American mothers on several mother–child interaction variables. Mexican-American mothers did less "instruction," operated at a slower pace, asked more questions, were less verbal, and used less variety in instructing their children. The sample sizes in this study were very small and socioeconomic status (SES) was not controlled. Laosa (1980) compared Mexican-American and Anglo middle- and low-SES mothers interacting with their 4-year-old children. He found Mexican-American mothers used less praise and inquiry, but more negative physical contact when interacting with their children than Anglo mothers did. However, these differences were nonsignificant when differences in maternal educational levels were statistically controlled.

These studies provide a context for our research, but it must be emphasized that our research is not a cross-cultural study in that our results are for one ethnic or cultural group only. However, the present report may facilitate cross-cultural comparisons and help to understand the contribution of culture to variation in HOME scores. We would warn, nevertheless, that the assumption of uniformity of culture of the present group may not be warranted. Although all are of low income, families vary greatly on the generation–in–the–United States dimension; that is, they may differ greatly in degree of assimilation into the United States, English-speaking, majority culture.

A second concern has to do with the individual items that comprise HOME. We have found no reports in the literature of item analyses of

HOME. It is quite possible that some items may receive nearly 100% positive responses, or that some may receive nearly total negative responses. If near unanimity of response is found for many items overall or for certain factors, there would be a seriously restricted range of variation and correlational studies would be necessarily affected.

Third, although most research has used HOME as an independent variable, the question of determinants of HOME scores is also of interest. What are the characteristics of mothers who have high or low HOME scores? This question is explored with PCDC data.

Fourth, we examine how HOME is related to measures of parent–child behavior. Our evaluation design included one other construct-related measure, a measure of mother–child interaction. A comparison of the relationship of the scores on the two measures provides information on the validity of certain aspects of HOME.

Fifth, a major potential use of HOME is as a program evaluation instrument, but relatively few reports of this use have appeared. HOME was selected for the PCDC project as one of many procedures to be used in evaluating the program and the results are reported.

Finally, the use of HOME scores as predictors of child cognitive development is also explored. There have been numerous reports of this use of HOME and the results are mixed. It is apparent that predictability is a function of subject and group characteristics, but the parameters of these influences are not yet known. Our data provide an opportunity to contribute to understanding predictive relationships.

Parent–Child Development Center

Family Characteristics

It is tempting to describe the Mexican-American family as an entity with certain culturally determined characteristics that distinguish it from other families. To do so would be an exercise in stereotyping because, as has been demonstrated by Murillo (1971) in his excellent discussion of the Mexican-American family, these families vary as a function of acculturation, geography, SES, and individual preferences.

The most relevant description of the Mexican-American family we can offer is a presentation of characteristics of families that have participated in the PCDC. Program selection-criteria required that they be low-income, urban families who had a 1-year-old child, and agreed to participate in a rather demanding and extensive study. Background characteristics of these families may not generalize to other families not having these features.

Background characteristics of PCDC families for program and control groups, fathers and mothers, are shown in Tables 1 and 2. These results are for Cohorts I and II at the time of intake.

Children

Boys and girls were evenly represented in program and control groups. On the average, families had about three children at time of entering the project.

Marital Status

All of the participants in the project were married for the first time. This is in sharp contrast to the marital status of participants in other projects for low-income parents with different ethnic groups (Andrews, Blumenthal, Ferguson, Malone, Johnson, Kahn, Lasater, & Wallace, 1982). Fathers married at about age 24 years and mothers were about 20 when they married. Prior to intake, fathers and mothers were, at intake, 30 and 26 years of age, respectively, and had been married 6 years, on the average.

Housing

Families typically live in detached dwellings with access to outdoor play space. Most rent these homes. All families had indoor bathrooms with hot and cold running water. Houses were relatively small with about five rooms, including two bedrooms. All families had TV. Many families had another adult, often more than one, living with them. This was nearly always a relative.

Income and Occupation

Family incomes were at low levels, as required by funding agency guidelines stipulating eligibility. As may be seen, the program-group mean income was significantly higher than that of the control group, but per capita income, a better measure of family resources, was not significantly higher. Fathers were the principal wage-earners. Nearly all fathers and few mothers were employed. This is to a large extent a function of eligibility requirements, which required that mothers be available for program participation. This requirement did not affect control mothers. Nevertheless the two groups did not differ on this characteristic. Most men worked at jobs classified in the Hollingshead

TABLE 1
Background Characteristics of PCDC Program and Control Families

Characteristic	Program	Control
N	96	118
Index child—% male	56	54
Number of children ($\overline{X}$)	3.0	2.9
Marital status (%)		
Married	86.3	88.6
Single	3.2	4.4
Separated	6.3	4.4
Divorced	2.1	2.6
Widowed	2.1	0.0
Previous marriages (%)		
Yes	18.9	16.4
No	81.1	83.9
Years married ($\overline{X}$)	6.6	6.2
Type of dwelling (%)		
Detached house	70.5	57.9
Apartment	28.4	40.4
Public housing	1.1	1.8
Home ownership (%)		
Rent	79.8	72.7
Own	12.1	21.8
Live with someone else	8.1	5.5
Outdoor play area (%)		
Yes	81.1	85.1
No	18.9	14.9
Number of people in household ($\overline{X}$)	5.7	5.5
Number rooms in house ($\overline{X}$)	5.4	4.9
Number of bedrooms ($\overline{X}$)	2.2	1.8
Annual family income ($) ($\overline{X}$)	6629	5983
Level of significance	$F = 2.13$ (1201), $p < .05.$	
Per capita family income ($)($\overline{X}$)	1491	1318
Level of significance	$F = 2.18$ (1201), $p = .14.$	
Main source of income (%)		
Father	89.5	88.7
Mother	11.6	7.8
Other	3.2	1.7
Savings account (%)	39.8	27.7
Checking account (%)	24.7	24.1
Credit cards (%)	53.6	69.4
Mean and level of significance	$\overline{X} = 4.78, p < .05.$	
Life insurance (%)	51.6	44.5
Health insurance (%)	46.2	45.9

TABLE 2

Background Characteristics of PCDC Program and Control Fathers and Mothers

Characteristic	Fathers		Mothers	
	Program	Control	Program	Control
N	95	113	96	118
Age ($\overline{X}$)	30.5	30.2	26.4	26.9
Age when married ($\overline{X}$)	24.0	23.7	20.3	20.7
Presently employed (%)	91.0	89.3	13.7	5.9
Reason not employed (%)				
Cannot find work	40.0	22.2	4.5	4.3
Medical reasons	40.0	55.6	0.0	3.2
Other	20.0	22.1	6.0	1.1
Not looking	0.0	0.0	89.6	91.4
Work full time (%)	97.7	98.2		
Hourly pay rate (%)				
$3.00 or more	57.2	51.0	4.4	0.0
$4.00 or more	29.8	23.6	0.0	0.0
Work more than 45 hours per week				
(%)	19.9	25.2	13.7	9.8
Belong to a union (%)	24.7	29.5	4.7	3.9
Eligible for retirement benefits (%)	39.0	47.4	4.7	7.8
Place of birth (%)				
Houston	17.9	8.0	27.1	13.6
Other city in Texas	40.0	34.5	32.3	31.4
Other state in United States	5.4	11.7	6.3	9.5
Mexico	29.3	43.2	33.7	39.7
Other country	1.1	1.8	1.1	1.7
Mean and level of significance	$\overline{X}$ = 13.26, df = 4, $p < .01$.			
Plan to stay in USA (%)	96.2	96.1	100.0	98.0
Registered to vote (%)	43.7	20.9	32.7	25.0
Mean and level of significance	$\overline{X}$ = 8.33, df = 1, $p < .01$.			
Has had major accident or illness				
(%)	18.9	26.8	8.4	5.3
Has permanent medical handicaps				
(%)	14.0	13.4	4.0	10.0
Has regular medical checkup (%)	38.5	33.6	54.3	53.4
Language used now (%)				
Spanish	25.5	26.4	37.9	35.6
English	2.1	0.0	0.0	0.0
Both	72.3	73.6	62.1	64.4
Language preferred (%)				
Spanish	39.0	54.7	29.5	38.6
English	28.6	24.4	39.3	20.5
Both	32.5	20.9	31.1	41.0
	$\overline{X}$ = 6.14, df = 2, $p < .05$.			
Years of education ($\overline{X}$)	7.9	7.5	7.8	7.6

(continued)

TABLE 2 (*Continued*)

Characteristic	Fathers		Mothers	
	Program	Control	Program	Control
Location of elementary school (%)				
Houston	28.6	15.0	32.6	26.7
Other city in Texas	27.5	29.0	22.8	23.3
Other state in United States	2.2	0.0	3.3	1.7
Mexico	41.8	55.1	41.3	46.6
Other country	0.0	0.9	0.0	1.7
Location of secondary school				
N	59	66	63	71
Houston (%)	44.1	28.8	52.4	45.1
Other city in Texas (%)	27.1	33.1	20.6	28.2
Other state in United States	1.7	1.5	3.2	1.4
Mexico (%)	25.4	30.3	23.8	22.5
Other country (%)	0.0	1.5	0.0	2.8
Religion (%)				
Catholic	90.1	93.8	88.2	90.7
Protestant	7.7	5.4	10.8	7.6
Other	0.0	0.9	0.0	1.7
None	2.2	0.0	1.1	0.0
Religious participation (%)				
At least once per week	22.7	28.1	27.8	30.7
Once a year or less	28.6	28.1	27.8	23.9

occupational system as Level 2 or 3; that is, semiskilled or unskilled workers. Nearly half of the fathers were paid less than three dollars per hour. Only about one-fourth were union members and only a few more had retirement benefits. The women who were employed tended to be paid less than two dollars per hour. Men who were unemployed tended to have medical problems or difficulty in finding work. Women typically reported they were not seeking employment.

Participant families reported infrequent use of checking or savings accounts. Their use of credit cards and both health and life insurance was somewhat higher. These results suggest prudent management of very limited financial resources.

Place of Origin

Most fathers and mothers were born in Mexico or in places in Texas outside of Houston. If the latter, this usually meant that they were born in the Rio Grande Valley. Most parents were born in rural areas. Just prior to moving to Houston, most had lived in the Rio Grande Valley or in Mexico. Most had lived in Houston less than 12 years. A significant difference appeared for fathers: more control than program men had moved to Houston from Mexico. Fewer than half of the fathers and only one-fourth of the mothers were registered to vote. Although many are immigrants, nearly all planned to stay in the United States.

Health

Somewhat more fathers than mothers had had a major illness or accident. For fathers these were largely work-related. Mothers more often had regular medical examinations, usually in connection with prenatal visits.

Language

A majority of parents used both English and Spanish, indicating that they are bilingual to some degree. Preferences for English and Spanish were about the same for the two groups, but mothers more often preferred Spanish and fathers tended to prefer English. Within the groups of mothers, those entering the program preferred English and the control mothers preferred Spanish. The first language for all parents was Spanish.

Education

Educational levels were low for fathers and mothers, with the mean falling within the elementary school level. Relatively large numbers attended elementary school in Mexico, but if they did go on to high school, they did so in Houston.

Religion

The great majority of parents were Roman Catholics. Regular participation, once a week or more, was reported by one-fourth to one-third of the families, but a similar percentage reported participation of once a year or less.

Summary

A profile of a "typical" low-income Mexican-American PCDC family includes the following salient features: The family consisted of a father, mother, and three children. The father was present and employed, although his income is very low. He was employed as a semi- or unskilled worker. The parents had less than an eight-grade education. Taking occupation and education together, the family was classified at the lowest two socioeconomic ranks. The family rented a small house, and outdoor play space was available. Many families had one or more other people living with them, usually a relative. Spanish was the first language for all of the parents, but most became bilingual to some extent. Fathers reported more proficiency in English than mothers. Parents tended to be relative newcomers to Houston, having moved from Mexico or South Texas. Most families were Catholic, but participation in formal religion was not high.

Background and Overview

The program was developed in 1969 in reaction to the Westinghouse report that Head Start programs were ineffective. It seemed to many developmental psychologists and educators then that the reasons for ineffectiveness might be that Head Start began too late in the child's life, after the effects of poverty had already had their impact, and that Head Start lacked continuity. The PCDCs, originally located in Birmingham, Houston, and New Orleans, would correct both of these shortcomings. It began earlier in the child's life, from birth to age 3 years, and it provided continuity by training the mother to be the teacher of her young child. PCDCs also were to acknowledge the destructive effects of poverty on family life and partially ameliorate these by providing a variety of social welfare and medical services.

The program development process has been discussed in detail elsewhere (Johnson, 1975) and it is sufficient now to say that the program format chosen was the outcome of two kinds of information: (1) discussion with many Mexican-American residents of the target area about their desired goals for children and parents, their family customs, and their opinions about intervention, and (2) a survey of the child development literature, especially as it related to the development of competence in young children. Major decisions made were to limit the program to 2 years instead of 3 to reduce the length of the time commitment by families, and to begin at child age 1 year, ending at age 3.

Another decision was to have a two-stage program. The first year of program participation was carried out in the mother's home by in-home teachers. This was done because there was a strong opinion in the community that Mexican-American families would not attend community programs. Perhaps by first going to their homes, they could gradually be drawn into the full program.

The Houston PCDC developers believed that low-income families do not always have knowledge of community resources available to them. Some parents need encouragement and more skills so that they can work with their children, and so that they can communicate with the schools regarding their children's needs. At the time the program began, surveys indicated that the public-school dropout rate for Mexican-Americans was more than 70% in some parts of the Southwest.

The Houston PCDC, located in a Mexican-American neighborhood, attempts to help families gain access to the information and resources they may need. It serves low-income families who have at least one child under three years of age. Its goal has been to develop and demonstrate ways of strengthening families and enabling parents to optimize the intellectual, social, and physical development of their young children. The maintenance of gains over a long period of time is an important aim. Two objectives are to build the skills of the parent and to increase his confidence in working with the schools and with his child. Recognition is given to the importance of parenting skills as they affect the development of the young child.

Families are recruited by workers who go door-to-door. If the family meets income guidelines and is interested, when the child is 1 year of age a community worker visits the home to explain the program and the control groups. Then during this first program year an In-Home Educator visits the home, meeting weekly with the child and the mother. The program focus is on facilitating the development of the mother's skills as an effective teacher of her child. The mother and In-Home Educator share their resources, with the mother contributing personal experience and knowledge. The mother and Educator explore and discuss ways in which the mother can promote the child's development in language, motor coordination, social relations, and self-confidence. Toys and books are lent or given to the family, and mothers are encouraged to make toys. While the child explores a toy or book, the mother and the Educator together find ways to enhance the child's enjoyment of learning. The focus is on such questions as What is the child learning? What else could he or she learn while using this book or toy? How can he or she learn such relational concepts as big and little, up and down? How can the mother use other objects in her home to teach the child such concepts? Thus, the mother is helped to generalize teaching to the home situation.

During this first program year, the entire family is involved in several family socials and workshops. Each family is invited to at least four family-workshops, usually held at the center for a full day on a weekend. The focus here is on building the strengths of the family. Discussions and activities explore communication in the family, decision making, problem solving, and role relationships within the family and between the family and the community.

During the second program year, when the child is 2 years old, mother and child attend the center-based program four mornings each week. The children are involved in nursery school activities designed to promote their cognitive, language, social, motor, and self-concept development. One-to-one teacher–child and mother–child interaction is a part of each daily session. Particular emphasis is placed on language and concept learning.

The mother's curriculum consists of work with the child, as well as adult sessions. Half of the adult sessions center on home-management activities such as budgeting, health, nutrition, consumer purchasing, cooking, and sewing. Through these the mother can manage family resources more effectively. Driver education, which is popular, enables the mother to become more self-sufficient in meeting her family's needs.

The rest of the adult sessions are devoted to studying and discussing child development and education, including such topics as discipline, children's self-concept, and the augmentation of children's learning. Mothers become aware of the effects they have on the child's present and future development. In small groups discussion sessions, the mothers share their experiences, with the Child Development Educator facilitating discussion and occasionally supplying information from research and practice.

Microteaching, a videotape technique, is used to improve the mothers teaching skills. Each mother and child pair is videotaped interacting with toys and books. The mother helps the child explore and learn. She views this tape for self-feedback, and then, with her permission, it is shown to the other mothers. Discussion centers on the positive things the mother does to help the child learn and to enjoy learning.

Evening sessions are held twice monthly with fathers and mothers attending together. Both parents have an opportunity to choose topics of interest to them. These range from consumer buying and program purposes and practices to resources they can use in the community and ways to develop effective interactions with the public schools.

Bilingual language activities are important. During the in-home year, the educator and mother discuss ways the mother can stimulate the child's language, with the mother urged to interact with the child in the language in which she is most comfortable. In the second year, the teachers speak to the 2-year-old in his or her dominant language, because he or she is just beginning to master it. This provides a natural bilingual environment because some children are spoken to in Spanish, some in English. The child hears and begins to grasp both languages. In the adult groups, the parents conduct most of their activities in Spanish, changing to English if they so desire or to meet individual needs. English-language classes are offered during both program years to aid mothers in contacts with community and schools. An effort is also made to include English terms in other areas of the curriculum. Thus the goal has been not to impose English, but rather to encourage the effective use of both Spanish and English. Value is placed both on the cultural and language patterns of the home community and on the acquisition of language and skills necessary in society.

Access to community resources is facilitated. Families are encouraged to enroll in the local community health clinic where each program child is given a medical examination with appropriate laboratory tests and follow-up. Families can consult project Community Workers about various problems and are referred to community agencies for such needs as legal aid, food stamps, and counseling.

Program Evaluation Procedures

Families for the project were recruited through a door-to-door survey. They were invited to participate if they had a 1-year-old child, met poverty guidelines, mother was not working and if there was no obvious evidence of mental retardation or neurological disorder for the child. If interested, they were assigned randomly to program or control group by a coin flip. The implications of this assignment were then presented to the mother. After the first two cohorts, prior to group assignment, a detailed description of the implications of program or control participation were given and a commitment to participate regardless of group assignment was requested.

Each program year, about 88–100 families were assigned to a cohort and a program evaluation was carried out with seven of the annual cohorts. The first two cohorts included were pilot groups (each of which had about half as many program hours as later groups) and were primarily involved in order to help develop curriculum materials, offer staff training experience, and enable the evaluation staff to pilot-test new procedures. The present report makes major use of data from these first two cohorts because the children in these were the only ones who were all administered Bayley Scales of Infant Development. This test was not used routinely with Cohorts III–V. These cohorts were incompletely assessed largely because funding uncertainties resulted in loss of the entire evaluation staff for several months and the process of recruiting and training new personnel. However, the program was functioning very well for Cohorts VI and VII and these groups received a full assessment battery.

Program assessment was carried out annually beginning when the index child was 1 year of age. This chapter deals only with program years one, two and three, but follow-up of children is expected to continue through the school years.

Assessment procedures were carried out in Spanish or English, depending on subject preference, by bilingual, bicultural data-collectors. All materials used were translated into both languages using the back-translation technique to assure comparability. Assessments were done in the home or in the evaluators' offices. A wide range of assessment procedures were used and not all of them are relevant for this report. Only those used here are listed.

Home Observation for Measurement of the Environment (HOME)

HOME (Caldwell & Bradley, 1979) was used to assess the organized cognitive stimulation available to the infant in the home. It consists of a 45-item checklist divided into six subscales and a total score. The scales are as follows: I. Emotional and Verbal Responsiveness of Mother (responsivity), II. Avoidance of Restriction and Punishment (avoid restrictions), III. Organization of Physical and Temporal Environment (organization), IV. Provision of Appropriate Play Materials (toys), V. Maternal Involvement with the Child (involvement), and VI. Opportunities for Variety in Daily Stimulation (variety).

The procedure is carried out in the home and scores are based on both direct observation (e.g., Item 12, "Mother does not shout at child during visit") and interview (e.g., Item 42, "Mother reads stories to child at least three times weekly.") Interobserver reliability for HOME in the PCDC research has consistently been above .90.

Comprehensive Family Data Interview (CFDI)

This interview was used at intake (child-age 12 months) to collect background information on the family as a whole and individual family members. It included information on family income, number of children and their ages, and occupation and education of parents.

Mother–Child Interaction (MCI)

Mother and child were videotaped as they interacted in several assigned tasks, which varied in length and nature as a function of child's age. Thus, at age 1 year, the tasks were "book task" (4 minutes), "teaching toys" (4 minutes) and "free play" (8 minutes). At age 2, the tasks were "book task" (4 minutes), "animal sort" (4 minutes), "block sort" (4 minutes), "play village" (8 minutes), and "free play" (8 minutes). At age 3, two sessions were used. The first comprised "free play" (20 minutes) and second of "book task" (6 minutes), "block sort" (12 minutes), "block design" (6 minutes) and "teaching toys" (12 minutes). The tasks differed greatly in the degree of structure the instructions imposed on the mothers (see Johnson, Kahn, & Davila, 1981, for details). Thus, the sorting and design tasks were highly structured (e.g., "Teach your child to solve this problem"), whereas the free play, book, and play village tasks were relatively unstructured (e.g., "Play together with your child.")

Ratings were made of the videotapes at one-minute intervals on the following scales: (1) Affection, (2) Praise, (3) Criticism, (4) Control, (5) Reasoning, (6) Mother's Verbal Encouragement and (7) Child Verbal Responsiveness. Observer reliability was checked frequently and reliabilities were all above .80.

Receptive Vocabulary (RV-S)

The mother's vocabulary knowledge in English and Spanish was tested at intake with the Peabody Picture Vocabulary Test and a translated adaptation of the test in Spanish. As all of the mothers were fluent Spanish-speakers and only a few were fluent in English, the Spanish version was used as the measure of intelligence. Raw scores were used.

Traditional Family Ideology (TFI)

The TFI (Levinson & Huffman, 1955) is a 12-item attitude scale used to assess the mother's agreement with traditional ideas about home and family. A five-point response scale is used. Responses for each item are summed to produce a single score for the entire scale. Levinson & Huffman report a test–retest reliability of .93. This was administered at intake.

Index of Achievement Values (IAV)

The IAV (Strodtbeck, 1958) is a seven-item attitude scale used at intake to assess the mother's valuation of independence and achievement. It is scored in a manner similar to the TFI. Reliability has not been reported.

Child Rearing Beliefs (CRB)

This is a new measure developed by the Houston PCDC research staff to measure changes in child-rearing beliefs. Items were selected to assess the mother's views regarding developmental change and her sensitivity to the baby's emotional state and developmental level. The reliability has not been determined. This was administered at intake.

Psychological Well-Being Scale (PWB)

The PWB, developed by Bradburn (1969), is used to assess the general morale of the mother. It was administered at intake, at the same session in which the child is tested. The PWB consists of 25 items, including 4 general questions, a list of all possible worries, and 10 specific feeling states. Data consist of responses to individual items, as well as the total number of worries expressed.

Locus of Control Scale (LCS)

This is an adapted version of the children's locus of control measure developed by Nowicki and Strickland (1973). It is used here to measure mothers' locus of control. Reliabilities have not yet been determined. It was completed at intake.

Bayley Scales of Infant Development

The Bayley scales are used to assess the general development of the child. Scores are obtained for the Mental Development Index (MDI), and the Psychomotor Development Index (PDI). Test–retest reliability of the MDI and PDI for one week as reported in the test scales is good. They were administered at 12 and 24 months of age.

Stanford–Binet Intelligence Scale (SB)

Often used in the evaluation of children in early compensatory education programs, this test is highly regarded for its ability to predict school achievement. The reliabilities are very high. It was administered at 36 months of age.

Concept Familiarity Index (CFI)

This measure was specifically designed to serve as a criterion test of the child's acquisition of the concept-training portion of the program. It was developed by Palmer (1970) and used successfully in his Harlem project. Reliabilities are reported to be satisfactory. It was administered at 36 months.

Item Analysis

Continuing in our attempt to understand the meaning of HOME score variation in Mexican-American families we turn next to an analysis of the frequency with which individual items receive positive or negative scores. For this analysis we used 163 HOME protocols taken at child age 12 months.

The results appear in Table 3 with items shown in rank order of positive score. Item numbers and factor categories are also shown. The content statements are abbreviations of the actual observation or interview questions.

TABLE 3
Rank Order of HOME Item Frequency at 12 Months
$(N = 163)$

Rank	HOME Item (number)	Factor	Number positive	Percent positive	Content
1	11	I	162	99	Mo[a] positive emotion
2	4	I	161	99	Mo clear speech
3	10	I	161	99	Mo caress Ch[b]
4	13	II	161	99	Mo not shout
5	12	II	160	98	Mo initiates exchange
6	16	II	160	98	Mo not scold Ch

(continued)

TABLE 3 (*Continued*)

Rank	HOME Item (number)	Factor	Number positive	Percent positive	Content
7	9	I	159	98	Mo positive voice
8	14	II	156	96	Mo not slap Ch
9	35	V	156	96	Mo keeps Ch close
10	6	I	155	95	Mo good conversation
11	25	III	155	95	Ch play environment good
12	21	III	154	95	Ch to grocery
13	1	I	152	93	Mo spontaneous vocalizes
14	22	III	151	93	Ch out 4 times/week
15	36	V	149	91	Mo talks to Ch
16	31	IV	148	91	Cuddly toys
17	44	VI	147	90	Family visits relatives
18	17	II	145	89	Mo not restrict Ch
19	41	VI	138	85	Fa[c] daily Ch care
20	20	III	135	83	Regular babysitters
21	26	IV	134	82	Muscle activity toys
22	15	II	132	81	Little physical punishment
23	2	I	131	80	Mo responds Ch vocalize
24	8	I	129	79	Mo spontaneously praises Ch
25	28	IV	127	78	Stroller, walker, or kiddie car
26	24	III	121	74	Special place Ch's "treasures"
27	27	IV	121	74	Push toy available
28	30	IV	120	74	Toy table, play pen
29	43	VI	120	74	Ch eats with family
30	7	I	115	71	Mo permits "messy" play
31	29	IV	113	69	Mo provides toys during interview
32	5	I	101	62	Mo asks O[d] questions
33	23	III	98	60	Ch regular medical checkup
34	3	I	87	53	Mo names object for Ch
35	37	V	75	46	Mo encourages development
36	38	V	66	41	Mo attentive to special toys
37	32	IV	61	37	Fit-together coordination toys
38	33	IV	52	32	Receptacle coordination toys
39	40	V	48	29	Challenge toys
40	39	V	47	29	Mo structure Ch play
41	19	II	44	27	Family has pet
42	34	IV	33	20	Toys for music & literature
43	18	II	31	19	10 books present
44	45	VI	29	18	Ch has 3 books of own
45	42	VI	16	10	Mo reads to Ch 3 times/week

[a] Mo = Mother.
[b] Ch = Child.
[c] Fa = Father.
[d] O = Observer–interviewer.

As we have noted earlier, the home environments of PCDC families tend to obtain high HOME scores. This appears in the item analysis in the fact that so many items receive positive scores for such a large number of respondents. It may be seen that 17 of the items were positive for 90% or more of the mothers and half of the items were at or above the 80% level. Certainly, the mothers are remarkably uniform on many items. They tend to be more uniform on scales for responsivity, avoidance of restriction, and organization, and more diverse on toys and on variety.

The low frequency items present two fairly definite patterns: the first has to do with reading and the second with structured play. The first is no surprise in view of the fact that the mean level of education for the mothers is below the eighth grade and many have had no schooling at all. Furthermore, most mothers are Spanish-speaking and although Spanish-language children's books are somewhat available in Houston, these books are expensive and not readily available.

The second pattern, of providing less structured play involves Items 32, 33, 40, 39, and 34. These items seem to focus on the mother's concern for providing play opportunities that promote curiosity, exploration, and problem solving. Other play materials are present, but not the kind that are deliberately selected to encourage learning or cognitive advance.

It is readily apparent that parent-education programs with this population could expect greater effect on HOME toys, involvement, and variety scales than on the first three scales. Two-thirds or more mothers have already achieved high scores on the latter factors, but the former factors leave much room for change.

We would also expect higher correlations between these factors and various other measures simply because the score range of responsivity, avoidance of restriction, and organization is so restricted.

Determinants of Home Scores at Child-Age 12 Months

In this section we explore the antecedents and possible causes of HOME score variation. We are especially concerned with mothers' characteristics that lead to behavior determining HOME variation. We view the mother as the manager of the home environment. She attempts to shape the child's behavior to conform to her standards, selects settings for interaction, rewards adequate performance, punishes misbehavior, lays out work to be done: in short, she extensively organizes the child's life. Because the younger child is more completely under direct parental control (Barker & Wright, 1955) her immediate impact on the infant and young child is, of course, greater than on the other child. We assume, too, that her performance of this managerial role is a function of her personal abilities, attitudes, beliefs, and the resources that she provides to her family.

This analysis of HOME determinants is limited by the kinds of measures available to us in the PCDC data bank and by requirements of the project. For example, we did not examine the effect of maternal employment, a potentially interesting variable because few of the mothers were employed. The role of alternative caretakers in the family may also have been of interest, but we did not have information on this matter. Also of great interest are the effects of characteristics of the child as determinants of HOME scores, but such analysis is too complex to be included here. It might be noted, however, that with the exception mentioned in the section on program evaluation, child's gender was not related to any HOME scores.

Family Resources

A set of variables consisting of family income, father presence, number of children in the household, and household crowding have been found relevant in child development research. Indeed, this is so often the case that White and Duker (1973) have advocated that such measures should be routinely reported in all child research and Bell and Hertz (1976) suggest that they have value as marker variables.

Family income indexes the potential availability of many material and experiential resources (e.g., the availability of books, newspapers, toys, and travel all depend to some degree on the amount of money a family has at its disposal).

Father presence in the home is of undoubted importance for the management of the child's learning environment. He not only provides material resources but offers the mother his emotional support. As he is also a manager of this environment his influence of some HOME scores is direct.

The number of children in a household has a bearing on how family resources are distributed. Most previous research has found an inverse relationship between family size and sibship and child cognitive abilities (Zajonc, Markus, & Markus, 1979).

While it would seem that crowding as measured by the ratio of rooms per person, would be closely related to both family income and number of children, we have found that this is true only for number of children (−.49). The correlation with income is only .06.

We expect high HOME scores to be associated with high family income, father presence, low number of children, and low crowding.

HOME scores were found to be related to all of the family resources measures, but the pattern of significant correlations was different for each measure (see Table 4). Income was related to the subscales for responsivity, involvement, variety, and total. Only the variety scale, which includes material goods such as books was directly related to income level.

Father presence was related only to the variety subscale. It is also the only scale that calls for information about the father's direct role in child rearing (e.g., "Father provides some caregiving each day"). Correlations with other scales may have been affected by the fact that a very high proportion of the families in this study included father presence.

Number of children and crowding yielded the same pattern of relationships with HOME scores. Although several correlations were reliable all were low. The scores for organization and for toys and the total scores were significantly related to the number of children and crowding. Involvement was also significantly associated with number of children.

TABLE 4
Family Resources and HOME Correlations

HOME	Family income	Father presence	Number of children	Crowding
N	85	519	511	497
Scales				
1. Responsivity	26*	08	00	07
2. Avoid restriction	20	−01	01	03
3. Organization	20	05	−15*	16*
4. Toys	06	−10	−17*	19*
5. Involvement	23*	−11	−16*	11
6. Variety	26*	36**	−11	10
Total	22*	13	−14*	17*

*$p < .05$.
**$p < .01$.

Mothers' Personal Resources

As mothers handle child-rearing tasks they must draw on their resourcefulness, problem solving abilities, and coping skills. The PCDC data bank includes several measures that may appropriately assess some of these resources. We have selected mother's years of education, vocabulary level, and morale.

The mother's years of education indexes the degree to which various educational resources are available to her, how well informed she is, and may say something about her educational values. Women in this study tend to have been educationally deprived. While women in the United States today typically have at least a high school degree, women in the project had less than an eighth grade education on the average. That the educational level of the mother has been found to be one of the most reliable correlates of child school achievement (Marjoribanks, 1979) is not surprising. If she is illiterate she is necessarily isolated from a vast array of information of potential value in rearing her children. With literacy more of these resources are available to her and with higher educational levels her cultural horizons are greatly expanded and she is more able to affect the level of educational achievement of the entire family.

Although no formal measure of intelligence was administered to the women in the project, the RV-S score provides a rough indicator of vocabulary level and therefore, of intellectual level. For this analysis, vocabulary knowledge in Spanish was used. The validity of this version of PPVT is not known.

The mother's morale was measured with the PWB scale. The PWB includes a list of worries and this was used to indicate her morale on the assumption that many worries would mean low morale. We have further assumed that if she is worried and if her morale is low she will be a less effective manager of her environment than if her morale is high.

As shown in Table 5, mother's years of educational attainment was related to the organization, the toys, the involvement and the total scores. Better-educated mothers are especially sensitive to the potential that children's toys hold for promoting competence in children.

The relationship between mothers' vocabulary level and HOME scores was the strongest overall in the entire study. As may be seen in Table 5, all of the correlations were significant and most were between .36 and .44. Apparently, mothers of higher vocabulary levels who are presumably more intelligent take action to make their baby's home environment more stimulating.

TABLE 5
Personal Resources and HOME Score Correlations

HOME	Years of education	RV–S (vocabulary)	PWB (morale)
N	492	173	257
Scales			
1. Responsivity	09	41***	−07
2. Avoid restriction	08	40***	−04
3. Organization	15*	36***	−01
4. Toys	27**	36***	−04
5. Involvement	15*	16*	03
6. Variety	11	44***	03
Total	22*	43***	−05

*p < .05.
**p < .01.
***p < .001.

None of the PWB morale correlations even approached significance. Whether worried and of low morale or not, mothers carried out their infant-care functions quite independently.

Mothers' Attitudes and Beliefs

The relationship between maternal attitudes and actual behavior has been the subject of numerous studies (Hess, 1970) and while it appears that this relationship is weaker for lower socioeconomic groups than for higher ones (Moss & Jones, 1977; Tulkin & Cohler, 1973; Zegiob & Forehand, 1975) there is still reason for supposing that HOME scores might vary as a function of maternal attitudes and beliefs. We argue that her behaviors as manager of the child's environment are a product of choices made and these in turn are based, at least in part, on her belief system.

Four measures were selected for this analysis: (TFI), (IAV), (CRB), and (LCS).

The mothers in our study vary greatly in the degree to which they hold attitudes or beliefs that are traditional or modern. It seems to us quite likely that these attitudes or orientations should be relevant for the kinds of activities that make up HOME scores. This is suggested by the work on traditionalism–modernism conducted by Inkeles and associates (Inkeles & Smith, 1974). This work was done in six countries with young men. Although women were not included in their study and there were no measures of child-rearing behaviors the general orientations described seem equally relevant for women. As summarized by Werner (1979) the "modern individual has these characteristics:

1. openness to new experience, both with people and with new ways of doing things such as family planning and birth control;
2. assertion of increasing independence from the authority of traditional figures such as parents;
3. belief in the efficacy of science and medicine and an abandonment of passivity and fatalism in the face of life's difficulties;
4. ambition for oneself and one's children to achieve higher occupational and educational goals" (p. 289).

If the more modern mothers have these views, it seems they should be active in providing an intellectually stimulating environment for their children, and thus, earn higher HOME scores. The TFI and IAV both were used as measures of traditionalism. Both are correlated with mother's place of birth, as mothers born in Mexico hold more traditional values.

A central issue in the mother's role as manager is her belief that developmental change is possible. If she regards the child's development as a predetermined unfolding of a natural course and minimizes the role environment and her own actions might have on the course of development, then HOME scores should be relatively low. But if she believes that the course of development is susceptible to environmental influence, and especially, that her own efforts on behalf of the child will have an effect on the child's development, we would expect higher HOME scores.

The CRB was used to assess the strength of these beliefs. The questionnaire calls for responses to such statements as: "Children aged 12 months often cry without reason" (−); "A mother can help her young child learn by providing play materials that awaken his curiosity" (+).

A measure of the mother's locus of control (LCS) orientation is included here to examine the notion that an effective manager should hold an expectation that she affects her environment. We expect mothers with an internal locus of control to take action to achieve their goals, whereas the woman who is externally oriented is expected to wait for desired results to happen. In a sense, the LCS measure resembles the CRB in that both deal with perceived influence, but the LCS is a measure of generalized expectancy whereas the CRB deals specifically with child rearing.

The results, shown in Table 6, indicate that mothers who hold traditional values tend to obtain lower HOME scores. The pattern of correlations with HOME was similar for the TFI and IAV, but the

TABLE 6
Mother Attitudes and Beliefs and HOME Score Correlations

HOME	TFI	IAV	CRB	LCS
N	327	327	80	341
Scales				
1. Responsivity	10	16*	16	01
2. Avoid restriction	13	11	27*	06
3. Organization	10	19*	21	−10
4. Toys	21*	25*	44*	−10
5. Involvement	21*	18*	07	−02
6. Variety	11	17*	04	−06
Total	24**	29**	38**	−01

*p < .05.
**p < .01.

correlations were slightly higher for the IAV. This suggests that it is the achievement-orientation aspect of modernism that is of importance for HOME scores. Total and toy scores were most highly correlated with these measures.

The measure of beliefs regarding developmental change, the CRB, was rather substantially related to toys and to total scores and to a lesser degree related to avoidance of restriction scores.

Contrary to our expectations, HOME and LCS scores were not related.

Summary

In order to better understand variability in HOME scores for mothers of 1-year-olds, the relationship of these scores to three kinds of information about the mothers were examined. Nearly all of the variables selected for analysis were related to at least some of the HOME factors. The background factors found to be significantly related to the HOME factors were as follows:

HOME factors	Background correlates
1. Responsivity	Family income
	Vocabulary level
	Achievement orientation
2. Avoidance of restriction	Developmental change and sensitivity
	Vocabulary level

(continued)

(Continued)

HOME factors	Background correlates
3. Organization	Number of children (−)
	Crowding
	Education
	Vocabulary level
	Achievement orientation
4. Toys	Number of children (−)
	Crowding
	Education
	Vocabulary level
	Traditionalism
	Achievement orientation
	Developmental change and sensitivity
5. Involvement	Family income
	Number of children (−)
	Education
	Vocabulary level
	Traditionalism
	Achievement orientation
6. Variety	Family income
	Father presence
	Vocabulary level
	Achievement orientation
Total	Family income
	Number of children (−)
	Crowding
	Education
	Vocabulary level
	Traditionalism
	Achievement orientation
	Development change and sensitivity

From these results it is apparent that the provision of a stimulating home environment is a function of available resources, both material and personal. If a mother's access to resources is limited, her ability to provide a stimulating environment for her child is also limited. Too little money, too many children, and living in a crowded household had effects on several factors. Limited education was associated with decreased scores on three factors. A lower vocabulary-level was correlated with generally lower HOME-scores.

While the resources available to the mothers are of obvious importance, their values and beliefs had at least as much effect on their management of the home learning-environment, they were involved in all factors and yielded some of the strongest correlations. The results demonstrate that child-rearing behaviors exist in a network of meaning and value. The mothers differed in their views of what was "good" or "right" in child-rearing and family relationships and these differences were reflected in their child-rearing behaviors.

The Construct Validity of HOME

The construct validity of HOME has been investigated by Ramey and Mills (1977) and Barnard and Gortner (1977). The first study compared HOME scores with laboratory mother–child interactions. Ramey and Mills found significant correlations for four of the HOME factors and the total score. Barnard and Gortner also found significant correlations between HOME and mothers and infants interacting at home. Although significant, the correlations were low, suggesting HOME and the other measures assessed somewhat different aspects of the home environment.

Our contribution to the construct validity of HOME used a method similar to that used by Ramey and Mills, but instead of coding discrete behaviors, we used rating scales to describe mother–child interactions. Our mother–child interaction procedure is described earlier in this chapter.

An examination of HOME items within each factor revealed few obvious correspondences with MCI scales. For example, Item 23, "child gets out of house at least four times a week" is a content not tapped by MCI. On the other hand, Item 8 "mother spontaneously praises child's qualities or behavior during the visit" is closely comparable to the MCI Praise scale.

Concurrent correlations at child age 12, 24, and 36 months for MCI and HOME scores are shown in Table 7. Only control-group participants were included to eliminate possible program effects on the correlations. Correlation panels boxed in are those for which at least two HOME items appeared to overlap MCI scales. Only boxed panels were expected to include significant correlations. Four of the six boxes had at least one significant correlation, but other significant correlations may be seen scattered across the overall matrix.

At 12 months, only two correlations were significant. As expected, the HOME avoid restriction scale was negatively related (−.32) to the MCI criticism. Although not predicted, the HOME toys scale was related to the MCI verbal encouragement subscale (.31).

Three significant correlations were obtained at 24 months, two of which were predicted. Again, the HOME avoid restriction scale was

TABLE 7

Concurrent HOME and Mother–Child Interaction Correlations[a]

HOME scales (age in months)	Mother–Child Interaction Scales					
	Affection	Praise	Criticism	Control	Reasoning	Verbal encourage- ment
1. Responsivity						
12	07	12	− 20	11	16	16
24	− 09	01	01	− 04	03	− 09
36	16	31*	− 07	07	11	32*
2. Avoid restriction						
12	− 02	− 04	− 32**	− 03	− 29*	− 05
24	19	24*	− 34**	15	19	14
36	24	14	23	17	− 22	04
3. Organization						
12	.09	− 02	− 17	− 11	03	16
24	− 08	03	− 01	11	07	12
36	11	12	− 23	− 09	09	21
4. Toys						
12	12	13	− 04	06	08	31*
24	02	14	− 02	06	05	17
36	13	24*	− 08	16	11	42**
5. Involvement						
12	00	− 13	− 09	02	− 10	03
24	− 02	07	02	25*	04	08
36	− 02	15	− 06	01	− 05	39*
6. Variety						
12	12	08	− 03	08	21	17
24	02	06	− 02	− 21	04	00
Total						
12	09	05	− 21	05	19	21
24	05	19	− 17	12	14	12
36	12	33*	04	06	03	44**

[a] At 12 months, $N = 73$; at 24, $N = 94$; at 36, $N = 50$.

*$p < .05$.

**$p < .01$.

related to criticism (− .34). The HOME involvement scale was related to the MCI control scale (.25). Unexpectedly, MCI praise was related to HOME avoid restriction (.24).

The 36-months correlations produced seven that were significant, but only two of six predicted correlations were reliable. The HOME responsivity scale was significantly related to the MCI praise (.31) and verbal encouragement scales (.32). Not predicted, but significant, were the HOME toys and the MCI praise (.24) and verbal encouragement scales (.42). HOME involvement was also related to MCI verbal encouragement (.39). HOME total was related to MCI praise (.33) and to verbal encouragement (.44).

No significant correlations were expected for three HOME factors: organization, toys, and variety; for organization and variety, that expectation was realized. The HOME toys scale was related to MCI praise and verbal encouragement.

The pattern of scattered correlations found offers little support for the idea that the two measures really tap the same aspects of parent–child relationships.

Program Evaluation

HOME was used along with several other measures to evaluate the effectiveness of the PCDC. For each of the measures the questions were essentially the same: (1) Was there any evidence of group differences at intake when the children were 12 months of age? (2) Was there evidence of program effect after the first year when the child was 24 months old? and (3) Was there evidence that the entire two-year program had an effect?

Families entered the project in annual cohorts. There were seven cohorts in the study, but for this analysis we report the results for the first two cohorts and the last two. The three middle cohorts are omitted because assessment data were less completely collected owing to budget problems and consequent staff shortages. The early cohorts are included to show the results of a new program, trying out new curriculum materials and novel pedagogical procedures. The last cohorts are included to provide a contrast to this novelty. It would seem that after 5 years any lingering Hawthorne effects would have been minimal.

Evaluation of the program depends on the success of the initial random assignment of participants to the program or control conditions. The evaluation is complicated by the fact that not all participants completed the program or were available for the postprogram testing and interviews. The drop-out percentage rates for the cohorts examined here were 50, 57, 50, and 48 for program and 47, 49, 33, and 44 for controls. That the rates are higher for program families is expected because greater demands were made on them for time and effort and if program mothers went to work during the day they had to drop out.

The major reason for dropping out overall was that families moved away from Houston, usually to South Texas or to Mexico.

The results of the initial randomization process were examined by comparing program and control families on a large number of background variables: total income, per capita income, number of children, parental education, and language use. Only one significant difference appeared: Cohort I program families had higher total incomes than controls, but this difference was not found for later cohorts. There were no systematic differences between groups.

When the question of whether differential attrition had occurred, that is, whether participants having certain characteristics tended to drop out of one group more often than in the other group, the answer was the same: There was no evidence of bias.

The analysis with background characteristics was repeated with measures taken at child age 12 months. No evidence of randomization or differential attrition bias was found for mother–child interaction, or any of the verbal–attitudinal measures. There were two significant differences between program and control groups on the HOME organization and variety scales for Cohort VII, both favoring the control group (see Table 8). One significant sex difference also appeared for Cohort VII. Mothers of girls had higher scores than mothers of boys on the avoid restriction score ($p < .03$). There was no evidence of attrition bias on HOME.

The results for HOME at 24 months, after the first program year, appear in Table 9. As may be seen, there were several significant differences between groups. No differences were found for responsivity and avoidance of restriction scores. For organization, the difference obtained for Cohort II favored the control group. All other differences showed an advantage for the program group. Toys scores showed differences for Cohorts I and VI; for involvement, there were differences for Cohort VI. Cohorts II, VI, and VII all showed group difference on variety scores. Total scores were significantly different for Cohorts I and VI. Thus, HOME differences were found for all four Cohorts on some factors.

The results at the end of the entire program appear in Table 10. There were 14 significant differences. All demonstrated an advantage for the program group. These appeared on five of the six scales and the total score; only organization scores remained without differences. The results were not uniform across cohorts; there was less evidence of program impact on Cohort I than on later cohorts. There was no evidence of a diminishing of effect as might be predicted by the Hawthorne-effect notion; indeed, the results suggest greater effects for later cohorts.

TABLE 8

Program and Control Group HOME Scores for Early and Late Cohorts at 12 Months

HOME Scales	Early cohorts				Later cohorts			
	I		II		VI		VII	
	P[a]	C[b]	P	C	P	C	P	C
N	48	67	50	49	34	45	37	37
1[c]	7.5 (2.3)[d]	7.7 (2.6)	9.0 (1.9)	9.6 (1.3)	8.5 (2.7)	7.8 (2.5)	9.8 (3.1)	8.2 (2.9)
2[e]	6.1* (1.4)	5.5 (1.6)	6.2 (0.9)	5.7 (1.5)	4.5 (1.8)	4.5 (1.8)	5.5 (1.4)	5.5 (1.6)
3[f]	4.4 (1.3)	4.5 (1.2)	4.9 (1.1)	5.2 (0.9)	4.3 (1.4)	4.0 (1.6)	4.1* (1.4)	4.8 (1.1)
4[g]	4.6 (2.6)	4.7 (2.1)	5.5 (1.9)	5.8 (1.7)	4.0 (2.2)	4.2 (2.0)	4.1 (2.5)	4.2 (2.0)
5[h]	2.6 (1.7)	2.9 (1.9)	3.6 (1.6)	3.9 (1.3)	3.0 (1.5)	2.9 (1.7)	3.7 (1.5)	4.2 (1.5)
6[i]	2.6 (1.4)	2.7 (1.0)	2.6 (2.7)	1.1 (1.0)	2.8 (1.1)	2.8 (1.1)	2.8* (0.8)	3.2 (0.8)
Total	27.9 (7.5)	27.4 (7.3)	31.9 (5.5)	33.0 (4.5)	27.1 (7.2)	25.6 (7.0)	28.5 (7.4)	30.0 (7.1)

[a] P = Program.
[b] C = Control.
[c] Responsivity.
[d] Standard deviations in parentheses.
[e] Avoid restriction.
[f] Organization.
[g] Toys.
[h] Involvement.
[i] Variety.
* $p < .05$.

These results indicate that the program was effective in changing HOME scores for participating mothers. That HOME is a valid program evaluation measure receives support from parallel results from the other measure of mother–child relationships: the videotaped mother–child interaction sessions. With Cohorts I and II, ratings of mother behavior on the MCI were significantly higher for program mothers on affectionateness, and encouragement and lower on her use of criticism (Andrews et al., 1982). Similar analyses for the last two cohorts have not been completed.

These evaluation results for HOME are in general accord with those of Field, Widmayer, Stringer, and Ignatoff (1980); Metzl (1980); and Ramey, Farran, and Campbell (1979); all of whom found program effects using HOME. Garber (1975) found no differences between program and

TABLE 9

Program and Control Group HOME Scores for Early and Late Cohorts at 24 Months

	Early cohorts				Later cohorts			
	I		II		VI		VII	
HOME	P[a]	C[b]	P	C	P	C	P	C
N	33	44	32	27	33	25	11	9
Scales								
1[c]	10.1	9.6	9.0	9.9	9.2	8.6	9.5	10.0
	(1.0)[d]	(1.5)	(1.9)	(1.2)	(2.3)	(1.9)	(1.5)	(1.0)
2[e]	6.1	6.1	6.2	6.0	5.7	5.7	6.8	6.4
	(1.3)	(1.2)	(1.3)	(1.0)	(1.4)	(1.2)	(0.6)	(0.9)
3[f]	5.4	5.3	4.8*	5.3	4.5	4.9	5.6	5.2
	(0.9)	(0.8)	(1.1)	(0.8)	(1.3)	(1.1)	(0.5)	(1.4)
4[g]	7.2*	6.4	7.7	7.1	6.8***	4.6	7.1	7.0
	(1.6)	(1.7)	(1.9)	(1.7)	(2.0)	(2.2)	(1.4)	(2.3)
5[h]	4.8	4.0	3.6	3.5	4.5**	3.7	3.8	4.0
	(1.1)	(1.5)	(1.7)	(1.4)	(1.3)	(1.2)	(1.3)	(1.6)
6[i]	3.5	3.0	4.0	3.1	4.6***	3.6	4.4*	3.6
	(1.2)	(1.5)	(0.9)	(0.9)	(0.8)	(1.1)	(0.7)	(0.9)
Total	37.1*	34.4	35.2	35.0	35.2***	30.9	37.2	36.2
	(4.2)	(5.2)	(5.4)	(4.0)	(4.9)	(5.2)	(3.0)	(5.5)

[a] P = Program.
[b] C = Control.
[c] Responsivity.
[d] Standard deviations in parentheses.
[e] Avoid restriction.
[f] Organization.
[g] Toys.
[h] Involvement.
[i] Variety.
* $p < .05$.
** $p < .01$.
*** $p < .001$.

control mothers on HOME, but this is hardly surprising as the Milwaukee project that he was evaluating, in contrast to those reporting significant effects, did not emphasize parent education and all of the other programs did.

It is our experience that HOME is a satisfactory and useful program evaluation instrument. It appears to be sensitive to program effects, but is also quite consistent across time. In an earlier study, Johnson (1981), HOME was found to be moderately stable from 12 to 36 months on the total score (.37), and slightly higher from 12 to 24 months and from 24 to 36 months on the total score (.45 and .44). These correlations were for the control group. As might be expected, the program group scores showed little stability.

TABLE 10

Program and Control Group HOME Scores for Early and Late Cohorts at 36 Months

	Early cohorts				Later cohorts			
	I		II		VI		VIII	
HOME	P[a]	C[b]	P	C	P	C	P	C
N	23	38	17	27	15	9	16	13
Scales								
1[c]	9.6	9.5	10.3**	8.1	10.5*	9.1	10.9*	10.5
	(1.1)[d]	(1.4)	(1.1)	(3.0)	(0.5)	(1.8)	(0.3)	(0.5)
2[e]	6.4	6.1	6.1	4.6	6.9*	6.0	6.9	6.4
	(1.3)	(1.3)	(2.4)	(2.6)	(0.8)	(1.2)	(0.9)	(0.5)
3[f]	5.1	4.9	5.1	5.1	5.7	5.7	5.8	5.7
	(0.9)	(0.8)	(1.0)	(1.1)	(0.5)	(0.5)	(0.4)	(0.5)
4[g]	7.6*	6.7	8.1**	6.5	8.5***	6.0	8.9**	7.2
	(1.3)	(1.8)	(1.0)	(2.0)	(0.8)	(1.9)	(0.3)	(1.8)
5[h]	3.8	3.6	3.5	3.9	4.5*	3.2	2.9	2.7
	(1.7)	(1.8)	(1.8)	(1.6)	(1.3)	(1.3)	(1.4)	(1.3)
6[i]	3.9	3.4	3.9	3.4	4.7**	3.9	4.2*	3.6
	(1.1)	(1.4)	(0.8)	(1.2)	(0.5)	(0.8)	(0.4)	(0.9)
Total	36.4	34.1	37.0*	30.8	40.7***	33.9	39.6**	36.2
	(3.6)	(5.2)	(5.0)	(9.3)	(2.4)	(4.3)	(2.0)	(3.4)

[a] P = Program.
[b] C = Control.
[c] Responsivity
[d] Standard deviations in parentheses.
[e] Avoid restriction.
[f] Organization.
[g] Toys.
[h] Involvement.
[i] Variety.
 *$p < .05$.
 **$p < .01$.
 ***$p < .001$.

As a program-evaluation measure, HOME has certain clear advantages over the MCI; it is much easier and quicker to use and is certainly less expensive. The MCI requires expensive equipment and a lot of coder time. The MCI does, however, offer a virtually unlimited range of interaction variables and this versatility is often desirable.

Cognitive Prediction

The relationship between HOME scales and measures of child cognitive abilities was examined in two ways. In the first section Pearson correlations are reported. This approach is consistent with much of the research literature and is used here to facilitate comparisons of our work with that of others. However, as the HOME–cognitive-test relationship is undoubtedly a complex one, we elected to explore the relationship through a series of multiple regression analyses.

Univariate Analyses

In some other studies, HOME was found to be reliably correlated with measures of child intellectual abilities. Elardo, Bradley, and Caldwell (1975) found this to be the case at 12 months of age for the toys and involvement scales and for total score. In contrast, Gottfried and Gottfried (1981) found no reliable relationships between 12-month HOME and Bayley MDI. Stevenson and Lamb (1979) found only responsivity scores related (.42) to Bayley MDI in a middle-SES sample.

There seem to be no reports of concurrent relationships between HOME and Bayley scores at 24 months or HOME and S-B at 36 months.

Apparently the relationship between HOME and child cognitive measures for the 1–3 year age period has not been established. It may be that the apparent lack of consistency is a function of the use of subject samples that differ greatly in degree of homogeneity.

We have examined these relationships in our own subject groups and the results appear in Table 11. The means and standard deviations for these analyses appear in Table 12. The numbers differ from those in Tables 8, 9 and 10 because Table 12 includes only those children available at all three time points. Correlations with 24- and 36-month child scores are not shown for the combined groups because of the possible effect of program participation on the correlations. Means and standard deviations are shown in Table 12. At 12 months, concurrent measures show significant correlations for the combined groups for responsivity, organization, toys, involvement, and total scores. The correlations are very similar to those reported by Elardo et al. (1975).

At 24 months, no significant correlations were found between HOME and Bayley MDI scores for either control or program groups. As noted before, there are apparently no prior reported studies at this age. Why significant relationships should appear at 12 months and not at 24 months is not at all obvious.

No significant correlations were found between HOME and S-B (Stanford-Binet) or CFI (Concept Familiarity Index) scores at 36 months. Again, there are no other results for this age reported in the literature.

The prediction of 24-month Bayley MDI scores with 12-month HOMEs yielded no significant correlations for the control group, and

TABLE 11
Correlations between HOME Scores and Child Cognitive Scores at Three Ages[a]

HOME	Control (age in months) N = 47				Program (age in months) N = 38				Combined (age in months) N = 85
	12 MDI	24 MDI	36 S–B	36 CFI	12 MDI	24 MDI	36 S–B	36 CFI	12 MDI
12 Months									
1[b]	25	19	18	35*	31	36*	13	34*	27*
2[c]	00	28	−09	07	02	08	−15	−14	01
3[d]	33*	28	02	15	09	20	09	−12	22*
4[e]	34*	12	11	27	40*	08	18	15	39***
5[f]	35*	25	36*	33*	06	06	16	05	22*
6[g]	−12	−03	−14	−03	15	28	22	08	02
Total	40*	29	17	34*	36*	26	25	18	35***
24 Months									
1	20	−07	01	−04	−15	−08	13	−35*	
2	03	−21	−21	25	23	05	01	−03	
3	20	20	04	−01	−15	−11	01	−36*	
4	31*	22	04	04	05	−17	03	−28	
5	17	16	−01	04	−01	−05	13	−16	
6	28	14	−01	18	18	19	19	−04	
Total	34*	14	−04	12	04	−07	14	−35*	
36 Months									
1	08	26	04	−09	05	18	19	16	
2	−23	−11	−11	−07	38*	17	13	02	
3	18	29	02	24	11	36*	−05	−09	
4	18	26	−03	12	18	17	26	17	
5	17	23	23	16	12	−21	19	01	
6	14	−12	−03	28	25	13	27	00	
Total	12	22	03	13	37*	18	32	01	
Mother's education									10
Number of children									−27*
Family income									03
Rooms: person ratio									−12

[a] Decimals omitted.
[b] Responsivity.
[c] Avoid restriction.
[d] Organization.
[e] Toys.
[f] Involvement.
[g] Variety.
  * $p < .05$.
 ** $p < .01$.
*** $p < .001$.

TABLE 12
Means and Standard Deviations of HOME and Child Intelligence Test Scores
at Three Time Points

Variables	Program (age in months) N = 38			Control (age in months) N = 47		
	12	24	36	12	24	36
HOME	8.30	9.63	9.92	8.43	9.72	9.26
1[a]	(1.90)[b]	(1.36)	(1.02)	(2.28)	(1.38)	(1.70)
2[c]	6.05	6.11	6.26	5.89	6.02	5.91
	(1.00)	(1.27)	(1.87)	(0.97)	(1.17)	(1.73)
3[d]	4.66	5.24	5.11	4.65	5.28	5.02
	(1.28)	(1.02)	(0.95)	(1.14)	(0.83)	(0.79)
4[e]	4.95	7.42	7.82	4.87	6.72	6.64
	(2.25)	(1.70)	(1.25)	(2.15)	(1.78)	(1.72)
5[f]	3.42	4.29	3.68	2.96	4.15	3.79
	(1.77)	(1.51)	(1.69)	(1.69)	(1.47)	(1.78)
6[g]	2.92	3.87	3.89	2.70	3.04	3.30
	(1.10)	(1.07)	(1.03)	(0.87)	(1.40)	(1.41)
Total	30.43	36.55	36.71	29.50	34.94	33.87
	(5.71)	(4.76)	(4.30)	(6.30)	(4.87)	(5.48)
PDI	99.68	107.66	—	98.77	104.77	—
	(9.65)	(13.78)	—	(10.83)	(13.75)	—
MDI	103.66	99.00	—	102.70	91.26	—
	(9.36)	(13.85)	—	(9.69)	(10.54)	—
S–B	—	—	107.37	—	—	103.8
	—	—	(12.17)	—	—	(12.48)
CFI	—	—	34.68	—	—	33.66
	—	—	(6.04)	—	—	(6.73)

[a] Responsivity.
[b] Standard deviations in parentheses.
[c] Avoid restriction.
[d] Organization.
[e] Toys.
[f] Involvement.
[g] Variety.

one, responsivity, for the program group. When 12-month HOME was used to predict 24-month MDI, Siegel (1981b) found significant correlations for toys, involvement, variety and total scores. Her sample included both preterm and full-term infants.

The prediction of 36-month S-B and CFI scores with 12-month HOME was a little better. Controls showed one significant correlation with the S-B (involvement) and the CFI scores were predicted for controls by responsivity, involvement, and total scores and for the program group by responsivity. None of these correlations accounted for more than 13% of the variance, but it is apparent that a relationship does exist.

Elardo *et al.* (1975) reported much stronger 12–36-month predictions, with all factors significantly related to S-B IQ. Siegel (1981a), in contrast, found no significant relationships for her group of mothers of full-term infants, but she did obtain several significant relationships for her sample of preterm babies.

Predicting 36-month test scores with 24-month HOMEs was unsuccessful for the control group, but significant correlations were obtained for the experimental group for responsivity, organization, and total scores with the CFI. Unfortunately, and incredibly, they were all negative, suggesting that for families in the PCDC program, high home-environmental-stimulation at 24 months was predictive of a child's low conceptual-abilities at 36 months. This relationship was not found for the S-B.

Elardo *et al.* (1975) obtained very different results in that they found that all HOME scales predicted S-B scores and at rather high (.41 to .64) levels.

Multivariate Analyses

A series of stepwise, hierarchical regression analyses (Cohen & Cohen, 1975) were performed to investigate relationships among HOME scales and cognitive measure at 12, 24, and 36 months. In order to take into account any possible group and gender differences in both HOME and cognitive measures, dummy coded-variables for children's program-status (omitted from the preintervention 12-month analysis) and for gender were entered prior to the HOME factors in each of the regression analyses. This procedure allows for an evaluation of associations among various HOME and cognitive scores that is statistically independent of differences due to gender or to program involvement. Clearly, because the PCDC program was intended to have an effect on both the home environment and cognitive development, relationships among these variable domains might clearly differ between groups. Therefore, group and gender interactions with each HOME subscale were tested to determine whether HOME and cognitive measure relationships were heterogeneous across conditions—tests that cannot be made if separate regression equations are derived for each group (Kerlinger & Pedhazur, 1973).

In addition, we wished to compare the explanatory power of the HOME subscales with that of certain more global variables generally thought to reflect nonspecific environmental resources for children's cognitive growth (Walberg & Marjoribanks, 1976). Consequently, number of children, crowding, maternal education, and family income were introduced prior to HOME scores in each regression equation to determine whether the HOME could account for any significant additional variance in cognitive scores.

MDI: 12 months.

Of the four nonspecific environmental factors, only *sibsize* (number of siblings in the family) was significantly related to 12-month MDI scores ($p < .02$). Lower cognitive-performance was associated with larger sibsizes. An additional 12% of the variance in MDI scores, however, was accounted for significantly ($p < .001$) by the toys HOME scale. Trends were also noted for the responsivity and variety scales ($p < .12$ and .10, respectively). In all three instances, higher HOME scores predicted superior MDI performance.

MDI: 24 months.

In the subsequent analyses for 24- and 36-month cognitive measures, the preintervention, 12-month MDI scores were employed as covariates. (The early MDI scores were significantly correlated with cognitive scores at 24 months ($r = .32, p < .005$), and with 36-month scores on the CFI ($r = .40, p < .001$) and the S-B ($r = .41, p < .001$). The next series of analyses examined the ability of the 12-month environmental measures to account for significant additional variance in cognitive performance beyond that explained by children's initial performance levels. In this sense, each analysis compares the HOME and global environmental variables as predictors of intellectual change or development.

In contrast to the significant relationship revealed at 12 months, no global environmental variables significantly contributed to the variance explained in 24-month MDI scores. Taken together this set of variables could account for only 1.8% further variance in MDI scores beyond that portion due to subjects' prior 12-month performance and to their gender and group status. A trend ($p < .10$) toward a positive relationship between scores on the responsivity scale and change in MDI was noted, however. Although no other HOME scale independently approached significance, a significant ($p < .05$) interaction between 12-month MDI and toys scale scores was observed. Superior 24-month cognitive performance was predicted as a joint function of higher initial MDI and HOME subscale scores.

S-B and CFI: 36 months.

As with the 24-month analysis, the total set of global environmental indicators could not account for a significant increase in the explained variance of the 36-month S-B IQ scores beyond that percentage attributable to early MDI and group differences. An additional 5% of the 36-month IQ variance was significantly ($p < .05$) explained by scores on the 12-month involvement HOME scale, and the Avoidance of Restriction scale accounted for a further 4.16% of the variance ($p < .05$) in S-B scores. The multiple R was .51 ($p = .007$). Superior cognitive performance was predicted by higher involvement-scores and by lower avoid-restriction-scores. In contrast to the 24-month finding, the MDI and maternal involvement score interaction did not reach significance ($p < .11$) at 36 months.

Two significant interactions with early cognitive performance were found, however. Both the toys and responsivity scales positively interacted with 12-month MDI scores ($p < .03$, .05 respectively.) Superior 36-month S-B performance was predicted as a joint function of higher 12-month MDI and of each of the two HOME subscales. No significant three-way interactions were found.

The regression equation for the 36-month CFI scores revealed a different pattern of predictive relationships than those identified for the concurrent S-B IQ scores. A significant, positive association ($p < .025$) between maternal education and CFI scores was found even after preintervention cognitive performance and group differences were statistically controlled. In addition, the HOME involvement scale significantly ($p < .02$) accounted for an additional 5.6% of the variance in CFI scores. As with the regression equation for the Binet, increased maternal involvement was related to higher cognitive ability at 36 months. No significant interactions (i.e., either two- or three-way interactions) among any of the predictor variables were indicated. Finally, a trend ($p < .10$) toward a positive relationship between CFI and the responsivity HOME scale was observed.

Discussion

In a series of reports, the HOME has been shown to relate significantly to changes in infants' early cognitive ability (see Elardo & Bradley, 1981). The findings of the present study, based on a larger, culturally distinct sample, parellel those of previous investigations.

Bradley and Caldwell (1976) found that both early (i.e., 6-month) scores on the involvement and the toys scales were significant predictors of increases in cognitive performance. Increases were estimated through comparisons of 6-month MDI and 36-month S-B IQ scores. These HOME scales were also observed to be significant predictors of cognitive change in our sample. Bradley and Caldwell did not examine or control for possible sex differences among the 77-child sample; however, our results suggest that relationships among measures of cognitive ability and aspects of the home environment are independent of sex differences.

Although somewhat different SES indicators were employed, our results are also consistent with those of Bradley, Caldwell, and Elardo (1977), who found HOME to be a superior predictor of 36-month S-B IQ scores. In our sample, the Toys scale accounted for a significant increment in the variance explained for 12-month MDI scores beyond that portion due to maternal education, family income, sibsize, and crowding. Interacting with 12-month MDI performance, this scale was also positively related to 24-month MDI and 36-month S-B scores. Twelve-month scores on the avoidance of restriction, involvement, and responsivity scales, the last interacting with 12-month MDI, also accounted for a significant percentage of the variance in S-B scores beyond that due to SES or nonspecific environmental factors.

No variable from the global environmental–SES group was a consistent predictor of cognitive ability at each time period. This may be a consequence of the restricted range of such variables in the present low-income sample. In addition, that sibsize was not a reliable predictor of cognitive development suggests that other variables (e.g, sibling spacing) of Zajonc's confluence model be included in future studies (Zajonc et al., 1979). In any case, aspects of the home environment, as measured by HOME, were shown to be significantly related to cognitive ability even when differences due to a variety of background variables were statistically controlled.

Finally, the strongest environmental–cognitive associations were among 12-month HOME scores and the 36-month S-B IQ performance. This result parallels, although at a lower level, those of Elardo et al. (1975), who conclude that the HOME

> measures a complex of environmental forces which are perhaps prerequisites to later performance on cognitive tasks, and is measuring those forces at a time in the infant's life prior to the period in development in which such environmental forces have affected the infant's measured development [p. 75].

A similar interpretation can be advanced for the present results.

Although generally consistent with previous reports, our findings do differ in some respects. In contrast to Bradley and Caldwell (1976), we found that 12-month scores on the avoid restriction scale were significantly related to 36-month cognitive outcome. Increased parental restrictiveness was associated with *higher* S-B IQ scores. While perhaps only characteristic of our particular sample, this finding agrees with other reports (McCall, Appelbaum, & Hogarty, 1973). In addition, the percentage of variance in cognitive scores explained by HOME was somewhat less than has been previously observed, but in our study the variance due to program status, sex, initial cognitive performance, and other variables was first evaluated. Consequently, less variance was available for explanation. That HOME significantly adds to the variance accounted for, however, seems to underscore its utility as a measure of "the adequacy of the environment to support child development" (Elardo & Bradley, 1981, p. 121).

Perhaps the most interesting departure from past results was the identification of significant interactions between early cognitive ability and certain aspects of the home environment. The presence (or absence) of such interaction effects may have important implications for the design of preventive or remedial interventions. Our findings, for instance, suggest that independent of their cognitive performance in the first year, infants are likely to benefit from increased maternal involvement. Bright children in particular, however, will make the most of greater access to appropriate play materials. In addition, although all two- and three-way intereactions among the HOME factors were tested, none significantly improved the regression equations for any time period. In this sample, cognitive–environmental relationships appear to occur independently of other measured environmental factors.

Parenthetically, we must stress that the presence of significant interaction terms represents statistical confirmation of a symmetric relationship between predictor variables. No causal order is established. Hence, all of the preceding significant interactions are consistent with at least two interpretations: Children with superior home environments are more likely to benefit from early cognitive advantages, or brighter infants are more likely to benefit from enriched home environments. These are not, of course, mutually exclusive possibilities. The essential point is that 12-month MDI scores and certain HOME scales are not independently related to later cognitive performance.

Finally, evaluation of interactions between predictors and infant's sex or program status did not reveal significant differences in environmental–cognitive relationship among groups. In view of the increased power and additional information provided, the use of dummy-coded variables for groups seems to have much to recommend it over separate analyses for each group.

Summary

Although HOME has been used widely with Anglo and black families, there has been little use with Mexican-American families. This chapter has reported on results obtained with HOME in the evaluation of a 2-year parent–child education program for low-income Mexican-Americans. In addition, several other issues concerning HOME were explored.

The analysis of HOME items revealed that in this sample, many items were scored positively by 80% or more of the mothers. The implications of this degree of uniformity, for evaluation research and correlational studies, was discussed.

HOME scores obtained by mothers of 12-month-old children were found to be related to several variables having to do with family resources and the mother's personal resources and values. Strongest correlations were obtained for vocabulary level and her child-rearing beliefs. Her educational level, traditionalism, and achievement orientation, and family income, father presence, and number of children in the home also produced significant correlations with HOME factors. Level of morale and locus of control were not related to HOME.

Construct validity of HOME was assessed by examining correlations of HOME scores with those obtained by rating mother–child interaction videotapes. Although some significant correlations were found, relatively few of these had been predicted. It appears that HOME and the mother–child interaction scales measure different aspects of the parent–child relationship.

HOME was used in the evaluation of the PCDC with highly favorable results. Significant differences between program and control groups were found on each of the HOME factors except organization, and were also found on total scores. Greatest differences appeared on toys and on total scores. Because these results paralleled those obtained with other measures, it was concluded that HOME is a useful, sensitive measure of program effects.

Two approaches were taken in exploring the relationship of HOME scores to measures of child cognitive abilities at 12, 24, and 36 months. Both concurrent and predictive relationships were examined. Pearson correlations indicated that a number of significant correlations existed at 12 months, but very few were found at later concurrent periods. The predictability of later cognitive abilities by early HOME scores was also very limited. A multiple regression approach, with program status and sex controlled, indicated that HOME factors contributed to child cognitive level beyond that explained by maternal background and earlier child cognitive measures. S-B IQ at 36 months was predicted by a combination of program status, Bayley MDI at 12 months, and HOME high involvement and low avoidance of restriction.

References

Anderson, J. G., & Johnson, W. H. Stability and change among three generations of Mexican-Americans: Factors affecting achievement. *American Educational Research Journal,* 1971, *8,* 285–309.

Andrews, S. R., Blumenthal, J. B., Ferguson, C. J., Malone, P. E., Johnson, D. L., Kahn, A. J., Lasater, T. M., & Wallace, D. B. Parent–Child Development Centers: Evaluation of program effects. *Monographs of the Society of Research in Child Development,* 1982, *47,* (61 Serial No. 198).

Barker, R. G., & Wright, H. F. *Midwest and its children.* New York: Harper, 1955.

Barnard, K. E., & Gortner, S. R. *Child health assessment:* (Vol. 2) *Results of the first twelve months of life.* U.S. Department of Health, Education and Welfare, DHEW Pub. No. (HRA) 75–30. Bethesda, MD, 1977.

Bell, R., & Hertz, T. Toward more comparability and generalizability of developmental research. *Child Development,* 1976, *47,* 6–13.

Bradburn, N. M. *The structure of psychological well-being.* Chicago: Aldine, 1969.

Bradley, R. H., & Caldwell, B. M. Early home environment and changes in mental test performance in children from 6 to 36 months. *Developmental Psychology,* 1976, *12,* 93–97.

Bradley, R. H., Caldwell, B. M., & Elardo, R. Home environment, social status, and mental test performance. *Journal of Educational Psychology,* 1977, *69,* 697–701.

Caldwell, B. M., & Bradley, R. *Home Observation for Measurement of the Environment,* Little Rock, AR: University of Arkansas, 1979.

Cohen, J. & Cohen P. Applied multiple regression/correlation analysis for the behavioral sciences. Hillsdale, N.J.: Lawrence Erlbaum Associates, 1975.

Durrett, M. E., O'Bryant, S., & Pennebaker, J. W. Child-rearing reports of white, black and Mexican-American families. *Developmental Psychology,* 1975, *11,* 871.

Elardo, R. & Bradley, R. H. The Home Observation for Measurement of the Environment (HOME) Scale: a review of research. *Developmental Review,* 1981, *1,* 113–145.

Elardo, R., Bradley, R., & Caldwell, B. M. The relation of infants' home environments to mental test performance from six to thirty-six months: A longitudinal analysis. *Child Development,* 1975, *46,* 71–76.

Field, T. M., Widmayer, S. M., Stringer, S., & Ignatoff, E. Teenage, lower-class, black mothers and their preterm infants: An intervention and developmental follow-up. *Child Development,* 1980, *51,* 426–436.

Garber, H. L. Intervention in infancy: A developmental approach. In M. J. Begab & S. A. Richardson (Eds.), *The mentally retarded and society: A social science perspective.* Baltimore: University Park Press, 1975.

Gill, L. J., & Spilka, B. Some nonintellectual correlates of academic achievement among Mexican-American secondary school students. *Journal of Educational Psychology,* 1962, *53,* 144–149.

Gottfried, A. W., & Gottfried, A. E. *Home environment and mental development in middle-class infants in the first two years.* Paper presented at the meeting of the Society for Research in Child Development, Boston, April 1981.

Henderson, R. W. Environmental predictors of academic performance of disadvantaged Mexican-American children. *Journal of Consulting and Clinical Psychology*, 1972, 38, 297.

Henderson, R. W., & Merritt, C. B. Environmental backgrounds of Mexican-American children with different potentials for school success. *Journal of Social Psychology*, 1968, 75, 101–106.

Hess, R. D. Social class and ethnic influences on socialization. In P. H. Mussen (Ed.) *Carmichael's Manual of Child Psychology*. New York: Wiley, 1970.

Inkeles, A., & Smith, D. H. *Becoming modern*. Cambridge, MA: Harvard University Press, 1974.

Johnson, D. L. The development of a program for parent–child education among Mexican-Americans in Texas. In B. F. Friedlander, G. M. Sterritt, & G. E. Kirk (Eds.), *Exceptional infant* (Vol. 3): *Assessment and intervention*. New York: Brunner/Mazel, 1975.

Johnson, D. L. The influence of an intensive parent education program on behavioral continuity of mothers and children. *Child Study Journal*, 1981, 11, 187–199.

Johnson, D. L., Kahn, A. J., & Davila, R. Instructions for the administration of the Maternal Interaction Structures Situation (MISS). *Resources in Education* 1981, 16, 173. (Eric Document Reproduction Service No. ED 194 538)

Kagan, S., & Ender, P. Maternal response to success and failure of Anglo-American, Mexican-American and Mexican children. *Child Development*, 1975, 46, 452–458.

Kerlinger, F., & Pedhazur, E. J. *Multiple Regression in Behavioral Research*, New York: Holt, Rinehart & Winston, 1973.

Laosa, L. M. Maternal teaching strategies in Chicano and Anglo-American families: The influence of culture and education on maternal behavior. *Child Development*, 1980, 57, 759–765.

Levinson, D. J., & Huffman, P. E. Traditional family ideology and its relation to personality. *Journal of Personality*, 1955, 23, 251–273.

Marjoribanks, K. *Families and their learning environments*, London: Routledge & Kegan Paul, 1979.

McCall, R. B., Appelbaum, M. I., & Hogarty, P. S. Developmental changes in mental performance. *Monographs of the Society for Research in Child Development*, 1973, 38(3, Serial No. 150)

Metzl, M. N. Teaching parents a strategy for enhancing infant development. *Child Development*, 1980, 51 583–586.

Moss, H. A., & Jones, S. J. Relations between maternal attitudes and maternal behavior as a function of social class. In P. H. Leiderman, S. R. Tulkin, & A. Rosenfeld (Eds.), *Culture and infancy*. New York: Academic Press, 1977.

Murillo, N. The Mexican-American family. In N. N. Wagner & M. J. Naug (Eds.), *Chicanos: Social and psychological perspectives*. St. Louis: Mosby, 1971.

Nowicki, S., & Strickland, B. R. A locus of control scale for children. *Journal of Consulting and Clinical Psychology*, 1973, 40, 148–154.

Palmer, F. H. Socio-economic status and intellective performance among Negro preschool boys. *Developmental Psychology*, 1970, 3, 1–9.

Ramey, C. T., Farran, D. C., & Campbell, F. A. Predicting IQ from mother–child interactions. *Child Development*, 1979, 50, 804–814.

Ramey, C. T., & Mills, P. Social and intellectual consequences of day care for high risk infants. In R. Webb (Ed.) *Social development in childhood*. Baltimore: Johns Hopkins Press, 1977.

Saldate, M. *Factors influencing academic performance of high and low achieving*

Mexican-American children. Unpublished doctoral dissertation, University of Arizona, 1972.

Sequesta, E. *Reading achievement as influenced by certain home factors in Mexican-American homes*. Unpublished doctoral dissertation, University of Southern California, 1976.

Siegel, L. S. *Home environmental influences on cognitive and language development in the first three years*. Paper presented at the meeting of the Society for Research in Child Development, Boston, April 1981. (a)

Siegel, L. S. Infant tests as predictors of cognitive and language development at two years. *Child Development*, 1981, *52*, 545–557. (b)

Stevenson, M. B., & Lamb, M. E. The effects of infant sociability and the caretaking environment on infant cognitive performance. *Child Development*, 1979, *50*, 340–349.

Steward, M., & Steward, D. The observation of Anglo- Mexican- and Chinese-American mothers teaching their young sons. *Child Development*, 1973, *44*, 329–337.

Strodtbeck, F. L. Family interaction, values, and achievement. In D. C. McClelland, A. L. Baldwin, U. Bronfenbrenner, & F. L. Strodtbeck (Eds.), *Talent and society*. New York: Van Nostrand, 1958.

Strom, R., Griswold, D., & Slaughter, H. Parental background: Does it matter in parent education? *Child Study Journal*, 1981, *10*, 243–260.

Tulkin, S. R., & Cohler, B. J. Childrearing attitudes and mother–child interaction in the first year of life. *Merrill-Palmer Quarterly*, 1973, *19*, 95–106

Walberg, H., & Marjoribanks, K. Family environment and cognitive development: Twelve analytic models. *Review of Educational Research*, 1976, *45*, 527–552.

Werner, E. E. *Cross-cultural child development*. Monterey, CA: Brooks/Cole, 1979.

White, M. A., & Duker, J. Suggested standards for children's samples. *American Psychologist*, 1973, *28*, 700–703.

Zajonc, R. B., Markus, H., & Markus, G. B. The birth order puzzle. *Journal of Personality and Social Psychology*, 1979, *8*, 1325–1341.

Zegiob, L. E., & Forehand, R. Maternal interactive behavior as a function of race, socioeconomic status and sex of the child. *Child Development*, 1975, *46*, 564–568.

6

Home Environmental Influences on Cognitive Development in Preterm and Full-term Children during the First 5 Years

Linda S. Siegel

Introduction

The development of an individual child has typically been assumed to be a result, at least in part, of the child's environment. For example, a measure of the environment, the HOME scale, has been found to predict subsequent cognitive and language development (e.g., Bradley & Caldwell, 1976a, 1976b, 1977; Bradley, Caldwell, & Elardo, 1977, 1979; Elardo, Bradley, & Caldwell, 1975, 1977). An alternate model of development, proposed by Bell (1968) and Bell and Harper (1977), describes children as having significant effects on parents and other adults. That is, children may be, at least in some cases, determinants of the type of environmental stimulation provided by the parents. In this chapter, I examine the mutual influences of parents and children. In addition, I consider two sources of possible stress within the parent–child relationship and how these might relate to the patterns of parent–child interaction. The first of these is preterm birth; the second is developmental delay.

The birth of a very low birthweight preterm child represents a significant event in the life of the family. The early birth is often unexpected and, in the case of a very small infant, typically necessitates an extended hospital stay and numerous medical interventions. Parent–child interaction is limited during the neonatal period because of the conditions under which the infant receives medical treatment. The child must live in an oxygen-, temperature-, and humidity-controlled environment, often with mechanically administered feeding and respiration. Relatively little is known about the influences of this atypical situation on subsequent parent–child interactions. A number of studies have found differences between the parents of preterm and full-term children in the interaction with their children in the early months (See Goldberg, 1978, for a review of some relevant literature.) While a great deal of data are not available concerning long-term differences in interaction, some of these differences may persist throughout the first 2 years (e.g., Crawford, 1982; Field, Dempsey, & Shuman, 1981).

In addition to the stresses of the early days, it may be that the developmental consequences of preterm birth are responsible for differences in interaction patterns. Preterm infants are more likely to be developmentally delayed (e.g., Hunt, 1981; Siegel, 1982a, 1982b, 1983; Siegel, Saigal, Rosenbaum, Morton, Young, Berenbaum, & Stoskopf, 1982), so it may be the presence of a child with delays, rather than the effects of the early atypical environment, that result in different parent–child interaction patterns.

In this study the Home Observation for Measurement of the Environment (HOME) scale was used as a measure of the children's environment and the type of stimulation and responsiveness provided by the parents. One purpose of this study was to determine whether the environments of preterm and full-term children would differ significantly during the first 5 years of postnatal life. The extent to which parents may respond differentially to developmentally delayed children, whether they were preterm or full-term, was also examined. Some models of parent–child interactions, such as those proposed by Bell (1968), Bell and Harper (1977), and Sameroff and Chandler (1975) stress the bidirectionality of child–caretaker effects. That is, the child and the parent mutually influence each other. Bell and his colleagues emphasize the role of the child in determining the course of the interaction. Parental influences are important but they are not the sole determinants of the course of the interaction. Sameroff and Chandler recognize these mutual influences and note that the course of the interaction may change because the nature of the child and the environment are continuously changing over time, each having an impact on the other. One way of studying this question is to examine differential parental response to children with and without developmental delays. Would delayed children elicit different patterns of parental stimulation than nondelayed children? Some clues to the nature of mutual and transacting influences might be gained from these analyses.

Another purpose of this study was to examine the relationship between the environment and subsequent cognitive development. Environmental factors have been shown to be correlated with the outcome of preterm birth (e.g., Caputo, Goldstein, & Taub, 1981; Sigman, Cohen, Beckwith & Parmelee, 1981). These studies have typically used global measures of socioeconomic status (SES), which may not adequately capture the variability within a particular SES. As McCall (1976) has noted, "SES may be too abstract and far removed from the actual functional parent–child interactions" (McCall, p. 107). In previous studies of full-term children, the HOME scale has been found to predict cognitive and language development (e.g., Bradley & Caldwell, 1976a, 1976b, 1977; Bradley et al., 1977, 1979; Elardo et al., 1975, 1977). In addition, it has been previously found that infants who demonstrated delayed early development, but who showed normal cognitive and language development at age 2 or 3 years, came from homes with more stimulating environments, as measured by the HOME (Siegel, 1979, 1981). Conversely, infants who appear to be developing normally early in infancy, but who were delayed later in development, came from homes with lower scores on the HOME scale. This study examines the possibility that the HOME scale scores might contribute significantly to the prediction of development at 5 years.

Method

Subjects

The children in this study were part of a longitudinal study of preterm and full-term children who were followed from infancy through early childhood. There were 2 samples: the 1975–1976 cohort was composed of children born between July 1975 and June 1976 and the 1977–1978 cohort was composed of children born between July 1977 and June 1978. Both cohorts were composed of preterms and full-terms matched on SES (Hollingshead two-factor), gender, parity, and maternal age at the time of the child's birth.

The demographic characteristics of the children in the two cohorts who had been administered the HOME at any point are shown in Table 1. There were no significant differences between the preterms and the full-terms in each cohort, with the exception of gestational age and birthweight. The two cohorts were not significantly different from one another on the demographic variables. The children were from intact blue-collar families, and were predominantly white. HOME scores were not obtained for a number of the children in the total sample due to

TABLE 1
Demographic Characteristics of the Children Administered the HOME
in the Two Cohorts

| | Cohort | | | |
| | 1975–1976 | | 1977–1978 | |
Characteristic	Full-term	Preterm	Full-term	Preterm
N	63	50	58	67
Gender (% males)	58.7	60.0	50.0	53.7
SES (% white collar)	31.6	16.3	24.1	18.5
Firstborn (%)	34.9	40.0	43.1	31.8
Maternal age $(\overline{X})$	25.5	25.9	25.6	25.7
Gestational age (weeks) $(\overline{X})$	40.0	30.3	39.7	30.0
Birthweight (grams) $(\overline{X})$	3370	1230	3410	1120

geographical factors, budget cutbacks, illness of the child, and so on. The Ns in the table represent the number of children in that cohort and group who were administered the HOME at any point in time.

Developmental Tests

The children and their families were administered the following tests:

Bayley Scales

The scales are composed of two subscales, the Mental Development Index (MDI), which contains items concerning perceptual and cognitive abilities, and the Psychomotor Development Index (PDI), which contains items measuring gross and fine motor development. These scales were administered at 4, 8, 12, 18, and 24 months of age.

Kohen–Raz Scoring of the Bayley Scales

The Kohen–Raz (1967) scoring of the Bayley was used. This system separates the Bayley MDI score into a set of five subscales. They are (1) eye–hand coordination ("reaches for dangling ring," "puts three or more cubes in cup"); (2) manipulation ("simple play with rattle," "fingers holes in pegboard"); (3) conceptual ability, originally called "object relations" by Kohen–Raz ("uncovers toy," "exploitive paper play"); (4) imitation–comprehension ("responds to verbal request," "imitated crayon strokes"); (5) and vocalization–social ("repeats performance laughed at," "says 'da-da' or equivalent").

Uzgiris–Hunt Scale

These are tests (Uzgiris–Hunt, 1975) of cognitive capacities of infants, based on Piagetian theory. The following scales were used: (1) Schemes—a test of the type and variety of activities that a child exhibits with objects (e.g., car, doll); (2) Visual Pursuit and Object Relations—test of the child's ability to visually and/or manually search for objects that are hidden; (3) Means—the extent that a child tries to influence and solve problems in the environment by, for example, using tools such as a stick to obtain an object beyond his or her reach; (4) Concepts of Space—the capacity of the child to understand and use containers and recognize obstacles; (5) Gestural Imitation—the ability of the child to imitate familiar (e.g., stirring a spoon in a cup) and unfamiliar (e.g., scratching a surface) gestures; (6) Vocal Imitation—the ability of the child to imitate familiar and unfamiliar sounds and words; and (7) Causality—the ability of the child to understand and try to activate some environmental event (e.g., pulling a string to make a music box work). These scales were administered at 4, 8, 12, and 18 months.

Reynell Developmental Language Scales

These scales (Reynell, 1969) measure language comprehension and expression and have norms for children 1½- to 6-years-old. This test was administered at 2, 3, and 4 years of age. Scores are expressed in terms of standard scores.

Stanford-Binet

This test (Terman & Merrill, 1973) provides a measure of IQ, based on verbal, memory and performance items. It was administered at 3 years of age.

McCarthy Scales of Children's Ability

The McCarthy is a set of 5 scales that can be administered to children 2½ to 8½ years of age. The Verbal scale measures the child's language comprehension and expression, and includes items involving the definition of words and verbal fluency. The Quantitative scale measures the understanding of numerical concepts, including counting and words related to number. The Memory scale measures memory for digits, pictures, and numbers. The Perceptual-Performance scale has items involving perception and eye–hand coordination, such as puzzle solving, and copying simple designs. The Motor scale measures a child's coordination, gross motor functions, and the ability to imitate actions. In the normative group, the mean $(\overline{X})$ of these scales is 50. The standard deviation (SD) is 10. A General Cognitive Index can be calculated based on the Verbal, Perceptual-Performance, and Quantitative scales. The mean of this scale is 100; the SD is 15. This test was administered to the 1975–1976 cohort at 5 years of age.

Home Observation for Measurement of the Environment (HOME)

The HOME-scale measures several dimensions of the child's environment in a structured interview of 45 questions that take place in the home. It is composed of 6 subscales: (1) Emotional and Verbal Responsivity (e.g., "Mother responds to child's vocalizations with a verbal response"); (2) Avoidance of Restriction and Punishment (e.g., "Mother does not shout at child during visit"); (3) Organization of Physical and Temporal Environment (e.g., "Child's play environment seems safe and free of hazards"); (4) Provision of Appropriate Play Materials, (e.g., "Provides eye–hand coordination toys . . . stacking or nesting toys, blocks or building toys"); (5) Maternal Involvement with Child, (e.g., "Mother tends to keep the child within visual range and look at him often"); and (6) Opportunities for Variety in Daily Stimulation, (e.g., "Mother reads stories at least three times weekly"). This version was administered to both cohorts at 1 year of age.

The HOME scale (3–6 year version) is composed of eight scales as follows: (1) Stimulation through Toys, Games, and Reading Materials (e.g., "Toys to learn colors and sizes and shapes"); (2) Language Stimulation (e.g., "Parent encourages child to relate experiences"); (3) Physical Environment (e.g., "Building has no potentially dangerous structural or health defect"); (4)Pride, Affection, and Warmth (e.g., "Mother answers child's questions or requests verbally"); (5) Stimulation of Academic Behavior (e.g., "Child is encouraged to learn colors"); (6) Modeling and Encouragement of Social Maturity (e.g., "Child can express negative feelings without harsh reprisal"); (7) Variety of Stimulation (e.g., "Family members have taken child on one outing at least every other week"); and (8) Avoidance of Physical Punishment (e.g., "No more than one instance of physical punishment occurred during the past week"). The version was administered to both cohorts at 3 years and the 1975–1976 cohort at 5 years. (The 1977–1978 cohort was not old enough). Reliability analyses were conducted on 5% of the administrations. The percentage agreement ranged from 85–100%.

Correction for Prematurity

The preterm children were tested as a function of their chronological age. For tests in which it was possible to do so, a score was calculated which was corrected for degree of prematurity. Therefore, calculations were conducted on the corrected and uncorrected scores. In most cases the uncorrected scores were more accurate predictors of subsequent development, except in the early months.

Results

Consistency of HOME Scores

One of the important issues about measurement of the environment is the consistency of measures of the environment. It is important to know whether the HOME scores remained stable. As the HOME scale was administered at various points the consistency could be examined. The correlations between the HOME scores at various points are shown in Table 2. There were statistically significant but moderate correla-

TABLE 2

Correlations of the HOME Scale (Total Score)
Administered at 12 Months and at 3 and 5 Years

Age of child	3 Year	5 Year
12 Month		
1975–1976 full-term r	.33 ***	.41 ***
N	47	39
1975–1976 preterm r	.41 **	.39 *
N	16	14
1977–1978 full-term r	.50 ****	
N	46	
1977–1978 preterm r	.78 ****	
N	22	
3 Year		
1975–1976 full-term r		.40 ***
N		36
1975–1976 preterm r		.71 **
N		13

* $p < .08$.
** $p < .06$.
*** $p < .01$.
**** $p < .001$.

tions among the scores. The exception to this is in the case of the 1975–1976 preterm infants, in which the correlations between the 12-month HOME and the 3- and 5-year HOME were not significant. This may be a result of the small sample-size or it may be due to the greater changes in the environment of the preterms. On the whole, however, the HOME scores were reasonably consistent in the time interval studied.

Relationships of the HOME scores to SES

Another consideration is whether the HOME measures aspects of the environment independent of SES. The correlations between the HOME scores and SES are shown in Table 3. As can be seen from the data presented in Table 3, there are many significant correlations between the HOME and SES. In the case of the 1975–1976 sample, SES was not significantly correlated with the 12-month HOME scores, except in a few instances. However, in the 1977–1978 sample, there were many significant correlations between the 12-month HOME scores and the SES. A more restricted range of SES scores in the 1975–1976 sample may have accounted for this. In the case of the 3-year HOME scores, the results were somewhat consistent in the two samples. The total score was significantly correlated with SES. The toys and play materials subscale was correlated with SES. The most notable differences between the preterm and full-term groups were that the social maturity and punishment subscales were significantly correlated with SES in both preterm samples but not in either full-term sample. Many of the 5-year HOME subscales, as well as the total HOME score at 5 years, were significantly correlated with SES. While there is some variation, the HOME scale is significantly correlated with SES in many cases, although these correlations increase as the child gets older. Possibly, the influences of SES are more obvious in the items on the later scales, which may reflect a family's economic status; for example, toys and opportunities available. However, as we see from the multiple regression results discussed later on in this chapter, there is some evidence that the HOME contributes to the prediction of subsequent development independently of SES.

Gender Differences and Similarities

Another issue is whether there are gender differences on the HOME scale. There was only one gender difference on the HOME scale at 12 months for the full-term group on the 1975–1976 sample. Males had

TABLE 3

Correlations of SES with the 12-Month, 3-Year, and 5-Year HOME Scores

HOME subscales and total scores	1975–1976 Sample		1977–1978 Sample	
	Full-term	Preterm	Full-term	Preterm
12-Month				
N	66	26	53	28
Maternal responsivity	.06	.15	.17	.32*
Avoidance of restriction	.02	−.35*	.27*	.58***
Organization of environment	.16	.09	.21	.47**
Play materials	.36**	.08	.44***	.43**
Maternal involvement	.15	.06	.52***	.46**
Variety of stimulation	.12	.15	.19	.60***
Total	.21*	.08	.49***	.70***
3-Year				
N	43	17	51	59
Toys & play materials	.45***	.41*	.45***	.34**
Language stimulation	.15	.37	.11	.28*
Physical environment	.18	.10	.36**	.08
Pride, affection, & warmth	.51***	.25	.21	.31**
Stimulation of academic behavior	.02	.34	.10	.22*
Social maturity	.05	.53*	.18	.39***
Variety of stimulation	.22	.31	.12	.17
Physical punishment	.24	.53*	.14	.24*
Total	.42**	.54*	.37**	.39***
5-Year				
N	37	38		
Toys & play materials	.52***	.40**		
Language stimulation	.02	.40**		
Physical environment	.36*	.35*		
Pride, affection, & warmth	.21	.28*		
Stimulation of academic behavior	.27*	.37*		
Social maturity	.26	.34*		
Variety of stimulation	.50***	.57***		
Physical punishment	.03	.19		
Total	.47**	.62***		

*$p < .05$.
**$p < .01$.
***$p < .001$.

significantly higher scores on the organization of environment scale. In the 1977–1978 sample the full-term males had higher scores on the maternal responsivity scale. There were no differences on the HOME scale at 12 months between the males and females of the preterm groups in either sample, but it should be noted that the numbers were very small. There were no gender differences when the males and females of the total group were compared.

There were some gender differences in the 3-year HOME scores. In both the preterm and the full-term groups in the 1975–1976 sample, the females had higher total scores. The females also had higher total scores when the scores of males and females of the entire group were compared. In the 1975–1976 sample, at 3 years of age in the preterm group the females had higher scores on the social maturity and variety of stimulation subscales. When the scores of the entire 1975–1976 sample were compared, the females had higher scores on the toys and variety of stimulation subscales. In the 1977–1978 sample at 3 years, the female preterms had higher scores on the language stimulation scale than male preterms, but there were no other significant gender difference.

At 5 years there are no significant differences in the preterm or full-term groups or when the groups were combined. While there were some slight gender differences there do not seem to have been any differences that were consistent in the two samples. Also, there were no significant differences in the magnitude of the correlations reported subsequently for males and females.

Birth-Order Differences and Similarities

A comparison of firstborns and later-borns did not yield a consistent pattern either. In the 1975–1976 sample there were no significant differences between first- and later-borns on 12-month HOME scores. There were some significant differences in HOME scores at 12 months in the 1977–1978 sample as a function of birth order. Of the firstborns, full-term children had higher scores on the maternal involvement and total scores and preterms had higher scores on the maternal involvement and variety of stimulation scale; in the total group firstborns had higher scores on play materials and maternal involvement scales and on the total score.

At 3 years there were few birth-order differences in the 1975–1976 sample. The firstborn full-terms had higher scores on the language stimulation and academic subscales and the second-born preterms had higher scores on the social responsiveness scale. There were no significant birth-order differences for the entire group. The picture was somewhat different for the 1977–1978 sample. The full-term firstborns had higher scores on the toys, language stimulation, and total scores and the preterm firstborns had higher scores on the academic subscale. For the entire 1977–1978 sample the firstborns had higher scores on the toys, language stimulation, academic, and variety of stimulation subscales and on the total score.

At 5 years there were no significant differences when first- and later-borns were compared.

In general the lack of gender and birth-order differences may be a result of the relatively small sample size by the time gender and birth order were considered.

Environmental Differences and Similarities: Preterms versus Full-terms

One of the primary questions of this study was whether there were any differences between the preterm and full-term groups in the environment as measured by the HOME scale. These data for the HOME at 12 months are shown in Table 4. There were few significant differences between the preterm and full-term groups. The preterms did have significantly lower scores on the provision of play materials and organization of the environment scales in the 1977–1978 sample. Goldberg, Brachfeld, and Divitto (1980) report that they did not find differences in HOME scores between preterm and full-term children at the first year.

The 3-year HOME scores are shown in Table 5. As can be seen in Table 5, there were only two instances in which the preterm group

TABLE 4
12-Month HOME Scores

HOME		1975–1976 Sample		1977–1978 Sample	
		Full-term	Preterm	Full-term	Preterm
N		61	27	53	29
Maternal responsivity	$\overline{X}$	9.2	9.1	8.8	8.8
	SD	1.8	1.4	2.2	2.3
Avoidance of restriction	$\overline{X}$	6.3	6.2	6.3	6.1
& punishment	SD	1.3	1.6	1.3	1.1
Organization of physical &	$\overline{X}$	5.3	5.1	5.3	4.7*
temporal environment	SD	.9	1.2	1.0	1.0
Provision of play materials	$\overline{X}$	7.5	7.0	7.8	6.4**
	SD	2.0	1.9	1.3	1.9
Maternal involvement	$\overline{X}$	3.8	3.4	3.9	3.9
	SD	1.5	2.0	1.7	1.7
Variety of stimulation	$\overline{X}$	3.2	2.9	3.4	2.9
	SD	1.4	1.4	1.3	1.1
Total	$\overline{X}$	35.3	33.8	35.6	32.8
	SD	5.6	6.4	5.2	6.4

*$p < .05$.
**$p < .001$.

TABLE 5
3-Year HOME Scores

HOME		1975–1976 Sample		1977–1978 Sample	
		Full-term	Preterm	Full-term	Preterm
N		48	18	51	61
Toys & play materials	$\overline{X}$	8.6	7.0**	8.5	8.0
	SD	1.8	2.5	1.8	2.0
Language stimulation	$\overline{X}$	6.3	5.9	6.5	6.4
	SD	.9	.9	.8	1.0
Physical environment	$\overline{X}$	6.8	6.7	6.3	6.2
	SD	.6	.9	1.3	1.4
Pride, affection, warmth	$\overline{X}$	5.6	5.6	5.6	5.7
	SD	1.2	1.2	1.2	1.5
Stimulation of academic behavior	$\overline{X}$	3.6	3.2	3.9	3.7
	SD	1.3	.9	.9	1.1
Social maturity	$\overline{X}$	3.3	2.8	3.4	3.2
	SD	1.1	1.2	1.1	1.2
Variety of stimulation	$\overline{X}$	7.0	6.9	6.9	6.7
	SD	1.4	1.3	1.2	1.4
Physical punishment	$\overline{X}$	3.4	3.4	3.6	3.7
	SD	.7	.8	.7	.6
Total	$\overline{X}$	44.4	41.6*	44.7	43.8
	SD	4.7	6.4	5.2	7.0

*$p < .05$.
**$p < .01$.

had lower scores than the full-term group in the 1975–1976 sample: the toys and play materials scale and the total scores. There were no significant differences in the 1977–1978 sample.

The 5-year HOME scores for the 1975–1976 sample are shown in Table 6. In this case, the scores of the preterms and full-terms were not significantly different except on one scale, physical punishment, in which the preterms had significantly higher scores.

In summary, while there were a few cases in which the full-term group had higher scores on some scales, and one case in which the reverse was true, there do not seem to have been significant environmental differences between the preterm and full-term infants. Preterm birth, by itself, does not seem to be a significant contribution to parent–child interactions.

Relationship to Developmental Level

As we have just noted, preterm birth may not be a significant variable in parent–child interactions. It is possible that the parents may

TABLE 6
5-Year HOME Scores

HOME		Full-term	Preterm
N		41	37
Toys & play materials	$\overline{X}$	9.6	8.9
	SD	1.7	1.6
Social responsiveness	$\overline{X}$	6.8	6.9
	SD	.6	.5
Physical environment	$\overline{X}$	6.6	6.7
	SD	.8	.6
Pride, affection, warmth	$\overline{X}$	5.6	5.5
	SD	1.1	1.1
Stimulation of academic behavior	$\overline{X}$	4.5	4.4
	SD	.8	.9
Social maturity	$\overline{X}$	3.3	3.4
	SD	1.2	1.1
Variety of stimulation	$\overline{X}$	7.5	5.5
	SD	1.0	1.1
Physical punishment	$\overline{X}$	3.6	4.1*
	SD	.8	1.5
Total	$\overline{X}$	47.8	47.0
	SD	4.4	4.7

*$p < .05$.

be responding to the level of the child and the type of stimulation may reflect the cues (or lack of them) provided by the child. The question then is whether the HOME scores are correlated with the child's concurrent developmental functioning. The relationship between HOME scores and concurrent developmental functioning are shown in Tables 7–9. For the sake of economy of presentation, only the tests with any significant correlations were included. The evidence on this point is confusing. For the 1975–1976 full-term group, there were some significant correlations between the 12-month Bayley and Uzgiris–Hunt scales and the 12-month HOME scores, but these correlations were typically of a low magnitude (e.g., Maternal responsivity and Bayley PDI, $r = .22$, $p < .05$). Three subscales, maternal responsivity, organization of the environment, and appropriate play materials were correlated with concurrent Bayley and Uzgiris–Hunt scores. The Bayley scheme subscale correlated with maternal responsivity ($.34$, $p < .01$), and organization of the environment ($.41$, $p < .001$).

The pattern of correlations was similar for the preterm group with the exception that the Bayley and Uzgiris–Hunt scales were also correlated with maternal involvement. However, there were a number of cases in which the HOME scales were significantly *negatively* correlated with the infant test-scores. These are shown in Table 7. While

TABLE 7

Correlations between the 12-Month HOME Scores and the 12-Month Tests

Scales	Maternal responsivity	Avoidance of restriction	Organization of environment	Play materials	Maternal involvement	Variety of stimulation	Total
			1975–1976 Sample—fullterm (N = 62)				
Bayley							
MDI	.18	.21*	.12	.23*	−.02	−.05	.17
PDI	.22	ns[a]	ns	ns	ns	ns	.22*
Uzgiris–Hunt							
Schemes	.34**	ns	.41***	ns	ns	.21*	.27*
Object permanence	.23*	ns	.22*	ns	ns	ns	ns
Total	.24*	ns	.25*	ns	ns	ns	ns
			1975–1976 Sample—preterm (N = 26)				
Bayley							
MDI (Corrected)	.24	−.06	.36*	.24	.39*	.40*	.14
PDI	ns	ns	ns	ns	ns	ns	ns
PDI (Corrected)	.34*	ns	ns	ns	.38*	ns	.38*
Uzgiris–Hunt							
Vocal imitation	ns	ns	−.39*	ns	ns	ns	ns
Gestural imitation	.35*	ns	ns	ns	.37*	ns	.39*
Object permanence	ns	ns	ns	ns	.37*	ns	ns
Total	ns	ns	ns	ns	.35*	ns	ns
			1977–1978 Sample—fullterm (N = 53)				

210

Bayley						
MDI	.09	-.24*	-.06	.03	.00	.08	-.09
PDI	ns	ns	ns	ns	-.22*	ns	ns
Uzgiris–Hunt						
Vocal imitation	ns	ns	ns	.22*	ns	.33*	ns
Gestural imitation	ns	ns	ns	ns	ns	.23*	ns
Total	ns	ns	ns	.28*	ns	.22*	ns
1977–1978 Sample—preterm (N = 29)						
Bayley						
MDI (corrected)	.32*	-.19	.05	.13	.26	-.10	.18
PDI (corrected)	.53**	ns	ns	ns	.34*	ns	.35*
Uzgiris–Hunt						
Schemes	ns	ns	ns	ns	ns	-.33*	ns
Object permanence	-.41*	-.45**	ns	-.46**	-.35*	-.36*	-.52**
Vocal imitation	-.34*	-.39*	-.38*	-.32*	ns	-.39*	-.46**
Total	-.37*	-.46**	-.32*	-.32*	ns	-.36*	-.50**

[a]Not significant referred to as ns.

  * $p < .05$.
 ** $p < .01$.
*** $p < .001$.

211

TABLE 8

Correlations of the 3-Year HOME and 3-Year Stanford-Binet and Reynell Language Scores[a]

	Play materials	Language stimulation	Physical environment	Pride, affect., warmth	Stimul. acad. behavior	Social maturity	Variety stimulation	Physical punishment	Total
Stanford-Binet									
1975-1976									
Full-term (N = 45)	.37**	.38**	ns[b]	.39**	ns	ns	ns	ns	.48***
Preterm (N = 15)	ns	ns	ns	ns	.45*	ns	ns	.66**	ns
1977-1978									
Full-term (N = 47)	.47***	ns	.36**	.38**	.25*	.34**	ns	.32**	.54***
Preterm (N = 53)	.30*	ns	.24*	.22*	.46***	ns	.30*	ns	.38**
Reynell Language Comprehension									
1975-1976									
Full-term (N = 45)	.37**	.37**	.52***	.44***	ns	ns	ns	ns	.50***
Preterm (N = 16)	ns	ns	ns	ns	ns	ns	ns	.50*	ns
1977-1978									
Full-term (N = 47)	.42**	ns	.41**	.26*	ns	.30*	ns	.29*	.45***
Preterm (N = 54)	.32**	.46***	ns	.35**	.43***	ns	.44***	ns	.46***
Reynell Language Expression									
1975-1976									
Full-term (N = 46)	.28*	.34**	ns	.24*	ns	ns	ns	.36**	.41**
Preterm (N = 16)	ns	ns	ns	ns	ns	ns	ns	.43*	ns
1977-1978									
Full-term (N = 47)	.32**	.25*	.37**	.27*	ns	ns	ns	ns	.39**
Preterm (N = 51)	.33**	.26*	ns	.27*	.41***	ns	.28*	ns	.37**

[a]
[b] Not significant.
    * p < .05.
   ** p < .01.
  *** p < .001.

TABLE 9

Correlations of 5-Year HOME Scores and 5-Year McCarthy Scores

HOME	McCarthy					
	Verbal	Quantitative	Memory	Perceptual performance	Motor	GCI
Full-term (N = 38)						
Toys & play materials	.55***	.34*	.36*	.33*	ns[a]	.52***
Language stimulation	.27*	.28*	ns	.37**	ns	.35*
Physical environment	ns	.28*	ns	.28*	ns	.29*
Pride, affection, & warmth	ns	ns	.48***	ns	ns	ns
Stimulation of academic behavior	ns	ns	ns	ns	.37**	ns
Social maturity	.42**	.42**	.35*	ns	ns	.43**
Variety of stimulation	.54***	.40**	.40*	.36*	ns	.57***
Physical punishment	ns	ns	ns	.27*	ns	.30*
Total	.66***	.57***	.57***	.44**	.27*	.69***
Preterm (N = 35)						
Toys & play materials	ns	ns	ns	ns	ns	.28*
Language stimulation	.34*	ns	ns	ns	ns	.35*
Physical environment	.39**	ns	ns	.33*	.45**	.41**
Pride, affection, & warmth	.27*	ns	ns	ns	ns	ns
Stimulation of academic behavior	.40**	ns	ns	.31*	.30*	.35*
Social maturity	.42**	ns	.38*	ns	ns	ns
Variety of stimulation	ns	ns	ns	ns	ns	.33*
Physical punishment	ns	.37*	.35*	ns	ns	ns
Total	.41**	ns	.31*	ns	.30*	.42**

[a]Not significant.
* p < .05.
** p < .01.
*** p < .001.

213

there were statistically significant but low positive-correlations between the HOME and the concurrent cognitive tests for the full-term group, the comparable correlations were negative for the preterm group. That is, the mothers were providing more stimulation to more delayed children. However, there were some exceptions to this trend. The corrected MDI and PDI scores were *positively* correlated with the HOME scores (see Table 7). The parents seem to be responding to the more delayed children with more attempts at stimulation in the preterm group. That is, when the correction for preterm birth was not used, the more delayed children had higher HOME scores. However, there was some tendency for parents to respond to the child's developmental level when the corrected scores were used. In the first year, the corrected scores may be a more adequate measure of the child's functioning and parents are apparently responding to it.

At 3 years, there was a clearer relation between the concurrent developmental scores, in this case Reynell Language Comprehension and Expression score and Stanford-Binet IQ scores (see Table 8), and the HOME scores. The relation with the corrected scores were very similar, so they are not reported here. The fewer significant correlations in the preterm group may be a result of the smaller N. A similar trend was found for the 5-year HOME scores and 5-year McCarthy scores. Many of the concurrent correlations are significant, more so for the full-term than the preterm group. Early in development the relationships between a child's development and the environment appear to be less strong than later in development.

HOME Scores as Function of Delayed Development

In order to determine the influences that delayed development might have on the type of environment provided by the parents, the HOME scores of the children who were delayed at a particular point in time were compared with those who were not delayed to determine whether there would be any measurable environmental differences as a function of developmental level. Developmental delay was defined as a score of one standard deviation below the mean (e.g., Bayley MDI, PDI, or McCarthy GCI < 85, Reynell score < -1.00). In the 1975–1976 sample for the 12-month scores, there were too few delayed full-term for a meaningful analysis. However, the 12-month HOME scores of the delayed preterms (MDI) were significantly higher than those of the nondelayed ones on the avoidance of restriction scale ($t[21] = 2.48$, $p < .05$). Therefore, consistent with the negative correlations between

HOME scores and developmental level, parents may be providing more stimulation to delayed infants. In the 1975–1976 sample, when the PDI scores were used to determine delay, there were no differences between the delayed and nondelayed full-terms. However, the preterms who were delayed on the PDI had lower HOME scores on the variety of stimulation scale $(t[21] = 2.59, p < .05)$. To the extent that these are reliable findings, parents are responding differently to the cognitive and motor development of the infant.

Using the corrected 12-month Bayley scores, the HOME scores of the preterm children who were delayed were compared to those who were not delayed. In the 1975–1976 sample, the delayed preterms had significantly lower scores on the organization of the environment $(t[25] = 2.31, p < .05)$ and the variety of stimulation $(t[25] = 2.49\ p < .05)$ scales. However, these comparisons were not significant in the 1977–1978 sample. In general, it did not appear that the HOME environments of the delayed and nondelayed children were very different at 12 months.

For the 1977–1978 sample, the full-terms who were delayed on the PDI at 12 months had lower scores on the organization of environment scale $(t[51] = 2.11, p < .05)$.

While there were not many differences in HOME scores between the delayed and nondelayed children at 12 months, there were many significant differences at 3 years. In the 1975–1976 sample the full-term children who were delayed at 3 years in the Stanford-Binet had lower scores on the following scales: Pride, Affection and Warmth $(t[43] = 2.81, p < .01)$, and total score $(t[43] = 3.24, p < .01)$. The difference between the delayed and nondelayed children on the toys scale did not reach conventional levels of statistical significance $(t[43] = 1.91, p < .07)$. There were few preterm children in the 1975–1976 sample who were administered the HOME at 3 years. The delayed preterms had significantly lower scores only in one case, the punishment scale $(t[13] = 2.96, p < .01)$. In the 1977–1978 sample, the full-terms who were delayed in the Stanford-Binet had lower scores on the modeling $(t[45] = 2.08, p < .05)$ and the total $(t[45] = 1.94, p < .05)$. The preterms in the 1977–1978 sample who were delayed on the Stanford-Binet at 3 years had lower scores on the physical environment $(t[52] = 1.00, p < .05)$, stimulation of academic behavior $(t[52] = 2.34, p < .05)$ and total scores $(t[51] = 2.41, p < .02)$.

Children who were delayed in language comprehension or expression on the Reynell Developmental Language Scales at 3 years had lower scores on many of the 3-year HOME scales than those who were not delayed. There were too few preterms in the 1975–1976 sample who were administered the HOME and there were too few delayed full-terms in the 1977–1978 sample for any meaningful comparisons. The 3-year-olds who were delayed in language comprehension had lower scores than those who were not on the following scales: full-term, 1975–1976, toys ($t[43]$ = 2.65, p < .05), language stimulation, ($t[43]$ = 2.53, p < .05), physical environment ($t[43]$ = 6.74, p < .001), affection, ($t[43]$ = 2.74, p < .01), total ($t[43]$ = 4.15, p < .001), and the preterms, 1977–1978, language stimulation ($t[53]$ = 2.85, p < .01), affection ($t[53]$ = 2.48, p < .05), stimulation of academic behavior ($t[53]$ = 2.00, p < .05), variety of stimulation ($t[52]$ = 2.14, p < .05), total ($t[52]$ = 2.35, p < .05).

There were fewer significant differences between the children who were delayed in expressive language—full-term, 1975–1976 sample: language stimulation ($t[44]$ = 2.22, p < .05), punishment ($t[44]$ = 2.71, p < .05), total ($t[44]$ = 2.05, p < .05); preterm, 1977–1978 sample: Variety of Stimulation ($t[49]$ = 2.14, p < .05).

At 5 years the fullterms who were delayed on the McCarthy GCI had lower scores on the following HOME scales at 5 years: toys ($t[37]$ = 3.40, p < .01), language stimulation ($t[37]$ = 2.40, p < .05), and total ($t[37]$ = 3.27, p < .01). The preterms showed a very similar pattern. The preterms who were delayed on the McCarthy GCI at 5 years had significantly lower scores on the following scales: language stimulation ($t[32]$ = 2.42, p < .05), physical environment ($t[32]$ = 2.93, p < .01), variety of stimulation ($t[32]$ = 1.98, p < .05), and total ($t[32]$ = 2.29, p < .01). The delayed child may be providing insufficient cues to the family as to the appropriate toys and activities and may be less responsive.

Although few studies have analyzed differential responsiveness of delayed and nondelayed children, Cohen, Beckwith, and Parmelee (1978) compared interactions between two groups of mother–child dyads, when the child was 21 months. The two groups differed in their receptive language scores at 24 months. The mothers of the children with lower scores engaged in fewer positive interactions. In addition, the children with higher scores vocalized more and there was more reciprocal interaction in the dyads with higher scores. While the observations of language competence and mother–child interaction were not made at exactly the same point in time, the data illustrate some reciprocal influences of a child's language on adult behavior and the adult interaction on child vocalization.

Early in development, the parents may be engaged in what Bell and Harper (1977) have called a lower-limit control-reaction in an attempt to stimulate the aspects of the child's behavior that are insufficient in some way. Later in development the parents may resort to an upper-limit control-reaction, that is an attempt to reduce or redirect behavior. In each case, the parents of the delayed children are behaving differently than those of the children who are not delayed. If the parents were continuously not providing the appropriate environment, then the delayed children should have been expected to have lower scores at whatever point in time it is being measured. As this was not consistently the case, delayed development is not directly related to environmental stimulation.

HOME, SES, and Mental Tests as Predictors of Stanford–Binet and Reynell Scores at 3 Years

The correlations of 12-month HOME scores, SES, and the infant test-scores with the Stanford-Binet scores and Reynell Language Comprehension and Expression at 3 years are shown in Tables 10–12. Nonsignificant correlations between the HOME and the 3-year tests have been included to facilitate comparisons with other samples.

For the full-term groups in both samples, there were no significant correlations between the 12-month HOME scores and the 3-year Stanford- Binet scores. However, some of the 12-month HOME scales were correlated with the 3-year scores in the preterm group in both samples, specifically maternal involvement, variety of stimulation and the total scores. These results are shown in Table 10. The difference between the preterm and the full-term groups may represent differential sensitivity to environmental stimulation. The infant tests were predictive in both groups but in the preterm group the correlations between the HOME scale and the 3-year IQ scores were higher than the infant test-scores. For the full-term group, the infant test-scores were more highly correlated than the HOME with the 3-year Stanford-Binet. For the preterm group, the HOME scores were more highly correlated with the 3-year IQ than SES was.

As in the case of the Stanford–Binet at 3 years, there were many more significant correlations in the preterm than in the full-term group between the 3-year Reynell Language Comprehension Scores and the 12-month HOME scores, as shown in Table 11. Provision of play materials, maternal involvement, and variety of stimulation were correlated in both samples. The HOME scores were more highly correlated than SES for the preterm group. Again, the infant test-scores were more highly correlated than the 12-month HOME scores were, with the 3-year language comprehension scores.

TABLE 10
Correlations of SES, the 12-Month Bayley, Uzgiris–Hunt, and HOME with 3-Year
Stanford-Binet Scores

12-Month	1975–1976 Sample		1977–1978 Sample	
	Full-term (N = 49)	Preterm (N = 20)	Full-term (N = 43)	Preterm (N = 21)
HOME				
Maternal responsivity	.05	.41*	.12	.32
Avoidance of punishment	.07	.46*	−.04	.07
Organization of environment	−.15	.26	.09	.11
Play materials	.17	.46*	.16	.32
Maternal involvement	−.03	.55**	.14	.52**
Variety of stimulation	.09	.49*	.13	.49*
Total	.09	.66**	.01	.45*
Bayley				
MDI	.31*	ns[a]	.55***	.40**
Corrected MDI	—	.38*	—	.38**
PDI	.33**	ns	.26*	.29*
Corrected PDI	—	.29*	—	.42**
Kohen–Raz				
Eye–hand coordination	ns	.30*	.64***	.34**
Manipulation	ns	ns	ns	.24*
Conceptual abilities	ns	ns	.40**	.29*
Imitation–comprehension	ns	ns	ns	.45***
Vocalization–social	ns	ns	.26*	.29*
Uzgiris–Hunt				
Gestural imitation	ns	.34*	.34**	.30*
Space concepts	ns	ns	.24*	ns
Means	ns	ns	.39**	ns
Total	ns	ns	.32*	.22*
SES	.30*	ns	.25*	.23*

[a]Not significant is referred to as ns.
 *$p < .05$.
 **$p < .01$.
 ***$p < .001$.

None of the 12-month HOME scores were correlated with 3-year Reynell Language Expression in either full-term group sample, as shown in Table 12. For the preterm 1975–1976 group only, organization of the environment, appropriate play materials, and total score were significantly correlated.

I have reported previously (Siegel, 1982c) that three of the 12-month scores appropriate (play materials, variety of stimulation and total scores) were significantly correlated with 4-year language

TABLE 11
Correlations of SES and 12-Month HOME and Intelligence Test Scores with 3-Year
Reynell Language Comprehension Scores

12-Month	1975–1976 Sample		1977–1978 Sample	
	Full-term (N = 48)	Preterm (N = 22)	Full-term (N = 43)	Preterm (N = 21)
HOME				
Maternal responsivity	.02	.19	.23	.06
Play materials	.31*	.59**	−.12	.54**
Avoidance of punishment	−.15	.31	−.07	.12
Maternal involvement	.17	.36*	.26*	.35
Organization of environment	−.02	.26	.05	−.03
Variety of stimulation	.14	.38*	.00	.37*
Total	.15	.55**	.06	.35*
Bayley				
MDI	ns[a]	.37*	.42**	.44**
Corrected MDI	—	.38**	—	.30*
PDI	.25*	ns	ns	.28*
Corrected PDI	—	ns	—	.34**
Kohen–Raz (Bayley MDI)				
Eye–hand coordination	.32*	ns	.46***	.31**
Manipulation	ns	.26*	ns	.36**
Conceptual abilities	ns	ns	.43**	.28*
Imitation–comprehension	.23*	.31*	ns	.47***
Vocalization–social	ns	ns	.24*	.38**
Uzgiris–Hunt				
Schemes	ns	ns	ns	.30**
Object permanence	ns	ns	ns	.27*
Space concepts	ns	ns	ns	.24*
Means–end thinking	ns	ns	ns	.26*
Gestural imitation	ns	ns	ns	.26*
Total scores	ns	ns	ns	.39**
SES	ns	ns	.26*	ns

[a]Not significant.
*p < .05.
**p < .01.
***p < .001.

comprehension scores on the Reynell Developmental Language Scales. None of the 12-month HOME scores were significantly correlated with language expression. However, the 3-year HOME scores (both total HOME and many of the subscales) were significantly correlated with 4-year Reynell Language Expression and Comprehension scores. These correlations were significant when SES was partialled out.

In the case of language development, environmental influences ap-

TABLE 12
Correlations of SES and the 12-Month HOME and Intelligence Test Scores
with Reynell Language Expression

12-Month	1975–1976 Sample		1977–1978 Sample	
	Full-term ($N = 49$)	Preterm ($N = 22$)	Full-term ($N = 43$)	Preterm ($N = 20$)
HOME				
Maternal responsivity	.14	−.03	.07	.08
Organization of environment	−.03	.38*	.03	.16
Avoidance of punishment	.07	.22	−.14	.05
Play materials	.17	.45*	−.03	.20
Maternal involvement	.09	.15	.18	.08
Variety of stimulation	.09	.23	.09	.34
Total	.16	−.06	−.05	.20
Bayley				
MDI	ns[a]	ns	.34**	.34*
Corrected MDI	—	ns	—	.26*
PDI	.34**	ns	ns	.29*
Corrected PDI	—	ns	—	.40**
Kohen–Raz				
Eye–hand coordination	ns	ns	.43**	ns
Imitation–comprehension	ns	ns	ns	.25*
Vocalization–social	ns	ns	ns	.34**
Uzgiris–Hunt				
Schemes	ns	.28*	.37**	ns
Vocal imitation	ns	ns	ns	.26*
Object permanence	ns	ns	.28*	ns
Space concepts	ns	ns	.43***	ns
Total	ns	ns	.37**	.24*
SES	ns	ns	.26*	ns

[a]Not significant.
*$p < .05$.
**$p < .01$.
***$p < .001$.

pear to be more significant later in development. This pattern is consistent with the results reported earlier in that the environmental effects seem to be stronger later in development. Gottfried and Gottfried (this volume) also reported that the environmental influences appear to be more significant later in development. Earlier child characteristics such as infant test scores are a better predictor of subsequent development.

Early in development, the environmental correlates were more apparent for the preterm group. The infant tests were better predictors for the full-term group. The correlation of the HOME scores with Stanford-Binet and Reynell Language scores appears to be greater for the preterm group. In all cases for the preterms, the HOME correlations are higher than SES. For the full-term group, the HOME test scores were typically not significantly correlated with subsequent scores. However, the infant test scores and SES were significantly correlated with subsequent scores. This may be a result of the greater heterogeneity in HOME scores in the preterm group. Overall, few of the 3-year scores were significantly correlated with SES and even when the correlations were statistically significant, they were of low magnitude.

HOME, SES, and Cognitive Tests as Predictors of McCarthy Scores at 5 Years

The relationship of SES, HOME, and test scores to the 5-year McCarthy scores are shown in Table 13. As can be seen in Table 13, the correlations of the HOME with 5-year scores are higher for the preterm group. More of the correlations were significant and the absolute magnitude was higher for the preterm group. For the full-term group, SES was typically at least as highly correlated (sometimes even more highly correlated) as the HOME, with the exception of the motor and perceptual performance scores, which have less verbal material than the other scales. The infant tests were more highly correlated with SES than with the motor scales. The infant tests, or subscales derived from them, were correlated with the McCarthy scores in both groups.

The more verbal scales of the McCarthy, Verbal Quantitative, General Cognitive, and Memory were very significantly correlated with SES. The Perceptual-Performance and the Motor scales were not. The latter type of development is probably less influenced by environmental factors.

The relationships between the 3-year scores and the 5-year scores are shown in Table 14. For both the preterm and full-term groups, the 3-year Stanford-Binet and Reynell Language scores were significantly correlated with the 5-year McCarthy scores.

The 3-year HOME scores were significantly correlated with the 5-year McCarthy scores for the full-term group. This was not true for the preterm group, with the exception of the punishment scale. However, the small number of preterms with 3-year HOME scores and with 5-year McCarthy scores make it difficult to draw any conclusions on the basis of these findings.

The 5-year scores were not typically correlated with SES, with the exception of the Verbal Scale and the GCI, which have many items that depend on specific language experience. The Quantitative and Memory Scales were also correlated with SES, in the full-term group. These scales have many verbal items.

TABLE 13
SES and the 12-Month Correlations of HOME, Intelligence Tests, with 5-Year McCarthy Scores

12-Month	Verbal	Quantitative	Memory	Perceptual performance	Motor	GCI
Full-term (N = 38–40)						
HOME						
Maternal responsivity	.14	−.08	−.04	−.01	0	0
Avoidance of punishment	.03	.13	.05	.12	.21	.11
Organization of environment	.10	−.09	−.07	−.17	−.13	−.06
Play materials	.21	.38**	.17	.29*	.06	.34*
Maternal involvement	.07	0	−.04	−.19	−.34	−.05
Variety of stimulation	.03	.17	.09	.31*	.15	.21
Total	.17	.18	.06	.13	−.08	.18
Bayley						
MDI	ns[a]	ns	ns	ns	.50***	ns
PDI	ns	ns	ns	ns	ns	ns
Kohen-Raz						
Eye-hand	.31*	.42*	ns	.33*	.25*	.39*
Manipulation	ns	ns	ns	ns	.25*	ns
Conceptual abilities	ns	ns	ns	ns	.28*	ns
Imitation–comprehension	ns	ns	ns	ns	.25*	ns
Uzgiris-Hunt						
Means–end thinking	ns	ns	ns	.39**	.40**	.35*
Gestural imitation	ns	ns	ns	ns	.35*	ns
SES	.41**	.40**	.37**	ns	ns	.42**

Preterm (N = 14–16)

HOME						
Maternal responsivity	.12	−.21	−.17	0	.27	.10
Avoidance of punishment	.28	.25	.31	.09	0	.23
Organization of environment	.47*	.20	.57*	.33	.25	.45*
Toys & play materials	.41	.39	.51*	.05	0	.33
Maternal involvement	.50*	.26	.33	.12	.31	.38
Variety of stimulation	.30	0	.32	.15	.23	.26
Total	.50*	.26	.47*	.16	.18	.42
Bayley						
MDI	.47**	.47**	.30*	.26	ns	.43**
Corrected MDI	.43**	.44**	ns	.43**	ns	.46**
PDI	.38*	.60	.47**	.31	ns	.45**
Corrected PDI	ns	.44**	.30*	.30*	ns	.32*
Kohen–Raz						
Eye-hand	.28*		ns	ns	ns	ns
Imitation–comprehension		.31*	ns	ns	ns	ns
Uzgiris–Hunt						
Object permanence	ns	.35*	ns	ns	ns	ns
Space concepts	.49**	.39*	.36*	ns	ns	.36*
Gestural imitation	ns		ns	ns	ns	ns
Vocal imitation	ns	.33*	ns	ns	.32*	ns
Total	ns	.45**	ns	ns	ns	ns
SES	.32*	.26	.23	.14	.13	.28*

[a]Not significant.
* p < .05.
** p < .01.
*** p < .001.

TABLE 14
Correlations of the 3-Year HOME, Intelligence Tests and SES with 5-Year McCarthy Scores

3-Year	Verbal	Quantitative	Memory	Perceptual performance	Motor	GCI
Full-term						
HOME						
Toys & play materials	.43***	.53***	.35*	.48***	.31*	.56**
Language stimulation	ns[a]	.35*	ns	ns	ns	.30*
Pride, affection, warmth	.51***	.36*	ns	ns	ns	.47**
Variety of stimulation	.36*	.27*	.28*	ns	ns	.38**
Total	.51***	.50***	.29*	.32	.32*	.55**
Stanford-Binet	.63***	.62***	.60***	.55***	ns	.70**
Reynell						
Comprehension	.67***	.62***	.55***	.43**	ns	.62**
Expression	.37***	ns	ns	ns	ns	.29*
SES	.41**	.40**	.37**	ns	ns	.42**
Preterm[b]						
HOME						
Physical punishment	.68**	ns	.57*	ns	ns	.56*
Stanford-Binet	.56***	.38*	.44**	.36*	ns	.54**
Reynell						
Comprehension	.67***	.30*	.42**	.39*	.46**	.61**
Expression	.65***	.45**	.64***	.36*	ns	.60**
SES	.32*	ns	ns	ns	ns	.28*

[a] Not significant.
[b] $N = 12$ for preterm group (HOME).
* $p < .05$.
** $p < .01$.
*** $p < .001$.

Correlations of HOME Scores with Cognitive Tests
(Preterms and Full-terms Combined)

In order to provide an estimate of the relationships between the environment and cognitive-test scores for the entire group, the correlations were calculated for the preterm and full-term groups combined. These results are shown in Tables 15–17. The trends are basically the same as those for the groups separately. The 12-month toys and play materials scores are significantly correlated with the 3- and 5-year scores, while few of the others are. The 3-year toys and play materials scale is also correlated with the 5-year scores. The total score at 3 years is correlated with all of the 5-year scores. As noted previously, environmental influences seem stronger later in development.

Prediction of Developmental Functioning

To determine the relative usefulness of the HOME, SES, and the 12-month test scores in predicting the 5-year McCarthy GCI, a series of stepwise linear multiple regression analyses were conducted with these variables at 12 months and also at 3 years. At 12 months there were not enough preterms who had been administered the HOME scale to conduct the multiple regression analyses. The results of the multiple regression analyses for the full-term group at 12 months are shown in Table 18. Typically, SES and various infant test scores are entered into the regression equations before the HOME, but the HOME still contributed to the prediction.

In order to determine the relative contributions of HOME scores, of SES, and of tests at 3 years toward the 5-year McCarthy scores, stepwise linear multiple regression analyses were conducted for these variables and the McCarthy GCI and the Perceptual-Performance and Verbal Scales. There were not enough preterm children who had been administered the HOME to conduct these types of analyses. As can be seen from the regression analyses in Table 19, the 3-year cognitive and language tests were more highly correlated than the HOME scale. A notable exception is in the case of the McCarthy Verbal Scale, in which the HOME contributed significantly to the 5-year scores.

Transactions

In the transactional model, children and adults show mutual influences on each other. A child's functioning influences the parent's behavior, which in turn influences the child's subsequent behavior,

TABLE 15
Correlations of the 12-Month HOME Scores with 3-Year Stanford-Binet and Reynell Language Scores for the 1975-1976 and 1977-1978 Cohorts (Total Group)

| | Stanford-Binet | | Reynell | | | |
| | | | Comprehension | | Expression | |
12-Month HOME	1975-1976	1977-1978	1975-1976	1977-1978	1975-1976	1977-1978
N	69	64	70	64	71	63
Maternal responsivity	.16	.19	.06	.17	.11	.08
Avoidance of restriction	.19	.04	.04	.03	.12	-.01
Organization of environment	.02	.17	.12	.11	.16	.16
Toys & play materials	.29**	.40***	.44***	.31**	.33**	.26*
Maternal involvement	.19	.24*	.27*	.25*	.16	.14
Variety of stimulation	.23*	.33**	.24**	.19	.19*	.25*
Total	.31**	.22*	.33**	.19	.28**	.09

* p < .05.
** p < .01.
*** p < .001.

TABLE 16

Correlations of 12-Month HOME Scores with 5-Year McCarthy Scores for the Total Group (1975–1976 Cohort) (N = 55–57)

HOME	Verbal	Quantitative	Memory	Perceptual performance	Motor	GCI
Maternal responsivity	.07	−.10	−.10	−.06	0	0
Avoidance of restriction	.16	.16	.14	.07	.10	.15
Organization of environment	.21	.03	.19	.09	.07	.16
Toys & play materials	.35**	.36**	.31**	.31**	.10	.41***
Maternal involvement	.21	.07	.08	−.03	−.17	.14
Variety of stimulation	.15	.13	.15	.31**	−.02	.24*
Total	.30*	.19	.20	.18	.01	.29*

* $p < .05$.
** $p < .01$.
*** $p < .001$.

TABLE 17

Correlations of the 3-Year HOME Scores with 5-Year McCarthy Scores for the Total Group (1975–1976 Cohort)

3-Year HOME	Verbal	Perceptual performance	Quantitative	Memory	Motor	GCI
Toys & play materials	.39**	.42***	.44***	.35**	.32*	.49**
Language stimulation	.24*	.25*	.31*	.13	.24*	.30*
Physical environment	−.01	−.03	−.01	−.05	.04	−.01
Pride, affection, & warmth	.43***	.10	.26*	.23*	−.04	.34**
Stimulation of academic behavior	.21	.10	.13	.11	.21	.20
Social maturity	−.05	.04	.03	−.09	.32*	−.03
Variety of stimulation	.33**	.15	.15	.17	.14	.32*
Physical punishment	33**	.15	.13	.22	.20	.26*
Total	.48***	.34**	.40**	.30*	.36**	.50**

* $p < .05$.
** $p < .01$.
*** $p < .001$.

TABLE 18
The Results of Multiple Regression Analyses
of 5-Year McCarthy Scores Using 12-Month Scores
(Full-term N = 37)

	Multiple R
GCI	.61
SES	
Uzgiris–Hunt means	
Kohen–Raz: eye–hand coordination	
Bayley PDI	
HOME: variety of stimulation	
Verbal	.46
SES	
Bayley	
Perceptual-performance	.61
Uzgiris–Hunt – means	
Kohen–Raz: eye–hand coordination	
Bayley PDI	
HOME: play materials	
SES	

which influences the parent's behavior, and so on. The environment
and the child are continuously interacting and changing. The appropriate way to study these changes is with measures of the child and
the environment at several points in time.

I have reported earlier (Siegel, 1979, 1981) that the children of the

TABLE 19
The Results of Multiple Regression Analyses
of 3-Year Variables and 5-Year McCarthy Scores
(Full-term N = 30)

	Multiple R
GCI	.81
Stanford–Binet IQ	
Reynell comprehension	
HOME: Variety of Stimulation	
Verbal	.78
Reynell comprehension	
HOME: Variety of Stimulation	
Stanford–Binet IQ	
Perceptual-performance	.68
Stanford–Binet IQ	
Reynell comprehension	
Reynell expression	
HOME: Play Materials	

1975–1976 sample who were delayed early in development but who were not delayed at 2 or 3 years (called the *false positives*) had significantly higher 12-month HOME scores than the children who were delayed both early and later in development. We attempted to determine if this was true for the 1977–1978 sample. As with the 1975–1976 group, there were too few false positives in the full-term group for any meaningful comparisons. However, in the 1977–1978 preterms the false positives (that is children who were delayed on the Bayley MDI at 12 months but who were not delayed at 3 years on the Stanford-Binet) had significantly higher scores on the maternal involvement $(t[12] = 3.02, p < .01)$ and total $(t[12] = 2.35, p < .05)$ HOME scores at 12 months.

The *false negatives* were children who performed in the normal range on the Bayley MDI at 12 months but subsequently had scores in the delayed range on the Stanford-Binet at 3 years. In the 1977–1978 cohort there were too few false negatives in the preterm group for any meaningful comparisons but in the full-term group the false negatives had lower scores than the true negatives on the following HOME scales: maternal responsivity $(t[40] = 2.42, p < .05)$, and organization of the environment $(t[40] = 2.60, p < .05)$. As the infant tests were reasonably accurate at predicting delayed development at 5 years, there were too few false negatives and false positives for any meaningful analyses.

It appears that more stimulating environments as experienced by the false positives may contribute to the modification of developmental delay while less stimulating ones experienced by the false negatives may contribute to the development of cognitive delays.

Conclusions

In spite of very different early neonatal environments for preterm and full-term infants, these differences were not manifested in parental interaction patterns later in childhood. However, there was evidence in this study of parents responding differently to delayed and nondelayed children. Differences in parental responses to delayed and nondelayed children were more marked later in development. There is no way to infer causal directions on the basis of these data. We cannot tell whether the environment contributes to delayed development or the delayed child fails to provide the cues that the parents need in order to provide the appropriate experiences and play materials. Two trends were clearly evident in these data: (1) the environments of delayed children are different from those of children who are developing normally; (2) children who are delayed early in development but who are functioning normally later on come from more stimulating homes than those who remain delayed and children who are functioning normally in the early months but who are delayed later in development come from less stimulating homes. These two trends suggest a transactional model in which environment and constitutional factors operate in an interacting fashion.

The HOME scale seems to contribute something to measures of subsequent development, although the contribution of cognitive tests and SES is significant also—in some cases more significant. The most accurate prediction was achieved by using a combination of factors, including cognitive tests, SES, and the HOME.

Environmental factors are clearly significant in development. But they do not operate totally independently of the level at which the child is functioning, as measured by cognitive tests, or the attitudes and values of the parents, as measured by SES.

Summary

The aims of this study were (1) to examine some environmental influences on cognitive development and (2) to clarify the role of the child in determining the type of environment provided by parents. Two samples of full-term and very-low-birthweight preterm children (birthweights < 1501 grams) were administered a series of developmental tests and the HOME scale. The 1975–1976 cohort, composed of children born between July 1975 and June 1976, was administered the Bayley at 1 year, the Stanford-Binet at 3 years, the McCarthy at 5 years, and the HOME at each of these times. The 1977–1978 cohort, composed of children born between July 1977 and June 1978, was administered the same tests and the HOME at 1 and 3 years. There were few significant differences in HOME scores between the preterm and full-term children, indicating that preterm birth, by itself, was not a source of differential parental stimulation. There were few significant differences in HOME scores as a function of gender or birth order. However, delayed development had a more significant impact. The HOME scores of delayed children were significantly lower than those of the nondelayed children at each age, although these differences were more pronounced later in development. Therefore, the delayed children may not be providing parents with sufficient cues as to what might be the appropriate stimulation.

In addition, there was evidence of environmental influences in that children who showed early developmental delay, but at 3 years functioned normally came from more stimulating environments, as measured by the HOME. Conversely, infants who appeared to be developing normally at 1 year, but who were delayed at 3 years, came from less-stimulating environments as measured by the HOME. Therefore, the most accurate prediction of subsequent development is achieved by the use of both cognitive test-scores and measures of the environment.

These data illustrate the reciprocal nature of the relationships between environment and cognitive development. The parents respond differentially to the delayed children and therefore do not provide the most stimulating environment. In some cases, however, stimulating home environments appear to reduce the probability of developmental delay, and less-stimulating environments appear to increase it. Development appears to be a process of mutual stimulation between parent and child.

Acknowledgment

This research was supported by grants from the Ontario Mental Health Foundation and the National Foundation. I would like to thank Kathy Deyo, Lorraine Hoult, and Wendy McHugh for help with the data collection and analyses, and the parents and children who have participated in the study.

References

Bell, R. Q. A reinterpretation of the direction of effects in studies of socialization. *Psychological Review*, 1968, *75*, 81–95.

Bell, R. Q., & Harper, L. V. *Child effects on adults*. Hillsdale, N.J: Erlbaum, 1977.

Bradley, R. H., & Caldwell, B. M. Early home environment and changes in mental test performance in children 6 to 36 months. *Developmental Psychology*, 1976, *12*, 93–97. (a)

Bradley, R. H., & Caldwell, B. M. The relation of infants' home environments to mental test performance at 54 months: A follow-up study. *Child Development*, 1976, *47*, 1172–1174. (b)

Bradley, R. H., & Caldwell, B. M. Home observation for measurement of the environment: A validation study of screening efficiency. *American Journal of Mental Deficiency*, 1977, *81*, 417–420.

Bradley, R. H. Caldwell, B. M., & Elardo, R. Home environment, social status, and mental test performance. *Journal of Educational Psychology*, 1977, *69*, 697–701.

Bradley, R. H., Caldwell, B. M., & Elardo, R. Home environment and cognitive development in the first two years: A cross-lagged panel analysis. *Developmental Psychology*, 1979, *15*, 246–250.

Caputo, D. I., Goldstein, K. M., & Taub, H. B. Neonatal compromise and later psychological development: A ten year longitudinal study. In S. L. Friedman & M. S. Sigman (Eds.), *Preterm birth and psychological development*. New York: Academic Press, 1981.

Cohen, S. E., Beckwith, L., & Parmelee, A. H. Receptive langauge development in preterm children as related to caregiver–child interaction. *Pediatrics*, 1978, *61*, 16–20.

Crawford, J. Mother–child interaction in premature and fullterm infants. *Child Development* 1982, *53*, 957–962.

Elardo, R., Bradley, R., & Caldwell, B. The relation of infants' home environments to mental test performance from six to thirty-six months: A longitudinal analysis. *Child Development*, 1975, *46*, 71–76.

Elardo, R., Bradley, R., & Caldwell, B. M. A longitudinal study of the relation of infants home environments to language development at age three. *Child Development*, 1977, *48*, 595–603.

Field, T. M., Dempsey, J. R., & Shuman, H. H. Developmental follow-up of pre- and postterm infants. In S. L. Friedman & M. Sigman (Eds.), *Preterm birth and psychological development*. New York: Academic Press, 1981.

Goldberg, S. Prematurity: Effects on parent–infant interaction. *Journal of Pediatric Psychology*, 1978, *3*, 137–144.

Goldberg, S., Brachfeld, S., & Divitto, B. Feeding, fussing, and play: Parent–infant interaction in the first year as a function of prematurity and perinatal medical problems. In T. M. Field, S. Goldberg, D. Stern, & A. M. Sostek (Eds.), *High-risk infant and children: Adult and peer interactions*. New York: Academic Press, 1980.

McCall, R. D. Toward an epigenetic conception of mental development in the first three years of life. In M. Lewis (Eds.), *Origins of intelligence*. New York: Plenum, 1976.

Reynell, J. Reynell Developmental Language Scales Windson Berks, England: NFER, 1969

Sameroff, A. J., & Chandler, M. J. Reproductive risk and the continuum of caretaking casualty. In F. D. Horowitz (Ed.), *Review of Child Development Research*. Chicago: University of Chicago Press, 1975.

Siegel, L. S. Infant perceptual, cognitive, and motor behaviors as predictors of subsequent cognitive and language development. *Canadian Journal of Psychology*, 1979, *33*, 382–395.

Siegel, L. S. Infant tests as predictors of cognitive and language development at two years. *Child Development*, 1981, *52*, 545–557.

Siegel, L. S. Reproductive, perinatal, and environmental factors as predictors of the cognitive and language development of preterm and fullterm infants. *Child Development*, 1982, *53*, 963 = 973. (a)

Siegel, L. S. Reproductive, perinatal, and environmental variables as predictors of development of preterm (< 1501 grams) and fullterm children at 5 years. *Seminars in Perinatology*, 1982. (b)

Siegel, L. S. The prediction of possible learning disabilities in preterm and fullterm children. In T. Field & A. Sostek (Eds.), *Infants born at risk: Physiological and perceptual processes*, 1983. (a)

Siegel, L. S. Early cognitive and environmental correlates of language development at 4 years. *International Journal of Behavioral Development*, 1982, *5*, 433–444. (c)

Siegel, L. S., Saigal, S., Rosenbaum, P., Morton, R. A., Young, A., Berenbaum, S., & Stoskopf, B. Predictors of development in preterm and fullterm infants: A model for detecting the at risk child. *Journal of Pediatric Psychology*, 1982, *7*, 135–148.

Sigman, M., Cohen, S. E., Beckwith, L., & Parmelee, A. H. Social and familial influences on the development of preterm infants. *Journal of Pediatric Psychology*, 1981, 6, 1–13.

Terman, L. M., & Merrill, M. A. Stanford-Binet Intelligence Scale Form L–M. Boston: Houghton Mifflin, 1973.

Uzgiris, I., & Hunt, J. Mc.V. Assessment in infancy: Ordinal Scales of psychological development. Urbana: University of Illinois Press, 1975.

7

Home Environment and Cognitive Competence in Preterm Children during the First 5 Years

Leila Beckwith
Sarale E. Cohen

Introduction

The infant develops within a social matrix, in almost all cases, the nuclear family. The nature of the family influences what is learned and how the infant feels about it (Clausen & Williams, 1963). In the present chapter, we examine how differences in the ways families interact with their infants, beginning early in the infant's life and continuing to age 2 years, affect the child's cognitive test performance at age 5 years. Early home environment has been shown to be important for the cognitive performance of children born full-term and healthy (Ainsworth & Bell, 1973; Beckwith, 1971; Clarke-Stewart, 1973; Clarke-Stewart, Van Der Stoep, & Killian, 1979; Elardo, Bradley, & Caldwell, 1975; Yarrow, Rubenstein, Pederson, & Jankowski, 1972). In the present chapter, we investigate the relationship in a biologically at-risk population—infants born preterm with varying severities of illness. Does the early home environment ameliorate biological risk?

To pose such a question is to take a position in the nature–nurture controversy, that has raged over childhood IQ performance. The data that exist, although substantial, continue to be considered inconclusive and the effects of environment on intellectual ability continue to be debated. As Lewis (1976) points out, the nature–nurture controversy now centers on the issue of heritability coefficients, the estimates of which tend to be quite high. Yet, a high degree of heritability does not imply that environment can have no or little effect (Lewis, 1976; McCall, 1976). The example reported by Lewis states that children with the same genotype, even if the heritability index is as high as .80, may differ by as much as 25 IQ points when one is reared in an enriched environment and the other in a more deprived one (Cronbach, 1971).

ISBN 0-12-293460-1

Surprisingly, the nature–nurture argument reemerges in the study of biologically at-risk infants. Whereas the normal infant may be considered to be malleable and subject to social environmental influences, the biologically at-risk infant may not. The biological given, nature, is no longer operationally defined by heritability but by biological trauma. The question then becomes, does the early biological trauma so affect the nervous system that intelligence is predoomed to be deficient and unaffected by experience? Our position is that despite evidence of increased risk for an infant who has experienced prenatal and perinatal hazards, the infant's development cannot be predicted independently of subsequent caretaking experiences. The at-risk infant is not different from the normal infant in the effects of experience on the growth of intelligence in infancy (Beckwith, Cohen, Kopp, Parmelee, & Marcy, 1976).

Our position is consistent with prospective studies that indicate that the outcome for all babies is more strongly related to environment than to prenatal and perinatal difficulties (Drillien, 1964; Sameroff & Chandler, 1975; Werner, Bierman, & French, 1971; Wiener, Rider, Oppel, Fischer, & Harper, 1965). That is not to say that the environment can repair serious neurological or sensory problems, as in cerebral palsy or blindness. Nonetheless, it may compensate for more subtle neurological dysfunctioning, the kind that is speculated about, but not clearly identified. Additionally, for children without neurological problems, environment may seriously impede or enrich cognitive development.

Many investigators (Caputo, Goldstein, & Taub, 1979; Hunt, 1981; Siegel, in press) find that at-risk infants, as a group, perform normally on cognitive tests. Our studies are consistent. Born too soon, being subject to complications of labor and delivery, to postnatal illness, and to adverse medical interventions does not predoom infants to deficient cognitive test performance, either within the first year of life or later. Even very-low-birthweight infants, less than 1500 gm at birth, may do no more poorly than preterm infants born heavier and less sick (Cohen, Sigman, Parmelee, & Beckwith, 1982).

That is not to say that to be sick or born preterm does not matter. Even for children with IQs within the normal range, there is always the possibility that the IQs might have been higher, but for the earlier insults. It is also possible that global IQ scores mask deficits in specific abilities. There is some evidence that perceptual–motor skills (Caputo et al., 1979) may be deficient despite normal IQs.

In our own studies, we found that by postdicting, looking backwards, it could be seen that only those children who had suffered the most severe postnatal complications (in English-speaking families) performed below the normal range at age 5 years. On the other hand, approximately three-fourths of their peers, those children who also had the most severe postnatal complications, later scored within the normal range. Thus, even for the group of children with severe perinatal complications, the future was not sealed, despite the increased risk (Cohen et al., 1982).

If the future is not sealed, then there is ample opportunity for postnatal experience—specifically early home environment—to influence development. The nature of the early home environment is of particular interest with biologically at-risk infants because biological risk may alter the relationships between parents and infants. Parents of at-risk infants face many problems, including the question of the survival and long-term health of their babies, and guilt as well as loss of self-esteem for their babies' problems (Caplan, Mason, & Kaplan, 1965; Kaplan & Mason, 1960). Moreover, the poor condition of the infant at birth means that the parents are denied access to the physical intimacy and emotional commitment of caring for the child, a denial that precludes the usual process of neonatal bonding, one of the identified factors in helping parents appropriately focus loving attention on the infant (Klaus & Kennell, 1976; Minde, 1980). Thus, the parents may feel less confident (Leifer, Leiderman, Barnett, & Williams, 1972) and perhaps act less joyfully.

Although most parents of infants at biological risk do cope with their emotional distress concerning their babies, they may still find it difficult to maintain a gratifying relationship with their children. Hazardous birth may prove as stressful for infants as for parents. Perinatal problems may so affect infants that they enter the relationship with altered or diminished behavioral capacities. Under those circumstances, at-risk infants may be inadequate social partners in their natural role in initiating, maintaining, and promoting caregiving (Field, 1978; Goldberg, 1979).

The research described in this chapter was part of a larger longitudinal prospective study of at-risk development. The aim of the study was to improve assessment of risk factors and to identify ameliorative processes by including detailed, multiple measurements of medical, social, and developmental variables. The goals, the procedures, and the sample have been described in several publications (Parmelee, Kopp, & Sigman, 1976; Parmelee, Sigman, Kopp, & Haber, 1975; Sigman & Parmelee, 1979). In this chapter, we focus on the contribution of social factors, particularly caregiver–infant interaction, to children's cognitive test performances within the first 5 years of life.

Method

Subjects

The subjects in this study were preterm infants born at the UCLA hospital or transferred to the nursery shortly after birth. All preterm infants cared for in the UCLA nurseries between July 1972 and December 1974 were potential subjects for the study. The parents of preterm infants were asked to participate in this study as soon as their infant's condition was stable and it was expected the infant would survive. The infants were required to be free of obvious congenital anomalies or syndromes, of a gestational age of 37 weeks or less, and of a birthweight of 2500 grams or less.

A sample of 126 infants was studied throughout the infants' first 2 years of life. One hundred of the children were retested at age 5 years. The sample represented a broad range of ethnic and social class backgrounds. The Hollingshead Four-Factor Index of Social Status score ranged from 8 to 66, with a mean score of 40.0. The parental occupations ranged from manual laborers to professors and physicians, and parental years of education from 1 to more than 18. Many of the children were being raised in single-parent families and the divorce or separation rate by the time the child was seen at age 5 was about 25%. At age 5, approximately 56% of the mothers were working full or part time.

Of the 100 children seen at age 5 years, 62 were from English-speaking homes, 28 from Spanish-speaking homes and 10 from families who had immigrated recently to the United States from other countries, such as Korea, India, and so forth. For the purposes of this chapter, data from three cerebral palsy children and one child who was placed for adoption were excluded from analyses, resulting in a sample of 59 children from English-speaking families and 27 from Spanish-speaking families. Although the Spanish-speaking and other language groups were both immigrant groups, they differed in a number of ways that made it advisable to divide the foreign language subgroup into two groups. For example, those families labeled as others had a mean of 12.4 years of mother's education, whereas the Spanish-speaking group had a mean of 6.5 years of education. In this chapter the sample is divided into English- and Spanish-speaking groups for all analyses. The group of other speaking children was too small for meaningful analyses.

It was necessary to consider separate statistical analyses for each language sample because, although language background factors played a relatively minor role in test performance up to age 2 years (Sigman,

Cohen, & Forsythe, 1981), by age 5, language background was a major factor in test performance, when using the Stanford-Binet as the outcome measure (Cohen *et al.*, in press). Performance on the Stanford-Binet was related to cultural assimilation and facility with English. Despite mean differences in the outcome score at age 5 years, between English- and Spanish-speaking groups, in this chapter the Spanish-speaking group serves as a replication for the examination of the relationship between home environment and competence.

In spite of the fact that all of the infants were born preterm, there was a great deal of variability in the infants' condition. Many infants suffered respiratory distress (38%); yet, on the other hand, there were some infants who were hospitalized for only a short time and were quickly cared for in their own homes. The average length of hospitalization was 24 days (range was 2 to 88 days). *Gestational age* (defined as the time from mother's last menstrual period, as reported by the mother, until time of birth) ranged from 25 to 37 weeks and birthweight ranged from 800 to 2500 gm. Twelve of the infants were small for gestational age. Mothers' age at the time of birth of the preterm infant varied from 17 to 39 years.

Table 1 presents descriptive information for each language group. Overall there was a 79% return from ages 2–5 years, with the following return rate by language groups: English, 82%; Spanish, 76%. No family refused testing. Those subjects lost to follow-up either could not be located or had moved out the area. Multivariate tests, Hotelling T^2, were used to compare the return groups within each language subgroup to those who did not return for testing. The first set of variables consisted of birthweight, gestational age, length of hospitalization, years of maternal education, gender, and birth order. The second set of Hotelling T^2 compared the groups on the diagnostic measures administered in the first year of life. None of the Hotelling T^2 values were significant ($p > .10$). For the English-speaking group the individual t values indicated that the return group differed from the no-return group on two single variables. The return group was lighter in birthweight and had mothers who had more years of education ($p < .05$).

Measures

Assessments used in the longitudinal project included measures of neurophysiological, sensory, and behavioral parameters of the child, as well as of the caregiving and home environment. In this chapter the focus is on the relationships between home environment measures and standard development tests.

TABLE 1
Description of Sample

Variable	English speaking (N = 59)			Spanish speaking (N = 27)		
	Mean or %	SD	Range	Mean or %	SD	Range
Hollingshead social status index	43.9	14.2	15.5–66.0	17.9	5.6	8–27
Maternal education (years)	13.2	2.1	8–17	6.0	3.0	1–12
Maternal age	25.7	5.5	17–39	24.1	5.2	17–37
Gender—% male	56%	—		59%	—	
Birth order—% firstborn	51%	—		48%	—	
Medical factors Birthweight (gm)	1774.4	492.5	800–2495	2007.7	389.3	1020–2500
Gestational age (weeks)	32.2	3.3	25–37	34.1	2.6	28–37
Days in hospital	26.5	21.5	2–88	16.0	14.0	2–57
Obstetrical complications scale[a]	82.2	15.9	50–121	87.0	18.2	50–112
Postnatal complications scale[a]	86.7	29.5	55–160	109.1	33.4	67–160
Low birthweight— ≤ 1500 gm	30%			15%		

[a] Higher scores are optimal. Scale was standardized with a mean of 100 and a standard deviation of 20.

Home Environment Measures

Assessments of the infant's social experience were based on naturalistic home observations and a semistructured laboratory situation, in which specific social transactions were counted. Observations were made by one of a pool of four observers both in the home during daily routines and in the laboratory. All observations were made at equivalent conceptional ages for all infants. The observations were made at 1, 8, 21, and 24 months after the infants' expected date of birth. The ages for these assessments were selected to correspond to the time periods for the developmental assessments in order to study concurrent, as well as long-time relationships.

At each observation, frequencies of specific discrete behaviors directed to the infant or shown by the infant were noted by continuous time sampling every 15 seconds on precoded checklists or by event sampling. In addition to behaviors of talking, touching, holding, presenting objects, and social play, we noted *reciprocal social transac-*

tions—that is, interactions that occurred mutually or in response to infant's gaze, smile, vocalization, or gesture.

The interactions of the primary caregiver (in 95% of the cases, the mother) with the infant were given primacy. Nonetheless, the behaviors of other adults and children interacting with the infant were noted. The interactions with the infant that involved any person were analyzed, as well as the interactions involving only the primary caregiver. As the majority of interactions involved the primary caregiver, results were not found to be different by recording more broadly (Cohen & Beckwith, 1977).

At the 1-month home visit, the babies were observed through a cycle of waking from sleep, being fed, and all other activities that occurred until they were asleep again for more than ½ hour. The average duration of the infants' awake time during the observation was 74 minutes. At the 8-month visit, 1½ hours of awake time plus the feeding was observed (Beckwith *et al.*, 1976). The laboratory observation at 21 months was of 14 minutes duration, and consisted of four tasks varying in structure. The caregiver and child were videotaped as they engaged in a dramatic play situation and three teaching tasks (Cohen, 1978). At the 24-month visit, 50 minutes of play time were observed by continuous event sampling (Beckwith & Cohen, 1980). The coding system was adapted from the approach system (Caldwell & Honig, 1971), with additional variables suggested by the work of White and Watts (1970).

The laboratory assessment of caregiver–infant interaction at 21 months was included, in addition to home observations, in order to broaden the scope of the observations. Laboratory observations have the advantage of standardizing the situation for all participants and equalize the opportunity for all caregivers to interact with the target children, free of the distractions and demands made in the home by other individuals and by situational circumstances. It was thought that the laboratory assessment could add information as to the potential of the caregiver to interact with the child whereas the naturalistic observation in the home was designed to assess how the caregiver typically interacted with the child. The 21-month assessment was not analyzed for the Spanish-speaking subjects.

Reliability of Caregiver–Infant Observations

Observer reliabilities for the home observation were determined during pilot work by computing Pearson correlation coefficients for the total frequency of a specific behavior each observer had recorded in an observation. Coefficients obtained ranged from .80 to .98 with the majority being greater than .90 (Beckwith *et al.*, 1976). For the laboratory assessment, observer reliability was determined on the basis of 10 cases. Reliability was calculated by the percentage of agreement for each behavior per dyad. Agreement between two independent assessments for the 10 cases averaged 92%, and only behaviors with greater than 85% agreement were used in analyses (Cohen, 1978).

The observers of the caregiver–infant interactions were naive regarding the child's medical history and the results of the developmental assessments.

Data Reduction

A large number of caregiver and infant behaviors were observed at each age, in order to provide a meaningful data base in an attempt to understand the processes in the infant's adaptation to the home environment. Both proximal and distal behaviors of the caregiver were included, as well as behaviors at each age period that represented reciprocal, positive, social interchanges between caregiver and infant, as well as infant behaviors that were communicative signals to others.

In order to conceptualize more global and stable dimensions, it was useful to have summary scores of caregiver–infant behaviors, in addition to the individual behaviors. The individual behaviors were used to derive composite scores in two ways. The first strategy involved a single overall home score for each age period. A few variables were selected, a priori, that characterized responsive caregiving.

The five variables selected at one month were (1) the percent of the baby's awake time in which the caregiver interacted socially by touching, or holding, or talking, or mutual gazing; (2) the percent of time the caregiver and baby were in the en face position; (3) the percent of time during which the caregiver talked to the baby in the en face position; (4) the percent of time the baby was held in an upright position; (5) the percentage of fuss or crying episodes to which the caregiver responded within 45 seconds. Variables at 8 months were similar, except that the caregiver's vocal imitation or response to the baby's babbling was included, rather than the caregiver's response to distress, and the percentage of time the baby was allowed on the floor replaced time the baby was held in the upright position. Three variables at 24 months were selected as analogues to the first-year variables: (1) the degree to which the caregiver interacted socially with the child by touching, talking, presenting a toy, or engaging in reciprocal play; (2) the degree to which either the child or the caregiver responded to each other, either verbally, as in a conversation, or nonverbally, as in rolling a ball back and forth one to the other; (3) the amount of time the child spent during the observation in looking at books and/or listening to records, and /or playing with sand, water, and blocks, and/or engaging in pretend play. The variables at each age period were converted to standardized scores for all subjects and the standardized scores were summed to make a single score per observation for each child, with a mean score of 100 and standard deviation of 20.

Factor scores were the second strategy used in obtaining a summary score. The individual behaviors at each age period were entered into a principal component-factor analysis, with varimax rotation (rotation to the maximum degree of variation) to orthogonal structure. The factors were derived from the first 50 babies in our sample from English-speaking homes. Weights derived from this sample were then used to generate factor scores on the entire sample. We have published previously on factor scores derived from factor analysis at each age period (Beckwith & Cohen, 1980; Beckwith et al., 1976). In this chapter, we have selected the first principal component factor to be used as an additional summary score of caregiving. The first factor at each age basically represented a positive responsive attentiveness and accounted for the following amount of variance: 1 month, 31%; 8 months, 32%; 21 months, 52%, and 24 months, 61%.

Developmental Assessments

The children were tested on a variety of developmental measures during the first 2 years. Those reported in this chapter are standard infant-development tests and include the Gesell Developmental Schedules, administered at 4, 9, and 24 months. At age 5 years the children were administered the Stanford-Binet Intelligence Test, Form L-M, using the 1972 restandardization norms. All tests were given at corrected conceptional ages. Testing was done by independent examiners who were naive about the medical data and the results of previous examinations, as well as the results of the home observations.

Results

The results of this study are complex in that many variables have been assessed over a 5-year period. Further, the results are presented separately for two subsamples of the group—the children from English-speaking homes and those from Spanish-speaking homes. As explained previously, the latter is treated as a replication on a different population.

For each language sample, data are summarized for infant developmental scores, for caregiver variables, and for the relationship between the two sets of variables at different age periods. Competence was assessed at four age-periods that are analyzed in this Chapter: 4 months, 9 months, 24 months, and 5 years. Thus, the results are presented for short- and long-term relationships.

Results are presented for each language group as well as for differences as a function of socioeconomic status (SES), gender, and birth order. SES differences were analyzed in two ways: (1) by partialing out the effects of SES in correlational analyses, and (2) by statistical test of mean differences. The families were divided into lower and higher SES groups on the basis of the Hollingshead Four-Factor Index of Social Position score at 5 years. Scores of 40 or greater were considered to reflect higher SES; all the parents in these families had completed high school and in most cases had attended college for 1 or more years. Occupations were most frequently technicians, semiprofessionals, and professionals. Scores of less than 40 were considered lower SES and represented parents with, in general, less than 12 years of education and occupations ranging from manual laborers to clerical positions. Within the Spanish-speaking sample there was little variation in SES and it was not necessary to divide the sample or to do partial correlations.

English Language Sample

1- to 4-Month Data

Infant Development   Despite preterm birth and attendant complications, the infants, in general, performed in the average range, earning a mean DQ (Developmental Quotient) of 106.1 ($SD = 9$, range = 76–124) on the Gesell Developmental Schedules at 4 months (see Table 2). There were no significant group differences between boys and girls, first- and later-borns, or infants from families of higher or lower SES, as indicated on Table 3.

Caregiver–Infant Interaction   Summary variables of caregiver–infant interaction at 1 month (Table 4) indicated that the level and quality of caregiver–infant interaction was also solidly within the average range in the early months, as based on norms from pilot study. Differences between groups were tested by a series of two-way analyses

TABLE 2
Developmental Assessment Scores for English-Speaking Sample

Test	N	Mean	SD	Range
Gesell, 4 months	59	106.1	9.0	76–124
Gesell, 9 months	59	99.9	6.7	85–115
Gesell, 24 months	59	101.4	12.3	71–138
Stanford-Binet, 5 years	59	105.6	16.3	57–138

TABLE 3
Developmental Assessment Scores and Significant Differences by Gender, Birth order, and SES Groups for English-Speaking Sample

Test	Gender		Birth order		SES	
	Boys (N = 33)	Girls (N = 26)	Firstborn (N = 30)	Later-born (N = 29)	Lower (N = 26)	Higher (N = 33)
Gesell, 4 months	104.8	107.8	105.6	106.7	105.8	106.4
Gesell, 9 months	97.8 *	102.8	102.2 *	97.6	99.9	100.1
Gesell, 24 months	97.2 **	106.7	104.8	97.9	97.8 *	104.3
Stanford-Binet, 5 years	105.1	106.3	107.2	104.0	99.7 *	110.3

* Group difference $p < .05$.
** Group difference $p < .01$.

TABLE 4
Caregiver–Infant Interaction Scores for English-Speaking Sample: Summary Scores

Summary variable	Mean	SD	Range
Caregiver–infant interaction[a]			
1 Month (N = 59)	108.1	21.0	60.6–157.0
8 Months (N = 59)	99.2	13.6	70.7–129.3
24 Months (N = 41)[b]	103.7	20.3	70.1–151.1
Factor score			
1 Month F1—social (N = 59)	.34	1.30	−1.3–5.1
8 Months F1—mutual social (N = 59)	.15	.98	−1.35–3.2
21 Months F1—positive attentiveness (N = 41)	.00	1.00	−2.5–2.1
24 Months F1—positive attentiveness (N = 41)	.05	1.00	−1.17–2.4

[a] High scores are optimal. Score was standardized with a mean of 100 and a standard deviation of 20.
[b] It may be noted that a smaller number of subjects were tested at 21 and 24 months than at other age periods.

of variance (ANOVA) (gender × birth order) and by *t* tests for differences between SES. Three-way analyses of variance were not used, as some cell sizes would be too small for meaningful analyses. There were no significant differences between groups in the overall level of interaction at that age (Table 5) but there were in specific behaviors (Tables 6 and 7). As can be seen from Table 7, middle-SES caregivers spoke more, even to the 1-month-old infant, than did lower-SES caregivers; caregivers, regardless of SES, engaged in more en face behavior with their girls than with their boys; and firstborns were responded to more promptly than later-borns when fussing or crying. Within each group, however, variability was marked.

Relationships between Infant Development and Caregiver–Infant Interaction There was no evidence that individual differences in development at 4 months were related to caregiver–infant interaction, either for the English speaking sample as a whole (Tables 8 and 9), or for any of the subgroups (Tables 10 and 11). However, there was a significant link between infant behavior in the home at 1 month and the

TABLE 5

Caregiver–Infant Interaction Scores for English-Speaking Sample: Summary Scores and Significant Group Differences for Gender, Birth Order, and SES Groups

Summary variable	Gender		Birth order		SES	
	Boys (N = 33)	Girls (N = 26)	Firstborn (N = 30)	Later-born (N = 29)	Lower (N = 26)	Higher (N = 33)
Caregiver–infant interaction[a]						
1 Month	103.4	114.1	112.2	103.9	106.8	109.6
8 Months	95.9	103.4	105.4 **	92.8	94.7 *	102.7
24 Months	98.3	111.1	110.1	97.3	96.6 *	109.3
Factor score						
1 Month F1—social	.08	.66	.41	.27	.19	.46
8 Months F1— mutual social	−.06 *	.42	.30	−.01	−.30 **	.50
21 Months F1— positive attentiveness	N = 22 −.19	N = 19 .28	N = 20 .00	N = 21 .01	N = 18 −.37 **	N = 23 .26
24 Months F1— positive attentiveness	−.18	.35	.35	−.31	−.39 **	.42

[a] Higher scores are optimal. Score was standardized with a mean of 100 and a standard deviation of 20.

* Group difference $p < .05$.

** Group difference $p < .01$.

TABLE 6
Caregiver–Infant Interaction Scores for English-Speaking Sample:
Individual Behaviors

| Behavior | Interaction scores | | |
	Mean	SD	Range
1 Month[a] (N = 59)			
Total talk	.31	.20	.01–.91
Face-to-face talk	.07	.07	.00–.38
Contingent vocalization	.11	.12	.00–.43
Hold	.54	.22	.00–.98
Contingency to distress	.78	.23	.07–1.00
Mutual visual regard	.11	.09	.00–.49
Fuss cry (infant)	.13	.08	.00–.39
Nondistress vocalization (infant)	.16	.12	.00–.45
8 Months[a]			
Total talk	.23	.13	.04–.58
Face-to-face talk	.06	.04	.01–.24
Contingent vocalization	.08	.07	.00–.34
Hold	.10	.07	.00–.26
Contingency to distress	.89	.16	.29–1.00
Mutual visual regard	.09	.05	.02–.57
Fuss cry (infant)	.06	.05	.00–.25
Nondistress vocalization (infant)	.32	.11	.10–.54
Floor freedom	.43	.24	.00–.97
21 Months[b] (N = 41)			
Total talk	46.0	9.6	22–56
Reciprocal exchanges	29.0	10.3	5–52
Fuss cry (infant)	2.4	3.4	0–27
Nondistress vocalization (infant)	34.8	11.1	7–52
24 Months[c]			
Total talk	235.8	179.4	7–657
Reciprocal exchanges	68.0	67.1	0–261
Fuss cry (infant)	3.6	4.9	0–19
Nondistress vocalization (infant)	230.4	138.8	2–556
Time in intellectual tasks (secs.)	624.6	674.7	0–2070

[a] Percent of observation intervals of awake time.
[b] Number of 15-second intervals during 14-minute laboratory observation.
[c] Frequency of events during 50-minute home observation.

4-month developmental performance. One-month-olds who were more irritable, (spent a larger percentage of their awake time fussing or crying) were also less developmentally skillful 4-month-olds, whereas 1-month-olds who vocalized more in nondistress became more competent 4-month-olds (Table 9). The relationships were not significantly different across groups and were not diminished by partialing out SES.

TABLE 7

Caregiver–Infant Interaction Scores for English-Speaking Sample:
Individual Behaviors and Significant Group Differences by Gender, Birth Order, and SES Groups

Behavior	Gender		Birth order		SES	
	Boys (N = 33)	Girls (N = 26)	Firstborn (N = 30)	Later-born (N = 29)	Lower (N = 26)	Higher (N = 33)
1 Month[a]						
Total talk	.28	.36	.36	.27	.25	.36 *
Face-to-face talk	.05 *	.10	.07	.07	.07	.07
Contingent vocalization	.10	.12	.12	.10	.11	.11
Hold	.52	.56	.57	.50	.53	.54
Contingency to distress	.74	.83	.86 *	.70	.80	.76
Mutual visual regard	.09 *	.15	.11	.12	.11	.12
Fuss cry (infant)	.15	.11	.13	.14	.11	.15
Nondistress vocalization (infant)	.14	.18	.18	.13	.14	.18
8 Months[a]						
Total talk	.20	.27	.28 *	.18	.18	.27 **
Face-to-face talk	.05	.07	.07	.04	.04	.06 *
Contingent vocalization	.08	.09	.10	.07	.06	.10 *
Hold	.10	.10	.10	.10	.08	.11
Contingency to distress	.89	.90	.94 *	.84	.90	.88
Mutual visual regard	.07 *	.10	.10	.07	.07	.10
Fuss cry (infant)	.05	.07	.07	.06	.05	.07
Nondistress vocalization (infant)	.32	.32	.35 **	.29	.32	.32
Floor freedom	.41	.46	.47	.39	.43	.42

248

21 Months[b]	$N = 22$	$N = 19$	$N = 21$	$N = 20$	$N = 18$	$N = 23$
Total talk	45.0	47.1	45.2	46.8	41.6	47.3
Reciprocal exchanges	27.8	30.3	28.8	29.2	24.9	29.4
Fuss cry (infant)	3.0	1.8	2.2	2.6	2.9	3.1
Nondistress vocalization (infant)	32.5 *	37.4	33.6	36.0	33.5	33.1
24 Months[c]						
Total talk	205.4	270.9	313.3 **	154.4	191.4	270.9
Reciprocal exchanges	47.2	92.2	91.3	43.4	57.2	79.1
Fuss cry (infant)	3.4	3.9	3.2	4.1	4.8	3.4
Nondistress vocalization (infant)	211.1	252.8	270.7	188.2	225.4	241.8
Time in intellectual tasks (seconds)	473.4	799.7	545.0	708.2	266.7 **	794.6

[a] Percent of observation intervals of awake time.
[b] Number of 15-second intervals during 14-minute laboratory observation.
[c] Frequency of events during 50-minute home observation.
* Group difference $p < .05$.
** Group difference $p < .01$.

TABLE 8

Significant* Correlations between Caregiver–Infant Interaction Behaviors
and Developmental Tests for English-Speaking Sample: Summary Scores[a]

Summary variable	Gesell, 9 months	Gesell, 24 months	Stanford-Binet, 5 Year
Caregiver–infant interaction			
1 Month			
8 Month	.27	.43	
24 Month		.37[b]	.38
Factor score			
1 Month F1—social		.30	.26[a]
8 Months F1—mutual social		.35[a]	
21 Months F1—positive attentiveness		.60	.65
24 Months F1—positive attentiveness		.42	.34[a]

[a] No significant correlations were found between caregiver–infant interaction variables and Gesell at 4 months.
[b] No longer significant when SES was partialed out.
*$p < .05$.

TABLE 9

Significant* Correlations between Caregiver–Infant Interaction Behaviors
and Developmental Tests for English-Speaking Sample: Individual Behaviors

Behavior	Gesell 4 months	Gesell 9 months	Gesell 24 months	Stanford-Binet 5 Year
1 Month				
Total talk			.26[a]	.26[a]
Fuss cry	−.26		−.23[b]	
Nondistress vocalization	.28			
8 Months				
Total talk		.25[b]	.39	
Face-to-face talk			.39	
Mutual visual regard			.34[a]	
21 Months				
Total talk			.43[a]	.61
Reciprocal exchanges			.60	.63
Nondistress vocalization			.39	.44
24 Months				
Total talk				
Reciprocal exchanges			.38	.31[a]
Fuss cry			−.42	−.33[a]
Nondistress vocalization			.33	.31[a]
Intellectual tasks				.35[a]

[a] No longer significant when SES partialed out.
[b] Became significant when SES partialed out.
*$p < .05$.

TABLE 10

Significant * Correlations between Caregiver–Infant Interaction Behaviors
and Developmental Tests, by Gender: Summary Scores for English-Speaking Sample[a]

	Developmental assessments					
	Gesell, 9 months		Gesell, 24 months		Stanford-Binet, 5 years	
Summary variable	Boys	Girls	Boys	Girls	Boys	Girls
Caregiver–infant interaction						
1 Month						
8 Month				.55[b]		.55[b]
24 Month			.38[b]		.38[b]	.59
Factor score						
1 Month F1 social	.45		.34[b]			
8 Month F1 mutual-social				.49[b]		.41[b]
21 Months F1 positive attentiveness			.61	.60	.61	.78
24 Months F1 positive attentiveness				.53		.50

[a] No significant correlations were found between caregiver–infant interaction variables and Gesell at 4 months.

[b] No longer significant when SES partialed out.

* $p < .05$.

5- to 9-Month Data

Infant Development The infants, as a group, scored lower at 9 months than they did at 4 months, $(t[58] = 5.2;\ p < .001)$, but were still within the average range (mean 99.9; $SD = 6.7$; range = 85–115; see Table 2). Hunt (1976) has suggested that equating for conceptional age inflates scores obtained in the first few months for preterm infants. SES differences were not evident, but girls and firstborn infants were significantly more advanced than were boys and later-born infants (Table 3).

Caregiver–Infant Interaction Caregiver-infant interaction, derived from the summary scores, encompassed a smaller proportion of the infant's awake time at 8 months than it had at 1 month $(t[58] = 3.16,\ p < .05$; mean = 99.2; $SD = 13.6$, range = 61−158; see Table 4). SES differences were apparent, with caregivers from higher socioeconomic statuses providing more interaction than lower-SES caregivers. Similarly, caregivers provided more interaction to their firstborn infants than they did to their later-borns (Table 5).

TABLE 11

Significant * Correlations between Caregiver–Infant Interaction Behaviors
and Developmental Tests, by Gender: Individual Behaviors for English-Speaking Sample

Behavior	Gesell 4 months		Gesell 9 months		Gesell 24 months		Stanford-Binet 5 years	
	Boys	Girls	Boys	Girls	Boys	Girls	Boys	Girls
1 Month								
Total talk					.44[a]			.40[a]
Face-to-face talk								
Contingent vocalization								.40
Nondistress vocalization	.42							
8 Months								
Total talk						.55		.42[a]
Face-to-face talk						.48[a]		.43[a]
Contingency to distress								.50
Mutual visual regard						.44[a]		.44[a]
Fuss cry								
Nondistress vocalization					-.47			
Floor freedom								.52[a]
21 Months								
Total talk					.45[b]		.63	.60
Reciprocal exchanges					.67	.58	.60	.71
Fuss cry								
Nondistress vocalization					.52		.47	
24 Months								
Total talk								.48[a]
Reciprocal exchanges								
Fuss cry					-.56			
Nondistress vocalization								.53
Time in intellectual tasks								.57[a]

[a] No longer significant when SES partialed out.
* p < .05.

Developmental change in the individual behaviors between ages 1 and 8 months occurred primarily in the percentage of awake time that infants were held. Whereas at 1 month, holding was the most frequent caregiver–infant interaction and infants were held more than half of their awake time (54%), by 8 months they were held only 10% of their wakeful time (Table 6). Perhaps infants evoked less holding because they fussed and cried significantly less (from 13 to 6%). Additionally, caregivers responded more quickly to fuss–cry episodes (contingency to distress increased from 78% of the episodes at 1 month to 89% of the episodes at 8 months). Further, infants increased their nondistress vocalizations (16% at 1 month to 32% at 8 months).

Caregivers from the higher socioeconomic statuses talked more to their infants at 8 months as they had at 1 month, and did so more contingently to their infants' vocalizations and more in the en face position than did lower-SES caregivers. Caregivers also continued to engage in more mutual visual regard with their girls than with their boys. Additionally, firstborns' fussing and crying was responded to more quickly and they were talked to more than were later-borns. Firstborns vocalized more than did later-borns (see Table 7).

Relationships between Infant Development and Caregiver–Infant Interaction   Caregiver–infant interaction at 8 months was modestly related to developmental test performance 1 month later, such that those infants receiving more interaction performed more competently (Table 8). The relationship was significant for the group as a whole, whether or not SES was partialed out. No single interactional or infant behavior at 8 months was related to 9-month test performance, either for the group as a whole or for any subgroup except that total talk became significant when SES was partialed out (Tables 9 and 11).

21- to 24-Month Data

Infant Development   The 24-month-olds continued to perform, as a group, within the average range, with a mean DQ of 101.4, *SD* of 12.3, and a range of scores from 71 to 138 (Table 2). By this age, SES differences emerged in the infants' test performances, with infants from higher SES families performing more competently. Girls were also more advanced developmentally than boys; however, firstborn children no longer had an advantage over later-borns (Table 3).

Caregiver–Infant Interaction   Higher-SES caregivers continued, as they had at 8 months, to interact socially more with their infants than did lower-SES caregivers. Higher-SES infants also spent more time in "intellectual tasks" (i.e., with books, blocks, or sand and water play). Caregivers talked more to their firstborns than to their later-borns and girls were more talkative than were boys (Tables 5 and 7).

Relationships between Infant Development and Caregiver–Infant Interaction   The level of caregiver–infant interaction, as measured by summary and factor scores at 1, 8, 21, and 24 months was related significantly to test performance at 24 months. Infants who engaged in more social interaction with their caregivers performed more competently. The relationships were significant for the group as a whole, and the majority of correlations remained significant even after partialing out SES (Tables 8 and 10).

In contrast to the paucity of significant relationships between individual behaviors of the caregiver and infant test performance during the first year of life were the numerous associations between those caregiver behaviors and test performances 1 year later, at 24 months (Tables 9 and 11). That pattern of associations stood in contradiction to the usual expectation which is that the longer the elapsed period between one event and the other, the fewer the significant associations.

The associations although somewhat changed by the age of the infants, their subgroup membership, and whether or not SES was partialled out, made a consistent pattern. The frequency with which the caregiver talked to the baby at 1 month, 8 months, and at 21 and 24 months was linked to more optimum performance. Similarly, more frequent visual checks between caregiver and infant at 8 months were associated with more competency later. By the second year of life, at 21 and 24 months, in the laboratory and at home, the more frequent the *reciprocal exchanges* (one member of the dyad responds to an initiation of the other member of the dyad) the more skilled the test performance. Additionally, infants who were more irritable (spent a larger percentage of their observed time fussing at 1 and 24 months) performed more poorly in the test situation, whereas toddlers who vocalized more (either in jargon or in words), performed more competently during testing.

5-Year Data

Child Development   At age 5 years, the children born preterm to English-speaking families, earned a mean IQ of 105.6, with an *SD* of 16.3, with a range of scores from 57 to 138 (Table 3). Their scores on the Stanford-Binet were significantly higher than their scores had been on the Gesell test at age 2 years ($t[58] = 2.38$, $p < .05$). Most of the children performed well-within the average range and many performed at the superior level. The performance of the English sample could not be distinguished from the standardization sample for the Stanford-Binet.

SES differences were evident; children from lower-SES homes performed with a lower mean IQ (99.7, $SD = 17.3$, and range of 57–134) than did children from middle-SES homes (mean IQ of 110.3, $SD = 14$, and range of 72–138, $p < .05$). In contrast to younger ages, there was no evidence that girls performed more competently than boys, nor that firstborns were more skilled than later-borns (Table 3).

Relationships between Child Development at Age 5 and Caregiver–Infant Interaction The ways in which the caregiver interacted with the child at 1, 8, 21, and 24 months as measured by summary and factor scores were associated with test performance 3 and 4 years later. The associations were, in part, mediated by SES, and once the effects of SES was partialled out, only caregiver–child interaction at 21 and 24 months remained significantly linked to 5-year performance (Table 8). The pattern was the same across all English-speaking subgroups (Table 10).

When individual behaviors were considered, only a few scattered correlations were significant for the first year of life but there were numerous and consistent relationships between specific caregiver–child interaction behaviors in the second year of life and Stanford-Binet performance at age 5 years. Interestingly, the behaviors that were significant in the first year of life, after partialing out SES, were contingent ones, that is, contingent vocalization at 1 month and contingency to distress at 8 months and they were significant only for girls.

The laboratory situation at 21 months proved to be particularly powerful in describing individual differences that would be significant for child test-performance 3 years later. For all subgroups, the degree to which the caregiver talked to the child in that situation, the degree to which the child vocalized and the degree to which one member of the dyad responded to the other, vocally or nonverbally, were significant correlates of child performance. At home, at 24 months, only child behaviors achieved significance once SES was partialed out; girls who vocalized more and first borns who fussed less were more skillful later (Tables 9 and 11).

Continuity in Responsive Caregiver–Infant Interaction and Child Test-Performance In order to take into account the pattern of caregiver–infant interactions across time, rather than, as in the previous analyses, considering each period separately, the sample was divided into (1) those who were equal to or above 100 at all 3 home observations on the summary score of caregiver–infant interaction and (2) those who were below 100 at all observations or who shifted from one time period to another. Table 12 lists the number of subjects who fell within each group, their SES membership and the mean developmental score their infants earned at 24 months and at 5 years.

Almost one-third of the sample engaged in consistently responsive caregiver–infant interaction. However, the majority of the subjects shifted, and there were many who fell below the mean at succeeding observations even though their initial exchanges with their infants were quite responsive. It was possible to shift at any time, with some subjects being able to change from diminished interactions with their infants in the first year of life to enriched interactions in the second year.

The pattern of responsiveness was related to SES. SES did not determine the percentage of caregivers who were consistently unresponsive with their infants; only a few caregivers, of equal number from the lower and higher SES groups, behaved that way. Rather, SES determined the ability to be consistently responsive. Except for a very few, almost all those who were consistently responsive were middle- or upper SES caregivers, whereas those who were sometimes responsive were more frequently lower-SES caregivers.

The pattern of responsiveness altered the children's developmental test performance, within SES. If a caregiver was able to consistently engage in a very interactive and contingent way with the child, the child tended to perform significantly above the average, even within the lower SES. The power of consistent, contingent interactions was evident in 2-year test performance and was sustained at 5 years.

Excellent caregiving, however, was not a necessary cause of excellent performance. Some children managed to function effectively although they came from a lower SES and/or received impoverished caregiving.

TABLE 12

Developmental Scores by Degree of Responsive Caregiving over Time for each SES:
English-Speaking Sample

Developmental assessment	Consistently responsive caregiving	Lower SES			Higher SES		
		N	Mean	Range	N	Mean	Range
Gesell, 24 months	No	21	95.6	83–117	14	99.4	54–121
	Yes	3	116.3	104–125	15	107.5	83–138
Stanford-Binet, 5 years	No	21	96.6	57–134	14	104.0	80–123
	Yes	3	117.7	101–130	15	114.5	103–127

Table 13
Developmental Assessment Scores for Spanish-Speaking Sample

Test	N	Mean	SD	Range
Gesell, 4 months	27	105.0	11.5	88–141
Gesell, 9 months	27	98.5	8.9	80–118
Gesell, 24 months	27	93.3	7.6	79–104
Stanford-Binet, 5 years	27	82.7	10.5	64–105

Spanish Language Sample

Data from the Spanish-speaking sample, smaller in size than the English-, are treated across age periods rather than by each individual age.

Infant Development

At 4 months, infants born preterm to Spanish-speaking families performed somewhat above average (mean = 105.0, SD = 11.5, range = 88–141) (Table 13). Firstborn infants were significantly more developmentally advanced (Table 14), an advantage that did not emerge until 9 months in the English sample.

At 9 months, as in the English language sample, the infants, although performing at an average level (mean = 98.5; SD = 8.9; range = 80–118), significantly decreased their DQ scores from 4 months ($t[26]$ = 3.9, p < .001). Firstborns still maintained their developmental edge, similar to the English-language sample. In contrast, however, to the English-speaking sample, boys from Spanish-speaking homes were significantly more skillful than were girls at this age (Table 14).

By 24 months, DQ scores for the group as a whole were significantly below average (mean 93.3, SD = 7.6, range = 79–104) and significantly

TABLE 14
Developmental Assessment Scores and Significant Differences by Gender
and Birth order: Spanish-Speaking Sample

	Gender		Birth order		
Test	Boys (N = 16)	Girls (N = 11)	Firstborn (N = 13)		Later-born (N = 14)
Gesell 4 months	107.8	101.1	110.3	*	100.1
Gesell 9 months	101.9 *	93.6	102.3	*	95.0
Gesell 24 months	93.9	92.4	95.8		90.9
Stanford-Binet 5 years	85.2	79.2	79.6		85.6

* Group difference p < .05.

decreased from 9 months ($t[26] = 2.6$, $p < .02$). Boys and firstborn children no longer held an advantage.

At 5 years, performance on the Stanford-Binet, administered in Spanish, was significantly below average (mean 82.7, $SD = 105$, range = 64–105). The continuing downward trend in performance level from 4 to 9 to 24 months, seen also in the lower-SES English-speaking sample, continued to 5 years ($t[26] = 5.2$, $p < .001$), and was even more accelerated than in the lower-SES English-speaking sample.

Caregiver–Infant Interaction

The composite scores at 1, 8, and 24 months were lower for the Spanish-speaking sample than for the English-speaking sample. Analyses of variance were done comparing the two samples, using only lower-SES English speakers as the comparison group and the differences approached significance ($p < .10$). Differences in individual behaviors were found that indicated caregivers from the Spanish-speaking sample spoke less to the infant at all observations in the first year and held the infant less at one month (Table 16).

Caregivers from the Spanish-speaking sample showed differential treatment to boys and to girls, but the direction of the differences was contrary to that within the English-speaking sample (see Tables 5, 7, 17, and 18). When the 4 groups were compared with one another, boys from Spanish-speaking homes and boys from English-speaking homes received about the same frequency and quality of social interactions, but girls from English-speaking homes received significantly more than

TABLE 15

Caregiver–Infant Interaction Scores for Spanish-Speaking Sample: Summary Scores

Summary variable	Mean	SD	Range
Caregiver–infant interaction[a]			
1 Month ($N = 27$)	96.4	18.6	64.0–133.8
8 Months ($N = 27$)	88.1	16.1	64.3–113.3
24 Months ($N = 25$)	97.8	17.7	70.7–134.7
Factor scores			
1 Month F1—social ($N = 27$)	.25	.98	−.66–3.7
8 Months F1—mutual social ($N = 27$)	−.23	.83	−1.25–1.87
24 Months F1—positive attentiveness ($N = 25$)	−.22	.54	−.89–.81

[a] Higher scores are optimal. Score was standardized; with a mean of 100 and a standard deviation of 20.

TABLE 16
Caregiver–Infant Interaction Scores for Spanish-Speaking Sample:
Individual Behaviors

Behavior	Mean	SD	Range
1 Month[a] (N = 27)			
Total talk	.13	.11	0–.46
Face-to-face talk	.03	.04	0–.17
Contingent vocalization	.04	.05	0–.23
Hold	.34	.22	0–.69
Contingency to distress	.68	.27	0–1.00
Mutual visual regard	.09	.08	0–.24
Fuss cry (infant)	.20	.14	.02–.57
Nondistress vocalization (infant)	.17	.11	.02–.43
8 Months[a]			
Total talk	.15	.12	0–.43
Face-to-face talk	.04	.04	0–.16
Contingent vocalization	.07	.08	0–.31
Hold	.08	.09	0–.28
Contingency to distress	.79	.28	0–1.00
Mutual visual regard	.07	.06	0–.22
Fuss cry (infant)	.07	.05	0–.19
Nondistress vocalization (infant)	.34	.13	.13–.59
Floor freedom			
24 Months[b] (N = 25)			
Total talk	163.8	121.4	27–385
Reciprocal exchanges	53.0	41.0	10–155
Fuss cry (infant)	5.3	5.7	0–19
Nondistress vocalization (infant)	174.4	107.8	50–415
Time in intellectual tasks (secs.)	373.0	516.0	0–1605

[a] Percentage observation intervals of awake time.
[b] Frequency of events during 50-minute home observation.

any other group and girls from Spanish-speaking homes received significantly less. There was no evidence for differences in infant behavior (Tables 17 and 18).

There were differential interactions of Spanish-speaking caregivers with their firstborn and later-born infants. Birth-order differences were more apparent than gender differences. The pattern was the same as within the English-speaking sample, but emerged earlier, at 1 month rather than at 8 months, and included more behaviors. Firstborn infants, in contrast to later-born infants, from Spanish-speaking homes were held more, and held more in the en face position. Firstborn infants were also talked to more and their nondistress and distress vocalizations were responded to more contingently. At 8 months,

TABLE 17

Caregiver–Infant Interaction Scores and Significant Group Differences by Gender
and Birth order for Spanish-Speaking Sample: Summary Scores

| | Gender | | Birth order | |
| | Boys
(N = 16) | Girls
(N = 11) | Firstborn
(N = 13) | Later-born
(N = 14) |
Summary variable				
Caregiver–infant interaction[a]				
1 Month	99.7	91.6	109.4 *	84.4
8 Months	92.4	81.2	96.7 *	80.7
24 Months	100	94.6	96.7	98.8
Factor scores				
1 Month F1—social	.45	−.05	.57	−.06
8 Months F1—mutual social	−.12	−.40	.08	−.50
24 Months F1—positive attentiveness	−.21	−.23	−.03	−.44

[a] Higher scores are optimal. Score was standardized with a mean of 100 and a standard deviation of 20.

* Group difference $p < .01$.

firstborn infants within the Spanish sample, as within the English sample, vocalized more than did their later-born counterparts (Table 18).

Relationships between Infant Development and Caregiver–Infant Interaction

Caregiver–infant interaction at 1 month was modestly related to developmental test performance at 4 months and at 9 months (Table 19). In contrast to the English-speaking sample, infants who were held more at 1 month were more advanced developmentally at both 4 and 9 months. Further, infants who received more talking, who experienced more mutual visual regard, and whose distress was responded to more quickly, also performed more competently at 9 months. There were many more significant correlations in the first year of life between caregiver behavior and infant test performance in the Spanish- than in the English-speaking families. However, there were no links between infant behavior of fussing and crying or nondistress vocalizing and later test performance, whereas such links existed in the English-speaking sample (Table 20).

For both samples, more frequent reciprocal exchanges between the caregiver and the 2-year-old child was associated with more competent performance on the Stanford-Binet 3 years later.

TABLE 18
Caregiver–Infant Interaction Scores and Significant Group Differences by Gender
and Birth Order for Spanish-Speaking Sample: Individual Behaviors

Behavior	Gender		Birth order	
	Boys (N = 16)	Girls (N = 11)	Firstborn (N = 13)	Later-born (N = 14)
1 Month[a]				
Total talk	.14	.11	.18	* .08
Face-to-face talk	.05	.03	.06	* .02
Contingent vocalization	.04	.03	.07	* .01
Hold	.39	.26	.47	** .21
Contingency to distress	.72	.63	.79	* .58
Mutual visual regard	.10	.08	.14	** .05
Fuss cry (infant)	.22	.16	.21	.18
Nondistress vocalization (infant)	.18	.17	.19	.17
8 Months[a]				
Total talk	.18	* .10	.22	* .09
Face-to-face talk	.05	.03	.06	.03
Contingent vocalization	.09	* .04	.10	* .04
Hold	.08	.07	.10	.06
Contingency to distress	.83	.74	.92	* .68
Mutual visual regard	.08	.06	.10	.06
Fuss cry (infant)	.07	.06	.06	.07
Nondistress vocalization (infant)	.34	.34	.39	* .29
Floor freedom	.21	.11	.18	.17
24 Months[b]				
Total talk	187.6	136.2	183.9	140.5
Reciprocal exchanges	58.8	44.4	48.0	57.0
Fuss cry (infant)	5.9	4.5	6.6	4.4
Nondistress vocalization (infant)	163.4	187.2	203.1	140.8
Time in intellectual tasks (secs.)	406.0	323.5	338.2	400.4

[a] Percent of observation intervals of awake time.
[b] Frequency of events during 50-minute home observation.
* Group difference $p < .05$.
** Group difference $p < .01$.

Continuity in Responsive Caregiver–Infant Interaction and Child Test Performance The Spanish-speaking families in our study, with the least amount of education and the lowest SES of all ethnic groups, were similar to the lower-SES English-speaking sample in having only a few caregivers who were consistently responsive to their infants (Table 21).

Infants who received consistently impoverished social exchanges performed more poorly at age 2 years. Their disadvantage was not evident by age 5 years, however, whereas it was maintained in the English sample.

TABLE 19

Significant Correlations * between Caregiver–Infant Interaction Scores
and Developmental Tests for Spanish-Speaking Sample: Summary Scores

	Developmental assessment		
Summary variable	Gesell, 4 months ($N = 27$)	Gesell, 9 months ($N = 27$)	Gesell, 24 months ($N = 27$)
Caregiver–infant interaction			
1 Month		.57	
Factor score			
1 month F1—social	.54	.52	
8 months F1—mutual social		.54	
24 months F1—positive attentiveness			.73

* $p < .05.$

Discussion

Perinatal biological hazards, in our sample, had little impact, even on test performance within the first year. Early biological hazards did not correlate with test performance at any age. Furthermore, it did not appear that biological hazards caused an early developmental lag that was then outgrown, as mean scores for our subjects were not lower at 4 months than at 24 months.

Social factors were found to be as important to cognitive test performance of high-risk infants as previous research has indicated for normal, term infants. SES and its closely linked correlate, parental education, have been found to be major determinants of the cognitive development of children with and without perinatal complications after the age of 2 years (Deutsch, 1973; Drillien, 1964; Werner, Bierman, & French, 1971). Our findings are similar to those of most studies in finding no relationship between SES and infant test-performance in the first year, but a significant relationship by age 2 years and an even stronger relationship by age 5 for both males and females (Golden & Birns, 1976; McCall, Hogarty, & Hurlburt, 1972). The progressive decline from infancy to school age noted to occur for children from disadvantaged homes was apparent and over shadowed biological risk.

SES is a powerful marker both of the home environment and of cognitive test performance. Yet, SES by itself does not explain the complexities involved, nor does it explain the wide differences in cognitive test performance within an SES. Partialing out SES decreased, but did not negate the links between caregiver behavior and the child's later

TABLE 20

Significant Correlations* between Caregiver–Infant Interaction Scores
and Developmental Tests for Spanish-Speaking Sample: Individual Behaviors

	Developmental assessment			
Behavior	Gesell, 4 months $(N = 27)$	Gesell, 9 months $(N = 27)$	Gesell, 24 months $(N = 27)$	Stanford-Binet, 5 year $(N = 27)$
1 Month				
Total talk		.49		
Face-to-face talk		.44		
Contingent vocalization				
Hold	.58	.63		
Contingency to distress		.42		
Mutual visual regard		.41		
Fuss cry (infant)				
Nondistress vocalization (infant)				
8 Months				
Total talk		.77		
Face-to-face talk		.59		
Contingent vocalization		.57		
Hold				
Contingency to distress		.48		
Mutual visual regard		.62		
Fuss cry (infant)				
Nondistress vocalization (infant)				
Floor freedom				.58
24 Months				
Total talk			.57	
Reciprocal exchanges				.40
Fuss cry (infant)				
Time in intellectual tasks				

* $p < .05$.

TABLE 21

Developmental Scores by Degree of Responsive Caregiving
over Time for Spanish-Speaking Sample

Developmental assessment	Consistently responsive caregiving	N	Mean
Gesell, 24 months	No	20	91.9
	Yes	4	98.4
Stanford-Binet, 5 years	No	20	83.4
	Yes	4	84.0

cognitive test performance. Even after partialing out SES the majority of associations remained significant. The power of specific interactional patterns in affecting later cognitive test performance could not be explained, therefore, solely by the association with SES. Furthermore, partialing out SES increased the apparent contribution of the infant's early behavior to its later test performance. The results are consistent with the increasing evidence (Field, Hallock & Ting, 1978; Vaughn, Crichton, & Egeland, 1982; Vaughn, Taraldson, Crichton, & Egeland, 1980) that neonatal and early infancy behavioral organization have modest but significant predictive value for individual differences in later cognitive status. SES influences on development and parenting, however, may mask the infant's contribution, perhaps because the parent's contribution is more powerful than the infant's.

Families who differed in SES, but who interacted with their infants in similar ways were compared. The findings indicated that children who experienced consistently responsive interactions during their first 2 years of life—regardless of social class—performed significantly better at ages 2 and 5 years. Consistently responsive interactions were associated with high performance in both lower-SES and middle-SES children. Less responsive interactions were associated with poorer performance in both middle-SES and lower-SES children. The relationships were modest, however. Some children from lower-SES, English-speaking homes, with the most unresponsive caregivers, performed well, at average or above-average levels. Individual variability in test performance was large, not only across the entire sample, but within SES and within most interactional patterns. Interestingly enough, consistently responsive early caregiving in English-speaking homes acted not only to raise mean scores but also to reduce individual variability, as no scores below 100 were found in this group.

Detailing the sequential nature of the infant's experiences with the caregivers illuminated the question of whether early experiences contributed to later cognitive test performance, independent of later experience. Our data suggest that the optimality of the early social interactions did not influence later test-performance unless these experiences were maintained over time. Early experience contributed only through its association with later experience. The stability of effect then was dependent on periodic reinstatement of early experiences (Wachs & Cucinotta, 1971) or was directly related to the extent that the subsequent environment was reinforcing of given child characteristics (Yarrow, 1964). Inattention and lack of response from the social environment was deleterious regardless of the age at which it occurred. Rutter (1979) states, and we agree, that the evidence suggests that good experiences early do not protect children against the ill effects of later disadvantages. Children's cognitive test performance is sensitive to environmental change both early and later.

The relationship between caregiving and competency was only partly replicated in the Spanish-speaking sample. The differences were evident in two ways. First, for the Spanish-speaking sample, there were more associations between caregiving and first-year test performance. The degree to which the infant was held, the degree of contingency to distress and to nondistress vocalization, the degree of mutual visual regard, were significantly associated with enhanced test performance within the first year of life for the Spanish- but not the English-speaking sample. We speculate that the decreased amounts of such interactional behaviors within the Spanish-speaking group, in comparison to the English-speaking group, made individual differences in those behaviors more salient, because many families were below the minimum threshold.

A second difference was that the antecedent–subsequent relationships were of shorter duration in the Spanish-speaking sample and tended not to carry over to age 5 years. Children from more responsive homes did perform significantly better at age 2 years than did children with less responsive caregivers in both the English- and Spanish-speaking sample. By 5 years, however, all children within the Spanish-speaking group performed at a depressed level. Difficulties of bilingualism, cultural alienation, and the enormous stress and instabilities within the family may have swamped any individual differences associated with early experience. Or it may be that the Stanford-Binet, or any other intelligence test, is not an adequate measuring instrument for this sample at this age.

The contribution of infants to their own development may occur by eliciting differential caregiver behaviors or by modifying the response to experience. Infants, particularly boys, who spent a greater percentage of awake time fussing and crying performed less competently later. The effects on test performance did not appear to be mediated by adverse caregiver behavior as there was no correlation between caregiving and irritability. In a recent review, Bates (1980) found little evidence to support the proposition that difficult temperament causes adverse caregiver behavior, at least in the first 6 months of life. It is therefore tempting to speculate that the increased irritability was itself a sign of vulnerability within the infant.

On the other hand, increased nondistress vocalizing for girls and boys was associated with later increased competence in cognitive test performance. Nondistress vocalization is highly sensitive to social interaction (Rheingold, 1956; Rheingold & Bayley, 1959) and does occur with excitement, with pleasure, and with higher arousal levels (Jones & Moss, 1971; Kagan, 1969). Infants who are more vocal in their home environment may be at a more optimum arousal level and may be exposed to more enriched social experiences. Several investigators (Cameron, Livson, & Bayley, 1967; Kagan, 1971; McCall, *et al.*, 1972; Moore, 1968), but not all (Roe, 1978), have suggested that vocalization in infancy may have a special salience for females that it does not connote for males in predicting later cognitive test performance. We did not find this gender difference.

Some investigators, among them Kagan (1971) and Yang and Moss (1978), have suggested that caregiver behavior more powerfully influences girls' development, whereas boys' behavior may be more a function of congenital characteristics. We did find that the way in which caregivers interacted with girls during the first year of life was associated with the way in which girls performed on cognitive tests at ages 2 and 5 years, whereas few such relationships existed for boys. Moreover, the degree to which boys fussed or vocalized as young infants was related to later cognitive test performance. The findings were consistent with the hypothesis that gender differences exist in responsiveness to early social experience.

Another gender difference, the evident precocity of girls over boys, a difference often thought of as biological, was found in the English- and reversed in the Spanish-speaking sample. Caregivers in both samples showed differential treatment to boys and girls, but the direction of the differences was reversed in the two samples. Girls from English-speaking homes received significantly more contingent social interactions and girls from Spanish-speaking homes received significantly less. This set of results support an environmental, not a biological, gender difference.

In summary, we find that the early home environment does ameliorate biological risk. Yet, home environment explains only a small portion of the variation in test performance. We recognize that our measurements were limited. Perhaps changes in measuring procedures would have provided stronger relationships, or perhaps they would not, as all studies of disadvantaged children have noted wide variations in outcome (Rutter, 1979). Some children appear to be invulnerable to the most deprived homes and the most stressful experiences (Werner & Smith, 1982). The study of invulnerability and the factors which protect children, enabling them to develop normally in spite of increased hazards promises fruitful new findings.

Summary of Findings

1. Test performance was not associated with measures of perinatal complications but was related to social factors.
2. Group comparisons indicated that groups that received the most enriched, responsive caregiving also performed more competently.
   a. Lower-SES children showed progressive decline in cognitive test scores from 4 months to 9 months to 24 months to 5 years, whereas middle- or higher-SES children improved their test performance from 9 months to 2 years to 5 years.
   b. Middle- and upper-SES families talked more to the infant, even at 1 month, engaged in more mutual social exchanges at 8 months, and continued to be more positively attentive to the child at age 2 years. Lower-SES families were less able to maintain consistently responsive caregiving beyond the early months.
   c. First- and later-born children differed in test performance within the first year of life, but not beyond. Firstborn children were more developmentally advanced than were later-born children. The difference was evident by age 4 months within the Spanish- and at 9 months within the English-speaking sample.
   d. Early home environments differed for first- and later-born infants. Firstborn children experienced more talking, more contingency to distress, and more contingent response to nondistress vocalization.
   e. There were gender differences in test scores but the direction of differences differed in the English- and the Spanish-speaking sample. Within the English-speaking sample, girls performed more competently than boys at 9 and 24 months, whereas within the Spanish-speaking sample, boys were more competent than girls at 9 months. There were no gender differences at age 5 years.
   f. Caregivers interacted differently with boys and with girls but the direction of the differences diverged in the English- and Spanish-speaking sample. Essentially, girls being reared in English-speaking households experienced the richest and most responsive caregiving, whereas girls being reared in Spanish-speaking homes experienced the most deprived caregiving.

3. Further support for the link between caregiving and test performance was found within groups. Caregiver infant interactions were related to cognitive test performance, such that the more attentive and responsive caregivers had children who performed more competently. Within the English-speaking sample, caregiving in the first year related more to performance at age 2 years than to concurrent test performance. In contrast, within the Spanish-speaking sample, caregiving in the first year related *only* to concurrent test performance. Within the English-speaking sample, there were relations between 5-year test performance and earlier caregiver–infant interaction, whereas with the Spanish-speaking sample, such associations were fewer.

4. The infants' contribution to their own test performance, independent of caregiving, was indicated by correlations between infant irritability and infant nondistress-vocalizing in the first and second year and test scores. Within the English-speaking sample, infants who fussed less and vocalized more performed more competently.

Acknowledgments

We wish to thank Dr. Arthur H. Parmelee, the principal investigator for the longitudinal project from which these data were derived, for his continuing support. We also wish to thank the families and children who so willingly participated in the research. The study was supported by NIH-NICHD Contract No. 1–HD–3–2776 and William T. Grant Foundation Grant No. B771121. We also express appreciation to Irving B. Harris, whose support gave Leila Beckwith the opportunity to reflect on the meaning of social factors in the development of at-risk children.

References

Ainsworth, M. D. S., & Bell, S. M. Mother–infant interaction and the development of competence. In K. S. Connolly & J. S. Bruner (Eds.), *The growth of competence*. New York: Academic Press, 1973.

Bates, J. The concept of difficult temperament. *Merrill-Palmer Quarterly*, 1980, *26*, 299–318.

Beckwith, L. Relationships between attributes of mothers and their infants' IQ scores. *Child Development*, 1971, *42*, 1083–1097.

Beckwith, L., Cohen, S. E., Kopp, C. B., Parmelee, A. H. & Marcy, T. G. Caregiver–infant interaction and early cognitive development in preterm infants. *Child Development*, 1976, *47*, 579–598.

Beckwith, L., & Cohen, S. E. Interactions of preterm infants. In T. M. Field, S. Goldberg, D. Stern, & A. Sostek (Eds.), *Interactions of high-risk infants and children.* New York: Academic Press, 1980.

Caldwell, B. M., & Honig, A. Approach: A procedure to code responses of adults and children. *Catalogue of Selected Documents of Psychology,* 1971, *1*:1.

Cameron, J., Livson, N., & Bayley, N. Infant vocalizations and their relationship to mature intelligence. *Science,* 1967, *157,* 331–333.

Caplan, G., Mason, E. A., & Kaplan, D. M. Four studies of crises in parents of prematures. *Community Mental Health Journal,* 1965, *1,* 149–161.

Caputo, D. V., Goldstein, K. M., & Taub, H. B. The development of prematurely born children through middle childhood. In T. M. Field, A. M. Sostek, S. Goldberg, & H. H. Shuman (Eds.), *Infants born at risk.* New York: Spectrum, 1979.

Clarke-Stewart, K. A. Interactions between mothers and their young children: Characteristics and consequences. *Monographs of the Society for Research in Child Development,* 1973, *6–7.* (Serial No. 153)

Clarke-Stewart, K. A., Van Der Stoep, L. P., & Killian, G. A. Analyses and replication of mother–child relations at two years of age. *Child Development,* 1979, *50,* 777–793.

Clausen, J. A., & Williams, J. R. Sociological correlates of child behavior. In H. W. Stevenson (Ed.), *Child psychology. The sixty-second yearbook of the National Society for the Study of Education.* Chicago: University of Chicago Press, 1963.

Cohen, S. E. Maternal employment and mother–child interaction. *Merrill-Palmer Quarterly,* 1978, *24,* 189–197.

Cohen, S. E., & Beckwith, L. Caregiving behaviors and early cognitive development as related to ordinal position in preterm infants. *Child Development,* 1977, *48,* 152–157.

Cohen, S. E., Sigman, M., Parmelee, A. H., & Beckwith, L. Neonatal risk factors in preterm infants. *Applied Research in Mental Retardation,* 1982, *3,* 265–278.

Cronbach, L. H. Five decades of public controversy over mental testing. *American Psychologist,* 1971, *30,* 1.

Deutsch, C. P. Social class and child development. In B. M. Caldwell & H. N. Ricciuti (Eds.), *Review of child development research* (Vol. 3). Chicago: University of Chicago Press, 1973.

Drillien, C. M. *The growth and development of the prematurely born infant.* Baltimore: Williams & Wilkens, 1964.

Elardo, R., Bradley, R., & Caldwell, B. M. The relation of infants' home environments to mental test performance from six to thirty-six months: A longitudinal analysis. *Child Development,* 1975, *46,* 71–76.

Field, T. M. The three Rs of infant–adult interactions: Rhythms repertoires and responsivity. *Journal of Pediatric Psychology,* 1978, *3,* 131–136.

Field, T., Hallock, N., & Ting, G. A first-year follow-up of high risk infants: Formulating a cumulative risk index. *Child Development,* 1978, *49,* 119–131.

Goldberg, S. Premature birth: Consequences for the parent–infant relationship. *American Scientist,* 1979, *67,* 214–222.

Golden, M., & Birns, B. Social class and infant intelligence. In M. Lewis (Ed.), *Origins of intelligence.* New York: Plenum 1976.

Hunt, J. V. Environmental risk in fetal and neonatal life and measured infant intelligence. In M. Lewis (Ed.), *Origins of intelligence.* New York: Plenum 1976.

Hunt, J. V. Predicting intellectual disorder in childhood for preterm infants with birthweight below 1501 gm. In S. L. Friedman & M. Sigman (Eds.), *Preterm birth and psychological development.* New York: Academic Press, 1981.

Jones, S. J., & Moss, H. A. Age, state and maternal behavior associated with infant vocalizations. *Child Development,* 1971, *42,* 1039–1051.

Kagan, J. Continuity in cognitive development during the first year. *Merrill-Palmer Quarterly*, 1969, *15*, 101–119.

Kagan, J. *Change and continuity in infancy*. New York: Wiley, 1971.

Kaplan, D., & Mason, E. A. Maternal reactions to premature birth viewed as an acute emotional disorder. *American Journal of Orthopsychiatry*, 1960, *50*, 539–552.

Klaus, M. A., & Kennell, J. H. *Maternal–infant bonding*. St. Louis, MO: Mosby, 1976.

Leifer, A. D., Leiderman, P. H., Barnett, C. R., & Williams, J. A. Effects of mother–infant separation on maternal attachment behavior. *Child Development*, 1972, *43*, 1203–1218.

Lewis, M. What do we mean when we say, "Infant Intelligence Scores"? A sociopolitical question. In M. Lewis (Ed.), *Origins of intelligence*. New York: Plenum, 1976.

McCall, R. B. Toward an epigenetic conception of mental development in the first three years of life. In M. Lewis (Ed.), *Origins of intelligence*. New York: Plenum, 1976.

McCall, R. B., Hogarty, P., & Hurlburt, N. Transitions in infant sensorimotor development and the prediction of childhood IQ. *American Psychologist*, 1972, *27*, 728–748.

Minde, K. Bonding of parents to premature infants: Theory and practice. In P. M. Taylor (Ed.), *Monographs in Neonatology Series*. New York: Grune & Stratton, 1980.

Moore, T. Language and intelligence: A longitudinal study of the first eight years (Vol. 2). *Human Development*, 1968, *11*, 1–24.

Parmelee, A. H., Kopp, C. B., & Sigman, M. Selection of developmental assessment techniques for infants at risk. *Merrill-Palmer Quarterly*, 1976, *22*, 177–199.

Parmelee, A. H., Sigman, M., Kopp, C. B., & Haber, A. The concept of a cumulative risk score for infants. In N. R. Ellis (Ed.), *Aberrant development in infancy: Human and animal studies*. Hillsdale, NJ: Erlbaum, 1975.

Rheingold, H. L. The modification of social responsiveness in institutional babies. *Monographs of the Society for Research in Child Development*, 1956, *21*, (Serial No. 2)

Rheingold, H. L., & Bayley, N. The later effects of an experimental modification of mothering. *Child Development*, 1959, *30*, 362–372.

Roe, K. V. Infants' mother–stranger discrimination at 3 months as a predictor of cognitive development at 3 and 5 years. *Developmental Psychology*, 1978, *14*, 191–192.

Rutter, M. Maternal deprivation, 1972–1978: New Findings, new concepts, new approaches. *Child Development*, 1979, *50*, 283–305.

Sameroff, A., & Chandler, M. Infant casualty and the continuum of infant caretaking. In F. D. Horowitz, E. M. Hetherington, M. Siegel, & S. Scarr Salapatek (Eds.), *Review of Child Development Research* (Vol 4). University of Chicago Press, Chicago, 1975.

Siegel, L. S. Reproductive, perinatal, and environmental factors as predictors of the cognitive and language development of preterm and full infants. *Child Development*, in press.

Sigman, M., Cohen, S. E., & Forsythe, A. The relationship of early infant measures to later development. *In* S. L. Friedman & M. Sigman (Eds.), *Preterm birth and psychological development*. New York: Academic Press, 1981.

Sigman, M., & Parmelee, A. H. Longitudinal evaluation of the high-risk infant. In T. M. Field, A. M. Sostek, S. Goldberg, & H. H. Shuman (Eds.), *Infants born at risk*. New York: Spectrum, 1979.

Vaughn, B. E., Crichton, L., & Egeland, B. Individual differences in qualities of caregiving during the first six months of life: Antecedents in maternal and infant behavior during the newborn period. *Infant Behavior and Development*, 1982, *5*, 77–95.

Vaughn, B. E., Taraldson, B., Crichton, L., & Egeland, B. Relationships between neonatal behavioral organization and infant behavior during the first year of life. *Infant Behavior and Development*, 1980, *3*, 47–66.

Wachs, T., & Cucinotta, P. *The effects of enriched neonatal experiences upon later cognitive functioning.* Paper presented at Society for Research in Child Development, Minneapolis MN, April 1–4, 1971.

Werner, E. E., Bierman, J. M., & French, F. E. *The children of Kauai. A longitudinal study from the prenatal period to age ten.* Honolulu: University of Hawaii Press, 1971.

Werner, E. E., & Smith, R. S. *Vulnerable but invincible: A study of resilient children.* New York: McGraw Hill, 1982.

White, B. L., & Watts, J. C. *Experience and environment: Major influences on the development of the young child* (Vol 1). Englewood Cliffs, NJ: Prentice-Hall, 1973.

Wiener, G., Rider, R. V., W. Oppel, L. K. Fischer, & Harper, P. A. Correlates of low-birth-weight: Psychological status at 6–7 years of age. *Pediatrics,* 1965, *35,* 434–444.

Yang, R. K., & Moss, H. A. Neonatal precursors of infant behavior. *Developmental Psychology,* 1978, *14,* 607–613.

Yarrow, L. J. Personality consistency and change: An overview of some conceptual and methodological issues. *Vita Humana,* 1964, *7,* 67–72.

Yarrow, L. J., Rubenstein, J. L., Pederson, F. A., & Jankowski, J. J. Dimensions of early stimulation and their differential effects on infant development. *Merrill-Palmer Quarterly,* 1972, *18,* 205–218.

8

Proximal Experience and Early
Cognitive–Intellectual Development:
The Social Environment*

Theodore D. Wachs

Research Overview

In science, until sufficient data are collected, incorrect models (myths) of how things work are common. These myths are often strongly held and defended until sufficient evidence is gathered to generate new models that can replace the old ones. Thus, as Hunt (1961) demonstrated, in the study of behavioral development, for many centuries the doctrine of preformationism held sway. It was not until microscopes were invented and scientists were able to demonstrate that there was no homunculus contained in either the sperm or egg that the preformationistic myth disappeared. Similar examples can be shown in the fields of astronomy (the geocentric theory) and chemistry (the phlogiston theory). In most cases these myths are harmless way stations, marking our incomplete understanding of a phenomena (though these myths can be harmful if they are put into practice—see the problems associated with attempts to develop an agricultural system, based on the myth of acquired characteristics [Medvedev, 1969]).

In the area of human early experience we are only now beginning to realize that one of our existing models about the nature of early environmental action may, in fact, be nothing more than a myth. Specifically what I refer to is global environmental action. The myth of *global early environmental action* refers to the belief that "good" environmental stimulation will uniformly enhance all aspects of cognitive development at all ages for all children and that "bad"

*Funding for this project was made possible by a research grant to the author from NICHD (HD-04514) and from a David Ross Grant from Purdue University.

273

environmental stimulation will uniformly depress all aspects of development at all ages for all children (Wachs, 1981). Hunt (1977) traces the genesis of this myth to the early impact of psychoanalysis and Gestalt psychology upon the field of developmental psychology. A further historical determinant (Wachs &Gruen, 1982) lies in the relationship between individual (correlational) and general (experimental) psychology. As Cronbach (1967) has noted, after 1920, the experimental approach to psychology clearly became dominant. Within this mainstream approach, individual differences were essentially regarded as nothing more than error variance.

The myth that early environmental action was essentially global in nature was supported by the methodology used to study human early experience, particularly in the period prior to 1960. Differences between lower and upper socioeconomic status (SES) groups or between institutionalized and home-reared children, on global intelligence tests such as the Bayley or the Stanford-Binet, were used to support the myth that the environment acted in a unidimensional, all or none framework, for all children. Quasiexperimental nursery school or early intervention studies, where global experiences were applied to heterogeneous samples of children, were also used to support the myth. If significant differences were shown between experimental and control groups, the procedure was considered a success, regardless of how many children in the intervention sample failed to show changes; if an acceptable level of statistical significance was not reached, the early intervention procedure was considered a failure, regardless of how many children in the intervention group actually responded. Thus, the notion of functional equivalence of positive and negative environmental parameters continued to receive implicit support.

As with most myths, existing contradictory evidence was essentially ignored. Thus, data from cultural anthropology, indicating highly specific relationships between specific geographic or climatological conditions and the development of specific personality or cultural patterns (Moos, 1973), had little impact on the field of early experience.

What initially caused behavioral scientists to question the myth of global early environmental action was the growing critical mass of contrary theory and evidence. In a major review Wohlwill (1973) pointed out that early experience may subsume a number of specific conditions, all of which may have differential influences upon development. Along the same lines, in the field of intelligence, developmental studies clearly indicated the inadequacy of conceptualizing intelligence as a quantitatively changing global factor (McCall, Eichorn, & Hogarty, 1977). The work of Thomas and Chess (1976), in the area of early temperament, suggested the possibility that characteristics inherent in the individual may mediate the effects of the environment upon development.

In addition to theory and basic research data, what ultimately was most devastating to the global model of early environmental action was the failure of intervention studies based on this model. In these studies the avowed goal was to use enriched environmental stimulation as a means of overcoming social–cultural retardation. To accomplish this task, heterogeneous masses of stimulation, assumed to be good, were given to heterogeneous groups of children. In contrast to the major cognitive gains predicted to occur from these interventions, reviews indicated, at best, modest gains for children in these programs (Belsky & Steinberg, 1978). Even more critically, available reviews indicated a tremendous range of reaction of individual children to intervention. Some children showed major gains following intervention, while other children in the same classroom, showed little gain or even showed losses (Williams, 1977). Some researchers, perhaps reluctant to give up a global model, essentially threw the baby out with the bath water by questioning the validity of early experience as a parameter relevant to development (e.g., Kagan, Kearsley, & Zelazo, 1978). However, it now seems clear that the fault was in the model utilized and not the assumption that early experience is relevant to development (Wachs & Gruen, 1982). Interventions based on a global model of environmental action make sense only if the early environment is, in fact, global in nature. If the pattern of early environmental action is not global in nature, global interventions make little sense.

If, in fact, the early environment is not global in nature, the question must then be raised as to what is the nature of early environmental action. What we have proposed is a Bifactor Environmental Action Model (BEAM), (Wachs, 1979; Wachs & Gruen, 1982). Our BEAM model assumes two classes of environmental stimulation. The first class subsumes a *small subset of environmental parameters,* which influence *most areas of development* for most children in a given age span. The second class encompasses the *majority of environmental parameters,* all of which are *highly specific* in their influence on development. As part of our BEAM model for the second class of environmental stimuli, what we have proposed are three hypotheses about the nature of early environmental action.

1. *The hypothesis of Environmental Specificity:* It is postulated that different aspects of the environment will influence different aspects of cognitive development. This is in contrast to a global model

of early environmental action, which postulates *functional equivalence of all environmental stimuli* within a given class, with given classes being defined as either good or bad. In general, reviews of available evidence (Hunt, 1979; Wachs & Gruen, 1982) have indicated strong support for the environmental specificity model over that of functional environmental equivalence.

2. *The hypothesis of Age Specificity:* Specific aspects of the environment will have differential influences on development depending on the age at which the child encounters them. This is in sharp contrast to a global model of environmental action, which postulates functional equivalence for environmental stimulation encountered at different ages. Again, reviews of the early experience literature (Hunt, 1979; Wachs & Gruen, 1982) indicate strong support for the age specificity hypothesis, as opposed to global models of environmental action.

3. *The hypothesis of Organismic Specificity:* It is hypothesized that the impact of the environment on development will be mediated by the individual characteristics of the child upon whom the environment impinges. This hypothesis is in sharp contrast to a global environmental hypothesis, which postulates that specific environmental stimuli will have a similar impact on all children. Theoretically the hypothesis of organismic specificity resembles the distinction made between objective stimulation and effective environment (Uzgiris, 1980). Although available evidence is scarce on this hypothesis, what evidence is available (Wachs & Gruen, 1982) suggests that individual differences in reaction to the environment clearly do exist.

In addition to evidence supporting the existence of the preceding three types of specificity, some evidence is also available indicating that interactions between the different types of specificity also exist. Thus, evidence is available indicating the existence of age × environmental specificity (Radin, 1972; 1973; Siegel, 1979), of environment × organismic specificity (Honzik, 1967a, 1967b) and age × environment × organismic specificity (Wachs, 1979).

One major reason why there is only limited evidence available, particularly in terms of the organismic specificity hypothesis and of the existence of interactions among the various types of specificity, is that, until recently, few studies were designed to test for specificity. To adequately test all aspects of specificity a study must contain four design features: (1)*the use of multidimensional environmental predictors and multidimensional criteria;* (2)*the study of environment–development relationships at more than one age level, for both predictors and cri-*

teria; (3)comparison of environment–development relationships across distinct subgroups of children; and *(4)a comparison of environmental variables across the subgroups.* The last feature is necessary to determine if subgroup differences in environment–development relationships are due to genuine differential reactivity or to different environments being provided for the different subgroups.

Historically, most human early experience studies looked at unidimensional environmental (SES) and cognitive (IQ) measures, at a single age level, across a total sample. More recently, studies have incorporated some, but not all, of the preceding design features. For example, research from the Berkeley (Bayley & Schaefer, 1964) and Fels (Kagan & Freeman, 1963) studies, as well as the excellent work of Caldwell and her associates (Elardo, Bradley, & Caldwell, 1975; Bradley, Caldwell, & Elardo, 1979) have involved different aspects of the environment measured at different ages; however, these studies used global measures of cognitive development, thus ruling out any possibility of obtaining environmental specificity or any interactions involving environmental specificity. Other studies have used multi-dimensional predictors and criteria with different subgroups of children, but measured the environment only at one age (Honzik, 1967a, 1967b; Yarrow, Rubenstein, & Pedersen, 1975), thus eliminating any possibility of obtaining age-specificity data or any interactions involving age specificity. Studies using multidimensional predictors and criteria at different ages (Beckwith & Cohen, 1978; Beckwith, Cohen, Kopp, Parmelee, & Marcy, 1976) have not looked at environment development relationships across different subgroups of children. Studies looking at these relationships across different subgroups have either not studied their groups longitudinally (Pedersen, Rubenstein, & Yarrow, 1979; Wachs & Gandour, in press; Wachs & Peters-Martin, 1981) or did not use multidimensional predictors and criteria (MacPhee & Ramey, 1981).

Our review indicates only one study available that appears to meet all of the required design features. This study (Wachs, 1979) looked at the relationship between specific aspects of the infant's physical environment and specific aspects of Piagetian sensorimotor development for males and females between 12 and 24 months of age. What our results revealed were highly complex relationships between environment, age, gender, and development. These results supported not only the existence of the three types of specificity, but also the existence of various interactions between the different types of specificity. These results were, however, restricted only to physical environmental parameters and were thus somewhat out of the "mainstream" of human early experience research, which is primarily concerned with social interaction. Whether the same types of specificity and their interactions can also be found for the social environment is a question we hope to answer in the present chapter. Specifically, the results reported in this chapter are based on measurement of specific aspects of male and female sensorimotor development in the period between 12 and 24 months of age. Five questions were asked in the present research:

1. Does the overall pattern of environment–development relationships fit the pattern predicted by the BEAM model, as opposed to the pure specificity or global models of environmental action? If the pattern fits either the BEAM or the specificity models, then,
2. Is there evidence for environmental specificity in the relationship between social environment and sensorimotor development: that is, do different aspects of the social environment predict different aspects of sensorimotor development?
3. Is there evidence for age specificity: that is, Does the relationship between the social environment and sensorimotor development change at different ages?
4. Is there evidence for organismic specificity: that is, Is the relationship between the social environment and sensorimotor development different for males and females and, if so, is this due to specificity or to differences in the environments of males and females?
5. Is there evidence for interactions between the three types of specificity: Do different aspects of the social environment predict different aspects of sensorimotor development for male and female infants at different ages?

Method

Subjects

Subjects were 38 infants who were 11 months of age upon entrance into the study. Of the 38 infants, 24 were male, 14 were female.[1] All infants were within normal limits on gross motor development. Of the

[1] Discrepancy in sample sizes between the genders in our project was due mainly to our unfounded assumption that, by random sampling, the number of males and females would be equated. This assumption, for unknown reasons, was not borne out, causing

infants, 37 were white, and one infant was a product of a black–white marriage. To ensure a wide variety of home environments, infants were drawn from two sources. Nine of the infants (24%) came from the roles of the Tippecanoe County (Indiana) Welfare Department, having mothers who were supported by Aid to Families with Dependent Children (AFDC). The remaining 29 were obtained through random sampling of births in hospitals in the Tippecanoe County area. Infants in this group came from a wide variety of socioeconomic backgrounds ranging from lower-SES unskilled laborers through offspring of university faculty.[2]

Of the 38 infants in the sample, a total of nine dropped out (3 males, 6 females) before participating in the full 12 months of the project. Preliminary analyses revealed no systematic differences, in either home environments or developmental levels, between those infants remaining in the project and those dropping out.

---

an underrepresentation of females. One consequence of this underrepresentation of females was that it was more difficult to obtain statistically significant results for females. Hence, the greater number of significant environment-development correlations for males does not reflect a greater male sensitivity to the environment; rather, it reflects the larger male sample in our study.

[2] The editor of this volume recommended that all contributors utilize SES as part of their analytic strategy. I strongly disagree with this recommendation. SES may be useful in ensuring that there is a wide range of potential environments available, but as Yarrow et al. (1975) concluded; "Social class membership per se does not effect the infant's development; rather, it is the proximal variables, the kind of stimulation and pattern of care giving that are important." Our review of SES as a methodological factor (Wachs & Gruen, 1982) clearly indicates a tremendous diversity in environments even for children within the same SES. Further, available evidence comparing the predictive powers of SES versus more proximal measures of the environment (again, see Wachs & Gruen, 1982 for a review of this literature) clearly indicates that significant variance is associated primarily with directly measured environmental parameters and not with SES. It could be argued that SES is relevant as a predictor in terms of differential genotype, biomedical history, or nutritional status being associated with SES. A model for differential genotypes associated with SES has been demonstrated at the infrahuman level (Thoday & Gibson, 1970). At the human level, the change in gene frequency necessary to provide this type of differential genotype is a function of centuries, rather than of decades, and thus is not likely to be relevant at present. A greater incidence of risk conditions such as preterm birth has been demonstrated for lower-SES infants (Sameroff & Chandler, 1975). Because such biomedical problems influence motor, as well as cognitive, development and because our sample was within normal limits on gross motor development, this criticism does not appear to be relevant for our population. The impact of chronic mild malnutrition upon development appears to be mediated by environmental factors, as well as by nutritional status (Brozek, 1978), and hence would not appear to be of major relevance to our study. For these reasons, we have chosen not to utilize SES as a predictor.

Instruments

Infant's social environments were characterized using Section IV Codes of the Purdue Home Stimulation Inventory (PHSI). This inventory attempts to categorize the infant's social interactions through observations of the environment and child–adult interactions. In developing the PHSI we were not concerned with developing a theoretically coherent instrument; rather, we attempted to develop an instrument that would tap a variety of potentially relevant social- environment parameters. Thus, our social-environment codes were derived both from items in the early experience literature that have proven relevant to development, and from social interaction parameters which, theoretically, were postulated as being potentially relevant for cognitive development.

As initially developed, PHSI-IV consisted of 126 social interaction codes. Twenty of these codes were subsequently dropped, due to inadequate interobserver reliability (all codes with reliabilities below .45 were dropped). Another 13 codes were dropped due to a lack of variability in scoring, while 9 codes were dropped due to conceptual overlap with other codes. Finally, 24 code-items were condensed into more global code-scores. This left us with 60 observational codes. These 60 observational codes had a median interobserver reliability of .85 (range, .45–1.00). (If we include all items, including those initially dropped for a lack of reliability the median interobserver reliability = .71). A description, code number, and interobserver reliability for each of our 60 items can be seen in Table 1.

Measurement of infant's cognitive intellectual development was based on the infant's level of performance on the Uzgiris–Hunt Infant

TABLE 1
Items, Item Codes, and Interrater Reliabilities for PHSI–IV

Item code	Item	Interrater r
IE Series	Each time child makes an exploratory response to household objects, toys, books, code IE1–IE4:	
IE1	Sibs interfere.	.98
IE2	Adults interfere.	.96
IE3	No interference.	.76
IE4	Child's exploration encouraged.	.88
LS3S	Spontaneous sib vocalizations to child (number).	.98
LS3A	Spontaneous adult vocalizations to child (number).	.98
LS4A	Times object named for child.	.92
LS4B	Times object known to child is referred to.	.82
LS4C	Times child's ongoing activity named.	.80

TABLE 1 (*Continued*)

Item code	Item	Interrater *r*
DSI Series	Each time child vocalizes, code DS1–DS2:	
DS1	Individual vocalizing is actively doing something, but not with child.	.95
DS2	Individual vocalizing is actively doing something with child.	.95
LS5 Series	Each time child vocalizes, code LS5-1–LS5-T:	
LS5-1	There is no one present to respond to child's vocalization.	.50
LS5-2	Adult or older sib is present, but does not respond.	.66
LS5-3a	Nonverbal response to childs vocalization.	.76
LS5-4b	Child vocalization repeated by adult or older sib.	.82
LS5-4d	Child vocalization expanded by adult or older sib.	.86
LS5-4e	Child vocalization responded to by comment.	.93
LS5-4f	Child vocalization responded to by question.	.48
LS5-T	Total number of verbal responses to child vocalization.	*
VG	Verbal garbage: LS3S + LS3A/LS4A + LS4B + LS4C	*
VS13a	Number of times objects given or shown to child.	.80
VS13b	Number of times food or drink given to child.	.97
VS14b	Number of times how something works demonstrated or explained to child.	.71
VS15	Duration of time demonstration–explanation takes place	.57
HK1	Number of times child picked up and held.	.67
HK2	Duration of time child picked up and held.	.49
HK3a	Amount of time child actively played or interacted with.	.98
HK3b	Amount of time adult actively watches child.	.71
CE3 Series	Note number of times child tries to engage adult attention, code CE3R–CE3P	
CE3R	Adult rejects child's efforts.	1.00
C3EI	Adult ignores child's efforts.	.73
CE3P	Adult responds positively to child's efforts.	.65
CE4 Series	Adult requests to child and child reacts, code CE4R–CE4P	
CE4R	Adult rejects child's reactions.	.71
CE4I	Adult ignores child's reactions.	.57
CE4P	Adult responds positively to child's reaction.	.71
CE7-1	Times child in distress but adult not in room.	1.00
CE7-7	Times child in distress and adult responds to relieve distress.	.84
SC2	Amount of time until parent responds to relieve child's distress.	.66
S1	Units where parent interactions with child characterized by attempts at coercing child.	.92

(*continued*)

TABLE 1 (*Continued*)

Item code	Item	Interrater r
S2a	Units where parent interactions with child characterized by nonverbal demonstrations.	.47
S2b	Units where parent interactions with child characterized by nonspecific learning experiences.	.91
S2c	Units where parent interactions with child characterized by use of object names.	.96
S2d	Units where parent interactions with child characterized by specific learning experiences.	.75
S2T	S2a + S2b + S2c + S2d.	[a]
S3	Units where parent interactions with child characterized by denial of child's actions or requests.	.70
S4	Units where parent interactions with child characterized by acceding to child's actions or requests.	.60
S5	Units where parent interactions with child characterized by comments to child.	.90
S6	Units where parent interactions with child characterized by questions to child.	.98
S7	Units where parent interactions with child characterized by nonverbal interactions.	.81
S12	Units where parent interactions with child characterized by nurturance activities.	.45
S13	Units where parent interactions with child characterized by praise of child.	.99
SCE series	For parental instructional attempts with child, code SCE1–SCE2.	
SCE1	Instructional strategies used are very explicit.	.87
SCE2	Instructional strategies used are vague.	.82
SC3B	Units where parent shows child how to make discriminations.	.94
SC4B	Units where training stimuli used with child are not distinctive.	.94
PA Series	For each time unit, code PA123–PA67	
PA123	Parent affect characterized as positive.	.80
PA4	Parent affect characterized as neutral.	.87
PA67	Parent affect characterized as negative.	.81
PI Series	For each time unit, P12–P45	
PI12	Parent investment toward child characterized as low.	.91
PI45	Parent investment toward child characterized as moderate.	.56
NA	Units where no adult in same room with child.	.98

[a] Reliability is a function of the component units of the total score.

Psychological Development Scale (IPDS—Uzgiris & Hunt, 1975). The IPDS was developed in an attempt to operationalize and standardize the techniques used by Piaget in his study of intellectual development. As originally developed, the IPDS had seven ordinal subscales; in our work, for both conceptual and empirical reasons (Wachs & Hubert, 1981), we have separated out Foresight from Means–Ends performance. Thus, as we used the IPDS, eight separately scored subscales were employed. These are (1) Object Permanence, (2) Development of Means for Achieving Desired Environmental Events; (3) Development of Foresight; (4) Development of Schemes Relating to Objects; (5) Development of an Understanding of Causality; (6) Construction of the Object in Space; (7) the Development of Vocal Imitation; (8) the Development of Gestural Imitation. Each subscale consists of a number of separate ordinal steps, with each step delineating a stage of the ability measured by the subscale. As constructed, each of the IPDS subscales has significant observer reliability and the ordinality required for a Piaget-based infant scale (Uzgiris & Hunt, 1975). Evidence on construct validity and other psychometric aspects of the IPDS are reviewed by Uzgiris (1976).

Procedure

Initial contact with the parents of subjects was made when the child was 11 months of age. Several preliminary observations were made between 11 and 12 months to get children and parents acclimated to being observed. From 12 through 24 months of age, all infants were formally observed in their own homes (or in the homes of babysitters or relatives when the child was in one of these settings during it's scheduled observation), twice a month, for a period of 45 minutes per observation. Observations took place over a wide variety of temporal settings (daytime, evening, mealtimes). Observations consisted of the observer following the infant with a portable tape recorder, dictating into the tape recorder all child–environment, child–person interactions. These observations were transcribed and then coded, using the PHSI codes. A second observer was present during 10% of the observations to obtain reliability data. During observations, parents were requested to go about their normal routines; after every 15 minutes of observation, the observer would stop recording and would check off the appropriate categories for ongoing aspects of the infant's physical environment, as measured by Section III of the PHSI (for results on impact of the physical environment, see Wachs, 1978; 1979). To minimize observer effects by having the observer as familiar as possible, the same individual observed a child during the 12 months the child was in the project.

Available evidence suggests that while initial interaction distortions may occur as a result of the presence of an observer (Zegiob, Arnold, & Forehand, 1975), with repeated observations, the bias introduced by the presence of an observer is minimized (Yarrow, 1963; Weick, 1968), particularly if infants or young children are used as subjects (Lytton, 1973). These results were supported by anecdotal reports of our observers. These indicated that by the time our actual observations had begun, both parents and infants had clearly acclimated to the presence of an observer, as indicated by the presence of marker variables such as the occurrence of negative parent–child interactions in the presence of the observer (Lytton, 1973).

The IPDS was administered at 3 month (± 4 days) intervals, starting when the child was 12 months of age. All administrations were done in the child's home. More than one testing session was used if needed, though the overwhelming majority of IPDS data was collected in one test session. To avoid halo effects, the individual who observed the child was not the same one who tested the child. Further, whenever possible, the individual who initially tested the child did not retest the child until at least 6 months later.

Statistical Analysis

For each PHSI code, the data was collected into 3-month time blocks; 12–14, 15–17, 18–20, and 21–23 months. By basing environmental codes on repeated measurements, this procedure minimizes the chances of a single extreme event unduly influencing results. Further, this procedure meant that, although the ratio of subjects to code items was well below what would be normally desirable, each environmental codes-score in a given time-block was based on 270 minutes of observation. The problem of low-frequency items was minimized by dropping items with restricted variability; this mainly included items with a low frequency of occurrence.

Criterion variables were the child's level of performance on each of the eight IPDS subscales at each 3-month interval. For each IPDS subscale, the child's level of performance was the highest level a child achieved on that particular subscale, plus an additional proficiency score ranging from .1 to .3. The additional proficiency score was based on the procedure used by Wachs, Uzgiris, and Hunt (1971), and reflected the variability among infants in the number of trials it took infants to achieve criterion at a particular level on a specific IPDS sub-scale.

In analyzing our data, we first ran product–moment correlations among all PHSI variables within a given time block, against the infants IPDS performance at all subsequent test ages.[3] These analyses were computed separately for each gender. As one might expect, this analysis lead to the generation of large-scale correlational matrices and the possibility of significant chance correlations. One approach to the problem of large-scale matrices is to use multivariate statistics to reduce the data. Unfortunately, almost all multivariate procedures assume large sample sizes as a means of avoiding unreliability of findings due to shifting of weights (McCall, 1970). However, large sample sizes are precluded by the methodology utilized here, which involved intensive and repeated observations on a small number of subjects. Preliminary reduction of data through factor analytic techniques would share many of the same problems as use of multivariate techniques (Wachs & Gruen, 1982) and is thus not desireable with small samples.

A second approach to minimizing the existence of a Type I error with large scale correlational matrices is the cutting score approach, which we have utilized previously in our early experience research (Wachs, 1978, 1979; Wachs et al., 1971). The cutting score approach is not a statistical technique. It is rather a logical approach to the problem of avoiding significant chance correlations in a large-scale correlational matrix. The cutting score approach is based on the assumption that, in correlating environment with development, *items that are actually related to development will show a systematic and consistent pattern of relationships*. Items that are related by chance will show scattered and inconsistent relationships. This assumption may be invalid where both predictor and criterion variables show a high level of cross-time stability, because this allows the existence of artifactually consistent patterns of correlations. This situation does not occur in our data. The PHSI shows only moderate cross- time stability. There was little stability for the IPDS over time.[4] This lack of stability for

[3] Our presentation and discussion of results will be unidirectional, in the sense of relating environment to subsequent developmental level. An alternative approach would be to reverse the direction of lag and relate developmental level to subsequent environment. Our design allows us to do this; given the concerns of the present chapter on models of environmental action, any consideration of the reverse lag data must await a future publication.

[4] For males, the median PHSI stability correlation was .47 with the range from −.39 to .95. For females, the median PHSI stability correlation was .50, with the range from −.75 to .94. Stability data for the IPDS has been reported previously (Wachs, 1979). Readers wishing a detailed table containing stability data as well as means and standard deviations for each PHSI item can obtain this information by writing to the author.

the IPDS seems to be a function of qualitative changes in the nature of sensorimotor intelligence over the second year of life (Wachs & Hubert, 1981).

After obtaining the correlational matrix the second step of data analysis consisted of establishing a cutting score for each matrix. To maximize the importance of those items showing a pattern of relationships with development, for each IPDS subscale, the mean number of significant correlations of PHSI items with the subscale was obtained. The standard deviation of this distribution of significant items was also obtained. *Only those PHSI items having a frequency of significant correlations with a particular IPDS subscale at or about the* cut-off score *(mean plus one standard deviation [rounded to the nearest whole number] were considered as actually being related to development and considered for discussion.* In those cases where the *unrounded cut-off score* came to less than 2, the matrix was considered to be nonsignificant and was not discussed. Thus, for male object permanence that mean number of significant correlations across all PHSI items was 1.12; the standard deviation was 1.64. This meant that, for male permanence, the rounded cut-off score was set at 3. As a result, for males, only those PHSI item having 3 or more significant correlations with permanence (out of 10 possible significant correlations), were considered for discussion. Following identification of items on the basis of *consistency* of relationship, items selected as being consistent were then screened for *directionality*. To pass this screen, at least 75% of the significant correlations for a PHSI item had to be *either* positively *or* negatively related to a given IPDS scale. Items where less than 75% of relations were either positive or negative were also dropped from consideration. Thus, in the second phase of our data analysis, individual environmental items were selected for final discussion, based on their meeting our dual cutting-score criteria of consistency and directionality.

Our third step of data analysis involved detection of gender differences in reactivity. This analysis involved r–z transformation tests on the significance of the difference between *each* of the male and female environment–development correlations that were significantly different from zero and, which met our dual cutting-score criteria. Environment–development correlations for one gender, which were significantly different from their corresponding other-gender correlation, were regarded as indicating differences in environment–development relationships. As the final step of our analytic procedure, to determine whether males and females differed from each other on social environment variables we ran univariate t tests between male and female PHSI codes at each time block.[5] *Environment–development correlations that were significantly different from zero and from their corresponding other-gender correlations, and that were based on items where there was no frequency difference between males and females, could be used as evidence for differential reactivity of the genders, to the environment (organismic specificity).* Environment–development relations significantly different from zero, and from their corresponding other-gender correlations, which were based on items where there were significant differences between males and females, could be seen as evidence for the existence of transactional effects rather than as evidence for specificity.

Relationships between Social Environment and Cognitive–Intellectual Performance

Object Permanence

For males, 11.16% of the correlations in the PHSI-Permanence matrix were significant. The mean number of significant correlations between PHSI items and object permanence level was 1.12, the standard deviation was 1.64 and the rounded cut-off score was set at 3. For males, 12 PHSI items met our dual cutting-score criteria. These items are shown in Table 2.

A number of environmental items are negatively related to the development of object permanence through most of the second year of life. These include frequency of parental nonresponsivity to child's verbalizations (LS52), parental use of non-verbal responses to child's verbalizations (LS53a), parental emphasis on feeding the child (VS13b), ignoring the childs reactions (CE4I), and a predominately negative affectual tone by the parent (PA567). *Positively related* to object permanence through the second year of life are amount of adult verbal responsivity to childs vocalizations (LS5T), parental interactions with the child characterized by the use of questions (S6), and neutral parental affect (PA4).

---

[5] We had initially planned to use the multivariate Hotelling T^2 statistic for this test. However, idiosyncrasies in the SPSS T^2 program meant that any piece of missing data on a subject led to a loss of all information for this subject. Given this, and given the fact that the major problem with repeated univariate Ts is that of chance significance, we chose to use the univariate test. Chance significance would work against our preferred hypothesis of differential reactivity and would thus be a more conservative test of this hypothesis.

In contrast, a number of other environmental parameters appear to have an influence primarily before 18 months of age. Those items that are negatively related to acquisition of object permanence include amount of time parents watch, but do not interact with their infant (HK3B), percent of times parents reject their childs reactions (CE4R), and slow parental responses to their infants distress calls (SC2). During this time span, object permanence is *positively related* to the number of times parents repeat their child's verbalizations (LS54B).

For girls, the mean number of significant correlations was .87, the standard deviation was .93. Because the unrounded cut-off score was < 2, the overall matrix for female object permanence was considered nonsignificant. Inspection of the matrix indicated that, with the exception of slow parental response to child's distress (SC2), which was

TABLE 2

PHSI Items Meeting Cutting-Score Criteria for Predicting Male Object Permanence

Item	rPHSI:IPDS	(PHSI months)	(IPDS month)
LS52: Number of times parents fail	− .48 **	(12–14)	(15)
to respond to infant vocalizations	− .49 **	(12–14)	(18)
	− .41 *	(12–14)	(21)
	− .46 *	(15–17)	(18)
	− .49 *	(15–17)	(21)
	− .42 *	(18–20)	(21)
LS53A: Number of times parent	− .44 *	(12–14)	(15)
uses nonverbal response to child	− .45 **	(12–14)	(21)
vocalizations	− .52 **	(12–14)	(24)
	− .68 **	(21–23)	(24)
LS54B: Number of times parent re-	.35 *	(12–14)	(15)
peats child vocalizations	.48 *	(12–14)	(21)
	.40 *	(15–17)	(21)
LS5T: Total number of parent	.42 *	(12–14)	(21)
verbal response to child vocali-	.36 *	(15–17)	(18)
zations	.42 *	(15–17)	(21)
	.48 *	(18–20)	(21)
VS13b: Number of times parent	− .37 *	(15–17)	(18)
gives food or drink to child	− .53 *	(15–17)	(21)
	− .60 **	(15–17)	(24)
	− .63 **	(21–23)	(24)
HK3b: Amount of time parent ac-	− .64 **	(12–14)	(15)
tively watches child	− .47 *	(12–14)	(18)
	− .79 **	(12–14)	(21)
	− .45 *	(15–17)	(18)
CE4R: % of times parent rejects	− .39 *	(12–14)	(15)
child's response to adult request	− .51 *	(12–14)	(21)
	− .39 *	(12–14)	(21)

TABLE 2 (Continued)

Item	rPHSI:IPDS	(PHSI months)	(IPDS month)
CE4I: % of times parent ignores	− .42 *	(15–17)	(18)
child's response to adult request	− .80 **	(15–17)	(21)
	− .75 **	(15–17)	(24)
	− .53 *	(18–20)	(24)
SC2: Time of parent response to	− .43 *	(12–14)	(15)
child's distress signals	− .48 **	(12–14)	(18)
	− .64 **	(12–14)	(21)
	− .68 **	(12–14)	(24)
S6: Parent interactions character-	.36 *	(12–14)	(15)
ized by use of questions to child	.47 *	(12–14)	(21)
	.36 *	(15–17)	(18)
	.45 *	(15–17)	(21)
	.46 *	(18–20)	(21)
PA4: Parent affect rated as predom-	.49 **	(12–14)	(15)
inantly neutral	.40 *	(12–14)	(21)
	.49 *	(18–20)	(21)
	.45 *	(18–20)	(24)
	.44 *	(21–23)	(24)
PA567: Parent affect rates as pre-	− .36 *	(12–14)	(15)
dominantly negative	− .73 **	(18–20)	(21)
	− .70 **	(18–20)	(24)

*p < .05.
**p < .01.

negatively and consistently related to permanence level, most items had few consistent or significant correlations.

Development of Means

For development of means for males, the mean number of significant correlations per item was .97, the standard deviation was 1.01 which meant a cutting score below 2. Inspection of the PHSI-Means matrix indicated that, while a number of environmental items were correlated with means, few were consistently related. The exceptions were parental interference with childs exploration (IE2), which was negatively related to means–end performance, and number of times adults gives or shows objects to the child (VS13A), which was positively related.

For females, the mean number of significant correlations was .82, and the standard deviation was .93. Because the unrounded cutting score is below 2, this matrix was also considered to be nonsignificant. With the exception of three items, inspection of the female correlational matrix for development of means indicates generally scattered and inconsistent correlations. Three exceptions were consistently and negatively related to female development of means: items IE2 (parental interference with child's exploration of objects), SC2 (slow parental response to child's distress), and S3 (parental interactions with child characterized by denial.

Foresight

For the PHSI-Foresight correlational matrix for males, 10.5% of all correlations were statistically significant. For males, the mean number of significant correlations per item was 1.05; the standard deviation 1.08, which rounded to a cutting score of 2. Nineteen items were found to have 2 or more significant correlations with the infant's ability to anticipate consequences (foresight), as is shown in Table 3.

Inspection of the data shown in Table 3 indicates a very strong re-

TABLE 3

PHSI Items Meeting Cutting-Score Criteria for Predicting Male Foresight

Item	rPHSI:IPDS	(PHSI months)	(IPDS month)
LS3S: Number of spontaneous sib	.73**	(12–14)	(18)
vocalizations to child	.66*	(12–14)	(21)
	.66**	(15–17)	(18)
LS3A: Number of spontaneous parent vocalizations to child	.47*	(12–14)	(21)
	.51*	(18–20)	(21)
LS4A: Number of times object	.44*	(12–14)	(18)
named for child	.52**	(15–17)	(18)
	.51*	(18–20)	(21)
LS4B: Number of times object	.50*	(12–14)	(21)
known to child is referred to	.49*	(15–17)	(21)
	.52*	(18–20)	(21)
DS1: Number of times parent vocalizing to child while engaging in other activities	.39*	(12–14)	(18)
	.45*	(15–17)	(18)
LS52: Number of times parents fail	−.37*	(12–14)	(18)
to respond to infant vocalization	−.50*	(12–14)	(21)
LS53a: Number of times parent uses	−.45*	(12–14)	(24)
nonverbal response to child vocalizations	−.43*	(15–17)	(18)
LS54D: Number of times child	.35*	(12–14)	(15)
vocalization expanded by parent	.43*	(12–14)	(18)
	.51**	(15–17)	(18)
	.49*	(15–17)	(21)
LS54E: Number of times child vocalization commented on by adult	.40*	(15–17)	(21)
	.68**	(18–20)	(21)

TABLE 3 (*Continued*)

Item	rPHSI:IPDS	(PHSI months)	(IPDS month)
LS5T: Total number of parent ver-	.49*	(15–17)	(21)
bal responses to child vocaliza-	.57*	(18–20)	(21)
tions			
VS13b: Number of times parent	−.52**	(15–17)	(24)
gives food or drink to child	−.60**	(21–23)	(24)
HK3B: Amount of time parent ac-	−.37*	(12–14)	(18)
tively watching child	−.55**	(12–14)	(21)
	−.68**	(15–17)	(21)
SC2: Length of time of parent re-	−.40*	(12–14)	(21)
sponse to child distress signals	−.63**	(12–14)	(24)
S5: Parent interactions character-	.54**	(12–14)	(21)
ized by comments to child	.46*	(18–20)	(21)
S7: Parent interactions with child	−.43*	(15–17)	(21)
characterized by nonverbal inter-	−.37*	(21–23)	(24)
actions			
S12: Parents interactions character-	−.36*	(12–14)	(15)
ized by responding to physical	−.48*	(21–23)	(24)
needs of child			
SC4b: Parent does not make train-	−.47*	(18–20)	(21)
ing stimuli distinctive for child	−.39*	(21–23)	(24)
PA4: Parental affect rated as pre-	.43*	(12–14)	(15)
dominantly neutral	.42*	(18–20)	(24)
PA567: Parental affect rated as pre-	−.35*	(15–17)	(18)
dominantly negative	−.59**	(18–20)	(21)
	−.75**	(18–20)	(24)

*$p < .05$.
**$p < .01$.

lationship between the infant's vocal environment and subsequent level of foresight. Specifically, number of spontaneous sib (LS3S) and adult vocalizations (LS3A) to the child, adult use of comments to the child (S5), adults responding by expansions (LS54D) or comments (LS54E), as well as total number of adult responses to child vocalizations (LS5T), and the number of time parents name objects for the child (LS4A), or refer to objects known to the child (LS4B), are all *positively* and significantly related to the development of male level of foresight. *Negatively* related to male level of foresight are non-response (LS52) or nonverbal response (LS53a) to the childs vocalizations, the use of nonverbal interactions with the child (S7), slow adult responsivity to the child's distress (SC2), adults stressing food and drink (VS13B; S12), adults passively involved with the child (HK3B), negative adult affect (PA567), and the use of nondistinctive training stimuli (SC4B).

For females, the mean number of significant correlations was .62, the standard deviation 1.04 with an unrounded cut-off score below 2. Again, for females, scattered correlations are the rule with one exception. The one exception is Item SC2 (time it takes for adult to respond to child's distress), which from 12 to 20 months of age was consistently and negatively related to the child's level of foresight performance at 21 and 24 months of age.

Schemes in Relation to Objects

Overall, for males, 22.6% of the correlations in the matrix were significant. The mean number of significant correlations was 2.27; the standard deviation was 2.19 with the rounded cut-off score being set at 4. Seventeen PHSI items were found to have four or more significant correlations with the level of schemes used by boys in relating to objects. These data are shown in Table 4.

Summarizing the results in Table 4 indicates that through the second year of life, level of schemes is *positively* related to total amount of sib vocalizations to the infant (LS3S), various types of adult verbal responsivity to the infants vocalizations (LS54D, LS54E, LS5T), adult interactions with the infant characterized as instructional or educational in nature (S2B, S2C, S2D, S2T), adult use of questions with the child (S6) and moderate to high adult interactions with the infant (PI45). Similarly, a lack of adult response to infant vocalizations (LS52) and low adult responsivity (CE3I) and investment (PI12) are *negatively* related to the development of schemes through the second year. Spontaneous adult vocalizations (LS3A) and adult use of praise with the child (S13) are *positively* related to level of schemes *prior to* 18 months of age, whereas adults naming known objects (LS4B) and active adult

TABLE 4

PHSI Items Meeting Cutting-Score Criteria for Predicting Male Level of Schemes in Relation to Objects

Item	rPHSI:IPDS	(PHSI months)	(IPDS month)
LS3S: Number of spontaneous sib	.77 **	(12–14)	(15)
vocalizations to child	.65 *	(12–14)	(18)
	.80 *	(12–14)	(24)
	.51 *	(15–17)	(18)
	.59 *	(15–17)	(24)
	.69 *	(18–20)	(24)
	.63 *	(23–24)	(24)

TABLE 4 (*Continued*)

Item	r PHSI:IPDS	(PHSI months)	(IPDS month)
LS3A: Number of spontaneous parent vocalizations to child	.36 *	(12–14)	(15)
	.50 **	(12–14)	(18)
	.37 *	(15–17)	(18)
	.44 *	(15–17)	(24)
LS4B: Number of times object known to child is referred to	.35 *	(15–17)	(18)
	.54 **	(15–17)	(24)
	.48 *	(18–20)	(24)
	.53 **	(21–23)	(24)
LS52: Number of times parent fails to respond to infant vocalization	− .58 **	(12–14)	(15)
	− .42 *	(12–14)	(18)
	− .55 **	(12–14)	(24)
	− .58 **	(15–17)	(21)
	− .57 **	(15–17)	(24)
	− .48 *	(18–20)	(24)
	− .55 **	(21–23)	(24)
LS54D: Number of times child vocalization expanded by parent	.38 *	(15–17)	(24)
	.42 *	(18–20)	(21)
	.44 *	(18–20)	(24)
	.48 *	(21–23)	(24)
LS54E: Number of times child vocalization commented on by adult	.42 *	(12–14)	(18)
	.43 *	(15–17)	(18)
	.49 *	(15–17)	(21)
	.51 **	(15–17)	(24)
	.53 *	(18–20)	(24)
	.51 **	(21–23)	(24)
LS5T: Total number of parental verbal responses to child vocalization	.37 *	(12–14)	(18)
	.42 *	(15–17)	(18)
	.46 *	(15–17)	(21)
	.63 **	(15–17)	(24)
	.56 **	(18–20)	(24)
	.60 **	(21–23)	(24)
HK3a: Amount of time parent actively interacts with child	.43 *	(15–17)	(18)
	.54 **	(15–17)	(24)
	.41 *	(18–20)	(24)
	.43 *	(21–23)	(24)
CE3I: % of time parent ignores child's attempts to engage adult attention	− .41 *	(12–14)	(15)
	− .44 *	(12–14)	(24)
	− .64 **	(15–17)	(21)
	− .48 *	(15–17)	(24)
	− .54 *	(18–20)	(24)
S2B: Parent interactions characterized by providing child with general information about child's world	.43 *	(12–14)	(18)
	.53 **	(15–17)	(18)
	.49 *	(15–17)	(24)
	.47 *	(18–20)	(24)

(continued)

TABLE 4 (Continued)

Item	rPHSI:IPDS	(PHSI months)	(IPDS month)
S2C: Parent interactions character-	.43 *	(12–14)	(15)
ized by nonspecific naming of	.38 *	(12–14)	(18)
objects	.41 *	(12–14)	(24)
	.41 *	(15–17)	(21)
	.40 *	(15–17)	(24)
	.50 *	(21–23)	(24)
S2D: Parent interactions character-	.52 **	(12–14)	(15)
ized by teaching child specific	.46 *	(12–14)	(18)
concepts, names, rationales, etc.	.44 *	(12–14)	(24)
	.61 **	(15–17)	(24)
	.64 **	(18–20)	(24)
S2T: Total number of parent inter-	.51 **	(12–14)	(15)
actions characterized as instruc-	.53 **	(12–14)	(18)
tional in nature	.44 *	(12–14)	(24)
	.42 *	(15–17)	(18)
	.45 *	(15–17)	(21)
	.49 **	(15–17)	(24)
	.53 **	(18–20)	(24)
	.53 **	(21–23)	(24)
S6: Parent interactions character-	.41 *	(12–14)	(18)
ized by use of questions to child	.44 *	(12–14)	(24)
	.41 *	(15–17)	(18)
	.61 **	(15–17)	(24)
	.52 *	(18–20)	(24)
	.39 *	(21–23)	(24)
S13: Parent interactions character-	.39 *	(12–14)	(15)
ized by parent praising child's	.35 *	(12–14)	(18)
actions	.45 *	(15–17)	(18)
	.43 *	(15–17)	(24)
P112: Parent investment in child's	− .36 *	(12–14)	(15)
activities rated as minimal to low	− .51 **	(12–14)	(18)
	− .43 *	(15–17)	(24)
	− .69 **	(21–23)	(24)
P145: Parent investment in child's	.40 *	(12–14)	(18)
activities rated as moderate to	.46 *	(12–14)	(24)
high	.44 *	(15–17)	(18)
	.51 **	(15–17)	(24)
	.56 **	(21–23)	(24)

$* p < .05.$
$** p < .01.$

interaction (HK3A) appear to have an impact upon schemes mainly in the period *after* 15 months.

For females, 11.16% of the correlations in the matrix were significant; the mean number of significant correlations per item was 1.12; the standard deviation was 1.14 with a rounded cut-off score being set at 2. Twelve environmental items had two or more significant correlations with female level of schemes in relation to objects. These correlations are shown in Table 5.

For females the correlational pattern, though significant, is less clear than that for males. Many of the verbal factors relevant for male level of schemes are either irrelevant for females or are relevant, but in an opposite direction (e.g., LS4B). There also appear to be certain inconsistencies in the data, such as the *negative* relationship between schemes and rejection of the childs requests (S3) and interaction attempts (CE3R) versus the *positive* correlations between schemes and rejection of child's responses (CE4R). What is most consistent for females level of schemes is the *negative* influence of adult interaction while the child is exploring objects, be this interference (IE2) or encouragement (IE4). In addition, the *negative* influences of a passive (HK3B) or a coercive adult (S1) who stresses feeding of the child (VS13B) are also evident.

Causality

Overall, for males, 9.33% of the matrix was significant. For males, the mean number of correlations between PHSI and level of understanding of causality was .93; the standard deviation was 1.10 with a rounded cut-off score being set at 2. Eleven PHSI items met our dual cutting-score criteria. These items and their relation to level of understanding of causal relations are shown in Table 6.

The results shown in Table 6 indicate that most environmental influences on the development of understanding of causality occur in the first half of the second year of life. Specifically, our results indicate a *positive* relationship between level of understanding of causality and early adult-encouragement of child's vocalizations (LS54D) and the parents' use of specific educational strategies (S2D) or praise (S13) with the infant. Similarly, *negatively* related to the development of male infants understanding of causality are the use of nonverbal responses to the child's vocalizations (LS53A), an emphasis on feeding (VS13B) and holding (HK2) the child, and ignoring the infant's attempts to engage adult attention (CE3I). A few environmental parameters are also rele-

TABLE 5

PHSI Items Meeting Cutting-Score Criteria for Predicting Female Level of Schemes in Relation to Objects

Item	rPHSI:IPDS	(PHSI months)	(IPDS month)
IE2: Number of times parent inter-	−.71**	(12–14)	(18)
feres with child exploration of	−.54*	(12–14)	(21)
objects	−.49*	(15–17)	(18)
IE4: Number of times parent en-	−.58*	(12–14)	(21)
courages child exploration of	−.61*	(15–17)	(21)
objects			
LS4B: Number of times object	−.57*	(12–14)	(21)
known to child is referred to	−.58*	(15–17)	(21)
	−.56*	(18–20)	(21)
DS2: Adult actively doing some-	.55*	(12–14)	(18)
thing with child while vocalizing	.57*	(15–17)	(18)
to child			
VS13B: Number of times parent	−.48*	(12–14)	(15)
gives food or drink to child	−.47*	(15–17)	(18)
	−.57*	(15–17)	(21)
HK3B: Amount of time parent	−.76**	(18–20)	(21)
actively watches child	−.79**	(21–23)	(24)
CE3R: % of times parent rejects	−.61*	(12–14)	(21)
child's attempts to engage adult's	−.65*	(18–20)	(24)
attention			
CE4R: % of times parent rejects	.67*	(12–14)	(21)
child's response to adult request	.77*	(12–14)	(24)
	.85*	(21–23)	(24)
CE4P: % of times parent responds	−.65*	(12–14)	(21)
positively to child's response to	−.73*	(12–14)	(24)
adult request	−.71*	(15–17)	(24)
S1: Parent interactions character-	−.50*	(15–17)	(18)
ized by attempting to get child	−.63*	(15–17)	(21)
to fulfill adult requests	−.75**	(18–20)	(21)
S3: Parent interactions character-	−.73**	(12–14)	(18)
ized by adult denying child's	−.55**	(12–14)	(21)
specific request or need	−.75**	(15–17)	(18)
	−.55*	(18–20)	(21)
SC3B: Parent attempts to show	.73*	(12–14)	(24)
child how to make discrimina-	.71*	(21–23)	(24)
tions			

*$p < .05$.
**$p < .01$.

TABLE 6

PHSI Items Meeting Cutting-Score Criteria for Predicting Male Development of Understanding of Causality

Item	rPHSI:IPDS	(PHSI months)	(IPDS month)
IE4: Number of times parent en-	.41 *	(12–14)	(18)
courages child exploration of	.42 *	(12–14)	(21)
objects			
LS3S: Number of spontaneous sib	.81 *	(12–14)	(21)
vocalizations to child	.47 *	(15–17)	(18)
LS53A: Number of times parent	− .48 *	(15–17)	(21)
uses nonverbal response to child	− .43 *	(15–17)	(24)
vocalizations			
LS54D: Number of times child vo-	.63 **	(12–14)	(18)
calization expanded by parent	.61 *	(15–17)	(18)
VS13B: Number of times parent	− .55 **	(15–17)	(21)
gives food or drink to child	− .59 **	(15–17)	(24)
HK2: Amount of time child is held	− .61 **	(12–14)	(24)
by adult	− .69 **	(18–20)	(24)
CE31: % of time parent ignores	− .49 **	(12–14)	(15)
child's attempts to engage adult	− .39 *	(12–14)	(18)
attention	− .46 *	(12–14)	(21)
CE3P: % of time parent responds	.48 *	(12–14)	(15)
positively to child's attempts	.39 *	(12–14)	(18)
to engage adult attention			
S2D: Parent interactions character-	.44 *	(12–14)	(21)
ized by teaching child specific	.50 *	(18–20)	(21)
concepts, names, rationales, etc.			
S12: Parent interactions character-	− .35 *	(12–14)	(15)
ized by responding to physical	− .42 *	(12–14)	(24)
needs of child	− .46 *	(15–17)	(21)
	− .53 *	(15–17)	(24)
	− .43 *	(18–20)	(24)
S13: Parent interactions character-	.36 *	(12–14)	(15)
ized by parent praising child's	.45 *	(18–20)	(21)
actions			
PA4: Parent affect rated as pre-	.45 *	(18–20)	(21)
dominantly neutral	.42 *	(18–20)	(24)

*$p < .05.$
**$p < .01.$

vant after 17 months of age (HK2, S2D, S13), but only neutral ratings of parental affect (PA4) are consistently related.

For females, the mean number of significant correlations was .92; the standard deviation was .81. This led to a total cutoff score below 2, thus the overall matrix for females was considered to be nonsignificant. Inspection of the female data matrix indicated only scattered relationships between environment and development, with many of these relationships differing in directional sign, even for the same environmental item.

Construction of Objects in Space

Overall, for males, 18.33% of the correlation matrix was significant. For males, the mean number of significant correlations per item was 1.83; the standard deviation was 1.72 yielding a rounded cut-off score of 4. Twelve items were found to have four or more significant correlations with level of understanding of early spatial relationships. These items are listed in Table 7.

In contrast to causality, the data shown in Table 7 suggest that environmental influences on the infant's concept of objects in space are manifest all through the second year of life. Results particularly indicate the relevance of the infant's vocal environment, with level of performance on the space subscale *positively* related to spontaneous sib (LS3S) and adult (LS4A, LS4B, S6) vocalizations directed toward the child. Adult vocal responding to the child's vocalizations (LS5T) is also *positively* related, whereas lack of responsivity (LS52) is *negatively* related. In addition, active (HK3A), as opposed to passive (HK3B), adult interaction with the child is also relevant to the child's understanding of spatial relations, as is the adult use of instructional interactions (S2C, S2D, S2T) with the child.

For females, the mean number of significant correlations was .70 and the standard deviation was .89. Because the sum of these two numbers was below 2, the overall female matrix was considered nonsignificant.

TABLE 7

PHSI Items Meeting Cutting-Score Criteria for Predicting Male Construction of Objects in Space

Item	rPHSI:IPDS	(PHSI months)	(IPDS month)
LS3S: Number of spontaneous sib	.55 *	(12–14)	(18)
vocalizations to child	.72 *	(12–14)	(21)
	.60 *	(15–17)	(21)
	.75 *	(18–20)	(21)
LS4A: Number of times object	.58 **	(12–14)	(15)
named for child	.36 *	(12–14)	(18)
	.47 *	(12–14)	(24)
	.41 *	(18–20)	(24)
LS4B: Number of times object	.42 *	(12–14)	(21)
known to child referred to	.50 *	(15–17)	(24)
	.48 *	(18–20)	(21)
	.50 *	(21–23)	(24)

TABLE 7 (*Continued*)

Item	rPHSI:IPDS	(PHSI months)	(IPDS month)
LS52: Number of times parent fails to respond to child vocalization	−.48**	(12–14)	(18)
	−.55**	(12–14)	(21)
	−.55**	(15–17)	(24)
	−.53**	(21–23)	(24)
LS5T: Total number of parent verbal responses to child vocalizations	.40*	(12–14)	(21)
	.41*	(15–17)	(21)
	.45*	(15–17)	(24)
	.47*	(18–20)	(21)
	.47*	(18–20)	(24)
	.62**	(21–23)	(24)
HK3A: Amount of time parent actively interacts with child	.41*	(12–14)	(21)
	.48*	(15–17)	(24)
	.40*	(18–20)	(24)
	.38*	(21–23)	(24)
HK3B: Amount of time parent actively watches child	−.42*	(12–14)	(15)
	−.43*	(12–14)	(24)
	−.54**	(15–17)	(18)
	−.63**	(15–17)	(21)
	−.52**	(21–23)	(24)
S1: Parent interactions characterized by attempting to get child to fulfill adult requests	.45*	(12–14)	(21)
	.43*	(12–14)	(24)
	.45*	(15–17)	(24)
	.60**	(18–20)	(24)
S2C: Parent interactions characterized by nonspecific naming of objects	.44*	(12–14)	(21)
	.41*	(12–14)	(24)
	.42*	(18–20)	(24)
	.46*	(21–23)	(24)
S2D: Parent interactions with child characterized by teaching child specific concepts, names, rationales, etc.	.52**	(12–14)	(15)
	.56**	(12–14)	(24)
	.56**	(15–17)	(24)
	.59**	(18–20)	(21)
	.52*	(18–20)	(24)
S2T: Total number of parent interactions characterized as instructional in nature	.50**	(12–14)	(15)
	.51**	(12–14)	(24)
	.53**	(15–17)	(24)
	.49*	(18–20)	(21)
	.52*	(18–20)	(24)
	.49*	(21–23)	(24)
S6: Parent interactions characterized by use of questions to child	.44*	(12–14)	(15)
	.44*	(12–14)	(24)
	.59**	(15–17)	(24)
	.52*	(18–20)	(24)
	.44*	(21–23)	(24)

*$p < .05$.
**$p < .01$.

Inspection of the data matrix for females did indicate that, in contrast to males, whatever consistencies there were in the matrix were due to sib interference with child's exploration of objects (IE1), to adult physical contact (HK1), and to nonverbal interactions with the child (S7), all of which were negatively related to female level of understanding of objects in space.

Verbal Imitation

For males, 11% of the correlations in the PHSI-Verbal Imitation matrix were significant. The mean number of significant correlations per item was 1.10, the standard deviation was 1.12 with the overall cutting score being at 2. Twelve environmental items were found to have two or more significant correlations with males level of verbal imitation. Those items are shown in Table 8.

As might be expected, the results shown in Table 8 indicate a strong relationship between adult verbal interactions and the child's level of verbal imitation. The total number of verbal responses to the child's vocalizations (LS5T) is obviously one critical factor. However, in contrast to other sensorimotor abilities, adult repetition of child's words or vocalizations (LS54B) and the adults responding to the child vocalizations with a question (LS54F) also seem to be especially salient in predicting male-infant levels of verbal imitation. In addition, parents who charactistically ask questions of the child (S6) have boys with higher levels of verbal imitation. In addition to the language environment, parental use of praise for the child's actions (S13) is *positively* related to level of Verbal Imitation. *Negatively* related to male-infant levels of verbal imitation are passive adult interactions (HK3B), rejecting the child's reactions to adult requests (CE4R), and not making stimuli distinctive to the child (SC4B).

For females, 13% of the correlations in the PHSI-Verbal Imitation matrix were significant. The mean number of significant correlations was 1.30, the standard deviation was 1.08, with a rounded cutoff score being set at 2. Eighteen environmental items were found to have two or more significant correlations with female level of verbal imitation. These items are shown in Table 9.

Inspection of the results in Table 9 indicates that, like males, total adult responsiveness (LS5T) to the child's vocalizations are *positively* related to female-infant level of verbal imitation. However, in contrast to the male data, adult expansion of the child's vocalization (LS54D) and adult commenting upon the child's vocalization (LS54E) are the types of parental responses that are positively related to female-infant

TABLE 8

PHSI Items Meeting Cutting-Score Criteria for Predicting Verbal Imitation for Males

Item	rPHSI:IPDS	(PHSI months)	(IPDS month)
LS53A: Number of times parent	−.38*	(12–14)	(24)
uses nonverbal response to child	−.44*	(21–23)	(24)
vocalizations			
LS54B: Number of times parent	.49**	(12–14)	(18)
repeats child vocalizations	.38*	(15–17)	(24)
	.46*	(18–20)	(24)
	.40*	(21–23)	(24)
LS54F: Number of times parent re-	.46*	(12–14)	(24)
sponds with question to child	.59**	(18–20)	(21)
vocalization	.54**	(18–20)	(24)
	.51**	(21–23)	(24)
LS5T: Total number of parent ver-	.38*	(12–14)	(18)
bal responses to child vocaliza-	.41*	(15–17)	(18)
tions	.43*	(18–20)	(21)
	.50*	(18–20)	(24)
	.46*	(21–23)	(24)
VS14B: Number of times parent	−.43*	(12–14)	(21)
uses explanations with child	−.41*	(21–23)	(24)
HK3B: Amount of time parent ac-	−.49*	(15–17)	(24)
tively watches child	−.50*	(18–20)	(21)
CE4R: % of times parent rejects	−.42*	(18–20)	(21)
child's response to adult request	−.42*	(18–20)	(24)
	−.46*	(21–23)	(24)
CE4P: % of times parent responds	.48*	(18–20)	(21)
positively to child's response to	.46*	(18–20)	(24)
adult request			
S2T: Total number of parent inter-	.42*	(12–14)	(24)
actions with child, characterized	.40*	(18–20)	(24)
as instructional in nature			
S6: Parent interactions character-	.45*	(12–14)	(24)
ized by use of questions to child	.40*	(18–20)	(24)
S13: Parent interactions character-	.39*	(12–14)	(24)
ized by parent praising child's	.48*	(15–17)	(24)
actions			
SC4B: Units of time in which par-	−.54**	(18–20)	(24)
ent does not make training stim-	−.46*	(21–23)	(24)
uli distinctive for child			

*p < .05.
**p < .01.

level of verbal imitation. In addition, sib vocalizations (LS3S), adult use of explanations (VS14B), and adult comments to the child (S5) are also *positively* related to female-infant level of verbal imitation; *negatively* related are adult vocalizations that lack informational content

(VG). In addition to verbal parameters, sibs' interference with the child's exploratory activities (IE1) and a lack of adult presence (NA) are *positively* related to female-infants' vocal imitation, whereas positive adult affect (PA123) and moderate-to-high levels of adult investment (PI45) are negatively related.

TABLE 9

PHSI Items Meeting Cutting-Score Criteria for Predicting Female Vocal Imitation

Item	rPHSI:IPDS	(PHSI months)	(IPDS month)
IE1: Number of times sibs	.60*	(12–14)	(21)
interfere with child's exploration	.56*	(15–17)	(21)
of objects	.56*	(18–20)	(21)
IE2: Number of times parent inter-	−.64**	(12–14)	(18)
feres with child's exploration of	.61*	(15–17)	(21)
objects	−.74*	(18–20)	(24)
	−.81**	(21–23)	(24)
LS3S: Number of spontaneous sib	.84*	(15–17)	(21)
vocalizations to child	.72*	(15–17)	(24)
	.73*	(18–20)	(21)
LS4B: Number of times object	−.65*	(12–14)	(21)
known to child is referred to	−.65*	(18–20)	(21)
DS2: Number of times parent vocal-	−.53*	(12–14)	(15)
izes to child while engaging in	−.65*	(21–23)	(24)
other activities			
LS52: Number of times parent fails	−.47*	(12–14)	(15)
to respond to child vocalizations	−.91**	(12–14)	(24)
LS54D: Number of times child	.63*	(12–14)	(24)
vocalization expanded by parent	.62*	(18–20)	(24)
LS54E: Number of times child	.49*	(12–14)	(15)
vocalization commented on by	.77*	(12–14)	(24)
adult	.65*	(21–23)	(24)
LS5T: Total number of parental re-	.51*	(12–14)	(15)
sponses to child vocalizations	.74*	(12–14)	(24)
VG: Ratio: total number of adult	−.48*	(15–17)	(18)
vocalizations and vocalizations	−.62*	(18–20)	(24)
containing informational content			
VS14B: Number of times parent	.46*	(12–14)	(15)
uses explanations with child	.62*	(15–17)	(24)
S1: Parent interactions character-	−.51*	(12–14)	(18)
ized by attempting to get the	−.60*	(12–14)	(21)
child to fulfill adult requests	−.55*	(18–20)	(21)
S2C: Parent interactions character-	.45*	(12–14)	(15)
ized by nonspecific naming of	.64*	(12–14)	(24)
objects	.62*	(18–20)	(24)
S3: Parent interactions character-	−.59*	(12–14)	(18)
ized by parents denying child's	−.55*	(18–20)	(21)
requests			

TABLE 9 (*Continued*)

Item	*r*PHSI:IPDS	(PHSI months)	(IPDS month)
S5: Parent interactions character-	.46*	(12–14)	(15)
ized by comments to child	.62*	(12–14)	(24)
PA123: Parent affect rated as pre-	−.54*	(15–17)	(21)
dominantly positive	−.67*	(18–20)	(21)
PI45: Parent investment in child's	−.47*	(12–14)	(18)
activity rated as moderate to high	−.70*	(18–20)	(21)
NA: Amount of time parents not in	.53*	(15–17)	(18)
room with child	.62*	(18–20)	(21)

*p < .05.
**p < .01.

Gestural Imitation

For males, 10.66% of correlations in the Gestural Imitation matrix were significant. The mean number of significant correlations between environmental items and level of gestural imitation was 1.07; the standard deviation was 1.23, with the rounded cut-off score being set at 2. The results for gestural imitation are shown in Table 10.

TABLE 10
PHSI Items Meeting Cutting-Score Criteria for Predicting Male Gestural Imitation

Item	*r*PHSI:IPDS	(PHSI months)	(IPDS month)
IE4: Number of times parent	−.57**	(12–14)	(15)
encourages exploration of objects	−.46*	(15–17)	(21)
LS3S: Number of spontaneous sib	.56*	(15–17)	(21)
vocalizations to child	.71*	(18–20)	(21)
LS52: Number of times parent fails	−.46*	(12–14)	(18)
to respond to child vocalizations	−.45*	(12–14)	(21)
	−.43*	(15–17)	(24)
LS53A: Number of times parent	−.45*	(15–17)	(18)
uses nonverbal response to child	−.44*	(21–23)	(24)
vocalizations			
LS54D: Number of times child	.38*	(15–17)	(18)
vocalization expanded by parent	.43*	(18–20)	(24)
LS54E: Number of times child vo-	.48*	(12–14)	(21)
calization commented on by	.44*	(12–14)	(24)
adult	.47*	(18–20)	(21)
	.47*	(18–20)	(24)
LS54F: Number of times parent re-	.53**	(15–17)	(24)
sponds with question to child	.61**	(18–20)	(24)
vocalization			

(continued)

TABLE 10 *(Continued)*

Item	ʳPHSI:IPDS	(PHSI months)	(IPDS month)
LS5T: Total number of parental ver-	.40*	(12–14)	(24)
bal responses to child vocaliza-	.37*	(15–17)	(24)
tion	.49*	(18–20)	(24)
VG: Ratio: Total number of adult	.43*	(15–17)	(21)
vocalizations/vocalizations con-	.46*	(18–20)	(21)
taining informational content			
HK3B: Amount of time parent ac-	−.50*	(12–14)	(24)
tively watches child	−.42*	(15–17)	(18)
S1: Parent interactions character-	.41*	(12–14)	(24)
ized by attempting to get child to	.40*	(15–17)	(24)
fulfill adult requests	.51*	(18–20)	(24)
S2C: Parent interactions with child,	.42*	(12–14)	(18)
characterized by nonspecific	.40*	(12–14)	(24)
naming of objects			
S3: Parent interactions character-	.39*	(12–14)	(18)
ized by parent denying child's re-	.39*	(12–14)	(24)
quests	.38*	(15–17)	(18)
	.42*	(15–17)	(24)
	.45*	(18–20)	(24)
PA123: Parent affect characterized	−.48**	(12–14)	(15)
as predominantly positive	−.37**	(15–17)	(18)
PA4: Parent affect characterized	.66**	(15–17)	(18)
as predominantly neutral	.56**	(18–20)	(24)
PI12: Parent investment in child	−.50**	(12–14)	(18)
rated as minimal to low	−.52**	(12–14)	(21)
	−.54**	(12–14)	(24)
NA: Amount of time parents not in	−.37*	(15–17)	(18)
room with child	−.43*	(18–20)	(24)

*p < .05.
**p < .01.

The results shown in Table 10 indicate that two groups of items appear to relate to the development of male gestural imitation. First, the results suggest that any type of adult responsivity to the child's verbalizations (LS52, LS54D, LS54E, LS54F, LS5T) or any type of spontaneous verbalizations (LS3S, VG, S2C) is relevant to the development of gestural imitation. Characteristic adult interactions involving demands (S1), and requests (S3) are *positively* related. However, a lack of adult involvement with the child (HK3B, PI12, NA) is *negatively* related to gestural imitation, as is encouragement of exploration (IE4).

For females, the mean number of significant correlations was .65, the standard deviation was .82. Because this total came to below 2, the overall female matrix for gestural imitation was considered to be nonsignificant. Inspection of the data matrix for females indicates generally scattered correlations.

Gender Differences in Reactivity to the Social Environment

For *all* male or female environment–development correlations which passed our cutting-score criteria, Fisher *r–z* transformation tests were used to compare the correlations for one gender with their opposite-gender correlations. Of the total matrix of male and female correlations thus analyzed, 13% were significantly different from each other. A cutting-score analysis was run on this matrix, with the mean number of significant correlations being 1.29, the standard deviation 1.12; the over-all cutting score was set at 2. Sixteen environmental items met our cutting-score criteria (because we were comparing items across cognitive scales, the directionality criteria was not used here). The male–female comparisons for these 16 environmental items are shown in Table 11.

Summarizing across Table 11, several patterns emerge. For 6 of our environmental items, correlations for males are positive and generally significant; the correlations for females tend to be negative in direc-

TABLE 11

PHSI Items Meeting Cutting-Score Criteria for Gender Differences, in Reactivity
to the Early Environment

PHSI item (Ages in months, when measured)	IPDS (Ages, in months, when measured)	Male r	Female r	z
IE1: Sibs interfere with child's exploratory behaviors				
(12–14)	Verbal imitation (21)	− .47 *	.60 *	2.61 **
(18–20)	Verbal imitation (21)	− .41	.56 *	2.27 *
LS3S: Number of spontaneous sib vocalizations to child				
(12–14)	Foresight (18)	.73 **	.16	2.02 *
(12–14)	Schemes (15)	.77 **	.18	2.20 *
(12–14)	Schemes (24)	.80 *	− .09	2.33 *
(12–14)	Causality (18)	.81 *	− .05	3.09 **
(15–17)	Verbal imitation (21)	.09	.84 *	2.45 *
LS4B: Number of times adult refers to object known to child				
(15–17)	Schemes (21)	.28	− .58 *	2.06 *
(15–17)	Space (24)	.50 *	− .58 *	2.37 *
(18–20)	Space (21)	.48 *	− .48	2.22 *
(18–20)	Verbal imitation (21)	.19	− .65 *	2.05 *

(continued)

TABLE 11 (Continued)

PHSI item (Ages in months, when measured)	IPDS (Ages, in months, when measured)	Male r	Female r	z
LS52: Number of times adult does not respond to child vocalizations				
(12–14)	Permanence (18)	−.49**	.24	2.05*
(12–14)	Space (21)	−.55*	.39	2.23*
(12–14)	Verbal imitation (24)	−.27	−.91**	2.45*
LS5T: Total number of adult responses to child vocalizations				
(15–17)	Schemes (21)	.46*	−.53	2.36*
(18–20)	Verbal imitation (21)	.43*	−.46	2.03*
VS13B: Number of times adult gives food or drink to child				
(15–17)	Schemes (21)	.27	−.57*	2.01*
(15–17)	Causality (24)	−.59*	.35	2.04*
CE3I: % times adult ignores child's attempt to obtain adult attention				
(15–17)	Schemes (21)	−.64**	.45	2.70**
(15–17)	Schemes (24)	−.48*	.61	2.41*
CE4R: % times adult rejects childs reaction to adult request				
(12–14)	Schemes (24)	−.24	.77*	2.48*
(21–23)	Schemes (24)	−.08	.85*	2.61**
CE4I: % times adult ignores child's reaction to adult request				
(15–17)	Permanence (21)	−.80**	−.04	2.30*
(18–20)	Permanence (21)	−.53*	.45	2.28*
CE4P: % time adult reacts positively to child's reaction to adult request				
(12–14)	Schemes (24)	.26	−.73*	2.34*
(18–20)	Verbal imitation (21)	.48*	−.39	1.98*
S1: Adult interactions with child characterized by adult attempting to get child to comply with adult requests				
(15–17)	Schemes (21)	.27	−.63*	2.21*
(18–20)	Schemes (21)	.22	−.75**	2.54*
(12–14)	Space (21)	.45*	−.88**	4.04**
(18–20)	Verbal imitation (21)	.31	−.55*	1.99*.

TABLE 11 (Continued)

PHSI item (Ages in months, when measured)	IPDS (Ages, in months, when measured)	Male r	Female r	z
S2C: Adult interactions with child characterized by adult naming objects for child				
(12–14)	Space (21)	.44*	−.68*	2.82**
(12–14)	Gestural imitation (18)	.42*	−.37	2.20*
S2T: Adult interactions with child characterized by adult teaching child				
(15–17)	Schemes (21)	.45*	−.48	2.19*
(12–14)	Space (15)	.50*	−.36	2.43*
S3: Adult interactions with child characterized by adult rejecting child's requests				
(12–14)	Schemes (18)	−.01	−.73**	2.41*
(15–17)	Schemes (18)	.00	−.75**	2.56*
(12–14)	Verbal imitation (18)	.10	−.59*	2.04*
PI12: Adult investment with child rated as minimal–low				
(12–14)	Schemes (18)	−.51**	.22	2.07*
(12–14)	Gestural imitation (24)	−.54**	.40	2.01*
NA: Amount of time adult not in same room as child				
(15–17)	Verbal imitation (18)	−.38*	.53*	2.60**
(18–20)	Verbal imitation (21)	−.28	.62*	2.15*

*$p < .05$.
**$p < .01$.

tion, moderate in magnitude and, in some cases, statistically significant. Items showing this pattern include the number of times the parent refers to objects known to the child (LS4B), the total number of adult vocal responses to child vocalizations (LS5T), the percentage of time the adult makes a positive response to the child's reactions to an adult request (CE4P), adult attempts to get the child to conform to adult requests (S1), interactions with the child characterized by the naming of objects (S2C), and parents' attempting to teach the child (S2T). A second cluster consists of 4 items where the correlations for males are negative in direction and generally significant; the correlations for females are positive in direction, of moderate magnitude and, in some cases, statistically significant. Items exhibiting this pattern include the number of times sibs interfere with the infants exploratory behaviors (IE1), the percentage of time adults ignore the childs attentional bids (CE3I), adult interactions with the child characterized as being low in terms of investment (PI12), and the amount of time the adult is not in the room with the child (NA). For two items, a pattern emerges where the correlations for males are essentially zero order, whereas the correlations for females are statistically significant. Items here include the adult rejecting the child's reactions to an adult request (CE4R), and adult interactions with the child, characterized by denial of the child's requests (S3). In contrast, for item CE4I (adult ignores child reaction to adult request), the correlations for males are negative and significant, whereas the correlations for females are nonsignificant.

For the remaining codes, two items show a correlational pattern, suggesting the possibility of environment × organismic specificity. For the number of spontaneous sib vocalizations to child (LS3S), the correlation is positive and statistically significant for males and essentially zero order for females, except in the case of verbal imitation, where this pattern is reversed. A similar reversal is also seen for item VS13B (number of times adult gives food or drink to child). Ignoring the childs vocalization (LS52) may also be an example of environment × organismic specificity, though the pattern for this item does not lend itself to easy interpretation.

Major differences were also noted in the sensitivity of different sensorimotor scales to gender differences. Thus, object permanence (6% of differences significant), foresight (4%), and gestural imitation (9%) showed relatively little differential reactivity. In contrast, schemes (18%), causality (21%), and verbal imitation (20%) showed much greater differential reactivity. Objects in space showed moderate differential reactivity, with 13% of the correlations being significantly different.

The aforementioned results indicate that there is evidence for gender differences in reactivity to the social environment for a limited number of items. The next analytic step was to determine if these gender differences were a function of differential reactivity to similar environmental stimulation, or to different environments provided to male and female infants. This step was accomplished through comparison of the t values on environmental scores for each of the 16 environmental items that yielded gender differences. Results indicated that from 12 through 20 months of age, only one item indicated differential treatment of male versus female infants. Specifically, between 15 and 17 months, female-infant vocalizations were ignored significantly more often than those of male infants (LS52) ($t = 2.09$, $p < .05$). In contrast, between 21 and 23 months of age, 3 of the 16 items indicated significant differential treatment of male and female infants. Results indicated that, during this time period, male infants got more food and drink from adults than females (VS13B: $t = 3.23$, $p < .01$), and had more adult–infant interactions characterized by object naming (S2C: $t = 2.47$, $p < .05$), and by instructional activities (S2T: $t = 2.84$, $p < .01$) than female infants.

Discussion

Environment and Cognitive–Intellectual Development

The BEAM model of environmental action we have proposed (Wachs, 1979) hypothesizes that there are two classes of environmental stimuli. The first class is a small subset of environmental parameters that are relevant to most aspects of cognitive–intellectual development for most individuals. The second is a larger subset of environmental items, which are specific to particular cognitive abilities for particular individuals at particular ages. Prior to looking at specificity the first question to be raised is whether our present results have shown any environmental parameters that could be considered as global in nature.

Inspection of our results suggests that items tapping the language environment of the child most closely fit the definition of a global environmental factor. Given the emphasis on the child's language environment in the early experience literature (Bronfenbrenner, 1974; Lichtenberg & Norton, 1970; White, 1975), such a conclusion is by itself, not surprising. However, in contrast to previous statements on this topic, what is unique about our results is delineation of what specific parameters of the child's language environment most closely fit our definition of a global environmental parameter. What our results indicate is that only a few aspects of the infant's language environment predict most aspects of sensorimotor development for most individuals at most ages.

Specifically, while sib and adult vocalizations are extremely critical for cognitive–intellectual development in the second year of life, these vocalizations are predictive in different ways. For siblings our results suggest that any type of spontaneous vocalization by an older sib to an infant (LS3S), facilitates most aspects of cognitive–intellectual development. The relevance of sib vocalizations as a global environmental parameter, is one that has not appeared in the literature until recently. Zajonc (1976) has discussed the possibility of older siblings serving as "teachers" to younger sibs but has provided no firm data on this topic. Norman-Jackson (1982) has recently reported data indicating that successful readers in school came from homes where, as preschoolers, they had higher levels of verbal interaction with their older sibs than did unsucessful readers. Our results may be seen as a downward extension of the Norman-Jackson data, indicating the relevance of older sib vocalizations to cognitive development in the second year of life. These data can be viewed as confirming Zajonc's original speculations on the possible teaching role of older sibs.

In contrast, for adults, the *amount of vocalizations* (LS3A) appears to be much less relevant than the *contingency relationship* between adult and child vocalizations. The lack of adult *verbal responses* to child vocalizations (LS52) is consistently and negatively related to most aspects of sensorimotor development during the second year of life; the total percentage of adult verbal responses that follow the child vocalizations (LS5T) is consistently and positively related to most aspects of sensorimotor development in the second year of life. In contrast, other aspects of child language-environment, such as naming of objects, characteristics of adult verbal response to child vocalizations, or informational content of adult vocalizations, appear to be highly specific in their relationship to cognitive–intellectual development during the second year of life. The relevance of verbal responsivity as a global environment parameter is further highlighted by recent data comparing early environment–development relationships in adoptive and biological families (De Fries, Plomin, Vandenberg, & Kuse, 1981). These data indicate that the relationship of responsivity to early cognitive development may be independent of genetic correlations between parent and offspring.

The preceding results have dual implications for early cognitive intervention. First, the results suggest that one of the core aspects of programs for early cognitive intervention in the second year of life should be an emphasis on adult verbal responsivity to infant vocalizations, regardless of the content of the adult response. It must be stressed that adult responsivity must be verbal; nonverbal responsivity (LS53A) was consistently found to be negatively related to cognitive–intellectual development.

In addition our results also suggest that early home-based intervention programs may also wish to work with the childs sibs as well as with the childs parents. Our previous research has suggested a consistent and negative relationship between number of siblings in the home and early cognitive–intellectual development (Wachs, 1979). However, when sibs serve a teaching function, as when they vocalize to the child, sibs may serve to facilitate both early cognitive–intellectual development (our data) and later reading skills (Norman-Jackson, 1982). Hence, in home-based intervention programs, working not just with the parent–child dyad, but also with sibs, in terms of training them to vocalize to the target child, may also be useful as an intervention technique.

In addition to certain aspects of the child's language environment our present data also suggest two other parameters that might act in a global fashion. The first taps adult watching of the child or orientation toward the child (HK3B). This parameter is consistently and negatively related to most aspects of sensorimotor development across the second year of life. However, we are constrained in labelling active watching as a global factor by the variability of results in this area. Previous studies have reported that parental orientation toward the infant, after 12 months of age, is significantly and positively correlated with level of habituation (Lewis & Goldberg, 1969), of object permanence, and of Bayley performance (Clarke-Stewart, 1973), but is negatively related to performance on the Uzgiris–Hunt Object Relations in Space Scale (Clarke-Stewart, 1973). Given the inconsistency both between and within studies, it seems clear that further research must be done on this parameter before it can be classified as global in nature.

The other environmental factor that appears to qualify as a global parameter is number of times mother gives food or drink to the child (VS13B). In our results this parameter was consistently and negatively related to most aspects of sensorimotor development for most children. However, previous research on the relationship of parental caretaking to cognitive–intellectual development has generally been inconsistent (Wachs & Gruen, 1982). In contrast to our approach, previous studies have used global measures of parental caretaking, where feeding is included as part of a general caretaking dimension. Thus, inconsistency of results may be a function of combining a variety of environmental factors under a single label rather then looking at specific single environmental predictors. This interpretation is supported by the general lack of predictive power of our global nurturance measure (S12). We could hypothesize that parental emphasis on feeding and drinking activities with the children may mean less time for other, more cognitively facilitating interactions. This hypothesis is supported by data reported by Carew (1980), comparing the facilitation potential of different environmental parameters. However, given the inconsistencies in the literature, at this time we are reluctant to label this parameter as global in nature. Thus, at present, for the social environment, only the three aforementioned language-environment factors appear to act in a global fashion upon cognitive performance. This small number of global predictors is, of course, congruent with the BEAM model.

One implication of the BEAM model is that, in addition to environmental parameters that are globally predictive, it should also be possible to identify a subset of environmental factors that are unrelated to any aspect of cognitive–intellectual development. Obviously, these would be ones that should not be included in intervention programs. For the period between 12 and 24 months of age our results reveal a number of nonpredictive environmental parameters. These include adult naming of childs ongoing activities, (LS4C), adult giving or showing objects to the child (VS13A), use of nonverbal demonstrations to the child (VS15, S2A), explicitness of parental instructional activities with the child, (SCE1) and characteristics of adult responses to the child's distress signals (CE7).

On the surface, the lack of significance for characteristics of response to distress may seem somewhat surprising, given the importance placed on contingencies in the literature (Finkelstein & Ramey, 1977; Watson, 1967). The general lack of salience for response to distress between 12 and 24 months of age can be explained by reference to the concept of age specificity, as we will note shortly. For explicitness of parental instructional strategies, and non-verbal demonstrations, our nonsignificant results are congruent with previous research on the impact of parental teaching styles (Wachs & Gruen, 1982). In terms of giving and showing of objects our results may reflect the general lack of relevance of providing objects per se, as opposed to the greater importance of the characteristics of the objects themselves (Wachs & Gruen, 1982).

In addition to the preceding factors, one surprising finding was the generally low level and inconsistent pattern of results for sib and adult responses to the infants exploratory responses (IE series). In contrast to our results, the literature has shown a consistent and negative relationship between restriction of exploration and subsequent cognitive–intellectual development (Wachs & Gruen, 1982). The difference between our results and those of previous studies may, in part, be a function of the characteristics of the populations studied. In our sample, only a small subset of subjects came from extremely low-income or disadvantaged families. In contrast, many of the previous studies reporting consistent and negative relationships between restriction and cognitive development used populations where there was a high proportion of infants who were living in lower-SES or disadvantaged surroundings (Clarke-Stewart, 1973; Elardo, Bradley, & Caldwell, 1979; Williams & Scott, 1953). In more disadvantaged populations, higher levels of adult interference *and* physical restriction may be used in the second year of life, to restrict a child's exploratory activities (Clarke-Stewart, 1973; Klaus & Gray, 1968). In our sample, inspection of the means and standard deviations for IE1–4 indicated that, for the most part, the characteristic adult or sib response was to ignore the infants' exploratory attempts. Our earlier data on this sample (Wachs, 1979) showed a consistent and negative relationship between physical restrictions of the child's exploratory behavior (i.e., use of barriers) and cognitive–intellectual development in the second year of life. This suggests that our infants were restricted to a given space but, within this space were relatively free to explore without interference. Given this, we hypothesize that, at low levels, interference with exploration probably has little impact on early cognitive development; however, *at higher levels* there undoubtedly is a negative impact. What the specific distinction is between low and high levels remains a subject for future research.

Congruent with the assumptions of our BEAM model, our results have identified a small subset of environmental parameters, which act in a global fashion in terms of their relationship to development. However, the BEAM model also suggests that there will be a larger subset of environmental parameters that are relevant only for specific aspects of cognitive development, at specific ages, for specific individuals. It is to this question of specificity that our discussion now turns.

Environmental Specificity

The hypothesis of environmental–specificity predicts that different aspects of cognitive intellectual development will be influenced by different aspects of the environment. Looking either at cognitive or at environmental parameters, our results support this hypothesis. In terms of specific cognitive parameters, our results indicate that the development of object permanence by males in the second year of life is negatively influenced by adults' not verbally responding to the infant's vocalizations, passively watching the child, stressing feeding activities, rejecting or ignoring infant responses to adult requests, and failing to respond quickly to the infant's distress signals. Object permanence is positively influenced by adult use of questions and by neutral adult effect. For the development of understanding of causality by males, we again see the negative influence of giving food and drink and the positive influence of adult neutral affect. However, understanding of causality is also influenced by a number of factors that are unique to this sensorimotor ability. These include adult response to the infant's exploratory activities, rejection of the infant's attempts to engage adult attention, and use of specific adult strategies with the child.

Similar distinctions can be made for each of our environmental predictors. For each IPDS scale there is some overlap of predictive environmental factors, but each scale also has a unique core of environmental predictors. Thus, our results indicate that failure to respond to infant verbalizations (LS52) is relevant to the development of object permanence, foresight, schemes, and to gestural imitation, but not to causality or to verbal imitation. The use of adult expansion of the child's utterances in response to child vocalizations (LS54D) is relevant to the development of foresight, schemes, causality, and gestural imitation, but not to permanence, space, or verbal imitation. Speed of adult reaction to the child's distress signals (SC2) is relevant to the development of permanence, foresight, causality, and gestural imitation, but not to schemes, space, or verbal imitation. Similar delineations can be made for each PHSI item.

Given this evidence for environmental specificity, What are the implications for future research and intervention? For future research, our results clearly suggest the necessity of using multidimensional predictors and criteria. It seems obvious that many of the relationships we reported between specific environmental parameters and specific IPDS subscales would simply have vanished, were we to have collapsed IPDS subscales into a single performance measure. Similarly, these same relationships would have been lost had we collapsed all of our environmental measures into either global factor scores, or into a heterogeneous score supposedly describing the "goodness" of the infant's environment.

The results we have reported here are one more example of an increasing body of evidence (Wachs & Gruen, 1982) supporting the validity of the environmental-specificity hypothesis. As we have noted in our review on this topic, such specificity is not likely to be due to statistical or artifactual factors; rather, environmental specificity appears to be a function of the multidimensional nature of both intelligence (McCall, Eichorn, & Hogarty, 1977; Wachs & Hubert, 1981) and environment (Roff, 1949; Stern, Caldwell, Hersher, Lipton, & Richmond, 1969; Wachs, Francis, & McQuiston, 1979).

In terms of application of environmental specificity to early intervention, our results suggest that traditional global-intervention strategies are clearly outdated. Specificity implies that the most parsimonious approach to early intervention is to first determine what are the target cognitive abilities that most require intervention. Once this has been determined, stimulation programs should be set up emphasizing those environmental parameters that appear to be most relevant in influencing the development of the specific target abilities. In our previous writings (Wachs & Gruen, 1982) we have developed listings of environmental items that seem most salient for the development of specific intellectual abilities at different ages. The present results can simply be appended to our tables involving sensorimotor abilities between 12 and 24 months of age.

The preceding strategy may seem quite alien to those involved in early intervention. Most of the controversies in the early intervention area have been focused around what we might call structural variables (e.g., home-center-based intervention [Bronfenbrenner, 1974]), rather than on the nature of the experiences that are offered in either the home or the center. Our results indicate that less attention should be focused on the structure, and more on the nature of the experiences the child is receiving, whether these experiences are in a center or in the home.

The Strange Case of Means

In our previous research relating physical environmental parameters to sensorimotor development we reported little evidence for any impact of the physical environment upon the development of means (Wachs, 1979). At that time, based on infrahuman studies of tool using (Menzel, Davenport, & Rogers, 1970), we speculated that environmental influences on the development of means were more likely to be found in the realm of the social environment than in the physical environment. This speculation has not proved to be correct. Our results indicate a weak and inconsistent influence of the social environment upon the development of means, between 12 and 24 months of age. Thus, neither the physical nor the social environment appears to have a consistent influence on the development of means–end behavior.

In looking at our data we did note that means tended to have lower variability than any of the other sensorimotor scales. The lack of variability may account for the lack of relationship with the environment, but this also opens up another question: If lowered variability accounts for a lack of relationships with the environment, why should means–end performance have such low variability?

One explanation may lie in the nature of means–end behavior. Items found on this scale, between 12 and 24 months of age, tap the infant's ability to use tools to obtain goals. Tool using has a long evolutionary history for the human species (Bodmer & Cavalli-Sforza, 1976). Given this, there well may be an evolutionary bias toward acquiring tool-using capacities, which would be manifest in all but the most extreme environmental circumstances (e.g., Canalization, Scarr-Salapatek, 1976). If this hypothesis is correct we would predict that there would also be minimal genetic influence on means–end capacities, because most additive genetic variance would have been "used up" due to selection for tool-using skills over the course of evolution of the human species.

Age Specificity

The hypothesis of age specificity predicts that relevant environmental parameters change as the child develops. The pattern of results from the present study very nicely illustrate our bifactor model. Certain environmental factors are related to sensorimotor development from ages 12 through 24 months, whereas other environmental factors are relevant only during a specific portion of this age span. As an example let us look at the development of foresight. The amount of adult responsivity to child vocalizations, adult naming of objects for the child or referring to known objects, an emphasis on feeding the child, and negative adult affect, as measured between 12 and 23 months of age, are all related to the development of foresight. In contrast, the amount of spontaneous sib vocalizations, the use of expansions in response to the child vocalizations, watching without interacting with the child, and delayed responses to the child's distress calls are related to the development of foresight only when these environmental parameters occur between 12 and 17 months of age. Similarly, spontaneous sib vocalizations, adult responses to child vocalizations, and adult interactions with the child characterized by use of instructions or questions, are related to the level of schemes when measured between 12 and 23 months. In contrast, the number of spontaneous adult vocalizations and adult use of praise with the child are related to level of schemes only when these parameters occur between 12 and 17 months of age. Similar patterns of age specificity can be found for the other sensorimotor abilities as well.

In addition to demonstrating age specificity the present results also can be used to test certain predictions that were made in previous reviews regarding age changes in the relationship of specific environmental parameters to development. Thus, in reviewing the relationship of physical contact stimulation (e.g., handling) to cognitive–intellectual development, Wachs and Gruen (1982) propose a time-limited relationship, with the major influence of physical contact occurring prior to 6 months of age. Our review indicates a consistent, positive relationship between physical contact stimulation and cognitive–intellectual development, *prior to six months of age.* Supporting our prediction, the present results indicate that the relationship of physical contact to development, *after 12 months of age,* are either nonsignificant (HK1, HK2) or occasionally even negative (HK2 to causality). The consistent lack of relationship between physical contact parameters and cognitive–intellectual development after 12 months of age clearly supports our previous conceptualization on the time-limited salience of this parameter.

A second example of time-limited parameters occurs when we look at the relationship of different types of contingency responses to development at different ages. In our review on this topic we postulated a developmental progression in the relationship of contingencies and development, based on the hypothesis that contingent responses are relevant only when they create an expectancy by the infant that it can affect its environment (Wachs & Gruen, 1982). Specifically, we proposed that adult responses to distress signals would be most relevant for cognitive development during the first year of life, whereas adult responses to other signals, such as social or verbal interactions, would become more prepotent thereafter. Our results clearly support the hypothesized developmental progression. Specifically, none of the PHSI items involving type of adult response to distress were relevant to any aspect of sensorimotor development during the second year of life. Speed of adult response to distress calls was relevant to level of object permanence and foresight, but only during the 12–14-month period. In contrast, contingent adult responses to infant vocalizations were among the most salient environmental predictors of sensorimotor development throughout the second year of life. Adult responses to the infant's attempts to gain adult attention were less global, but did relate to the development of schemes and causality through the second year of life. Thus, our present results clearly support the notion of a developmental progression in the types of contingent responses that are relevant to cognitive–intellectual development at different ages.

The implications for intervention are obvious from these results. Not only must care be taken to provide stimulation that is appropriate to the developmental level of the child, but care must also be taken to change environmental parameters when research evidence suggests that these are no longer salient. Thus, a program emphasizing the use of physical contact stimulation with infants older than six months of age would not be doing these infants a service, because it would be minimizing their contact with more salient environmental parameters.

In addition to intervention, our data also has methodological implications for future longitudinal research. One prominent method for assessing the impact of early environment (Cohen & Beckwith, 1979; Tulkin & Covitz, 1975; Yarrow, Goodwin, Mannheimer, & Milowe, 1973) is to measure infant environment at a single age or set of ages and then follow the infant developmentally for a period of years, assessing the relationship between early environment and later development. When significant relationships occur between early experience and later development, it is difficult to know whether these effects are due to a lasting impact of the early experience itself or to the mediating impact of later environmental variables. Evidence exists for both the former (Bayley & Schaefer, 1964; Kagan & Moss, 1962) and the latter interpretations (Bradley & Caldwell, 1981; Olson, Bates, Pettit, & Bayles, 1981). A distinction between these two possibilities can be made *only* if there is a continuing follow-up of the infant's environment, in order to assess the continuing patterns of relationship between environment and development. In our present research, both kinds of environmental influence are seen. For casuality, most environmental influences occur in the period between 12 and 18 months of age. The fact that these early parameters influence development past 18 months of age, whereas environment after 18 months of age is predominately nonpredictive, suggests for Causality, a genuine longitudinal impact of the early environment. In contrast, for objects in space and verbal imitation, the consistency of relationships between later environment and development after 12–14 months suggests that the predictive value of 12–14-month environment is probably due to later environmental input.

The distinction between these two types of environmental action is of more than academic interest. In terms of intervention, if certain environmental parameters can be demonstrated as having a longitudinal influence, then it may be sufficient to provide these experiences only at certain points in time. In contrast, if other environmental parameters have a longitudinal impact primarily through cummulative action, then it may be necessary to continue providing these experiences, to avoid a wash-out of initial gains. Again, however, such distinctions can be made only if there is continuous follow-up of the relationship of environment to development over time.

Organismic Specificity

The hypothesis of organismic specificity postulates that different individuals will react in different ways to the environment. In terms of the present results, while the majority of male–female comparisons were nonsignificant, enough significant differences did occur to suggest the possibility of specificity for certain environmental dimensions. This is particularly true when we consider the two IPDS subscales where *both* the male and female matrices were considered significant (schemes and verbal imitation).

Specifically, our results are not supportive of the hypotheses that females are more sensitive to the verbal environment then are males (Hutt, 1972; Kagan, 1969). Rather, our results suggest that males and female are equally sensitive to the language environment, but in different ways. Males appear to be more sensitive to responsiveness (LS5-T), whereas females may be more sensitive to verbal naming of familiar objects (LS4B).

In addition to language, males seem to be more sensitive to adult ignoring of the child's attempts to obtain social interaction from adults (CE3I), more sensitive to a lack of adult interaction with the child (PI12), and more sensitive to instructional attempts by the adult (S2T). In contrast, females seem to be more sensitive to adult use of coercion (S1) or denial (S3), and to adult rejection of the infant's reactions to adult requests (CE4R). In short, males appear to be more sensitive to social interactions, whereas females are more sensitive to interations that deny the child's sense of autonomy. These patterns have been reported previously in the literature. Yarrow *et al.* (1973) have reported that males are more sensitive than females to specific training influences, and to positive emotional expressions from adults. Bradley and Caldwell (1980) have reported that males are more sensitive to adult encouragement for development, whereas, for females, level of punishment appears to be critical.

In interpreting the preceding results, the most critical question is not whether there is differential reactivity, but rather whether this differential reactivity can be seen as evidence for organismic specificity or for transactional environmental action. Differences in the environment of males and females across the preceding dimensions could be seen as evidence supporting a transactional model; a lack of differences could be viewed as evidence for the specificity model. The results of our analysis clearly suggest that both models may be relevant. Specifically, our results indicate that between 12 and 20 months of age, environmental differences for male and females are virtually nonexistent. It is only after 20 months of age that environmental differences begin to appear. This pattern suggests that gender differences in reactivity occurring prior to 20 months of age are due to organismic specificity. After 20 months of age the hypothesis that differences in reactivity are due to different environments becomes more probable.

Such a finding is not as surprising as it would seem. Research in the area of infant temperament has indicated no relationship between ratings of infant temperament and measurements of parent–infant interaction at 6 months of age (Bates, Olson, Pettit, & Bayles, 1982; Wachs & Gandour, in press), or at 13 months of age (Bates, Pettit, & Bayles, 1981). Relationships between environment and temperament only begin to appear around 24 months of age (Lee, 1981). What these data suggest is that differential parent treatment of infants differing in characteristics such as gender or temperament may not occur until after the parent has had time to build up a stable picture of each infant's characteristics. It is only after this picture has been drawn that differential treatment of infants may systematically occur. Given this, our results suggest that organismic specificity may well be the rule for the first 2 years after birth, in terms of interpreting differential reactivity to the environment. This interpretation is congruent with our previous research on differential reactivity by males and females, to the physical environment (Wachs, 1978, 1979), as well as with data by Pedersen, Rubenstein, and Yarrow, (1979) on gender differences in reactivity to social interaction.

The present pattern of results lend support to the growing body of evidence indicating the existence of differential reactivity to similar environmental circumstances by infants with different organismic characteristics. One implication of this type of specificity is the inadequacy of global experiential theories, based on concepts such as match, dependence drive, or stimulus deprivation. Rather, organismic specificity implies the need for minitheories, encompassing the differential reactivity of specific organisms to specific environmental parameters.

The relevance of organismic specificity for intervention also exists. The major implication of this hypothesis is that it is not sufficient simply to present an infant with a "standard" intervention program (whether at home or in a center), and hope that enough positive stimulus elements for this child are present in the program, to promote cognitive gains. The tremendous variability in response to early intervention (Stevenson, Parker, Wilkinson, Bonnevaux & Gonzalez, 1978; Williams, 1977); clearly shows the inadequacy of this strategy. Rather than global or group intervention strategies, what seems to be needed are intervention strategies, wherein stimulation appropriate to a child's particular organismic characteristics are provided. Unfortunately, what is currently lacking is a taxonomy of specific organismic characteristics that have been shown to mediate the individual's response to the environment. Evidence is available on gender and temperamental differences (Wachs & Gruen, 1982), and suggestions have been made for other types of organismic parameters that might serve as individual difference mediators (Wachs, 1977). However, at present, few empirical data are available. Until such data are available, perhaps the wisest course is to be alert for children's lack of reaction to particular intervention programs (plus not promising too much for early intervention until more is known).

In addition to implications for early experience per se, the hypothesis of organismic specificity provides a potential bridge between those interested in environmental factors and those interested in genetic biological factors (Wachs, 1983). The concept of gene–environment interaction (differential response to the environment by different genotypes [Bodmer & Cavalli-Sforza, 1976]) may be seen as one form of organismic specificity. Integrative studies, looking at how genotypically based individual differences mediate the response of the individual to the environment, may form a common meeting ground between those interested in biological factors and those interested in experience.

Higher-Order Specificity

As we noted earlier, in addition to the three major types of specificity, we must also consider the possibility of interactions among the various types. Our results, in fact, do yield a number of examples suggesting the existence of higher-order interactions.

Illustrating age × environmental specificity, sib vocalizations (LS35) are relevant for both causality and space concepts from 12 months through 17 months of age; however, after 18 months of age this variable is relevant only for the development of space concepts. Similarly, in terms of verbal versus gestural imitation, the influence of active parental watching of the child (HK3B) continues after 17 months of age for verbal imitation but not for gestural imitation.

In terms of age × organismic specificity, for verbal imitation, we find that percentage of adult verbal responses to child vocalizations (LS5T) is relevant for male verbal imitation between 12 and 24 months of age; for females, LS5T is relevant only between 12 and 14 months of age.

In terms of organismic × environmental specificity, we find that informational content contained in adult vocalizations (VG) is positively related to male gestural imitation, but negatively related to female verbal imitation. Comparing the environmental items relevant to male and female performance on development of schemes we find virtually no overlap in the types of environmental items related to male versus female performance on this scale.

In terms of environment × age × organismic specificity, our results indicate that spontaneous sib vocalizations to the child (LS3S) measured from 12 to 23 months are positively related to male performance on development of schemes. The corresponding correlations for females are zero order. In contrast, our results show a positive and significant relationship between sib vocalizations measured between 15 and 17 months of age and female verbal imitation; the corresponding correlations for males are zero order. A similar finding is seen in the percentage of time the adult reacts positively to the child's reactions to adult requests (CE4P). From 12 to 24 months of age, this item is significantly and negatively related to female performance on development of schemes; the corresponding correlation for males is zero order. In contrast, for verbal imitation between 18 and 20 months of age the correlation for males is positive and significant, whereas the correlation for females is zero order. Other examples of these various types of specificity can also be found in our tables.

Some Closing Thoughts on the Nature of Early Environmental Action

When we were operating under the dual assumptions of parsimony and global environmental action, for those interested in research or intervention, the idea of early experience was much more simple then it is now. We believe that the available evidence, contained both in this chapter and in other reviews of human early experience (Hunt, 1979; Wachs & Gruen, 1982) clearly indicate a much more complex process than had been previously envisioned. It is our belief that the nature of early environmental action is well described by the bifactor model we have proposed. There appear to be a limited set of environmental parameters that relate to most aspects of development for most children within a fairly wide age-range. Clearly, these are the environmental items that should form the core of any intervention attempt. However, in addition, to this class of global environmental parameters there are a larger set of specific environmental items. Some are specific only to certain developmental parameters; others are relevant to development only at certain ages; still others influence development only for certain individuals.

The critical point to note, given the evidence we have presented on the validity of the bifactor model, is the relevance of this model for future early experience research or environmental intervention. In terms of future research it seems clear that we must use multidimensional predictors and criteria at different ages. Longitudinal studies must involve repeated measures of both environment and development, in order to properly interpret results. Further, it is no longer sufficient to report results for a heterogeneous group of subjects. Rather, subjects must be divided on the basis of individual characteristics that may potentially act to mediate the impact of the environment upon the individual.

Similarly, in terms of intervention, it no longer appears sufficient to assume that the same intervention parameters that work for disadvantaged infants will work for preterm or Downs syndrome infants. It is doubtful if we can continue to assume that the same environmental factors that promote infants expressive vocabulary will be the same ones that promote their understanding of concepts, receptive vocabulary, or attention. Nor does it seem correct to evaluate the impact of intervention through measurement of gains on a global intelligence score, and report of mean differences, for a sample. Rather, what seems most critical is to look at the gains or losses for individual infants, in relationship to the goals of the program and the individual characteristics of the infants involved. More than anything else, it may well be that the failure to integrate into intervention programs current knowledge regarding the nature of early environmental action has led to the tremendous controversy regarding the efficacy of these programs (Wachs & Gruen, 1982).

It seems clear that we are now entering a new stage in the human early experience field. Until very recently we were concerned with establishing the relevance of early experience for development (the perennial heredity–environment controversy) and with attempting to show the social utility of early experience. It seems clear that both these aims have been well established. Given our current knowledge base the time is now right to move onto a new stage, characterized by a close interface between those interested in experience, biologically mediated individual differences, and social intervention.

For those interested in intervention the major goal should be an attempt to determine what aspects of the environment are most salient in facilitating or inhibiting specific aspects of development for specific individuals at specific ages. For those interested in basic problems the relevance of these data to questions such as how specific experiences result in specific developmental changes, or how individual differences act to mediate environmental impact, seems obvious.

Until recently, the preceding approaches would not have seemed valid, given the existing myth of global environmental action. It is painful to give up treasured myths, as any child who has stopped believing in Santa Claus or the tooth fairy can tell us. Comfortable as these myths are, after a certain time they outlive their usefulness. Perhaps, for those of us interested in the early environment it is time to act like the children we work with, and put away a treasured myth to face the world whose complexity we are only now beginning to grasp.

Acknowledgments

*The burden of data collection in this project fell on four individuals: Jean Cicirelli, Jan-Ellen Kaderabek, Rosemary Saluri-Morris and Eloise Stiglitz. For their help the author is most grateful. Special thanks go to Mary Jane Gandour for her heroic efforts to convince the computer that we wanted the data analyzed our way and not its way. Thanks are also due to Robert Plomin for his comments on canalization and to Allen Gottfried for his incisive editorial comments. Finally and most importantly our deepest thanks go to the parents of the infants used in our study. Without their continued, and even cheerful, cooperation, none of this would have been possible.

References

Bates, J., Olson, S., Pettit, G., & Bayles, K. Dimensions of individuality in the mother–infant relationship at six months. Child Development, 1982, 53, 446–461.
Bates, J., Pettit, G., & Bayles, K. Antecedents of problem behaviors at age three years. Paper presented at the Society for Research in Child Development, Boston April 1981.
Bayley, N., & Schaefer, E. Correlations of maternal and child behaviors with the devel-

opment of mental abilities: Data from the Berkeley Growth Study. *Monographs of the Society for Research in Child Development*, 1964, 29.

Beckwith, L., & Cohen, S. Pre-term births: Hazardous obstetrical and postnatal events as related to caregiver–infant behavior. *Infant Behavior and Development*, 1978, 1, 403–411.

Beckwith, L., Cohen, S., Kopp, C., Parmelee, A., & Marcy, J. Caregiver–infant interaction and early cognitive development in pre-term infants. *Child Development*, 1976, 47, 579–587.

Belsky, J., & Steinberg, L. The effects of day care: A critical review. *Child Development*, 1978, 49, 929–949.

Bodmer, W., & Cavalli-Sforza, L. *Genetics, evolution and man*. San Francisco: Freeman, 1976.

Bradley, R., & Caldwell, B. The relation of home environment, cognitive competence, and IQ among males and females. *Child Development*, 1980, 51, 1140–1148.

Bradley, R., & Caldwell, B. *The stability of the home environment and its relation to child development*. Paper presented at the International Society for the Study of Behavioral Development, Toronto, August, 1981.

Bradley, R., Caldwell, B., & Elardo, R. Home environment and cognitive development in the first two years: A cross-lagged panel analysis. *Developmental Psychology*, 1979, 15, 246–250.

Bronfenbrenner, U. *Is early intervention effective?* Department of Health, Education, and Welfare Publication No. (OHD)76–30025, Washington, DC, 1974.

Brozek, J. Nutrition, malnutrition and behavior. *Annual Review of Psychology*, 1978, 29, 157–178.

Carew, J. Experience and the development of intelligence in young children at home and in day care. *Monograph of the Society for Research in Child Development*, 1980, 45.

Clarke-Stewart, K. A. Interactions between mothers and their young children: Characteristics and consequences. *SRCD Monographs*, 1973, 38.

Cohen, S., & Beckwith, L. Pre-term infant interaction with the caregiver in the first year of life and competence at age 2. *Child Development*, 1979, 48, 152–157.

Cronbach, L. The two disciplines of scientific psychology. In D. Jackson & S. Messick (Eds.), *Problems in human assessment*. New York: McGraw-Hill, 1967.

De Fries, J., Plomin, R., Vandenberg, J., & Kuse, A. Parent–offspring resemblance for cognitive abilities in the Colorado Adoption Project. *Intelligence*, 1981, 5, 245–277.

Elardo, R., Bradley, R., & Caldwell, B. The relationship of infant's home environment to mental test performance from 6–36 months: A longitudinal analysis. *Child Development*, 1975, 46, 71–76.

Finkelstein, N., & Ramey, C. Learning to control the environment in infancy. *Child Development*, 1977, 48, 806–814.

Honzik, M. Environmental correlates of mental growth: Predictions from the family setting at 21 months. *Child Development*, 1967, 38, 337–364. (a)

Honzik, M. Prediction of differential abilities at age 18 from the early family environment. *APA Proceedings*, 1967, 2, 151–152. (b)

Hunt, J. McV. *Intelligence and experience*. New York: Ronald Press, 1961.

Hunt, J. McV. *Specificity in early development and experience*. O'Neill Invited Lecture, Meyer Children's Rehabilitation Instutite, University of Nebraska Medical Center, 1977.

Hunt, J. McV. Psychological development: Early experience. *Annual Review of Psychology*, 1979, 30, 103–143.

Hutt, C. Sex differences in human development. *Human Development*, 1972, 15, 153–170.

Kagan, J. On the need for relativism. *American Psychologist*, 1967, *22*, 131–142.

Kagan, J., & Freeman, M. Relation of childhood intelligence, maternal behaviors and social class to behavior during adolescence. *Child Development*, 1963, *34*, 899–911.

Kagan, J., Kearsley, R. B., & Zelazo, P. R. *Infancy: Its place in human development.* Cambridge, MA: Harvard University Press, 1978.

Kagan, J., & Moss, H. A. Birth to maturity: *The Fels study of psychological development.* New York: Wiley, 1962.

Klaus, R., & Gray, S. The early training project for disadvantaged children. *Monographs of the Society for Research in Child Development*, 1968, *33*.

Lee, C. *Perceived difficult temperament and mother-toddler interaction sequences.* Paper presented at the Society for Research in Child Development, Boston, April 1981.

Lewis, M., & Goldberg, S. Perceptual cognitive development in infancy: A generalized expectancy model as a function of the mother–infant interaction. *Merrill-Palmer Quarterly*, 1969, *15*, 87–100.

Lichtenberg, P., & Norton, D. *Cognitive and mental development in the first 5 years of life.* National Institute of Mental Health Report, Washington, DC, 1970.

Lytton, H. Three approaches to the study of parent–child interaction: Ethological, interview, and experimental. *Journal of Child Psychology and Psychiatry*, 1973, *14*, 1–17.

McCall, R. The use of multivariate procedures in developmental psychology. In P. Mussen (Ed.), *Carmichael's manual of child psychology.* New York: Wiley, 1970.

McCall, R., Eichorn, D., & Hogarty, P. Transitions in early mental development. *Monographs of the Society for Research in Child Development*, 1977, *42*.

Macphee, D., & Ramey, C. *Infant temperament as a catalyst and consequence of development in two caregiving environments.* Paper presented at the 14th Gatlinburg Conference, Gatlinburg, March, 1981.

Medvedev, Z. *The rise and fall of T. D. Lysenko.* New York: Columbia University Press, 1969.

Menzel, E., Davenport, R., & Rogers, C. The development of tool using in wild-born and restriction reared chimpanzees. *Folia Primat*, 1970, *12*, 273–282.

Moos, R. Conceptualizations of human environments. *American Psychologist*, 1973, *20*, 652–667.

Norman-Jackson, J. Family interactions, language development and primary reading achievement of black children in families of low income. *Child Development*, 1982, *53*, 349–358.

Olson, S., Bates, J., Pettit, G., & Bayles, K. *Antecedents of individual differences in children's cognitive and language competence at age two.* Paper presented to the Society for Research in Child Development, Boston, April 1981.

Pederson, F. A., Rubenstein, J. L., & Yarrow, L. J. Infant development in father-absent families. *The Journal of Genetic Psychology*, 1979, *135*, 51–61.

Radin, N. Father–child interaction and the intellectual functioning of four-year-old boys. *Developmental Psychology*, 1972, *6*, 353–361.

Radin, N. Observed paternal behaviors as antecedents of intellectual functioning in young boys. *Developmental Psychology*, 1973, *8*, 369–376.

Roff, M. A factorial study of the Fels Parent Behavior Scale. *Child Development*, 1949, *20*, 29–45.

Sameroff, A., & Chandler, M. Reproductive risk and the continuum of caretaking casualty. In F. Horowitz (ed.), *Review of child development research* (Vol. 4). Chicago: University of Chicago Press, 1975.

Scarr-Salapatek, S. An evolutionary perspective on infant intelligence. In M. Lewis (Ed.), *Origins of intelligence.* New York: Plenum, 1976.

Siegel, L. Infant perceptual, cognitive and motor behaviors as predictors of subsequent cognitive and language development. *Canadian Journal of Psychology*, 1979, *33*, 382–295.

Stern, G., Caldwell, B., Hersher, L., Lipton, E., & Richmond, J. A factor analytic sudy of the mother–infant dyad. *Child Development*, 1969, *40*, 163–182.

Stevenson, H., Parker, T., Wilkinson, A., Bonnevaux, B., & Gonzalez, M. Schooling, environment and cognitive development: A cross-cultural study. *Monographs of the Society for Research in Child Development*, 1978, *175*.

Thoday, J., & Gibson, J. Environmental and genetical contributions to class differences: A model experiment. *Science*, 1970, *167*, 990–992.

Thomas, A., & Chess, S. Behavioral individuality in childhood. In L. Aronson, E. Tobach, D. Lehrman, & J. Rosenblatt (Eds.), *Development and evolution of behavior*. San Francisco: Freeman, 1976.

Tulkin, S., & Covitz, F. *Mother–infant interaction and intellectual functioning at age 6*. Paper presented at the Biennial Meeting of the Society for Research in Child Development, Denver, 1975.

Uzgiris, I. Organization of sensorimotor intelligence. In M. Lewis (Ed.), *Origins of intelligence*. New York: Plenum Press, 1976.

Uzgiris, I. *Changing patterns of infant environment interaction at various stages of development*. Paper presented at the symposium on biosocial factors and the infant who is at high risk for developmental disabilities, University of Massachusetts Medical School, Worcester, MA., May 1980.

Uzgiris, I., & Hunt, J. McV. *Assessment in infancy*. Urbana, IL.: University of Illinois Press, 1975.

Wachs, T. D. The optimal stimulation hypothesis and early development. In I. Uzgiris & F. Weizmann (Eds.), *The structuring of experience*. New York: Plenum, 1977.

Wachs, T. D. The relationship of infants' physical environment to their Binet performance at $2\frac{1}{2}$ years. *International Journal of Behavioral Development*, 1978, *1*, 51–56.

Wachs, T. D. Proximal experience and early cognitive–intellectual development: The physical environment. *Merrill-Palmer Quarterly*, 1979, *25*, 3–41.

Wachs, T. D. Ten years of research on early experience and early intelligence Presented at the meeting of Ontario Psychological Association, Toronto, April 1981.

Wachs, T. D. The use and abuse of environment in behavior-genetic research. *Child Development*, 1983, *54*, 396–407.

Wachs, T. D., Francis, J., & McQuiston, S. Psychological dimensions of the infant's physical environment. *Infant Behavior and Development*, 1979, *2*, 155–161.

Wachs, T. D., & Gandour, N. J. Temperament, environment and six- month cognitive–intellectual development. *International Journal of Behavioral Development*, in press.

Wachs, T. D. & Gruen, G. *Early experience and human development*. New York: Plenum, 1982.

Wachs, T. D., & Hubert, N. Changes in the structure of cognitive–intellectual performance during the second year of life. *Infant Behavior and Development*, 1981, *4*, 151–162.

Wachs, T. D., & Peters-Martin, P. *Temperament, environment and twelve-month sensorimotor development*. Paper presented at the International Society for the Study of Behavioral Development, Toronto, August 1981.

Wachs, T. D., Uzgiris, I., & Hunt, J. McV. Cognitive development in infants of different age levels and from different environmental backgrounds. *Merrill-Palmer Quarterly*, 1971, *17*, 283–317.

Watson, J. S. Memory and "contingency analysis" in infant learning. *Merrill-Palmer Quarterly*, 1967, *13*, 55–76.

Weick, K. Systematic observational methods. In G. Lindzey & F. Aronson (Eds.), *Handbook of social psychology* (2nd ed.). Reading, MA: Addison-Wesley, 1968.

White, B. Critical influences in the origins of competence. *Merrill-Palmer Quarterly*, 1975, *21*, 243–266.

Williams, J., & Scott, R. Growth and development of Negro infants: Motor development and its relationship to child rearing practices in two groups of Negro infants (Vol. 4) *Child Development*, 1953, *24*, 103–121.

Williams, T. Infant development and supplemental care: A comparative review of basic and applied research. *Human Development*, 1977, *20*, 1–30.

Wohlwill, J. *The study of behavioral development*. New York: Academic Press, 1973.

Yarrow, L. J. Research in dimensions of early maternal care. *Merrill- Palmer Quarterly*, 1963, *9*, 101–114.

Yarrow, L. J., Goodwin, M., Mannheimer, H., & Milowe, I. Infancy experience and cognitive and personality development at 10 years. In J. Stone, H. Smith, & L. Murphy (Eds.). *The competent infant*. New York: Basic Books, 1973.

Yarrow, L. J., Rubenstein, J., & Pedersen, F. *Infant and environment*. New York: Wiley, 1975.

Zajonc, R. Family configuration and intelligence. *Science*, 1976, *192*, 227–236.

Zegiob, L., Arnold, S., & Forehand, R. An examination of observer effects in parent–child interactions. *Child Development*, 1975, *46*, 509–512.

9

Home Environment and Early Cognitive Development: Integration, Meta-analyses, and Conclusions

Allen W. Gottfried

The results of multivariate longitudinal investigations are complex and complicated. The purpose of this chapter is to put forth those findings that are comparable and generalizable across the longitudinal studies, as well as to highlight some specific findings presented in the foregoing chapters. This chapter deals first with the relationship of family demographic factors and home environment, and second with the relationship of home environment and cognitive development.

Home Environment

The data clearly demonstrated that assessments of proximal home environmental variables are reliable and valid indicators of the stimulation and experiences available to infants and young children. The investigators consistently reported high levels of interobserver agreement, with values typically in the high 80s and 90s. On the HOME, Bradley and Caldwell, and Barnard, Bee, and Hammond, reported internal reliability coefficients averaging .72 and .52, respectively, indicating a moderate to moderately high degree of homogeneity among items in this scale. Home environmental assessments showed a moderate level of stability across intervals of months and years during infancy and the preschool period. In the Bradley and Caldwell study, the average correlation across all HOME scales for intervals of 6–18-months was .46. Gottfried and Gottfried reported a correlation of .58 for HOME total scores, between a 2-year interval. The average coefficient across all HOME scales in the Barnard, Bee, and Hammond study was .58 for a 20-month interval. In the Johnson, Breckenridge, and McGowan study, the average correlation for the HOME total score was .42 for 1–2-year intervals. The study by Siegel, which presented correlations across the longest interval, 2–4 years on HOME total scores, had an average coefficient of .49. The foregoing studies have employed the HOME infant and/or preschool scales. Wachs reported median correlations on the Purdue Home Stimulation Inventory (PHSI) (IV) of .47 and .50 within a 1-year interval for males and for females, respectively. Across various samples, time intervals, home assessments, and types of coefficients employed in these studies, the average stability coefficient for home environmental variables during the early years is .50 (range = .42–.58 across studies).

Several trends emerged concerning the relationship of family demographic characteristics and home environment. The most pervasive finding involved the covariation of socioeconomic status (SES) and home stimulation. All of the researchers investigating this issue have reported a positive association between SES and home environment (Bradley & Caldwell; Gottfried & Gottfried; Barnard, Bee, & Hammond; Johnson, Breckenridge, & McGowan; Siegel; Beckwith & Cohen). Regardless of the SES indicator employed (parental income, education, paternal occupation, or a global index), the findings remained invariant. Thus, it is an empirical fact that children from relatively higher SES families receive an intellectually more advantageous home environment. This finding holds for white, black, and Hispanic children, for children within lower- and middle-SES families, as well as for children born preterm and full-term. As Bradley and Caldwell, and Beckwith and Cohen showed, the difference in home environment between white and black children and between English- and Spanish-speaking children was a function of socioeconomic factors, not race per se. Data also revealed that SES differences in home environment were evident as early as the first 4 months of age (Barnard, Bee, & Hammond; Beckwith & Cohen). Consistent with the relationship between SES and home environment, is the finding that mothers of relatively higher intelligence, as measured by vocabulary, provided a more enriched environment for their children. This was found in the predominantly white middle-SES sample of Gottfried and Gottfried, and in the Mexican-American lower-SES sample of Johnson, Breckenridge, and McGowan.

To ascertain the specific home environmental factors that were associated with SES across studies, those studies using the HOME scale were compared. Based on the sample characteristics described in each chapter, these studies were arranged in order of SES from low to relatively higher status. The Johnson, Breckenridge, and McGowan sample was the lowest (an entirely low SES group); the Bradley and Caldwell sample was next (a heterogeneous, but predominantly low SES group); the Siegel sample was third (an intact blue-collar working class); and the equivalent middle-SES samples (see Hollingshead Four-Factor Indexes) of Barnard, Bee, and Hammond, and of Gottfried and Gottfried were highest. The means and standard deviations on the HOME scales at 1-year for each study are presented in Table 1.

Examination of the individual scales revealed obvious trends. The lower- compared to middle-SES samples had lower scores on Emotional and Verbal Responsivity of Mother, Provision of Appropriate Play Materials, Maternal Involvement with Child, Opportunities for Variety in Daily Stimulation, and HOME total score. On most of these scales the trend was linear. The Beckwith and Cohen results are entirely in accordance with these findings. These investigators reported that middle- compared to lower-SES mothers spoke more to their children, were socially more involved, provided more intellectual tasks in terms of play materials, and showed consistently higher levels of caregiver responsiveness. There were no differences on Avoidance of Restriction and Punishment, and Organization of Temporal and Physical Environ-

TABLE 1
Means and Standard Deviations on 1-Year HOME Scales across Studies

HOME	Johnson Breckenridge McGowan (JBM)	Bradley Caldwell (BC)	Siegel (S)	Barnard Bee Hammond (BBH)	Gottfried Gottfried (GG)
1. Responsivity	8.5	8.0	9.0	9.7	8.7
	(2.1)[a]	(2.1)	(1.9)	(1.6)	(1.5)
2. Restriction and	5.4	5.3	6.2	5.4	6.4
punishment	(1.5)	(1.6)	(1.3)	(1.7)	(1.1)
3. Organization	4.5	4.9	5.1	4.8	5.2
	(1.3)	(1.2)	(1.0)	(1.0)	(0.9)
4. Play materials	4.6	6.4	7.2	7.9	8.6
	(2.1)	(2.4)	(1.8)	(1.5)	(0.7)
5. Involvement	3.4	3.3	3.8	5.0	4.0
	(1.6)	(1.6)	(1.9)	(1.3)	(1.2)
6. Variety	2.6	3.0	3.1	3.4	3.4
	(1.2)	(1.1)	(1.3)	(1.2)	(1.1)
Total	28.9	31.9	34.4	36.3	36.4
	(6.7)	(7.6)	(5.9)	(5.6)	(3.7)
N	367	67	170	169	129

[a] Standard deviations in parentheses.

ment, across the studies. Another pattern in Table 1 was the tendency for lower SES samples to be more variable than the middle-SES samples on maternal responsivity, organization, play materials, maternal involvement, and HOME total score. Thus, it may be that middle-SES families are more homogeneous in the home environment they create for their children or that the lowered variability was possibly the result of a ceiling effect in the scale.

The relationship of birth order to home environment also showed a generalizable finding. In the studies investigating this relationship, the data indicated that firstborns, compared to later-borns, received a more intellectually stimulating environment. Bradley and Caldwell reported that a substantial relationship exists between birth order and HOME scores at 12- and 24-months. Gottfried and Gottfried found differences between first and later-borns on the HOME at 15 and 39 months, PHSI (I–III) at 15 months, and Family Environmental Scale (FES) at 36 months. Beckwith and Cohen found advantages for firstborns, well within the first year, for both the English- and Spanish-speaking samples. Siegel reported that there were no consistent patterns in birth order between her cohorts or between the full-terms and preterms. She did note that it may have been due to the small sample-sizes involved in these comparisons. However, where differences did emerge at 12 and 36-months, they favored firstborns in all but one instance. Thus, the evidence is reliable that during infancy and the preschool years, firstborns compared to later-borns have environments that are advantaged for enhancing intellectual skills. This holds for children differing in race and SES, and who differed in gestational age. For the three studies using the HOME, there were no birth-order differences found on any scale across all three studies. However, differences were found in two of three studies for play materials, organization, maternal involvement, and variety of stimulation. There were no birth order differences in any of the three studies for maternal responsivity and for avoidance of restriction and punishment.

Two other family demographic or structure variables that consistently related to home environment were crowding (room:person ratio) and number of children in the family. Bradley and Caldwell reported that crowding was the strongest and most consistent correlate of the HOME. Crowding correlated with all of the HOME subscales at 12 months of age and all but maternal responsivity at 24 months. It is noteworthy that crowding remained significantly related to the HOME when other environmental factors were controlled. Johnson, Breckenridge, and McGowan also found positive correlations between crowding and 12-month HOME scales, in particular, organization, play materials, and HOME total score. Thus, it appears that the greater a young child's personal space in the home, the greater the quantity and quality of home stimulation. Across these two studies, crowding correlated most consistently with organization of the home and play materials in the home.

In line with these findings is the relationship between number of children in the family and home environment. Both Gottfried and Gottfried, and Johnson, Breckenridge, and McGowan, found negative correlations between number of children and scores on the HOME scales at 15 and 39 months, and 12 months, respectively. Furthermore, both studies showed highly similar relationships on the infant HOME scales. In both studies, there were negative correlations with organization, play materials, maternal involvement, and HOME total score. Across the array of family structure or configuration variables (birth order, crowding, and number of children), organization, play materials, and maternal involvement were most consistently related.

All of the investigators examined whether there were gender differences on the home variables. The findings are consistent with some minor exceptions. Those researchers employing the HOME scales (Bradley & Caldwell; Gottfried & Gottfried; Barnard, Bee, & Hammond; Johnson, Breckenridge, and McGowan; Siegel) have all reported that there were no gender differences at any of the ages assessed. Data in the Beckwith and Cohen and Wachs studies indicated that at most ages and on most variables there were no gender differences. However, some gender differences were noted and considered significant. Beckwith and Cohen found that caregivers in the English- and Spanish-speaking samples displayed differential treatment toward males and females, with the direction differing for the two samples. Compared to the males, females from English-speaking homes received significantly more and females from Spanish-speaking homes received significantly fewer contingent social interactions (e.g., mutual visual regard, contingent vocalization). Wachs found gender differences in social environment for a limited number of items. Of the 60 observational codes in his scale, there were differential correlations for the genders on 16, and when the genders were compared on these variables, there were gender differences on four variables. These differences involved female vocalizations being ignored significantly more than those of males, and males compared to females received more food and drink from adults, had more object-naming interactions, and more instructional activities with adults. Although the Beckwith and Cohen, and Wachs studies suggested that there may be subtle gender differences in caregiver–infant interactions, the predominance of evi-

dence in the present longitudinal studies did not show gender differences in early home environment.

Home Environment and Cognitive Development

All of the investigators have reported that proximal home environmental variables correlated with the cognitive development of young
children. Although the outcomes across studies showed variation with
respect to the specific factors that correlated with developmental tests
and the magnitudes of correlations, the studies did show comparability
of findings on several major theoretical issues.

Most of the investigators sought to determine whether home environmental variables contributed to cognitive development when SES
factors were controlled (Bradley & Caldwell, see Bradley, Caldwell, &
Elardo, 1977; Gottfried & Gottfried; Barnard, Bee, & Hammond; Johnson, Breckenridge, & McGowan; Siegel; Beckwith & Cohen). Analyses
were conducted by partial correlations and/or regression analyses. The
results invariantly showed that home environmental variables related
to cognitive development, independent of SES. While reductions in the
frequency of significant correlations were found when SES was partialed out (Gottfried & Gottfried; Barnard, Bee, & Hammond; Beckwith
& Cohen), the large majority of the correlations remained significant.
Reductions in magnitude, to nonsignificance, were typically found
with the weakest correlations, and were not associated with any particular home environmental variable, age, or developmental measure
(Gottfried & Gottfried; Barnard, Bee, & Hammond). The overall finding
showed that home environmental factors contributed significantly to
cognitive development, independent of their association with SES. It
should also be noted that SES correlated with cognitive development,
independent of home environmental factors (Gottfried & Gottfried;
Siegel).

Two studies have addressed the controversial issue of whether the
correlation between home environment and cognitive development is
accounted for by their relationship with mothers' intelligence (Gottfried & Gottfried; Barnard, Bee, & Hammond). In the study by Gottfried and Gottfried, the correlations with maternal intelligence
partialed out, as well as the series of stepwise and hierarchical regression analyses, revealed that the relationship between home environment and children's cognitive development is not spuriously due to
their relationship with mothers' intelligence. Furthermore, it was

found that the correlations between mothers' and children's intelligence is not independent of home environment. Although Barnard, Bee, and Hammond did not use a measure of intelligence, their findings are in accord with those of Gottfried and Gottfried. Barnard, Bee, and Hammond's results showed that when maternal education was partialed out of the correlations of home environment and children's cognitive development, 88% of the correlations remained significant. It is noteworthy that this high percentage of significant correlations, with maternal education partialed out, is comparable to the percentages of significant correlations with maternal intelligence partialed out in the Gottfrieds' study. These two investigations provided complementary evidence favoring the view that home environment is significantly and independently related to children's cognitive development, controlling for mothers' intelligence (or educational achievement).

In the investigations where children were assessed through the preschool years, there were two confluent trends that characterized the relationship between home environment and cognitive development, with respect to changes in age. These trends hold for the studies of Bradley and Caldwell, of Gottfried and Gottfried, of Barnard, Bee, and Hammond, of Siegel, and of Beckwith and Cohen, but not for those of Johnson, Breckenridge, and McGowan. The first trend showed that later, compared to earlier, assessments of home environment were more highly correlated with cognitive development. Home assessments conducted at age 2 years or later showed higher correlations with concurrent and subsequent measures of cognitive development than did assessments of home environment conducted within the first year. The second trend showed that later measures of cognitive development, in contrast to earlier measures, were more consistently and more highly associated with home environmental variables. Preschool intelligence tests correlated higher with home environment than did infant intelligence tests. Taken together, these two trends showed that a greater frequency of significant correlations and correlations of higher magnitudes were found predictively (e.g., 1-year HOME and 3-year Stanford-Binet) that were found concurrently (e.g., 1-year HOME and 1-year Bayley), and that correlations of greatest magnitudes were found between the last home assessments (around 2 years of age or later) and measures of cognitive development during the preschool years. There are several implications of these trends. First, the content of later assessments of home environment (e.g., educational materials, stimulation of academic skills), as in the case of the preschool compared to the infant version of the HOME, may be more similar to the tasks involved in assessing preschool intelligence. Second, preschool assessments of home environments may include variables that are more influential of intellectual development. Third, where the same home inventory was repeatedly used over time (e.g., infant version of HOME), the higher correlations with the later assessments may be due to the differential abilities among children exerting a greater influence on their home environments as they get older. With advancement in age, individual differences in intelligence among children may account more for differences in home environments. Fourth, the higher correlations with preschoolers compared to infants implies that the cognitive abilities assessed on tests for the former may be more sensitive to home stimulation than cognitive abilities assessed on tests for the latter.

Several of the researchers addressed the theoretical issue of whether the relationship between early home environment and subsequent cognitive development was due to early experiences per se, or to the cross-time consistency of home environment. As noted previously, assessments of home environment showed moderate stability during infancy and the preschool years. Most of the findings support the view that early home environment related to later intellectual development because of stability of home environment (Bradley & Caldwell; Gottfried & Gottfried; Barnard, Bee, & Hammond; Beckwith & Cohen contended that their results supported this view; Wachs reported that in his data there is evidence for this position as well). Furthermore, the findings showed that there was no additive or cumulative effect of early and later home environment in predicting intelligence in preschoolers (Gottfried & Gottfried; Barnard, Bee, & Hammond). However, Bradley and Caldwell, Barnard, Bee, and Hammond, and Wachs pointed out that there were some early specific age-related home factors that correlated with later development independently of the cross-time relationship in home environment. Stability of home environment accounted for most of the correlations between early environment and subsequent cognitive development, while there were some early specific age-related home experiences that had unique developmental predictive weight.

Differential correlational networks between home environmental variables and cognitive development, for particular sample characteristics, were examined. Gottfried and Gottfried reported no correlational differences between first- and later-borns. Barnard, Bee, and Hammond found no differences in children of mothers with low and high educational-achievement. Both Bradley and Caldwell and Beckwith and Cohen found some differences between racial groups. Bradley and Caldwell noted that there was a tendency for whites to show higher correlations than blacks on certain HOME subscales. Beckwith and Cohen reported that their English-speaking sample differed from their Spanish-speaking sample, in that the former, compared to the latter, had fewer concurrent relationships between caregiving and test performance within the first year, but more predictive relationships to age 5 years. In those studies that included children with perinatal complications, the data indicated that home environmental factors are as important to cognitive development as with children not at risk (Barnard, Bee, & Hammond; Siegel; Beckwith & Cohen). Barnard, Bee, and Hammond reported that there were no differences in strength or pattern of correlations between their zero- and their minimal-risk group. Siegel found more significant correlations for her preterm than her full-term group. Certainly more research is needed to determine whether trends exist on the preceding variables. Almost all of the investigators conducted analyses comparing the genders. In the investigations using the HOME scales there were no significant differences in the correlations between males and females (Bradley & Caldwell; Gottfried & Gottfried; Barnard, Bee, & Hammond; Siegel). However, Beckwith and Cohen as well as Wachs, reported findings that they interpreted as indicative of gender differences in responsiveness or reactivity to the social environment. Beckwith and Cohen found that caregiver interaction with females during the first year correlated considerably with performance at ages 2 and 5 years, whereas caregiver instructions with males in the first year showed fewer correlations with subsequent ages. Although 87% of the comparisons of the correlations between males and females were nonsignificant, Wachs noted that there was enough evidence to suggest the possibility of specificity for certain environmental variables. While the predominance of evidence does not show differential correlational networks for males and females, there may be some subtle differences, as indicated by the findings of Beckwith and Cohen and of Wachs. The lack of correlational differences between the genders was consistently found on the HOME, suggesting the possibility that the items on the HOME scales are not as sensitive as those used by Beckwith and Cohen and by Wachs for detecting differences between the genders. On the other hand, differential relationships for the genders in the Beckwith and Cohen and the Wachs studies could be the result of differential reliabilities for the genders on those items. This last point may hold where differential relationships are found on any of the preceding variables.

One of the most central issues in studying the relationship of home environment and cognitive development concerns which specific factors correlate with cognitive development and the magnitudes of their correlations. This information is important to establish for both theory construction and intervention research. As previously noted, there is variation across the studies in the specific home factors that correlated with cognitive development, as well as the amount of variance accounted for by these factors. In the study by Bradley and Caldwell, organization, play materials, maternal involvement, and variety showed the strongest relationships. Gottfried and Gottfried found variety and stimulation of academic behavior to have the most potent and pervasive relationship. Barnard, Bee, and Hammond found maternal responsiveness, restriction and punishment, play materials, and maternal involvement to have the highest and most consistent relationships. The last three variables were also the strongest in the Johnson, Breckenridge, and McGowan study. Siegel found play materials and variety to correlate the most highly. In these studies that used the HOME, no single factor (or scale) correlated with cognitive development across all of the studies. Play materials was reported as one of the most important in four of the five studies, and maternal involvement and variety in three of the studies. In the study by Beckwith and Cohen, frequency of reciprocal exchanges between caregiver and child at age 2 years was highly associated with cognitive development in both the English- and Spanish-speaking samples. Wachs found that items tapping the language environment of the child (e.g., spontaneous vocalization by sibs to infant, verbal responses to infants' vocalizations) showed a global relationship with cognitive development.

With respect to the amount of variance in cognitive development accounted for by home factors, significant correlations were typically in the low to moderate range. The lowest correlations were found in the Johnson, Breckenridge, and McGowan study and the highest correlations reported were by Wachs. The relatively higher correlations found in the Wachs study, compared to the other studies, could be the result of (1) the particular variables investigated, (2) the sample constructed to be broad in socioeconomic variation, and /or (3) aggregating the home data across blocks of time. It is difficult to compare all of the studies directly because of differences both in demographic characteristics and in home factors selected for investigation. However, across those studies using the HOME scale (i.e., infant version), it is feasible to ascertain the factors (or scales) that related most highly and consistently with cognitive development at the various ages investigated.

A meta-analysis (Glass, 1981) was conducted to provide a statistical integration or overview of the relationship of specific HOME factors and cognitive development and the amount of variance accounted for by these factors across the studies. It is important to emphasize that the purpose of the meta-analysis was not to reinterpret or to alter the integrity of the individual findings in the foregoing chapters. There are few longitudinal studies to date on the issue at hand and there were vast differences among the samples' characteristics with respect to SES, race, gestational age, and so on. However, the meta-analysis should serve to establish the strength of the relationships that can be expected.

The results are presented in Tables 2 and 3.[1] In table 2 are the bivariate correlations for each study contributing data on the relationship between the 1-year HOME and cognitive development at 1, 2, 3, and 3½–5 years. The magnitudes of the mean correlation (corrected for sample sizes)[2] for each HOME scale are presented for each test period. The mean correlations with the 1-year Bayley ranged from .02 to .18. The scales that correlated the most highly were play materials, HOME total score, maternal involvement, and maternal responsivity. With the 2-year Bayley, the mean correlations ranged from .16 to .32. The highest correlations were with the HOME total score, maternal involvement, variety, and play materials. The mean correlations with intelligence assessed at 3 years ranged from .11 to .34 with the HOME total score, maternal involvement, play materials, and variety showing the highest correlations. The mean correlations with intelligence between 3½ and 5 years ranged from .16 to .38. The highest correlations were found with the HOME total score, play materials, variety, and maternal involvement. The grand mean (based on 17 size-effects) was calculated to obtain an overall picture of the relationship between the 1-year HOME and cognitive development between 1 and 5 years. The grand mean correlations ranged from .12 to .30, with the highest mean correlations found with the HOME total score, maternal involvement, play materials, and variety. The metaanalysis revealed several important findings. First, the mean correlation between the 1-year HOME and cognitive development did not exceed a modest level of magnitude. Second, relatively higher mean correlations were found predictively (with preschool measures of intelligence) than concurrently (with infant measures of intelligence). This was a trend noted previously, from the individual studies. Third, the HOME total score did show a linear increase with advancement in age, and for the most part accounted for most variance at each age. Fourth, the maternal involve-

---

[1]Meta-analyses were not conducted on the HOME before 1 year or on the preschool version of the HOME, because there were too few studies to analyze.

[2]Meta-analyses were also conducted without corrected sample sizes. The results were virtually identical to the analyses with corrected sample sizes.

Allen W. Gottfried

TABLE 2
Correlations between 1-Year HOME and Cognitive Development[a]

		1-Year Bayley						2-Year Bayley			
HOME	BC	GG	BBH	JBM[b]	S[c]	Mean r	GG	BBH	JBM	S[d]	Mean r
Responsivity	.15	−.04	.10	.27*	.18	.12	.09	.29*	.19	.13	.17
Restriction and											
punishment	.01	−.06	.19*	.01*	−.05	.02	.08	.20*	.28	.14	.16
Organization	.20	−.07	.09	.22*	.10	.10	.00	.37*	.28	.08	.17
Play materials	.28*	−.13	.27*	.39*	.15	.18	.02	.36*	.12	.35*	.23
Involvement	.28*	−.05	.18*	.22*	.12	.14	.10	.39*	.25	.24*	.25
Variety	.05	.12	.20*	.02	.07	.10	.31*	.27*	−.03	.25*	.24
Total	.30*	−.07	.26*	.35*	.09	.17	.20*	.45*	.29	.32*	.32
N	77	129	165	85	170	626	128	155	24	148	455

[a]BC = Bradley & Caldwell; GG = Gottfried & Gottfried; BBH = Barnard, Bee, & Hammond; JBM = Johnson, Breckenridge, & McGowan; S = Siegel.

[b]Correlations based on control and program groups combined.

[c]Correlations based on full-terms, preterms, and cohorts combined (corrected for sample sizes); see Table 7 in Siegel chapter for significant correlations; a single significant correlation was reported for each subscale across the groups.

[d]Correlations taken from Siegel (1981, Table 4).

ment, play materials, and variety subscales tended to be most highly and consistently related to cognitive development between 1 and 5 years. The organization and restriction and punishment subscales consistently accounted for the least amount of variance.

The bivariate correlations for those studies contributing data on the relationship between the 2-year HOME and preschool cognitive development (36–54 month) are displayed in Table 3. The magnitudes of the mean correlations are presented and ranged from .21 to .50. In contrast to the consistently low mean correlations found with the 1-year HOME, the mean correlations with the 2-year HOME were of low to moderate magnitudes. These data support a second trend—that later home assessments correlated more highly with cognitive development than did relatively earlier assessments (even when the same scale is used). Like the 1-year HOME, the HOME total score showed the highest mean correlation. Furthermore, maternal involvement and play materials continued to yield the highest correlations, with maternal responsivity now showing an equally high relationship. The meta-analysis on the 1- and 2-year HOME revealed that (1) with increasing age, higher correlations emerged between home environmental factors and cognitive development, (2) the most consistent and highly correlated HOME factors during infancy and the preschool years were ma-

	3-Year intellectual performance[e]				3½–5-Year intellectual performance[f]					Grand Mean r[i]
BC	GG	JBM	S[g]	Mean r	BC	GG	BBH	S[h]	Mean r	
.39*	.18*	.18	.18	.23	.34*	.11	.27*	.00	.19	.17
.24*	.11	−.09	.12	.11	.21	.11	.29*	.15	.19	.12
.39*	.03	.02	.10	.13	.34*	.01	.18*	.16	.16	.14
.56*	−.05	.11	.35*	.24	.52*	−.04	.32*	.41*	.29	.23
.47*	.31*	.36*	.22*	.33	.36*	.16*	.35*	.14	.26	.24
.28*	.36*	−.14	.28*	.24	.32*	.40*	.18*	.24*	.28	.21
.58*	.33*	.17	.27*	.34	.53*	.26*	.44*	.29*	.38	.30
77	119	36	133	365	77	118	153	56	404	1850

[e] Based on Stanford-Binet IQ, except for GG, which was based on McCarthy General Cognitive Index.

[f] Based on Stanford-Binet IQ, except for GG and S, which were based on McCarthy General Cognitive Index.

[g] Correlations based on fullterms, preterms, and cohorts combined (corrected for sample sizes); see Table 15 in Siegel chapter.

[h] Correlations based on full-terms, preterms, and cohorts combined (corrected for sample sizes); see Table 16 in Siegel chapter.

[i] Grand Mean based on average of foregoing means and based on 17 size-effects and 1850 subject entries.

* = Indicates that the correlation reached a statistical level of significance in that particular study.

TABLE 3

Correlations between 2-Year HOME and Preschool Cognitive Development

	BC[a]	BC[b]	BBH[c]	JBM[d]	Mean r
Responsivity	.49*	.50*	.42*	.01	.38
Restriction and punishment	.41*	.28*	.56*	−.21	.29
Organization	.41*	.33*	.05	.04	.21
Play materials	.64*	.56*	.21*	.04	.37
Involvement	.55*	.55*	.37*	−.01	.38
Variety	.50*	.39*	.20*	−.01	.28
Total	.71*	.57*	.60*	−.04	.50
N	77	77	133	47	334

[a] 36-Month Stanford-Binet IQ, Bradley & Caldwell.

[b] 54-Month Stanford-Binet IQ, Bradley & Caldwell.

[c] 48-Month Stanford-Binet, Barnard, Bee, & Hammond.

[d] 36-Month Stanford-Binet, IQ on control group, Johnson, Breckenridge, & McGowan.

* Indicates that the correlation reached a statistical level of significance in that particular study.

ternal involvement and play materials, and (3) the maximum amount of variance accounted for by a single HOME subscale did not exceed 14% of the variance, with the HOME total score accounting for no more than an average of 25%.

References

Bradley, R., Caldwell, B., & Elardo, R. Home environment, social status, and mental test performance. *Journal of Educational Psychology*, 1977, *69*, 697–701.

Glass, G. V., McGaw, B., & Smith, M. L. *Meta-analysis in social research*. Beverly Hills, CA: Sage, 1981.

Siegel, L. S. Infant tests as predictors of cognitive and language development at two years. *Child Development*, 1981, *52*, 545–557.

10

Home Environment and Early Cognitive Development: Implications for Intervention

David MacPhee
Craig T. Ramey
Keith Owen Yeates

Introduction

Constructing intervention programs is as much an art as a science, requiring a creative interplay between existing cultural and political realities, prevailing scientific theories and paradigms, and the corpus of research data applicable to the processes or deficits to be modified. The task of this chapter is to explore methods for preventing developmental retardation. To do so, we examine current knowledge of theory and research pertaining to the home environment and cognitive development. Finally, we propose workable (hopefully) intervention strategies that are firmly grounded in contemporary theories and research on the processes of child development.

In the exuberance of the 1960s, many of the enrichment programs for disadvantaged children were based on untested assumptions about development and a determination to change society, rather than on basic research on the mechanisms of poverty and early experience (Zigler & Valentine, 1979). For example, it was thought that lower-socioeconomic-status (SES) homes suffered from stimulus deprivation when, in fact, many disadvantaged children were being *over*stimulated by their environments (Gray & Klaus, 1968). Assumptions about the malleability of development led to the expectation that a single summer enrichment program for lower-SES children would prevent school failure. With such tenuous assumptions, Head Start initially failed to fulfill its mandate. Now, however, we have additional empirical knowledge with which to work. One purpose of this chapter is to review this recently acquired body of data in order to lay the empirical groundwork for future intervention programs. That is, knowing the kinds of experiences that *do*—rather than *might*—influence cognitive development, how can these experiences be provided to children and families lacking them? We now seem to possess the necessary ingredients for intervention programs, but still need the formulae to combine them in meaningful, effective ways.

Our other purposes are more mundane, though no less important. One of the issues to be dealt with in any early experience paradigm is differential responsivity across populations or species (e.g., Scott & Fuller, 1965). In the particular case of research on the home environment, most of the earlier studies compared middle- and lower-SES homes, typically finding mean differences in a number of areas, including language (Bernstein, 1964), parent–child interaction (Hess & Shipman, 1965), and aspects of the physical environment (see Deutsch, 1973, for a review). The fact that cross-class mean differences in home environments exist, though, does not imply that similar processes may account for differences *within* social classes. If, in fact, cognitive development in lower- and middle-SES children *is* influenced in a like manner by the same experiences, the task of intervention is made easier because the core curriculum would be effective for children from all SES backgrounds. A second purpose of our chapters then, is to determine if the same dimensions of the home environment account for within- and across-class differences in cognitive development.

As we have suggested, intervention programs should emerge from a union of research and theory. Although the scope and effectiveness of previous programs were limited by the available data, we would argue that the greatest handicaps were the theoretical models of development and the experimental designs that grew out of them. Our comments on models of development are reserved until a later section; a consideration of design flaws deserves immediate explication.

Most contemporary research on the home environment has, by its naturalistic context, been restricted to the use of correlational designs. Often, the HOME scales simply are correlated with a variety of intellectual and linguistic outcome measures. The resultant matrices—some with 30 or 40 entries—are then searched for specific linkages between predictors and outcome. Such a strategy ignores possible relationships *within* the predictor and criterion sets. In addition, conservative alpha levels rarely are employed to control for chance relationships. Once correlations between the home environment and development are generated, often they are imprudently interpreted. Many relationships, although statistically significant, account for a small portion of the total variation in developmental outcomes. Furthermore, most of the correlational research on the home seems to conclude, implicitly or otherwise, that the direction of effects is from the environment to the child. The data in this book, though, affirm the principle of bidirectionality. The child's irritability, vocalizations (Beckwith & Cohen, Chapter 7, this volume), and intelligence (Johnson, Breckenridge, & McGowan, Chapter 5, this volume) actually may *shape* the home environment in different ways.

These results challenge previous assumptions about the direction of causality, and suggest that new research designs need to be incorporated into our arsenal. Quasi-experimental designs could be used to compare naturally occurring groups (e.g., boys vs. girls; first- vs. later-born children) on their creation of and responses to differences in the home environment. Experimental designs, using random assignment to various intervention groups, also could disentangle cause and effect. Clearly, a more adequate basis for intervention will evolve only when more rigorous, multivariate methods are embraced.

The final purpose of our chapter concerns the bases for deciding how, where, and when to intervene. The dictates of social policy are one such criterion. The cost effectiveness of alternative programs, as well as political expediency and philosophy, will determine the nature of intervention, whether it is directed at preschoolers in daycare, at parent education, or at income maintenance. Logistical considerations are a second basis. Decisions about what *should* be modified through intervention more often than not will be influenced by what demonstrably *can* be changed. For example, the mother's knowledge of developmental norms and principles may change much more readily with education than attitudes and values. Similarly, it will be easier to modify one aspect of the home environment than several dimensions at once. A final criterion is simply to choose variables that are known to be effective and incorporate them into the intervention program. This scientific basis assumes that we know which dimensions of the home environment are related to various aspects of cognitive functioning at given ages. Accordingly, the next section is devoted to a general review of experiences that enhance or impede cognitive development. Our discussion is organized by means of level of influence, beginning with the most direct—the inanimate environment—and proceeding to variables such as the family ecology, which operate in more complex and subtle ways.

The Empirical Bases for Intervention

The Inanimate Environment

Summary of Knowledge

Several dimensions of the physical environment are found to be consistently related to cognitive performance in childhood. One of the best general predictors of cognitive development is the presence of age-appropriate play materials (Bradley & Caldwell, Chapter 2; Johnson et al., Chapter 5, this volume; Wachs, 1978; 1979). An environment that permits visual and physical exploration (e.g., floor freedom; access to reading materials and windows) also is associated with greater cognitive skills, although meaningful variations on this dimension may be observed only in lower-SES homes (Gottfried & Gottfried, Chapter 3, this volume; Wachs, 1979). The amount of personal space or lack of crowding also is related to cognitive development, as is the temporal regularity of events (e.g., naps; meals) in the home (Wachs, 1978; 1979). Finally, variables defining an overstimulation cluster seem to have a detrimental effect on the child—these include a high rate of noise and confusion; a "barrage of unstructured stimulation" such as the television going full blast; and the lack of a stimulus shelter, or place where the child can escape for quiet moments alone (Gottfried & Gottfried, this volume; Wachs, 1979).

Several core principles of early experience can be extracted from these findings. As the "match hypothesis" (Wachs, 1977) predicts, there seems to be an optimal level of physical stimulation that provides an adequate amount of varied experiences without overly taxing the child's ability to assimilate them. Toys that are attractive, as well as contingently responsive, promote exploration and learning. In addition, predictability is an important facet of the daily schedule of the home. Giving the child opportunities to explore the environment, it is assumed, should inculcate independence and a sense of control over what is experienced. Overarching many of these processes—contingent responsivity, predictability, control, independence—is the development of a sense of effectance (White, 1959). As is discussed here later, most of these core principles can be observed in both the social and the physical environments, leading us to ask whether the parallel is coincidental or causal.

Unresolved Research Issues

Is there a confluence of independent streams of social and inanimate experience, or is the physical environment important only because it springs from and is filtered through social interactions? This central issue in the early experience literature is described clearly by Feuerstein (1979), who draws a distinction between direct and mediated learning:

> The [direct] learning process is conceived of as resulting from direct chance encounters with, and spontaneous manipulations of, objects and experiences of events, resulting in continuous modification of existent schemata. Mediated learning experience, on the other hand, is defined as the interactional processes between the developing human organism and an experienced, intentional adult who, by interposing himself between the child and external sources of stimulation, "mediates" the world to the child by framing, selecting, focusing, and feeding back environmental experiences in such a way as to produce in him appropriate learning sets and habits. The action of the adult and his activity in restricting the stimulational field and interpreting it to the infant or child constitute the major difference between mediated learning and nonmediated, direct exposure learning. [pp. 70–71].

Some authors argue that the caregiver's interpretation of experiences for the child is the critical aspect of the home environment. Clarke-Stewart (1973) and Carew (1980) found that neither the mere availability of play materials nor self-generated intellectual experiences in solitary, independent play were related to cognitive development. Instead, effective intellectual stimulation arose out of joint play or instances in which the caregiver proactively structured experiences for the child. Wachs (1979) asserts to the contrary that the physical and temporal aspects of the home environment influence cognitive development independent of socially mediated experiences.

Unfortunately, a definitive resolution of this issue will not be forthcoming until *both* categories of stimulation are included in the data. One question to be addressed in future research is how inanimate or direct experiences are related to mediated experiences. Do warm, responsive, stimulating parents also provide a home environment that has a variety of toys, is not crowded or confusing, and has a predictable daily routine? If correlations between different scales of the HOME are any indication, the answer would have to be affirmative. The data are meager but do show correlations on the order of .20–.40 between measures of the social (maternal involvement, and responsivity) and physical (organization of the environment) environments, measured at the same point in time (Bradley & Caldwell, this volume). The major question, though, concerns the relative potency of these two aspects of experience. Again the data are sparse and somewhat contradictory, with more evidence being presented in favor of the efficacy of mediated experiences than direct exposure to the inanimate environment.

Parental Characteristics

Summary of Knowledge

Within- and across-class research has documented different types of experiences associated with the child's intellectual competence. The most pervasively associated with cognitive development is a cluster of parental attitudes and activities that could be labelled *encouragement of development.* This constellation includes the following parental characteristics: achievement-motivation (McCall, Appelbaum, & Hogarty, 1973); engaging in intellectually stimulating activities (Beckwith & Cohen, this volume; Carew, 1980; Clarke-Stewart, 1973); and providing a variety of stimulating experiences for the child, including responsive play materials and field trips (Bradley & Caldwell, Chapter 2, this volume; Elardo, Bradley & Caldwell, 1977; Gottfried & Gottfried, Chapter 3; Johnson *et al.*, Chapter 5, this volume; Wachs, 1978; 1979). These variables, singly or in combination, typically account for a substantial portion of the variance in childhood cognitive performance. However, lumping together variables from different domains—parental attitudes, the social and physical environment—may obscure processes that influence cognitive development. Thus, we need to consider the more specific aspects of parental characteristics.

Social Stimulation The most parsimonious approach to describing the influence of social interactions on the child's cognitive development would be to describe the optimal caregiver. At the risk of oversimplification, we have synthesized findings from this volume (e.g., Beckwith & Cohen, Chapter 7; Bradley & Caldwell, Chapter 2; Johnson *et al.*, Chapter 5; Wachs, Chapter 8) and from other research on the social environment (e.g., Carew, 1980; Carew-Watts & Chan-Barnett, 1973; Clarke-Stewart, 1973; Elardo, Bradley, & Caldwell, 1975; 1977; Farran & Ramey, 1980) into a sketch of the stimulating caregiver.

The parent's involvement with the child is a critical aspect of the social environment that appears throughout the early-experience literature. Involvement actually may subsume several different continua: the level or amount of interaction, its reciprocity, and how intrusive or ignoring the parent is. Carew (1980) points out that the extremes of any of these dimensions may be harmful. For instance, completely reciprocal interactions between the child and caregiver may not be very beneficial to the child if it means the absence of structured, directed experiences. Similarly, a parent who is overly intrusive may have an effect on the child that is just as detrimental as an uninvolved caregiver. Although parent involvement is clearly related to the child's cognitive development, the reasons for these effects are not clearly understood.

The emotional tone of social interchanges also is important. Affective descriptors have included the caregiver's warmth, demonstrations of affection, and the use of praise and encouragement. There are several reasons why these variables should be related to the child's cognitive development. A child is more likely to identify with a warm, affectionate parent and thus imitate and obey the adult. In addition, the child's self-esteem and confidence will be enhanced if praise is used, perhaps resulting in greater effectance motivation.

Not surprisingly, parents who participate with their children in socially and intellectually stimulating interactions have children with relatively greater intellectual competence. As with any curriculum, this aspect of social experience involves both content and process. The process is one in which the caregiver serves a proactive, generative role (Carew, 1980), structuring and interpreting events for the child. Verbal interaction appears to be the primary vehicle for mediated experiences (Feuerstein, 1979), although to have a salutary effect it should be characterized by talking *with* the child rather than mere labelling, showing, or talking *at* the child.

Contingent verbal responsiveness to the child is perhaps the greatest single influence on early cognitive development. Virtually all studies including this variable have found that it is one of the best predictors of later intelligence (Beckwith & Cohen, Chapter 7, this volume; Clarke-Stewart, 1973; Wachs, Chapter 8, this volume), leading Beckwith and Cohen to remark that "inattention and lack of response from the social environment was deleterious regardless of the age at which it occurred." This variable is particularly potent because it combines verbal and social stimulation with contingent interaction, which should increase the child's sense of control and competence.

Disciplinary practices, including reasoning and restrictiveness, are not generally related to cognitive performance until later in development. Barnard, Bee, & Hammond (Chapter 4, this volume) and Elardo *et al.* (1977a), for example, found that avoidance of restriction and punishment did not correlate with cognitive skills until 2 years of age or later. Gottfried and Gottfried also found no effect, whereas Elardo *et al.* (1977) and Wachs (Chapter 8, this volume) found it only for females. These data, in conjunction with Baumrind's research on restrictive versus permissive control (Baumrind & Black, 1967), suggest that certain disciplinary practices may be age and organismic specific (Wachs, 1979).

In sum, optimal caregiving involves warmth and encouragement and interactions that are reciprocal yet directed and structured, involved yet not intrusive; the theme of the optimal caregiving interchanges is probably not as important as contingent verbal responsiveness and interpreting experiences for the child; and discipline at later ages is marked by reasoning and authoritative control. But are these characteristics of social stimulation separate factors independently related to cognitive competence, or only different facets reflecting from the same gem? What little research exists suggests that mothers tend to vary on a single dimension of responsive attentiveness (Beckwith & Cohen, Chapter 7, this volume), optimal caregiving (Clarke-Stewart, 1973), or dyadic involvement (Farran & Ramey, 1980), which subsumes most of the preceding caregiving factors (see also Bates, Olson, Pettit, & Bayles, 1982). Even so, it is desirable to have a better taxonomy of the social environment, and to determine how various dimensions of it correlate with specific cognitive skills at different ages and for different children.

Early Language   Although linguistic and social stimulation tend to be fused in the first years of the child's life, some aspects of the language environment deserve a separate, brief account. As previously noted, contingent *verbal* responsiveness by the caregiver, regardless of content, is strongly related to children's cognitive development; verbal labelling or demonstration is not (Wachs, Chapter 8, this volume). The same statement can be made in regard to verbal interactions with an older sibling after the child's first year (Wachs). Differences in the language environment emerge early—middle-SES mothers tend to talk to their infants more throughout the first year of life, and infants who vocalize more (especially around 2 years) have higher language and intellectual scores at 5 years (Beckwith & Cohen, Chapter 7, this volume). Finally, reading to the child begins to predict later cognitive development at 15–18 months, although the effect may be specific to only a few cognitive skills (Gottfried & Gottfried, Chapter 3, this volume; Wachs, 1979). These data highlight the pivotal role of early verbal interactions with the infant—the partner in the dyad can be a sibling or a parent—and the emerging importance of reading in the second year of life as the child's receptive and expressive language skills begin to blossom.

Unresolved Research Issues

One of the thornier issues in studying influences on development is that parental characteristics such as intelligence or education may have direct *and* mediated effects on ontogeny. The mother's IQ, for example, may influence the child's intellectual development through genetic as well as environmental pathways. Plomin, DeFries, and Loehlin (1977) have labelled this a *passive* genotype–environment interaction. Is the home environment then merely a reflection of the parents' intellectual level?

Although maternal IQ is correlated with characteristics of the home environment, each variable does make a unique contribution to children's intellectual development (Gottfried & Gottfried, Chapter 3, this volume; see also Yeates, MacPhee, Campbell & Ramey, 1983). The same pattern of relationships emerges when parent education or social class is substituted for parental IQ, with demographic variables rarely accounting for more than 25% to 50% of the variance in the home environment (Barnard et al., Chapter 4; Bradley & Caldwell, Chapter 2; Gottfried & Gottfried, Chapter 3, this volume). As with the glass that is half empty and half full, these data invite different interpretations. Gottfried and Gottfried speculate that the "half-full glass" may be a function of more knowledgeable parents being more sensitive to the child's changing needs and knowing what to do to stimulate development. The "half-empty glass," though, implies that other characteristics of the parent or child influence the home environment, independent of SES or the parent's education.

Previous studies of parental characteristics and the home environment provide some guidelines for future research. First, it is clear that distal influences on intellectual development, such as parent education or IQ, are related to, yet somewhat independent of, proximal determinants—the social and physical environment. *Both* types of variables, therefore, should be included in regression equations. Second, our own research (Yeates et al., 1983) as well as other's (e.g., Elardo et al., 1975; Wilson, 1978) demonstrates the advisability of studying the *changing* relationships among parent IQ (or SES), the home environment, and the child's cognitive development. Our final point concerns parental characteristics that may be at the core of variations in experience. For example, the parent's values, attitudes, and *instrumental beliefs* undoubtedly influence what experiences the parent thinks should be provided to the child, and how they should be presented (Stolz, 1967). The parent's *expectations and perceptions* of the child, in turn, probably influence interpretations of the child's readiness to benefit from given experiences (e.g., Bee, Barnard, Eyres, Gray, Hammond, Spietz, Snyder, & Clark, 1982; Ninio, 1979). As Carew (1980) astutely noted;

Much may depend on the caregiver's attitudes toward fairness to children, her appreciation of individuality, her interest in tailoring her behavior to her perceptions of individual needs in children, her beliefs about how important what she does is to their development. . . . Future research might profitably focus on factors affecting the caregiver's perceptions of children, their basis and degree of differentiation, and how these perceptions intersect with caregiver characteristics in influencing both the caregiver's general and individualized treatment of children [pp. 68–69].

In brief, what the parent thinks *should* be provided to children, and the parent's perceptions of the child's readiness for those experiences, should contribute to the characteristics of the home environment.

Social Ecology of the Family

Summary of Knowledge

Stresses and Supports Aspects of the family's broader social ecology (Cochran & Brassard, 1979) may have direct and indirect influences on the child's cognitive development. Researchers have been particularly interested in two facets of the family climate: (1) stresses and supports, and (2) family configuration. The family's material and social resources appear to be related to the child's cognitive development, although it is not clear how the effects are mediated. Gottfried and Gottfried (this volume), for example, discovered that children's cognitive development was correlated with family cohesion, expressiveness and an intellectual–cultural atmosphere. Similarly, social and emotional supports were strongly related to children's language and intellectual development in Bee *et al.*'s study (1982). Johnson *et al.* (this volume), however, found few correlations within a lower-SES sample between HOME scores and income or the father's presence.

These results, while tantalizing, leave significant lacunae in knowledge. The most fundamental issue is a definitional one: What are stresses and supports? Until we can better define the object of inquiry, we will have trouble studying its effects. Thus, empirical progress awaits theoretical advances. However, once the beast has been described and classified, we then must discern what it does. In short, how do stresses and supports influence the child's development? The affective and social environment would be an obvious place to begin examining this issue. In families where one parent has a psychiatric disorder (Baldwin, Cole, & Baldwin, 1982) or where marital discord is present (Belsky, 1981), stresses appear to be manifested in the reduced intensity, reciprocity, and warmth of interactions with the child. The emotional climate of the home, then, may be inseparable from the child's social experiences.

Family Configuration   Family configuration has been investigated in more detail than stresses and supports, perhaps because it is easier to define and measure. Two variables are used frequently—crowding (rooms:people ratio) and the child's ordinal position. The relationship between crowding and the HOME ranges from weak ($rs = -.11$ to $-.17$ using number of children; Johnson *et al.*, this volume) to moderate ($rs = .34$ to $.48$ for crowding, even with SES partialled; Bradley & Caldwell, this volume). Not surprisingly, crowding is negatively correlated with organization of the environment, play materials, and maternal involvement (Bradley & Caldwell), probably because of competition for material and emotional resources. The child's ordinal position also is related to HOME scores (Bradley & Caldwell, Chapter 2; Gottfried & Gottfried, Chapter 3, this volume) and especially to aspects of the parent-child relationships (Beckwith & Cohen, Chapter 7, this volume; see also Sigman, Cohen, Beckwith & Parmelee, 1981). The major difference appears to be in contingent responsiveness; first-born children are responded to more quickly than later-borns (Beckwith & Cohen; Bernal, 1972). They also receive more verbal, social, and object stimulation from the caregiver (Sigman *et al.*, 1981) and higher levels of achievement are expected from them (Marjoribanks, 1981).

Crowding and birth order are strongly associated with the child's cognitive development, independent of some other characteristics of the home environment. Wachs (1979) found that *personal space* (a stimulus shelter + lack of crowding) was one of the better predictors of the child's cognitive development. Gottfried and Gottfried (this volume) partially replicated Wachs' study in finding that higher rooms: people ratios and fewer siblings were correlated with higher DQs, although the presence of a stimulus shelter was not related to better cognitive performance. Finally, Sigman *et al.* (1981) concluded that the cognitive development of preterm infants was strongly influenced by ordinal position, even after taking SES into account; firstborn infants performed better on linguistic and intellectual assessments.

Although family configuration seems to be an important influence on cognitive development, we are far from understanding why. Recent developmental research on the confluence model challenges previously held assumptions about changes in the intellectual climate of the home as more children are added (Galbraith, 1982; Rogers, in press). It is not clear, for example, what family resources other than time or money are taxed by the addition of more children. Can two or three children get by with fewer toys if the parents emphasize sharing? Can an older sibling fulfill part of the parent's role as teacher and mediator of experiences? Perhaps the number of children is not as important as their spacing, the roles that are assigned to each by the parents, and the parents' attitudes toward sharing and competition among siblings.

The Child's Contribution   The physical and social environment obviously does not have a unitary influence across all ages and children. Therefore, all of the conclusions in the preceding sections must be qualified by considerations of children's receptivity to stimulation.

First, are *early* experiences critical to cognitive development or are later ones equally important? Virtually all of the research in this volume and elsewhere concludes that the early environment does not play a unique role in cognitive development, nor does it innoculate the child against later privations. Rather, experiences may have a cumulative effect on the child. However, correlations between early measures of the environment and cognitive development *do* increase after 24 months of age (Barnard *et al.* and Bradley & Caldwell, this volume). We have argued elsewhere (Yeates *et al.,* 1983) that these data support McCall's (1981) "scoop model" of cognitive development, whereby intelligence is relatively canalized until about 2 years of age. After 2 years, though, maturational forces ebb and genetic variability and environmental factors are, perhaps, more influential.

An elegant demonstration of age specificity is provided by Wachs (1979; Chapter 8, this volume) in which he found that some cognitive skills "show almost complete changes in the types of environmental variables they are related to at different ages" (1979, p. 32). These changes can be attributed in part to qualitative transformations in the nature of cognition, making children more receptive to some experiences in early infancy (e.g., physical contact before 6 months; appropriate play materials in the second 6 months) and to other experiences in late toddlerhood (reading to children, beginning at 15–18 months; disciplinary practices after 24 months). Part of age specificity, as pointed out by Bradley and Caldwell, also can be attributed to early cognitive abilities (attention; goal orientation) mediating the impact of early experiences on later cognitive development. As dialectical models such as General Systems Theory (Ramey, MacPhee, & Yeates, 1982; Sameroff, 1983) predict, there is feedback between what the child already knows and what he or she is able to acquire from particular experiences.

Characteristics other than developmental stage will influence how much the child benefits from the home environment. Postulates concerning organismic specificity (Wachs, 1979; Chapter 8) or the "goodness-of-fit" between child and environment (Lerner, 1982) integrate an individual-difference perspective with the more traditional early-experience literature. Two propositions generally are made: (1) There are individual differences in *responsivity* to stimulation that may vary with temperament, gender, biomedical status, and other factors; and (2) children differ in the types of stimulation they seek out. Differences in stimulus *selectivity*, which Plomin *et al.* (1977) have termed an *active* genotype–environment interaction (or niche building), do not appear to become important until late infancy. As Wachs (1979) noted, then, age and organismic specificity interact. Such an interaction will be an important consideration in designing curricula for intervention programs.

Finally, variations in an organism's environment often arise through their own efforts to modify the world they inhabit. Plomin *et al.* (1977) have discussed this principle in terms of an *evocative* genotype–environment interaction, whereby different child characteristics elicit different responses from the social and physical environment. Brighter infants, for example, receive different kinds and amounts of stimulation throughout childhood (Gottfried & Gottfried, Chapter 3, this volume; Bradley, Caldwell, & Elardo, 1979). The child's vocalizations and other cues also elicit differential caregiving which, in turn, is related to better cognitive performance later in childhood (Beckwith & Cohen, Chapter 7; Siegel, Chapter 6, this volume).

Unresolved Research Issues

Evidence indicating that children shape and are shaped by the environment still leaves the mechanisms unspecified. Which child behaviors elicit various caregiving patterns at different ages? What parental characteristics—perceptions, expectations, attitudes—influence their interpretations of and responses to the child? What options, as far as social and physical stimulation, do parents have in their repertoires, and how do they know that the child is primed for some experiences but not others? These questions acknowledge the child as a source of demands and subtle cues and the parent as an information processor. Which information is provided and processed, and what experiences then are provided, is a key in understanding the match between organism and environment (Wachs, 1977).

Because undirectional and univariate causal models of development have failed to account for the full complexity of ontogenic processes, there is a need to formulate improved models to guide intervention efforts. The next section summarizes an emerging perspective that we have found useful in understanding and preventing developmental dysfunctions. This model, developed by Ramey, MacPhee and Yeates (1982), is derived from General Systems Theory (Miller, 1978).

General Systems Theory as a Framework for Intervention

Major Principles and Features of General Systems Theory

Our current understanding of developmental risk and, hence, our theoretical and practical stance on intervention is based on several concepts of General Systems Theory that are the core of our approach to preventive intervention. They are as follows:

The Emergent Principle The developing child can be viewed as one product of a system of units that interact. According to Miller (1978), "the state of each unit is constrained by, conditioned by, or dependent upon the state of other units" (p. 16). In other words, the behavior of a system emerges out of the interaction of its components, such that there are multiple rather than unitary causes.

Levels of Analysis Living systems have different levels of complexity and functioning. Further, complex interactions can occur within each level as well as across levels. For example, societal processes such as economic conditions can influence functioning at the level of the family.

Range of Stability Each variable within a system has a range of stability (Miller, 1978); that is, each is maintained in equilibrium by transactions with the environment and other components of the system. Any variable that forces the system beyond its range of stability is called a strain, producing a stress in the system. According to Miller (1978), living systems have a limited repertoire of coping strategies to deal with strain, including (1) altering oneself by learning new skills; (2) altering the environment; (3) withdrawing to a more favorable environment; or (4) changing what one defines as stable.

Regulatory Mechanisms In the human, cybernetic processes operate to regulate behavior. In terms of development, this means that there is constant feedback and regulation such that the child continuously adapts to the environment. In cases where self-regulatory mechanisms are unable to cope with strain on the system, deficits or maladaptive behavior may result.

The Active Organism   This principle suggests that development is characterized by plasticity because adaptation occurs in the presence of changing demands. The child, furthermore, is seen as an active rather than passive agent, eliciting responses from the environment at the same time that he or she is adapting to its demands.

The Orthogenetic Principle   Development "proceeds from a state of relative globality and lack of differentiation to a state of increasing differentiation, articulation and hierarchical integration" (Werner, 1957, p. 126). This concept may account for the specificity of organism–environment relationships as well as qualitative shifts in cognitive development.

These six principles, then, are primary principles in our conception of development. We have integrated these principles within a General Systems Model of ontogeny that is presented schematically in Figure 1. Several terms in this model deserve further clarification. By the *history* of the component, we mean the effects of previous transactions

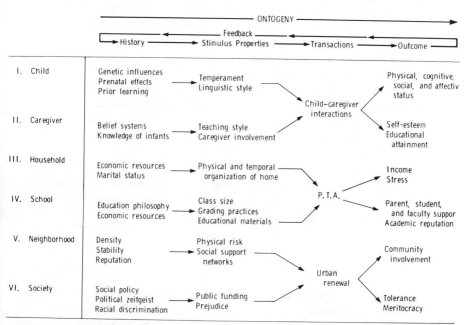

Figure 1. A General Systems Model for influences on development. The flow chart is illustrative of some important variables and processes but is not construed as exhaustive.

that are not manifested as observable behavior. Such effects can occur at any level of analysis, ranging from the child to the society. Historical variables are assumed to mediate or influence the behavior of a system but they cannot be observed directly. Thus, a central issue in the study of development is to determine how history (e.g., SES) is related to behavior (e.g., parent stimulation).

The specification of such relationships depends, in turn, on inquiry into how historical variables are translated into concrete behaviors and actions, or *stimulus properties*, which in turn influence transactions. *Transactions*, as used in the General Systems Model, imply an interactional process that is at least bidirectional and often multidirectional. The behavior of participants in transactions is the result of proximal and distal determinants, ranging from the behavior of the other participants to the individual's own history. It is important to note that transactions can occur between any two or more levels in the model, as well as within levels; a myriad of relationships, thus, is possible.

Finally, the endpoint of this stream of cause and effect would include a number of *outcome variables* that should be measured in an ecologically valid manner. In the case of developmental retardation, we would want to know about the child's competence in a number of settings, about his or her ability to adapt to the environment, and at another level, about how supportive the environment is.

In summary, developmental pathology, from a systems perspective, can result from a number of factors, including those at the level of the organism, the level of the family, their transactions, and so on. The value of General Systems Theory is that it forces an appreciation of development as a set of transactive forces operating to produce outcomes at a variety of levels of analysis. Its utility lies in its ability to help us see new relationships among variables and in its flexibility in helping to wed different theories about component processes to each other in order to explain behavioral development.

Intervention from a Systems Perspective

A major hurdle in preventing developmental dysfunctions is the translation of abstract, general models such as ours into viable intervention strategies. We have chosen to make the leap from theory to practice by incorporating research on the home environment—documenting processes of early experience—into the General Systems Model. The first task in the intervention process is to identify those who need it, and so we begin with a consideration of screening for developmental retardation.

Who Is in Need of Intervention?

Inherent to General Systems Theory is the concept that organisms possess a range of stability making them more or less vulnerable to adverse experiences. If we can combine measures of individual vulnerability with assessments of environmental forces that influence the range of stability (i.e., stresses and supports), we should be able to identify individuals who are at-risk for maladaptive or impaired functioning. The systems model thus provides the general framework for screening children who are at-risk for developmental retardation, while research on the home environment and on risk indexes supply specific variables that can be used to identify children who would benefit from intervention.

An effective, efficient screening program might involve two stages. First, demographic characteristics available from birth certificates are predictive of later school achievement; the best predictors are parent education, race, and the child's birth order (Ramey, Stedman, Borders-Patterson, & Mengel, 1978; Finkelstein & Ramey, 1980). Not coincidentally, the chapters in this volume found that parent education and the child's ordinal position predict cognitive performance independent of the contribution of the home environment. Several of these variables also are correlated with measures of the home and so provide a rough index of children's early experiences. Furthermore, they are readily available, thus requiring a minimum of time and money to collect and analyze. In the second level of screening, high-risk families defined by demographic criteria might complete an abridged HOME inventory (Frankenburg, van Doorninck, Liddel, & Dick, 1976). Data on the child's range of stability also could be gathered at this time, perhaps by using some combination of biomedical (e.g., birthweight, Apgar scores) and temperamental variables. The general strategy for identifying at-risk families, then, would be to utilize distal *and* proximal influences on cognitive development, with a minimal investment of professional time.

Form of Intervention

If one were to simply take all aspects of the social and physical environment that influence cognitive development and incorporate them into an intervention program, the result would be a scattershot, chaotic effort. The work in this volume, though, documents a few key processes operating at three levels of influence that could serve as the nucleus of intervention programs.

The family's social climate and support system should be the first target of intervention for, as Bee *et al.* (1982) noted, "providing a mother with information about normal child development, or about how to stimulate the child appears to be of little use unless the mother's own life circumstances are addressed first" (p. 1154). In a similar vein, evaluations of the effectiveness of early intervention (see Bronfenbrenner, 1975) typically have found that families whose children are most at-risk for school failure often benefitted the least from home-based programs because so much of the parent's energy was devoted to managing stress or to basic survival. Research on the home environment reaches the same conclusion: The family context, including emotional support (Bee *et al.*, 1982), cohesion, and expressiveness (Gottfried & Gottfried, Chapter 3, this volume), is correlated with children's intellectual scores.

We therefore recommend the following strategies directed toward modifying the family ecology. Some have been incorporated into approaches used by the Parent Child Development Centers (Andrews, Blumenthal, Johnson, Kahn, Ferguson, Lasater, Malone, & Wallace, 1982) and some are derived from our own work on preventive interventions. Social and material resources can be provided through community social service agencies, so contact with them should be facilitated, as one way to alleviate stress on the family. The family's financial resources will determine the number and types of educational materials that can be provided for the child. A way to circumvent this economic barrier in low-income families is to establish a lending library of books and toys; corporations and communities often can provide the necessary funding. The parent's educational level also places limits on the effective use of play materials and adequate linguistic stimulation through verbal interactions and reading. Encouraging the mother or father to complete high school, though difficult to achieve, should benefit both parents and children in the long run. Finally, efforts to strengthen family functioning may help. Johnson *et al.* (Chapter 5, this volume) employed a variety of tactics to accomplish this, including discussions of role relationships, problem-solving and communication, as well as driver's education to give the mothers more independence. In general, any effort to reduce stress on the family or to provide social and material supports will have multiple influences: (1) on marital and parent–child relationships; (2) on the parents' functioning as adults and thus on their receptivity to intervention; and (3) directly, on children's intellectual development.

Socially mediated experiences seem to be at the nucleus of influences on early cognitive development. These include not only the content of what caregivers do, but also their perceptions of the child's readiness for experiences, and the motive to provide these experiences (e.g., attitudes toward achievement and stimulation). Thus, teaching parents to be teachers should be a central goal of any intervention program. The parent-as-teacher role includes, first of all, goals and values for child-rearing, or *wanting* to enhance child development. To an extent that is possible, then, parents' attitudes toward intellectual achievement and beliefs in their efficacy as teachers should be instilled. Even though most parents want to encourage their children's development, many do not know *when* to provide the proper experiences. This aspect of the parent-as-teacher role includes knowledge of normal child development, and the ability to "read" children's readiness for given experiences. Parent education, it follows, should emphasize interpreting child behavior as it relates to the timing of experiences, especially for parents who may feel that infants and toddlers cannot benefit from early stimulation (Epstein, 1979). Parents also need to know *what* to provide in the way of stimulation—the "how to" or instrumental component of parenting. The curriculum, based on what we know about the home environment, could emphasize the following:

1. Contingent verbal responsiveness, regardless of content, to the child's overtures. Older siblings and parents can enhance cognitive development through verbal interactions with the child, so the intervention program also should include any older siblings.
2. Active, mutual participation in intellectual activities (e.g., reading, social games, toys). Because solitary play does not appear to be very beneficial, the use of playpens or using the TV as a babysitter should be discouraged. Sparling and Lewis (1979) have developed a number of inexpensive, age-appropriate games that parents can play with their children.
3. A warm, responsive relationship could be fostered by showing parents how to have fun with their babies. This might involve, at earlier ages, give-and-take social games, whereas later in development, mutual activities such as cooking, storytelling, and play could be the vehicles for parental involvement.
4. Disciplinary techniques that emphasize reasoning, consistency, and behavioral control (e.g., time-out, extinction, token economies) could be provided as more beneficial alternatives to restrictive or permissive approaches.

Many of these attitudes and skills could first be introduced in high school classes on parenting and family life, as Hawkins (1972) has suggested. If such classes were implemented in conjunction with an in-house daycare center, the dual problems of deficits in parental skills and the chronic shortage of daycare services could be partially solved.

Changes in the physical environment of the home may be more difficult to achieve because many facets of it ultimately are influenced by the family's economic resources. An absence of crowding, for instance, is linked to adequate housing, and providing varied stimulation takes money as well. Still, designating a corner of a room as the child's own "stimulus shelter" or play area might alleviate some of the stress of crowding. Overstimulation of the child could be prevented through judicious use of the television, and by fostering a predictable, regular routine in the home. Emphasizing the benefits of baby-proofing the home environment, rather than confining the child to long stretches in a playpen, would encourage safe physical exploration. Visual exploration could be enhanced with mirror games and homemade stabiles and mobiles (Sparling & Lewis, 1979). Finally, establishing toy and book lending library would help increase the variety and appropriateness of stimulation in the home.

Focus of Intervention

Merely describing aspects of the environment that *can* be manipulated to modify cognitive development, though, begs the policy issue of where intervention *should* be focused. Ideally, one would want a prevention strategy that produced powerful effects with a minimum of money and effort. Given existing data on age and organismic specificity, though, different intervention curricula may have to be designed for different stages of development and for various types of children (see Wachs & Gruen, 1982). Furthermore, we can infer from the emergent principle that intervention at several points simultaneously may produce synergistic effects (i.e., more dramatic changes than modifications of individual components). For example, Bronfenbrenner (1975), in reviewing the effects of early educational intervention programs, concluded that (1) center-based programs with cognitive curricula produced greater gains than play-oriented programs; (2) parent intervention yielded benefits that extended to younger siblings, and to the attitudes and feelings of the parents; and (3) families who are under the most economic and psychological stress are the ones least likely to become involved in an intervention program. This suggests that a *combination* of approaches may be the most effective. These might

363

include quality daycare, parent education, programs to loan education materials, and expanded social services that move the child and family into a broader social support network. The goal of preventing developmental retardation, in brief, should be to ensure a rearing atmosphere where the needs of children are attended to with flexibility and appropriate resources on the part of their caregivers.

A brief overview of previous early education programs illustrates the many foci of intervention (see reviews by Lazar, Darlington, Murray, Royce & Snipper, 1982; Ramey, Sparling, Bryant, & Wasik, 1982). Many of them, such as Head Start, the Abecedarian Project (Ramey, MacPhee, & Yeates, 1982), and the Milwaukee Project (Garber & Heber, 1977), primarily are child-centered. The strategy typically employed is to enroll the children in educational daycare at an early age, with the intention of enhancing their cognitive, linguistic and/or social development. Some daycare programs *do* attempt, as a secondary focus, to alleviate family stress in the high-risk participants, either through procuring social service assistance (e.g., Abecedarian Project) or with job training (e.g., Milwaukee Project).

Home-based programs, in contrast, often attempt to change a broader network of influences on development (Andrews *et al.*, 1982). The centerpiece of most of these programs is strategies to (1) foster positive social interactions between caregivers and children; and (2) teach caregivers how to stimulate their children's intellectual development, usually with age-appropriate materials that have been supplied (Gordon & Guinagh, 1978; Gray & Klaus, 1968; Madden, Levenstein, & Levenstein, 1976). Home-based programs primarily differ in how much the child or other family members are involved, whether discussions of adult and family crises are encouraged, and in the use of daycare as an adjunctive intervention. Few if any of these programs explicitly focus on parental attitudes, sensitivity to the children's readiness for experiences, or the inanimate environment. Rather, *techniques* for mediating experiences are the focus, implying that perhaps these are the most cost-effective intervention strategies, although no adequate comparative data exist to buttress this popular belief.

Specificity of Intervention

A major theme emerging from recent research on the home environment is that the effects of various experiences are age- and organismic-specific. The need to consider the child's stage of development when formulating intervention strategies can be derived from the General Systems Model, which implies that modifiability and learning tend to strike a balance over time (Bateson, 1979). While children may be viewed as dynamic individuals constantly adapting to changes in the environment, learning and hierarchical organization of behavior patterns also are taking place. This interplay of plasticity and learning has crucial significance for the reversibility of detrimental early experiences. Clarke and Clarke (1976), in discussing this issue, liken development to a wedge where there is "a greater potential responsiveness during early life . . . tailing off to little responsiveness in adulthood" (pp. 271–272). These theoretical statements plus empirical data on the home environment lead to two conclusions regarding the timing of intervention. First, consistent with McCall's (1981) "scoop model," early experiences (before 18 months) leave few indelible impressions on cognitive development. Second, experiences that are repeated and cumulative *are* correlated with later cognitive performance. Given that home environments are fairly stable over time, then, early intervention would seem to be the safest strategy if alterations in experience were to have an effect by age 2 years. Furthermore, periodic reinstatement of the intervention, or "booster shots," are advised if families cannot be enrolled continuously. These boosters might be timed to coincide with major developmental milestones so that the caregivers will adapt their stimulation techniques to the children's changing abilities, and so that the children will learn adaptive behavior patterns not demanded at earlier ages (see Ramey & Baker-Ward, 1982).

General Systems Theory also accounts for organismic-specificity in that it places equal emphasis on the contribution of the child to its own development and on the characteristics of the environment. As a consequence, the curriculum of an intervention program will need to be tailored not only to the children's stages of development, but to their preferences for stimulus modality, structure, and content as well. Contrary to Occam's razor, this suggests that intervention philosophies and practices will need to be shifted from a model that assumes uniform main effects to a perspective that emphasizes organism × environment interaction effects. More effective strategies, then, will be developed when we have derived a taxonomy of individual differences that mediate children's responses to experiences, and then implement *different* curricula with different types or clusters of children.

Conclusions

In closing, we recast some of the major research and intervention issues in terms of the General Systems Model. One proposition is that historical variables (distal determinants) such as SES should be related to proximal influences on development (stimulus properties). SES, in fact, does account for a substantial proportion of the variance in the home environment, yet 50% remains unaccounted for. A major research question, then, is what factors influence the home environment in addition to SES? Likely candidates include feedback from the child; parental attitudes and beliefs; and household characteristics such as crowding and stresses and supports. In terms of intervention, some of these distal influences on cognitive development can be combined into a first-line screening program.

A notable and frustrating deficiency in the General Systems Model has been the inability to specify the nature of transactions among levels (child; caregiver; family) that influence development. The data in this volume unravel some mysteries but leave us fit to be tied with other Gordian knots. Mediated experiences, for instance, are pivotal in the child's cognitive development. Caregivers who are warm, involved, contingently responsive, and engage in structured, verbal interactions appear to foster in children a sense of control and self-worth (effectance), and teach children information, cognitive skills, and language. Children also contribute to transactions with the environment by evoking different kinds of experiences, by differential responsiveness to the environment, and by seeking out compatible stimulation. The vehicles for these dialectical processes include biomedical factors, gender differences, temperament, language, and cognitive skills, all of which may change with accumulated experience. Intervention, then, should focus on mediated experiences provided by the caregiver, should be tailored to the child's proclivities, and should incorporate the notions of feedback and cumulative experience. The complex nature of influences on cognitive development also should spur the field into adopting more sophisticated multivariate, longitudinal research designs, and in developing mathematical models or statistical techniques that can treat the resulting data.

The central unresolved issue in this field, as we see it, concerns the match between the child's ability to assimilate information and the nature of stimulation in the environment. This issue is at the core of organism–environment transactions, and has implications for research and intervention. The essence of matched, mediated experiences is that the caregiver must be able to perceive the child's readiness for certain experiences and then provide them in a challenging yet comprehensible fashion. Global intervention strategies, from this perspective, are outmoded. Instead, cognitive abilities that are likely to exhibit deficits will need to be identified; the ages at which they are most susceptible to stimulation need to be explicated; and then programs will have to be designed that emphasize specific environmental parameters for the given abilities, ages and subgroups of children (see Wachs & Gruen, 1982). Research might profitably explore parents' abilities to interpret children's behavior accurately, parents' repertoire of games and intellectual activities, and why parents choose to engage in particular activities or to structure the physical environment as they do (Rheingold & Cook, 1975). If parents are the architects of the home environment, we need to know not only *what* they use as building blocks, but *why* they decide on a particular infrastructure and why they choose one material over another at a given time. An understanding of how differences in the home environment arise will provide the foundation for future intervention programs.

References

Andrews, S. R., Blumenthal, J. B., Johnson, D. L., Kahn, A. J., Ferguson, C. J., Lasater, T. M., Malone, P. E., & Wallace, D. B. The skills of mothering: A study of Parent Child Development Centers. *Monographs of the Society for Research in Child Development*, 1982, 47, (6, Serial No. 198).

Baldwin, A. L., Cole, R. E., & Baldwin, C. P. (Eds). Parental pathology, family interaction, and the competence of the child in school. *Monographs of the Society for Research in Child Development*, 1982, 47, (5, Serial No. 197).

Bates, J. E., Olson, S. L., Pettit, G. S., & Bayles, K. Dimensions of individuality in the mother–infant relationship at six months of age. *Child Development*, 1982, 53, 446–461.

Bateson, P. P. G. How do sensitive periods arise and what are they for? *Animal Behaviour*, 1979, 27, 470–486.

Baumrind, D., & Black, A. E. Socialization patterns associated with dimensions of competence in preschool boys and girls. *Child Development*, 1967, 38, 291–327.

Bee, H. L., Barnard, K. E., Eyres, S. J., Gray, C. A., Hammond, M. A., Spietz, A. L., Snyder, C., & Clark, B. Prediction of IQ and language skill from perinatal status, child performance, family characteristics, and mother–infant interaction. *Child Development*, 1982, 53, 1134–1156.

Belsky, J. Early human experience: A family perspective. *Developmental Psychology*, 1981, 17, 3–23.

Bernal, J. Crying during the first 10 days of life, and maternal responses. *Developmental Medicine and Child Neurology*, 1972, 14, 362–372.

Bernstein, B. B. Elaborated and restricted codes: Their social origins and some consequences. *American Anthropologist*, 1964, 66, 55–69.

Bradley, R. H., Caldwell, B. M., & Elardo, R. Home environment and cognitive development in the first two years: A cross-lagged panel analysis. *Developmental Psychology*, 1979, 15, 246–250.

Bronfenbrenner, U. Is early intervention effective? In M. Guttentag & E. L. Struening (Eds.), *Handbook of evaluation research* (Vol. 2). Beverly Hills, CA: Sage, 1975.

Carew, J. V. Experience and the development of intelligence in young children at home and in day care. *Monographs of the Society for Research in Child Development*, 1980, 45, (6–7, Serial No. 187).

Carew-Watts, J. V., & Chan-Barnett, I. C. The child's environment. In B. L. White, with I. Chan-Barnett, B. T. Kaban, J. R. Marmor, B. B. Shapiro, & J. Carew-Watts, *Environment and experience* (Vol. 1): *Major influences on the development of the young child*. Englewood Cliffs, NJ: Prentice-Hall, 1973.

Clarke, A. M., & Clarke, A. D. B. *Early Experience: Myth and evidence*. New York: Free Press, 1976.

Clarke-Stewart, K. A. Interactions between mothers and their young children: Characteristics and consequences. *Monographs of the Society for Research in Child Development*, 1973, *38*, (6–7, Serial No. 153).

Cochran, M. M., & Brassard, J. A. Child development and personal social networks. *Child Development*, 1979, *50*, 601–616.

Deutsch, C. Social class and child development. In B. M. Caldwell & H. N. Ricciuti (Eds.), *Review of child development research* (Vol. 3). Chicago: University of Chicago Press, 1973.

Elardo, R., Bradley, R. H., & Caldwell, B. M. The relation of infants' home environments to mental test performance from six to thirty-six months: A longitudinal analysis. *Child Development*, 1975, *46*, 71–76.

Elardo, R., Bradley, R. H., & Caldwell, B. M. A longitudinal study of the relation of infants' home environments to language development at age three. *Child Development*, 1977, *48*, 595–603.

Epstein, A. S. *Pregnant teenagers' knowledge of infant development*. Paper presented at the Biennial Meeting of the Society for Research in Child Development, San Francisco, April 1979.

Farran, D. C., & Ramey, C. T. Social class differences in dyadic involvement during infancy. *Child Development*, 1980, *51*, 254–257.

Feuerstein, R. *The dynamic assessment of retarded performers*. Baltimore: University Park Press, 1979.

Finkelstein, N. W., & Ramey, C. T. Information from birth certificate data as a risk index for school failure. *American Journal of Mental Deficiency*, 1980, *84*, 546–552.

Frankenburg, W. K., van Doorninck, W. J., Liddel, T. N., & Dick, N. P. The Denver Prescreening Developmental Questionnaire (PDQ). *Pediatrics*, 1976, *59*, 744–753.

Galbraith, R. C. Sibling spacing and intellectual development: A closer look at the confluence models. *Developmental Psychology*, 1982, *18*, 151–173.

Garber, H., & Heber, R. The Milwaukee Project: Indications of the effectiveness of early intervention in preventing mental retardation. In P. Mittler (Ed.), *Research to practice in mental retardation: Care and intervention* (Vol. 1). Baltimore: University Park Press, 1977.

Gordon, I. J., & Guinagh, B. J. A home learning center approach to early stimulation. *JSAS Catalog of Selected Documents in Psychology*, 1978, *8*, 6. (Ms. No. 1634)

Gray, S., & Klaus, R. The early training project and its general rationale. In R. Hess, & R. Bear (Eds.), *Early education*. Chicago: Aldine, 1968.

Hawkins, R. P. It's time we taught the young how to be good parents (and don't you wish we'd started a long time ago?). *Psychology Today*, 1972, November, 29–30, 36–40.

Hess, R. D., & Shipman, V. C. Early experience and the socialization of cognitive modes in children. *Child Development*, 1965, *34*, 869–886.

Lazar, I., Darlington, R., Murray, H., Royce, J., & Snipper, A. Lasting effects of early education: A report from the consortium for longitudinal studies. *Monographs of the Society for Research in Child Development*, 1982, *47*, (2–3, Serial No. 195).

Lerner, R. M. Children and adolescents as producers of their own development. *Developmental Review*, 1982, *2*, 342–370.

McCall, R. B. Nature–nurture and the two realms of development: A proposed integration with respect to mental development. *Child Development*, 1981, *55*, 1–12.

McCall, R. B., Appelbaum, M. I., & Hogarty, P. S. Developmental changes in mental performance. *Monographs of the Society for Research in Child Development*, 1973, *38*, (3, Serial No. 150).

Madden, J., Levenstein, P., & Levenstein, S. Longitudinal IQ outcomes of the mother-child home program. *Child Development*, 1976, *46*, 1015–1025.

Marjoribanks, K. Birth order and family learning environments. *Psychological Reports*, 1981, *49*, 915–919.

Miller, J. G. *Living systems*. New York: McGraw-Hill, 1978.

Ninio, A. The naive theory of the infant and other maternal attitudes in Israel. *Child Development*, 1979, *50*, 976–980.

Plomin, R., DeFries, J. C., & Loehlin, J. C. Genotype-environment interaction and correlation in the analysis of human behavior. *Psychological Bulletin*, 1977, *84*, 309–322.

Ramey, C. T., & Baker-Ward, L. Psychosocial retardation and the early experience paradigm. In D. Bricker (Ed.), *Intervention with at-risk and handicapped infants: From research to application*. Baltimore: University Park Press, 1982.

Ramey, C. T., MacPhee, D., & Yeates, K. O. Preventing developmental retardation: A General Systems Model. In L. A. Bond & J. M. Joffe (Eds.), *Facilitating infant and early childhood development*. Hanover, NH: University Press of New England, 1982.

Ramey, C. T., Sparling, J. J., Bryant, D. M., & Wasik, B. H. Primary prevention of developmental retardation during infancy. *Prevention in Human Services*, 1982, *1*, 61–83.

Ramey, C. T., Stedman, D. S., Borders-Patterson, A., & Mengel, W. Predicting school failure from information available at birth. *American Journal of Mental Deficiency*, 1978, *82*, 524–534.

Rheingold, H. L., & Cook, K. V. The content of boys' and girls' rooms as an index of parents' behavior. *Child Development*, 1975, *46*, 459–463.

Rogers, J. L. Confluence effects: Not here, not now! *Developmental Psychology*, in press.

Sameroff, A. J. Developmental systems: Contexts and evolution. In W. Kessen (Ed.), *History, theory, and methods* (Vol. 1), of P. H. Mussen (Ed.), *Handbook of child psychology* (4 Vols.). New York: Wiley, 1983.

Scott, J. P., & Fuller, J. L. *Genetics and the social behavior of the dog*. Chicago: University of Chicago Press, 1965.

Sigman, M., Cohen, S. E., Beckwith, L., & Parmelee, A. H. Social and familial influences on the development of preterm infants. *Journal of Pediatric Psychology*, 1981, *6*, 1–13.

Sparling, J. J., & Lewis, I. S. *Learningames for the first three years: A guide to parent–child play*. New York: Walker, 1979.

Stolz, L. M. *Influences on parent behavior*. Stanford, CA: Stanford University Press, 1967.

Wachs, T. D. The optimal stimulation hypothesis and early experience: Anybody got a match? In I. C. Uzgiris & F. Weizmann (Eds.), *The structuring of experience*. New York: Plenum, 1977.

Wachs, T. D. The relationship of infants' physical environment to their Binet performance at 2½ years. *International Journal of Behavioral Development*, 1978, *1*, 51–65.

Wachs, T. D. Proximal experience and early cognitive-intellectual development: The physical environment. *Merrill-Palmer Quarterly*, 1979, *25*, 3–41.

Wachs, T. D., & Gruen, G. E. *Early experience and human development.* New York: Plenum, 1982.

Watson, J. S., & Ramey, C. T. Reactions to response contingent stimulation early in infancy. *Merrill-Palmer Quarterly,* 1972, *18,* 219–227.

Werner, H. The concept of development from a comparative and organismic point of view. In D. B. Harris (Ed.), *The concept of development: An issue in the study of human behavior.* Minneapolis: University of Minnesota Press, 1957.

White, R. W. Motivation reconsidered: The concept of competence. *Psychological Review,* 1959, *66,* 297–331.

Wilson, R. S. Synchronies in mental development: An epigenetic perspective. *Science,* 1978, *202,* 939–948.

Yeates, K. O., MacPhee, D., Campbell, F. A., & Ramey, C. T. Maternal IQ and home environment as determinants of early childhood intellectual competence: A developmental analysis. *Developmental Psychology,* 1983, *19,* 731–739.

Zigler, E., & Valentine, J. (Eds.). *Project Head Start: A legacy of the War on Poverty.* New York: Free Press, 1979.

Author Index

Subject Index

DEVELOPMENTAL PSYCHOLOGY SERIES

Continued from page ii

GEORGE E. FORMAN. (Editor). *Action and Thought: From Sensorimotor Schemes to Symbolic Operations*

EUGENE S. GOLLIN. (Editor). *Developmental Plasticity: Behavioral and Biological Aspects of Variations in Development*

W. PATRICK DICKSON. (Editor). *Children's Oral Communication Skills*

LYNN S. LIBEN, ARTHUR H. PATTERSON, and NORA NEWCOMBE. (Editors). *Spatial Representation and Behavior across the Life Span: Theory and Application*

SARAH L. FRIEDMAN and MARIAN SIGMAN. (Editors). *Preterm Birth and Psychological Development*

HARBEN BOUTOURLINE YOUNG and LUCY RAU FERGUSON. *Puberty to Manhood in Italy and America*

RAINER H. KLUWE and HANS SPADA. (Editors). *Developmental Models of Thinking*

ROBERT L. SELMAN. *The Growth of Interpersonal Understanding: Developmental and Clinical Analyses*

BARRY GHOLSON. *The Cognitive-Developmental Basis of Human Learning: Studies in Hypothesis Testing*

TIFFANY MARTINI FIELD, SUSAN GOLDBERG, DANIEL STERN, and ANITA MILLER SOSTEK. (Editors). *High-Risk Infants and Children: Adult and Peer Interactions*

GILBERTE PIERAUT-LE BONNIEC. *The Development of Modal Reasoning: Genesis of Necessity and Possibility Notions*

JONAS LANGER. *The Origins of Logic: Six to Twelve Months*

LYNN S. LIBEN. *Deaf Children: Developmental Perspectives*